SOCIAL PROBLEMS AND SOCIAL CONTEXTS IN ADOLESCENCE

SOCIAL PROBLEMS AND SOCIAL CONTEXTS IN ADOLESCENCE

Perspectives across Boundaries

Klaus Hurrelmann and Stephen F. Hamilton

EDITORS

ALDINE DE GRUYTER

New York

About the Editors

Klaus Hurrelman is a professor in, and the dean of the Faculty of Health Sciences at the University of Bielefeld. Dr. Hurrelmann is the Director of Prevention and Intervention in Childhood and Adolescence, and has written and edited several books, most recently a new edition of the *Handbuch der Sozialisationsforschung* (Handbook of Socialization Research) and the *International Handbook of Adolescence*.

Steven F. Hamilton is a professor and chair of the Department of Human Development and Family Studies at Cornell University. As Director of the Cornell Youth and Work Program, he has been involved in research and development related to the School-to-Work Opportunities Act of 1994. Dr. Hamilton is the author of numerous journal articles and his latest book is *Apprenticeship for Adulthood: Preparing Youth for the Future*.

ALDINE DE GRUYTER
A division of Walter de Gruyter, Inc.
200 Saw Mill River Road
Hawthorne, New York 10532

This publication is printed on acid free paper

Library of Congress Cataloging-in-Publication Data
Social Problems and social contexts in adolescence : perspectives
  across boundaries / Klaus Hurrelman and Stephen F. Hamilton,
  editors.
       p.   cm.
   Includes biographical references and index.
   ISBN 0-202-36101-2 (paper : alk. paper)
   1. Adolescence.   2. Teenagers—Social conditions.   3. Adolescent
psychology.   I. Hurrelmann, Klaus.   II. Hamilton, Stephen F.
HQ796.S564   1996
305.23'5—dc20   96-4551
                                                             CIP

Manufactured in the United States of America

10 9 8 7 6 5 4 3 2 1

Contents

List of Contributors

Inge Bø

Rogaland University Center
Stavanger, Norway

Ana Mari Cauce

Department of Psychology
University of Washington

Frances Costa

Institute of Behavioral Science
University of Colorado

Nancy Darling

College of Human Ecology
Cornell University

Willem Doise

Department of Psychology
University of Geneva
Switzerland

John E. Donovan

Institute of Behavioral Science
University of Colorado

Edna Lomsky-Feder

Department of Sociology
University of Jerusalem
Israel

James Garbarino

Family Life Development Center
Cornell University

Nancy Gonzales

Department of Psychology
University of Washington

Benjamin H. Gottlieb

Department of Psychology
University of Guelph
Ontario, Canada

Stephen F. Hamilton   Department of Human Development
                                         and Family Studies
                                       Cornell University

Yumi Hiraga   Department of Psychology
                                       University of Washington

Klaus Hurrelmann   Dean
                                       Faculty for Health Sciences
                                       University of Bielefeld
                                       Germany

Richard Jessor   Institute of Behavioral Science
                                       University of Colorado

Gloria Liu   Department of Psychology
                                       University of Washington

Craig Mason   Department of Psychology
                                       University of Washington

Wim Meeus   Department of Psychology
                                       Utrecht University
                                       The Netherlands

Anne Petersen   Deputy Director
                                       National Science Foundation
                                       Washington, DC

Janita Ravesloot   Department of Sociology
                                       University of Leiden
                                       The Netherlands

Manuela du Bois-Reymond   Department of Sociology
                                       University of Leiden
                                       The Netherlands

Rainer K. Silbereisen   Department of Human Development
                                         and Family Studies
                                       Pennsylvania State University

Silvia Sörensen   Department of Human Development
                                         and Family Studies
                                       Pennsylvania State University

John C. Sylvestre   Department of Psychology
                                        University of Guelph
                                        Ontario, Canada

Wilma Vollebergh   University of Utrecht
                                        The Netherlands

Introduction

Adolescence is a critical phase of life, a time for crucial decisions and key experiences that resonate throughout the remainder of the life course. Although the characteristics we associate with adolescence and youth are distinctive in our era, nearly all known cultures have recognized a period between childhood and adulthood comparable to what we mean by adolescence. As the twentieth century draws to a close, the contexts and problems of adolescents continue to change.

Change makes adolescence an intriguing area of inquiry. Change is prominent in individual adolescents, in the definition of the phase, and in the prevailing roles and images of adolescents. The rate of growth adolescents experience is exceeded only by that of infants during their first year of life. Sexual maturation produces dramatic changes in emotions. Cognitive development yields new forms of thought. The increasing autonomy that accompanies adolescence in most modern societies enables young people to act and interact in ways that were not possible for them when they were younger. For most, opportunities to choose are wider than they will be later in life.

The compression of so much change into a period of about a decade intensifies interaction between the developing person and the environment. Such interaction characterizes development across the life course but is never again so vivid as it is during adolescence. Adolescents are acutely sensitive to the societal forces surrounding them. They are stamped indelibly with the marks of the period in which they come of age. Thus, adolescence is something of a barometer for society. Adolescents register impending changes that may not be fully established until they become adults. As a result, studying adolescents can yield information about social changes as they are unfolding. Comparisons of adolescent development in different countries are especially fruitful for this purpose because they make it easier to disentangle universal, cultural, and historical components of that development.

The study of adolescence can shed light on other issues as well. The extreme differences in access to resources and in future prospects found in modern capitalist economies result in dramatic differences among adolescents. Gender, income, race, class, urban/rural/suburban location, region, physical and mental impairments, and other characteristics distinguish the experiences and developmental trajectories of adolescents within as well as across societies. Although it is useful to refer to adolescents in general and to adolescents in particular countries, we must always keep in mind the many differences among adolescents that cut across their similarities.

One quality of adolescence that seems almost universal in modern societies is that adults view it as a problematic time of life. Adults' complaints of adolescents' indiscipline, moodiness, and self-indulgence are as old as the oldest written records. "The problems of youth" is a perennial topic of researchers, practitioners, and policy makers. Certain kinds of problem behavior are definitely more common during adolescence than in other periods of life. They include violence and illicit drug use. Some other behaviors, notably sexual behaviors, are defined as problematic primarily because of the age of those involved.

It is worth asking what problem behaviors do for adolescents. What constructive functions might they perform in adolescent development? Adolescents may perceive many such behaviors as conferring advantages that outweigh the disadvantages that are more evident to adults. Aggressiveness against a fellow student, for example, brings about a measure of respect and increased attention from the peer group. To achieve attention and respect, the adolescent accepts the sanctions from teachers, parents, even the police, that may result from his action. These sanctions may actually enhance the standing gained in some peer groups. Having a child out of wedlock is a second example. A young man who fathers a child has proved his manhood, just as a young woman has demonstrated her adulthood. Becoming a mother may confer a higher status on a disadvantaged teenager than any other action under her control. An adolescent in an affluent suburb may experiment with drugs to satisfy curiosity and overcome boredom. Alcohol consumption and delinquency may constitute declarations of independence from parents and other adult authorities.

Although adults may condemn these choices, adolescents may not believe other choices are available and preferable. Furthermore, most adolescents indulge in such activities to some degree for a limited time without disastrous consequences. Irreversible problem behavior is still relatively rare.

These reflections might imply that adolescent social problems are not serious, but one change in the social context of adolescence makes them more serious. That is the declining capacity of families to nurture and support adolescents. Divorce and the escalating demands of working life have left parents less able to protect and guide their sons and daughters. Simultaneously, at least some aspects of the larger social context have become more threatening, including drugs, violence, and sexually transmitted disease. What is worse, many parents themselves feel insecure and uncertain about values, behavior, and what the future will bring. Under such circumstances, experimental problem behavior that might once have proved relatively harmless can result in serious and permanent harm. One of the purposes of this volume is to examine both the threats and the supports available to adolescents. Only by understanding both can we reduce the former and increase the latter.

The following chapters were written under the auspices of a special research unit, Prevention and Intervention in Childhood and Adolescence, at the University of Bielefeld in Germany. Established to link research on the causes of problems with assessments of intervention measures and to foster longitudinal research, this unit has exploited international comparisons by regularly bringing together scholars from many nations to share their work and discuss its implications for such problems as poor school performance and disordered social behavior.

The book addresses some of the social contexts for adolescent development and some of the social problems adolescents encounter, with contributions from European and Israeli as well as American scholars. Although no attempt is made to provide direct comparisons, this combination provides some insights into similarities and differences among societies. Some of the topics cut across national boundaries, such as Wim Meeus's appreciative critique of Erik Erikson's theory of adolescent identity formation. Others are rooted in specific countries, such as the study of Dutch adolescents' sexual socialization by Manuela du Bois-Reymond and Janita Ravesloot and Edna Lomsky-Feder's research on young Israeli soldiers. Yet these contributions also raise the question of what is universal and what particular to a given society.

Part I provide theoretical perspectives for the study of adolescent problems and the social context of adolescent development, including biological and sociological as well as psychological orientations. Part II offers a relatively positive view, focusing on the human relations in which adolescents are embedded, both those with peers and those with parents and other adults. Part III explores adolescent problems, with an emphasis on the kinds of social environments that elicit problem behavior.

Social science is one product that the United States exports more than it imports. That is, social scientists outside the United States are much more familiar with U.S. literature than vice versa. A reading knowledge of English is practically required of social scientists around the world, and those who are most active internationally frequently publish in English. They tend to read journals and books from the United States regularly. However, what would be a "favorable balance of trade" in economic terms is unfavorable to science; it blinds scholars in the United States to contrasts and parallels with other countries that could enrich their research and theories. One purpose of this volume is to bring a sampling of research and researchers from other countries to the attention of Americans. This book will have succeeded if it reveals some unexpected similarities and differences in adolescent development in the United States and in other countries and if it piques readers' curiosity about phenomena and research in other parts of the world.

ACKNOWLEDGEMENTS

Persephone Doliner carefully edited all of the chapters, assuring their completeness and consistency of style, and created the index. Amy Tietjen Smith painstakingly corrected several generations of manuscripts and directed the work of multiple typists.

Klaus Hurrelmann
Stephen F. Hamilton

I

THEORETICAL APPROACHES TO ADOLESCENT DEVELOPMENT IN CONTEXT

The selections in Part I provide theoretical perspectives for the study of adolescent problems and the social context of adolescent development, including biological and sociological as well as psychological orientations. A brief description of Chapters 1–4 follows.

Adolescent Development:
A Global Perspective

Drawing on an impressively diverse literature, authors Petersen, Silbereisen and Sörenson provide a masterly review of recent research on adolescent development, primarily but not exclusively focusing on research conducted in the West. They note the insights yielded by longitudinal studies and new research topics and methods, and they emphasize biological factors. Their careful attention to the process of development and to the interplay among phenomena at the individual level and social contexts make this chapter an excellent overview of the issues addressed in this volume.

The Social World of Adolescents:
A Sociological Perspective

With its emphasis on the individual, the United States is a fertile field for psychology. Sociology seems stronger in Europe, where differences among social classes are more distinct and more widely accepted as real and inevitable. In this chapter Hurrelmann examines the ways in which social institutions such as schooling have changed the course of adolescent development over time. It pays special attention to the impact of "status inconsistencies" that might be seen as a more important source of adolescent confusion than any internal forces.

Social Psychology and the Study of Youth

Doise makes a strong case for three claims, describing exemplary studies to support each one. The first is that the psychological study of youth is inherently broader and more inclusive than research and theorizing in other domains of psychology. The second is that youth research links scientific and societal concerns. Third, he advocates combining four levels of sociopsychological explanation, which he explicates and then uses to analyze several of the studies previously cited.

Toward a Psychosocial Analysis of Adolescent Identity

No theory of adolescent development has been more influential in the second half of the twentieth century than Erik Erikson's. James Marcia has operationalized Erikson's theory with his schema of identity statuses. In this chapter Meeus conveys his appreciation for both Erikson and Marcia but also criticizes the limitations of their work, noting especially the need to incorporate information about social class into theories of adolescent identity formation.

1

Adolescent Development: A Global Perspective

Anne C. Petersen, Rainer K. Silbereisen,
and Silvia Sörensen

1. INTRODUCTION

Although scholars have written about adolescents for centuries, and a developmental phase called adolescence was identified at the beginning of this century, research on adolescence has been meager. Currently, however, many scientists throughout the world are at work on topics relevant to adolescent development. Although the bulk of recent research focuses on populations in the United States and Western Europe, research exists on diverse adolescent populations globally.

In the United States, there was a dramatic growth of the adolescent population during the 20-year period between 1955 and 1975 (United Nations Population Division, 1976), and some researchers thought that the almost-doubled size of the population aged 15 to 19 was at least one of the reasons for protest and unrest among youth. However, applying a cross-national perspective reveals that other countries, although they were also shaken by the youth rebellion of the late sixties and early seventies, had entirely different trends in the relative sizes of the young populations. In West Germany, for example, there was almost no change over these decades in the relative size of the population aged 15 to 18. In the mid-eighties, the percentage of children and adolescents below the age of 15 varied from 15 percent in West Germany to 48 percent in Algeria; the United States held a middle position with 22 percent (Statistisches Bundesamt, 1987). Subsequent decades will generally bring a reduction in the relative size of younger cohorts, with dramatic increases in the size of older cohorts, especially in highly industrialized countries such as the United States and those in Western Europe (Deutsches Institut für Wirtschaftsforschung, 1988; U.S. Bureau of the Census, 1982). This cohort shift will bring increasing pressure on younger cohorts to provide for older generations. This demographic shift has stimulated renewed interest in youth in some countries and a focus on the capacity of young people to be productive workers (e.g., Grant Foundation, 1988).

Basic theoretical and empirical advances in several areas have permitted the advance of research on adolescence. Some areas of behavioral science from which adolescence researchers have drawn are life-span developmental psychology, life-course sociology, social support, stress and coping, and cognitive development; important contributing areas in the biomedical sciences include endocrinology and adolescent medicine. The recent maturation to adolescence of subjects in major longitudinal growth studies (e.g., Baumrind, 1985; Block & Gjerde, 1987; Pulkkinen, 1982) has also contributed to the topic's empirical knowledge base. Research on adolescence has benefited from analyses of longitudinal data archives, such as the various Berkeley Growth Studies, begun in the 1920s (e.g., Elder, 1974), and the Newcastle Thousand Family Study, initiated in 1947 (Kolvin, Miller, Fleeting, & Kolvin, 1988), that are unique in terms of the ultimate time range they observed (30 to 40 years) and their focus on generations within the family.

Certain forces have impeded the scientific study of adolescence as well. Belief in the importance of early experience focused attention for decades on infancy and early childhood (e.g., Brim & Kagan, 1980; Clarke & Clarke, 1976). In addition, powerful beliefs about adolescence have undermined systematic work. For example, adolescents are often portrayed in the Western media as noisy, obnoxious, dirty, inarticulate, rebellious, and so forth. Such portrayals not only communicate to adolescents how they are expected to behave but also create expectations in the research community. Despite the paucity of research on this topic, most people believe they know what adolescence is like and are unreceptive to findings that challenge their beliefs (Brooks-Gunn & Petersen, 1984).

1.1. Major Areas of Current Scientific Activity

To provide clear information about some areas of knowledge about adolescence, this review is necessarily selective. This approach necessitates omitting several areas of research, but fortunately there are good textbooks and handbooks on adolescence for readers who would like to see a comprehensive review or who have interests in a topic omitted here (e.g., Adelson, 1980; Conger & Petersen, 1984; Santrock, 1987; Steinberg, 1985; Van Hasselt & Hersen, 1987).

Three major areas in which there has been a great deal of recent research on Western adolescence include (1) adjustment or turmoil, (2) puberty and its effects, and (3) adolescent-family relations. All three areas have long traditions of work, though in each case the current work is of a different nature, in part because of technological advances, such as the development of radioimmunoassay as a technique for measuring hormones and the use of audio and video technology for studying family interaction.

It is important to note that current research on adolescence is inherently interdisciplinary. The study of adolescence has developed with important contributions from psychology, biology, sociology, anthropology, and applied areas such as medicine (especially psychiatry and pediatrics). The interdisciplinary focus of this review draws primarily on both the life-span perspective (e.g., Baltes, Reese, & Lipsitt, 1980) and the ecological perspective (Bronfenbrenner, 1979) on development, which draw attention to the multifaceted nature of lives and their contexts. In addition, as Bronfenbrenner (1989) has stressed, research on human development can profit much by comparing developmental processes across macrocontexts, that is, belief systems and other variables indexing cultural differences. This is especially true for research on adolescence, as the quality and timing of this life stage, and the influence of social institutions on it, show variation among cultures and countries.

1.2. Definitions and Key Concepts

Age is the most convenient marker for developmental changes and phases but, as many have noted (e.g., Featherman & Peterson, 1986; Neugarten, 1979; Wohlwill, 1973), chronological age does not appropriately index many developmental phenomena. Since beginning puberty is a major developmental milestone of adolescence, it is considered by many to be the developmental change that signals the transition into adolescence from childhood (e.g., Brooks-Gunn & Petersen, 1984). Thus, one might conclude that pubertal change is the best way to index adolescent development. It is probably not appropriate, however, to consider pubertal development as the sole developmental marker in adolescence because of the strong organization of the period accomplished by educational institutions. Depending on the country considered, the second decade of life is usually structured by schooling and entry into work. These settings are largely age-graded, thus emphasizing the importance of chronological age, regardless of any other developmental status. In view of the salience of the social organization of schooling, and despite the great individual variability in various developmental statuses, such as puberty or cognitive development, it is convenient to identify some span of years as the scope of this discussion of adolescence. Although a great many conventions are used by writers and researchers, we focus primarily on the second decade of life.

A concept central to much current developmental research, particularly on adolescence, is developmental transition. A developmental transition is a period of life in which there is a great deal of change, both within the individual and within the social environment (Eichhorn, Mussen, Clausen, Haan, & Honzik, 1981).

Although the debate continues among developmentalists regarding whether continuity or discontinuity is dominant over the life course (e.g., Brim & Kagan, 1980; Rutter, 1987), an emerging perspective (e.g., Rutter, 1986) focuses on the importance of considering both aspects within this framework. Developmental transitions are thought to involve more discontinuity and less continuity than other periods. The movements from childhood to adolescence and from adolescence to adulthood have both been considered developmental transitions (Connell & Furman, 1984; Petersen & Ebata, 1987). It should be noted, however, that the transition into adulthood from adolescence is much more variable as to age and the markers of this change; in addition, legal conventions and social traditions for identifying adult statuses vary from country to country.

2. RESEARCH ON ADOLESCENCE

Although some have claimed that adolescence is a twentieth-century invention (e.g., Aries, 1962), reference to behavior stereotypic of adolescents can be found in the writings of both Plato and Aristotle. Turning away from the regressive views on development that charactererized the Middle Ages, in which children were thought to be small adults, Rousseau renewed the life-phase concepts of Plato and Aristotle, describing two phases that encompass the current view of adolescence.

Current research on adolescent development differs from earlier research in important respects. First, the quantity has dramatically increased. More important, and perhaps explaining the quantitative increase, are the qualitative changes in adolescent research. As with much developmental research, there has been a shift in research on adolescence from stage-oriented approaches to process-oriented approaches (e.g., Davis, Cahan, & Bashi, 1977; Keating, 1987; Munroe & Munroe, 1983; Visser, 1987). For example, many developmental domains, from secondary sex characteristic development to cognitive development, were conceptualized as involving a series of invariant stages. Although the validity of some of these progressions has not been questioned (e.g., secondary sex characteristic development, or "Tanner staging"; Tanner, 1974), validity has been an issue in other domains. Even with developmental change such as secondary sex characteristic development, the underlying process is assumed to involve fairly continuous, progressive changes, rather than transformations from one qualitative stage to another. Development in many domains is now conceptualized as involving more continual change, sometimes including regressions as a typical aspect. Even pubertal development, in which regressions are infrequent but possible, has been so conceptualized. Although there is still some controversy on the issue of the underlying course of development—qualitative stages versus more quantitative progressions (with possible regressions)—there seems to be accumulating evidence that stages inaccurately depict the processes involved in some domains and in others represent at best a categorical abstraction of what is actually a more continual process.

The more process-oriented approaches of current research on adolescent development also recognize that these processes must involve interactions between the individual and other people and contexts (e.g., Lerner, 1981). A return to recognition of the person-environment interaction is probably attributable to the significant contributions of the life-span and ecological perspectives on human development (e.g., Baltes et al., 1980; Bronfenbrenner, 1979; Hurrelmann, 1988). To fully understand even a biological developmental process such as puberty, it is important to know about the effects of nutrition, exercise, and the norms of the broader society regarding weight and body shape (e.g., Attie, Brooks-Gunn, & Petersen, 1987).

Similarly, after decades of neglecting the situation and environment, work in cognitive development is currently turning toward context effects to explain developmental findings (e.g., Keating, 1987). With processes such as social development, the importance of family, peers, and social environment is even clearer (Caspu, Downey, & Moorehouse, 1988). Furthermore, recent research involves increased analysis of settings frequented by adolescents (Eccles, Midgley, & Adler, 1984; Silbereisen, Noack, & von Eye, 1992).

In Europe, a new impetus for developmental research was provided by the emergence of structural reforms of the educational system (e.g., Fend & Schroer, 1985; Hurrelmann, Rosewitz, & Wolf, 1985), and other problems of high societal impact, such as drug use (e.g., Semmer, Dwyer, Lippert, Fuchs, Cleary, & Schindler, 1987; Silbereisen & Reitzle, 1992). Some studies have also examined the influence of change on the societal level; examples are studies of the impact of modernization in Iceland on sociocognitive development (Edelstein, Keller, & Wahlen, 1984) and of the effect of a socialistic educational system on personality development (Friedrich & Mueller, 1985). Studies of societal effects on individual development are scarce in the non-Western literature, although the effects of poverty and of large evaluations have been discussed (Antonovsky & Sagy, 1986; Offer, Ostrov, Howard, & Atkinson, 1988; Venkata Rami Reddy, 1979).

3. ADOLESCENT ADJUSTMENT VERSUS TURMOIL

As noted earlier, adolescent adjustment is an area of active research globally. Hall and the psychoanalytic theorists (e.g., Blos, 1962; Freud, 1958; Hall, 1904) had pervasive influence on the research on adolescent mental health. These theoretical perspectives established the still prevalent belief in normative turmoil during adolescence, that is, the belief that significant difficulties during adolescence represent normal, healthy development. As a result, difficulties during adolescence were not investigated and typically were not treated in any extensive way when they occurred.

In the 1960s and early 1970s, several research reports appeared that challenged the previous beliefs and resulting research and treatment practices. These studies documented the absence of significant psychological difficulties among at least some, if not the majority, of adolescents (Bandura, 1964; Douvan & Adelson, 1966; Grinker, Grinker, & Timberlake, 1962; Offer & Offer, 1975). At the same time, research demonstrated that difficulties manifested in adolescence often continued into adulthood, often resulting in serious mental illness (Rutter, 1980; Rutter, Graham, Chadwick, & Yule, 1976; Weiner & DelGaudio, 1976). Thus, it was clearly inappropriate to assume that psychological difficulties in adolescence were normal and something that young people grew out of.

By the mid-1970s, an interest in early adolescence had emerged (e.g., Hamburg, 1974; Lipsitz, 1977). It was thought that the studies described above had not identified normative turmoil because it occurred earlier, as a result of the effects of pubertal hormones (e.g., Kestenberg, 1968). This hypothesis was consistent with research identifying a dip in self-esteem in early adolescence (Simmons, Rosenberg, & Rosenberg, 1973).

The early adolescent turmoil hypothesis led to a set of new studies examining the development of mental health in relation to the social and biological changes of early adolescence. This research has demonstrated that although early adolescence may be a challenging life period, young people traverse it with varying degrees of difficulty, just as older people experience varying degrees of difficulty in later periods of life. For example, the percentages of youngsters having psychological difficulties in early adolescence, when compared to the percentages of those with psychological difficulties among high school youth and older youngsters (e.g., Offer & Offer, 1975; Offer et al., 1988), suggest that development during early adolescence is characterized by fewer rather than more difficulties. However, because each of the studies noted used different measures and statistical analyses, definitive conclusions await further replication; the conclusions appear, however, to be fairly universal across the several countries studied (Offer et al., 1988).

Given the belief that adolescence is characterized by moodiness, it is odd that there is little research on this topic. Larson and colleagues (Larson, Csikszentmihalyi, & Graef, 1980), using a method of random time sampling with automatic paging devices, found more mood variability among high-school students than among adults. In later research, Larson (personal communication) found a linear increase in mood variability from the fifth to the ninth grade among girls but not boys. Thus, in the little extant research on moodiness, there appears to be no support for the hypothesis that early adolescence involves more normative turmoil and difficulties than other life phases.

There is still a great deal to be learned about the development of mental health or psychological difficulties during adolescence. If not all adolescents experience difficulties, which ones do develop problems? Gender and class differences appear to be important here (Sudha & Tirth, 1986). Cross-national variations may also be illuminating.

A study of self-image in ten countries (Offer et al., 1988) found several marked gender differences. Boys overall seemed to evidence more self-confidence and adjustment. They reported better self-control, less vulnerability, more pride and positive feelings about their bodies, more interest in and positive feelings about sex, and a higher sense of subjective well-being. Girls appeared to have more social awareness, however, and a stronger commitment to a work ethic. Other non-Western studies on the development of self-concept and self-perception have shown contradictory results with respect to gender. Higher self-image is reported in older Malaysian boys than in younger ones, with the opposite being true for Malaysian girls (Chiam, 1985); this pattern is, however, the opposite of that found among Indian adolescents (Jogawar, 1982).

Adolescent boys with psychological difficulties are likely to have had problems in childhood; girls, in contrast, are more likely to first manifest psychological difficulties in adolescence (Ebata, 1987). As others have found (e.g., Rutter, 1986), girls appear to increase in depressive affect over the adolescent period, so that by age 17 they have significantly poorer emotional tone and well-being and more depressive affect than boys (Petersen et al., 1987). The causes of the different developmental patterns for boys and girls remain to be elucidated, but genes, hormones, and environmental stressors have been implicated (Rutter, 1986).

One hypothesis that may encompass the findings is that anxiety plays a role in the development of depression. Suomi (1987) has proposed that challenging situations together with high arousal in such situations may produce anxiety; individuals who feel little control or efficacy may subsequently become depressed. Both situational factors (e.g., uncontrollable situations) and personal response styles (e.g., negative expectancies [Seligman & Peterson, 1986] or low perceived self-efficacy [Bandura, 1982, 1987]) may play important causal roles in this process. To relate this hypothesis to the findings cited above, it has been found previously that achievement situations are more likely to produce anxiety responses in males, whereas interpersonal situations are more likely to produce anxiety in females (Frankenhaeuser, 1983). Girls are more likely than boys to experience particular challenging situations, such as pubertal change accompanied by simultaneous school change or parental divorce (Petersen & Ebata, 1987), with anxiety. Experiencing more challenge and responding less positively to challenge (e.g., Peterson & Seligman, 1984) may render girls more susceptible to anxiety, and thus to depressive affect, in adolescence. Other behavioral indexes suggest girls' greater susceptibility to affective disturbance. For example, Kirmil-Gray, Eagleston, Gibson, and Thoresen (1984) found that significantly more adolescent girls than boys reported sleep problems, and poor sleepers exhibited more cognitive and behavioral signs of daytime stress than good sleepers. Poor sleep, then, may be a marker of greater difficulties in adolescent girls. The gender difference in negative self-appraisal is widely found by middle adolescence (e.g., Chiam, 1985; Gove & Herb, 1974; Kandel & Davies,

1982; Petersen et al., 1987; Weissman & Klerman, 1977). Thus, the anxiety hypothesis for depressive feelings is consistent with the findings on gender differences in developmental patterns during adolescence.

3.1. Development of Mental Health in Adolescence: Discrepant Views

Although more recent normative research on adolescent mental health has revealed that some, if not most, adolescents traverse the period without significant psychological difficulties and that indicators such as self-esteem become steadily more positive over adolescence (e.g., Damon & Hart, 1982), the statistics on various other indicators make it clear that the proportion of young people who experience difficulties such as suicide, various kinds of substance abuse, and other psychological disorders (e.g., Green & Horton, 1982; Petersen & Hamburg, 1986) increases during the adolescent decade of life as well as from childhood to adolescence (Kaplan, Hong, & Weingold, 1984; Rutter et al., 1976; Weiner, 1980). Unfortunately, we could find no conclusive studies giving the prevalence of psychological disorders among youth in developing countries. The rosy picture of increasingly positive development over adolescence drawn from representative samples of subjects seems at odds with the statistics on increasing casualties over the period. How can these two pictures be reconciled?

The answer probably lies in the nature of the samples. Although the statistics document that troubles for some youth increase with age, none of the indicators identify a majority of adolescents in a given population as having difficulties. We note, however, that since less privileged adolescents and those in developing countries tend to report more psychological problems (e.g., Offer et al., 1988; Venkata Rami Reddy, 1979) more research on global mental health may produce a different picture of adolescent troubles. Similarly, although the psychoanalytic and clinical literatures frequently describe the kind of adolescent we have known, worked with, or perhaps been, such portraits represent a biased sampling of the population.

The representative samples are not without problems either. They are probably not useful for identifying or understanding those subgroups of youngsters who do develop difficulties during adolescence. The minority of adolescents with psychological difficulties may become lost in the overall group patterns and statistics. Indeed, statistics describing central tendencies in the overall distributions may represent no one in particular. Categorical and configural methods of data analysis may be more useful for identifying subgroups of individuals (Magnusson, 1988; von Eye & Brandtstaedter, 1988). In addition, patterns of change may be more illuminating than snapshots taken at single points of time. For example, there is an increasing divergence over the adolescent decade between those who can cope with the challenges of adolescent transition and those who cannot

(Petersen & Ebata, 1987; Petersen, Ebata, & Graber, 1987). The latter group may internalize their difficulties in depression or externalize them in delinquent behavior or substance abuse. Thus, the pictures of adolescence derived from clinical and normative developmental studies may describe two distinct groups of young people. The emerging field of developmental psychopathology (e.g., Cicchetti, 1984; Remschmidt, 1989; Rolf, Master, Cicchetto, Nuecchterlein, & Weintraub, 1987; Rutter, 1986) may help to integrate clinical and developmental perspectives on adolescent mental health.

4. PUBERTY AND ITS EFFECTS IN EARLY ADOLESCENCE

During the mid-1970s, two reports focused on the potential importance of early adolescence, the period of transition from childhood to adolescence in which puberty plays a central role. Hamburg (1974) first drew attention to the possibility that early adolescence represented a critical transition. Shortly thereafter, Lipsitz (1977) reported on this age period for the Ford Foundation. These two pieces stimulated a great deal of research that included puberty as a central variable.

4.1. Pubertal Change

The development of radioimmunoassay methodology in the late 1960s made it possible to study the hormones presumably responsible for gender differentiation and reproductive maturation (Faiman & Winter, 1974). Growth studies had already documented the increased rate of growth characteristic of puberty (e.g., Bayer & Bayley, 1959), but until the 1960s the endocrine basis for differences between men and women had not been demonstrated, and the endocrinology of pubertal change had not been described. Yet pubertal hormones were hypothesized to cause adolescent behavior, turmoil, moodiness, difficulties in parent-adolescent relationships, and hypersexuality (e.g., Kestenberg, 1968).

Endocrine studies documented the increases in pubertal hormones that generally paralleled changes in the development of secondary sex characteristics (e.g., Gupta, Attanasio, & Raaf, 1975). The most exciting work in pubertal endocrinology investigated the mechanisms that control puberty (e.g., Grumbach, Grave, & Mayer, 1974). Research on precocious puberty (e.g., Comite et al., 1987), a problem in which children as young as four or five develop secondary sex characteristics such as breasts or pubic hair, revealed that the mechanisms that control pubertal change develop prenatally. An apparent test of the system, involving the attainment of adult endocrine values, occurs just prior to birth (e.g., Grumbach et al., 1974). These high hormone levels are then suppressed until, in normal children, pubertal hormone levels begin increasing around seven years of age, with visible somatic changes typically appearing four or five years later. These somatic changes appear a year or two earlier in girls than in boys, depending on the specific characteristic examined (Marshall & Tanner, 1969, 1970).

Puberty, including growth to maturity and reproductive maturation, has been studied in many populations worldwide (e.g., Eveleth & Tanner, 1976). Pubertal change is a universal characteristic of adolescence and involves the most extensive and rapid change in postnatal life (Grave, 1974). The timing of pubertal changes, as well as the extent of growth attained, are constrained by factors related generally to socioeconomic status (Eveleth & Tanner, 1976). Particularly, adequacy of nutrition and health care have been linked to attaining optimal growth (e.g., Singh & Ahuja, 1979). Puberty is typically delayed when nutrition and health conditions are poor (Akinboye, 1984; duToit, 1987; Haq, 1984; Mallik, Ghosh, & Chattopadhyay, 1986). Rural-urban differences often index socioeconomic status, with rural girls' age at menarche, for example, typically being a year or two higher than that seen among urban girls within the same country or region (Eveleth & Tanner, 1976; Madhavan, 1965). Interestingly, the oft-noted secular reduction in age at menarche (e.g., Tanner, 1962) appears to be seen only in better-off populations, with little secular change seen among the rural poor (Malina, 1985). The historical trends toward earlier puberty are seen for pubertal status (e.g., Largo & Prader, 1983) as well as for age at peak growth and menarche (Akinboye, 1984; Haq, 1984).

Perhaps more important than the physical changes themselves are the responses of the self and others to the physical changes. Societal reactions to youngsters approaching physical maturity vary widely among cultures, although we note that this topic has been studied less frequently than the biological changes themselves. Differences in the treatment of adolescent boys and girls seem to be a universal phenomenon. For example, a number of ethnographic accounts clearly indicate that girls are subjected to more restrictions than boys at the onset of puberty. These can range from severe limits on their freedom of movement and dress (a result of religious beliefs regarding their chastity and social role) and menstrual taboos (Das, 1979; Diallo, 1982; Kitahara, 1983; Melikian, 1981), to less restrictive consequences, such as a decrease in the free time available to them resulting from increased household responsibilities. Boys are likely to be encouraged to pursue their education or be left with comparatively little supervision (Melikian, 1981; Saraswathi, 1988 personal communication).

Puberty brings reproductive maturation, thus raising issues of sex. In many societies, especially the Islamic, but also the Chinese, the discussion of issues related to sex is not considered appropriate, though it may occur among same-sex peers or directly preceding marriage, the typical context in which some knowledge of sex is acquired (Diallo, 1982; McClure, 1988; Melikian, 1981). Puberty rites, such as large celebrations, periods of seclusion, and circumcision for boys, and excision for girls, are fairly common, particularly in matrilocal societies (Kitahara, 1983; Weeks, 1973). On the whole, it can be concluded that although the physical development of adolescents in developing countries parallels that in industrialized nations, there are marked differences in the social consequences of maturing physically, especially for girls.

Adolescents are acutely aware of their changing selves. Two aspects of pubertal changes may be important to psychosocial functioning: *pubertal status,* the changes experienced by every individual as he or she matures physically; and *pubertal timing,* the timing of these changes relative to that for same-aged peers. Pubertal status effects could be direct results of hormonal changes, or they could be indirect effects mediated by social and psychological responses of the individual or of others in the social environment (Peterson & Taylor, 1980). Although timing effects could have a direct biological origin (for example, if earlier pubertal timing produced changes different from those of later timing), they are more likely to result from interaction between the timing of puberty relative to that of peers and the psychological and social responses of the individual and others.

Other processes may have an impact on psychosocial outcomes as well. Extreme asynchrony among pubertal changes could produce anxiety in an individual and perhaps physical difficulties as well (Eichorn, 1975). For example, feet typically grow before limbs, producing a clumsy individual for a time (Tanner, 1974).

4.2. Puberty and Psychosocial Functioning

Research linking pubertal change and psychosocial status has thus far found little evidence for pervasive pubertal effects on psychosocial variables, but these effects are specific and proximal. Not uniformly negative, they may enhance functioning. Finally, the effects on boys and girls appear to be different, but these differences may be culture-specific.

Only a few studies have examined the hypothesis that pubertal change increases psychological difficulties. Research on a U.S. sample, controlling for age effects, found that advancing pubertal status was related to enhanced body image and improved moods for boys but to decreased feelings of attractiveness for girls (Crockett & Petersen, 1987). As pubertal status advanced, both boys and girls became more interested in sex, and conflict increased in girls' relationships with their parents. Analyses of pubertal timing effects revealed improved psychological adjustment for later-developing boys and girls (Petersen & Crockett, 1985). These results corresponded well with others, as long as pubertal status was not confounded with chronological age. For example, Simmons and Blyth found that early pubertal development was related to better body image and higher self-esteem for boys in the United States (Blyth, Simmons, Bulcroft, Felt, Van

Cleave, & Bush, 1981), whereas for girls later development was associated with these positive psychological outcomes (Simmons, Blyth, Van Cleave, & Bush, 1979). These researchers hypothesized (Simmons, Blyth, & McKinney, 1983) that pubertal change is most stressful when it puts the young adolescent in a deviant status relative to his or her peers or when the changes are not seen as advantageous or desirable. Thus, although early-maturing boys tend to be more muscular, leading to social benefits such as strength and athletic ability (Simmons & Blyth, 1987), the pubertal changes manifested by girls (e.g., weight gain) are in conflict with some girls' desire for thinness.

However, a quite different relationship between pubertal development and psychological outcomes was seen in a German sample. Silbereisen, Noack, and von Eye (1989) found higher self-esteem among early-maturing girls. They speculated that the difference between this result and that for U.S. girls indicated the higher value of mature appearance as well as the greater openness to sex education in West Germany. However, this study also found that early-maturing girls were more likely to engage in problem behavior and associate with deviant peers, a finding that is in accord with results of Magnusson and colleagues (1985) on a Swedish sample.

Although many researchers acknowledge the importance of the social forces that mediate between pubertal development and psychosocial outcomes, other more direct links are possible. For example, Rutter (1980) found that although none of the prepubescent boys he surveyed reported depressed feelings, a small number of pubescent boys and almost one-third of postpubescent boys did report depressive affect. Rutter suggested that puberty rather than age may be the crucial factor in the development of psychological disorders, but he could not separate the influences of endocrine levels from those of psychological adaptations to sexual maturation.

Other research has attempted to address the effects of hormonal levels more directly. Nottelmann and colleagues (Nottelmann, Susman, Inoff-Germain, Cutler, Loriaux, & Chrousos, 1987), for example, reported that, especially for boys, adjustment problems were associated with a profile that may reflect later maturation (for boys, low sex steroid levels, low pubertal stage, and higher adrenal androgen levels in combination with greater chronological age). For both boys and girls, relatively high levels of adrenal androgen were associated with adjustment difficulties. Because adrenal androgen level is responsive to environmental stressors, the profile of lower levels of sex steroids and higher levels of both adrenal androgen and adjustment problems was interpreted as reflecting stress-related processes. In this case, the stress of later maturation may result from self-comparisons with same-age peers or from the effects of adrenal and gonadal hormones.

Therefore, research suggests that puberty per se does not bring psychological turmoil. Pubertal hormones may affect the behavior of boys, particularly agression (Olweus, 1979). Hormones may also affect sexual interest (e.g., Meyer-Bahlburg et al., 1985; Udry, Billy, Morris, Groff, & Raj, 1985; Udry, Talbert, &

Morris, 1986). Most of the observed effects, however, appear to be mediated by or interact with social, psychological, and physical factors, such as dieting or intense exercise (Brooks-Gunn & Warren, 1987). Becoming pubertal has meaning for an individual's emerging status as an adult, socially and sexually. Cultural standards for attractiveness in women, particularly the prevalent emphasis on thinness, appear to be implicated in the negative relationship between becoming pubertal and body image in girls (e.g., Faust, 1983; Garner & Garfinkel, 1980).

These general findings do not apply to certain subgroups of adolescents, for whom puberty may hold liabilities. For example, Simmons and colleagues (Zakin, Blyth, & Simmons, 1984) found that attractive girls were more anxious about becoming pubertal than were less attractive girls. Adolescents whose occupational goals involve a particular body shape, such as aspiring models, dancers, and athletes, may be disappointed or distressed when puberty produces some other shape and may be at risk for developing subsequent psychological difficulties.

Future research on puberty will continue to elucidate the mechanism of its effects on specific subgroups. The literature is already sufficient to suggest several hypotheses. For example, it seems reasonable to hypothesize that children who are having difficulties with issues of control, particularly those struggling to attain greater control of their lives (Block & Block, 1980; Brandtstaedter, Krampen, & Greve, 1987), will be likely to have negative reactions to pubertal change, a process typically beyond the control of the individual. On the biological side of the process, newer methods of endocrine assay afford the possibility of specifying the hormones most responsible for effects, both physical and psychological (e.g., Susman, Nottelmann, Dorn, Gold, & Chrousos, 1987). Social factors can be examined with pubertal change as well, to identify which family, peer, or cultural contexts produce which kinds of developmental processes (e.g., Magnusson, 1987; Magnusson, Stattin, & Allen, 1985).

5. ADOLESCENT-FAMILY INTERACTIONS

Although the relationship of adolescents to their families has been of interest for some time, recent research has benefited from the increase in attention to adolescence as a period of life and from technological advances such as computer-linked audio or video capability, which permits more efficient access to family interactions. Recent adolescent-family research is very much in the tradition of contextually based life-span psychology (e.g., Baltes et al., 1980; Bronfenbrenner, 1979; Lerner & Spanier, 1978), examining the reciprocal effects of the family on the developing individual (e.g., Block, Block, & Gjerde, 1986; Cooper, Grotevant, & Condon, 1983; Hauser et al., 1984) and of the developing individual on family processes (e.g., Steinberg, 1981; Steinberg & Hill, 1978). In addition to being consistent with the life-span perspective on human development (e.g., Lerner, 1984), the nature of recent adolescent-family research is also consistent with recent conceptualizations of parent-child relationships (e.g., Maccoby & Martin, 1983) as well as with family systems theory (Kaye, 1985; Schneewind, 1987).

5.1. Adolescent-Family Conflict

The traditional belief is that adolescents and their parents suffer from a "generation gap." Research has shown this belief to be incorrect (e.g., Bengtson, 1975; Lerner, Karson, Meisels, & Knapp, 1975). For example, parents and their children had more similar values and attitudes than did adolescents and their friends; adolescent-peer similarities were typically found in areas of "adolescent culture," such as dress and music (Kandel & Lesser, 1972). It is important to note, however, that cultures vary in the extent of autonomy granted to adolescents by parents. Asian and African cultures, for example, expect more conformity to parental views than do Western cultures (e.g., Poole, Cooney, & Cheong, 1986; Vandewiele & D'Hondt, 1983).

The view that adolescent-parent relationships are inevitably stormy has been advanced primarily by psychoanalytic theorists (e.g., Adelson & Doehrman, 1980; Blos, 1970) and has not been supported by research findings (see Montemayor [1983] for a review). The origins of adolescent-parent conflict were once thought to be adolescent difficulties, needs, and developmental changes (e.g., Blos, 1962; Erikson, 1968; Hall, 1904), but parental factors, such as parents' midlife status (Chilman, 1968; Hill, 1980), marital relationship (Wadkar, Gore, & Palsane, 1986), and maternal control (Turner, 1980) have now been identified as playing a role in adolescent-parent stress. Perceived agreement between parents and children is much higher than the actual agreement between them, with adolescents' accuracy of perception being an important mediational factor (Cashmore & Goodnow, 1985).

Recently, it has been typical for observers to consider the family system in relation to the developmental status of family members. In particular, the developmental changes and needs of adolescents are thought to disrupt the functioning of a family system, requiring a readjustment to achieve a new homeostasis. The limited existing research suggests that there is an increase in parent-adolescent conflict during early adolescence, with subsequent declines occurring until adolescents leave the parental home (Montemayor, 1983; Smetana, 1987). The manifestations of parent-adolescent conflict have changed little over the past century (e.g., Caplow & Bahr, 1979; Lynd & Lynd, 1929), involving primarily such mundane aspects of life as chores and hours. Potentially explosive issues, such as sex, tend not to be discussed.

The belief that parent-adolescent conflict is basically healthy is not supported by the relevant research. High levels of conflict are related to adolescents' moving away (Gottlieb & Chafetz, 1977), running away (Blood & D'Angelo, 1974;

Shellow, Schamp, Liebow, & Unger, 1967; Singh, 1984), joining religious cults (Kox, Meeus, & 't Hart, 1991; Ullman, 1982), marrying or becoming pregnant early (McKenry, Walters, & Johnston, 1979), dropping out of school (Bachman, Green, & Wirtanen, 1971), developing psychiatric disorders (Rutter et al., 1976; Hurrelmann, Engel, Holler, & Nordlohne, 1988; Rao, Channabasavanna, & Parthasarathy, 1982), attempting suicide (Jacobs, 1971), and abusing drugs (e.g., Kandel, Kessler, & Margulies, 1978; McCubbin, Needle, & Wilson, 1985). Similarly, low family cohesion has been related to poorer adolescent self-esteem (Silbereisen, Walper, & Albrecht, 1990), with a more open family climate related to greater resilience among adolescents (Loesel, Bliesener, Kaeferl, 1989; Mikesell & Sorensen, 1989) and better coping (Shulman, Seiffge-Krenke, & Samet, 1987).

The ability of parents to encourage mature problem solving and to allow adolescents to individuate has been linked to adolescents' psychological development as well. For example, Cooper and Grotevant (Cooper et al., 1983; Grotevant & Cooper, 1985) observed in a sample of U.S. high school seniors and their families that individuation, including both connectedness and individuality, was favorable for adolescents' development of role-taking skill and for identity development. In similar research, Hauser and colleagues (Hauser, Powers, Noam, Jacobson, Weiss, & Follansbee, 1984) linked patterns of discourse (whether discourse sequences progressed positively, regressed, terminated, or changed focus) and the use of enabling discourse (e.g., problem solving, empathy) rather than constraining discourse (e.g., devaluing, withholding) to higher ego development in adolescents.

The majority of non-Western studies of family relationships have surveyed adolescents' perceptions of their parents' personality or behavior (Dhammi, Sathyavathi, & Murthy, 1978; Rosenthal, Efklides, & Demetriou, 1988; Singh & Singh, 1986; Vandewiele, 1981). Generally, adolescents from less industrialized countries have reported more positive family relationships than those from Western nations (Offer et al., 1988).

5.2. Pubertal Change and Family Interaction

One of the interesting areas of research integrating the areas discussed thus far concerns the effects on family interaction of a child's becoming pubertal. The primary hypothesis is that pubertal change signals emerging adult size, shape, and reproductive potential and that this new status affects the nature of the child's interactions with mother and father. The theoretical perspectives that have been used as the framework for examining this set of relationships range from sociobiology (e.g., Savin-Williams, Small, & Zeldin, 1981; Steinberg, 1981), to family process (e.g., Papini & Datan, 1983), to gender role relationships (e.g., Hill, Holmbeck, Marlow, Green, & Lynch, 1985a, 1985b).

The results show that in families with two biological parents present, both boys and girls engage in more conflict with parents as they reach the middle of the pubertal process (e.g., Hill et al., 1985a, 1985b; Papini & Datan, 1983; Steinberg, 1981; Steinberg & Hill, 1978), although slight gender variations are found as well: Girls experienced decreased levels of conflict with and control by their mothers as they reached puberty (Anderson, Hetherington, & Clingempeel, 1986; Hill et al., 1985a).

For both girls and boys, the peak of pubertal change in family relationships is considerably earlier than the stereotypes of adolescent-parent conflict suggest. Rather than occurring in the late high school years, it is actually at around 12 years of age in girls and at around 13 years in boys. More research is needed to identify the aspects of parent-child relationships that change and why they change, but a common interpretation of these studies is that with an adolescent's increasing maturity and impending adult status, the adolescent-parent relationship needs to adjust. It is functional for an individual to begin to have more autonomy and responsibility within the family as he or she proceeds through adolescence, and puberty is an appropriate signal for the timing of this change.

Research with families involving stepparents or single parents suggests that pubertal effects on the adolescent-parent relationship are conditional on parental composition. For example, Hetherington and colleagues (Anderson et al., 1986) found that the patterns were entirely different with stepfathers and single or remarried mothers. For both boys and girls in single-mother or mother-stepfather families, there was less mother-child conflict at the pubertal apex and a generally more quiescent transition. The authors interpreted this result in terms of other results on the effects of divorce: Children in divorced families are expected to behave more maturely and responsibly than children in nondivorced families. A transformation in the parent-child relationship like that occurring with puberty may take place soon after a divorce. No relationship between pubertal status and conflict with stepfathers was seen; in general, stepfathers appeared to be disengaged from their stepchildren. Because these remarriages all took place within a year of data collection, the authors reasoned that pubertal effects were suppressed by the more potent process of incorporating the stepfather into the family. These results suggest that family context at puberty's onset influences the nature and intensity of adolescent-parent interactions. The strong effects of parental composition have been seen in other research as well (e.g., Dornbusch et al., 1985). We note, however, that the cross-national generality of these U.S. findings has not been established.

6. OTHER AREAS OF ACTIVE WORK

Four additional areas merit brief summaries: (1) cognition and achievement, (2) social development and peer relationships, (3) problem behavior, and (4) effects of economic hardship and unemployment.

6.1. Cognition and Achievement

There has always been a substantial amount of research on the cognitive development and achievement of adolescents (e.g., Bayley, 1949; Inhelder & Piaget, 1958). Recent research has provided new information on developmental trends. School achievement, in terms of marks assigned by teachers, appears to decline in U.S. samples over the adolescent years (e.g., Schulenberg, Asp, & Petersen, 1984; Simmons & Blyth, 1987). Grade decline is generally believed to result from increasingly stringent grading practices. In contrast, cognitive development and cognitive abilities increase over the years, with particular increase occurring in the capacity to think abstractly (e.g., Keating & Clark, 1980; Martorano, 1977; Petersen, 1983). Most studies have found a male advantage on the usual tests measuring formal operations or abstract thinking (e.g., Dulit, 1972; Sandhu, 1984), though the fact that not all have found such a difference (Huang, Yang, Liu, & Yao, 1985) suggests there may be cross-national variations. As mentioned earlier, cognitive development is frequently linked to contextual variables such as family size (Davis et al., 1977), birth order (Munroe & Munroe, 1988), and parental attitudes (Visser, 1987).

The possibility that cognitive change in adolescence is linked to pubertal change has been repeatedly examined (e.g., Kohen-Raz, 1974; Shuttleworth, 1939). Interestingly, a recent meta-analysis of the relationship between pubertal timing and IQ test performance supports the view that early maturers have a small but consistent advantage except on spatial tasks that require "disembedding" (Newcombe & Dubas, 1987). Waber's intriguing hypothesis (1976, 1977) that the earlier pubertal timing of girls produced sex differences in cognition has not been supported by subsequent work (see Linn and Petersen [1985] and Newcombe and Dubas [1987] for reviews).

6.2. Social Development and Peer Relationships

Adolescence involves systematic changes in social development and the nature of peer relationships (Bigelow & La Gaipa, 1975; Coleman, 1974, 1980; Douvan & Adelson, 1966). The peer group increases in size and complexity (Crockett, Losoff, & Petersen, 1984), with adolescents spending and enjoying more time with chosen friends than with classmates (Csikszentmihalyi & Larson, 1984; Palmonari, Pombeni, & Kirchler, 1989). Adolescents are more involved and intimate with peers than are children, increasingly sharing thoughts and feelings (Camarena, Sarigiani, & Petersen, 1992; Hartup, 1983; Youniss & Smollar, 1985).

Gottman and Mettetal's (1987) analysis of U.S. adolescents' conversations provides interesting and rich data on the processes involved in friendship. Their results led them to hypothesize that "developmental change in friendship occurs because of changes in the affective competence demands of the ecological niches children are forced by our culture to occupy and to maneuver within" (p. 193). Salient ecological niches of adolescents include school and cross-sex and same-sex peer cultures (cf. Dunphy, 1963). These researchers further proposed that qualitative change in cognitive competence accompanies the increasing social competence involved in friendship change.

Research on the "fourth environment" (Van Vliet, 1983), that is, settings such as street corners and shopping malls (Anthony, 1985), has revealed that contacts with peers and the formation of heterosexual friendships figure prominently among the motives and consequent behaviors of adolescents (Noack & Silbereisen, 1988). Furthermore, using longitudinal data on change in leisure preferences, Silbereisen, Noack, and von Eye (1992) reported a link between the desire for other-sex friendships and adolescents' preferences for settings that help to promote dating (Goodnow, 1988).

6.3. Problem Behavior

As noted earlier, several kinds of behavior thought to be problematic increase over the adolescent period. Research has focused especially on drug and alcohol use, cigarette smoking, sexual behavior, and delinquency (e.g., Farrington, 1986; Jessor & Jessor, 1977; West, 1982). Most of these behaviors would not be alarming in adults but are perceived as inappropriate for youngsters (Petersen, 1982). Excessive engagement in many of these behaviors, of course, can be problematic at any age.

Though research has been highly active in the field of adolescent problem behavior, relatively few approaches have realized appropriate designs and concepts with which to investigate the developmental processes. Following the model provided by U.S. normal population studies (e.g., Johnston, O'Malley, & Bachman, 1986), longitudinal research in other countries has focused on smoking and alcohol (e.g., Galambos & Silbereisen, 1987; Pulkkinen, 1983; Semmer et al., 1987; Sieber & Angst, 1981) and on illegal psychoactive drugs (Holmberg, 1985). Fillmore and colleagues (Fillmore, Golding, Leino, Ager, & Ferrer, 1991) reported a meta-analytic investigation of longitudinal data on alcohol consumption from more than a dozen countries. Cross-sectional studies (e.g., D'Hondt & Vandeweile, 1983, 1984; Kandel & Adler, 1981; Morales & Atilano, 1977; Soueif, El-Sayed, Darweesh, Hannourah, & Yunis, 1988; Teichmann, Rahav, & Barnea, 1987) are important because of their broad epidemiological approach. In-depth studies have also reported on the use of heroin (Projektgruppe Tudrop, 1984; Uchtenhagen & Zimmer-Hofler, 1987) and inhalants (Teck-Hong, 1986; Zank, 1988).

Most of these results suggest that problem behavior is related to coping with developmental tasks, decreasing controls by adults, and the increasing attraction of peer-related activities, all probably related to the transition to adulthood.

Moreover, Yamaguchi and Kandel (1985) found a reduction in the use of illegal substances concurrent with or even preceding the transition to adult family roles.

Silbereisen and colleagues (e.g., Silbereisen, Noack, & Eyferth, 1986) have proposed that these so-called problem behaviors are in fact purposive, self-regulating, and designed to cope with problems of development. Therefore, they play a constructive developmental role, at least over the short term (Kaplan, 1980; Silbereisen & Reitzle, 1992). Early sexual activity and even early child-bearing may have a similar function (Petersen, Ebata, & Graber, 1987). Nevertheless, the negative consequences of these behaviors over the long term, and often, lasting developmental effects, can be clearly documented (e.g., Baumrind & Moselle, 1985; Felsman & Vaillant, 1987; Furstenberg, Brooks-Gunn, & Morgan, 1987; Himmelweit & Turner, 1982; Kandel, Davies, Karus, & Yamaguchi, 1986; Pulkkinen, in press).

6.4. Economic Hardship and Unemployment

Research on the effects of economic hardship and unemployment on adolescents and their families has a long tradition. Jahoda, Lazarsfeld, and Zeisel (1933) were, in their study of an Austrian village, the first to emphasize the psychological significance of economic deprivation on the development of the young. The research by Elder and colleagues (e.g., Elder & Caspi, 1988) gives an exceptionally rich picture of the impact of the Great Depression on U.S. family life and adolescents' psychosocial development. The studies showed that adolescents' well-being and conduct were negatively influenced by financial loss, with increased strains in family relationships mediating the effects. Using West German data from the 1980s, research has confirmed the central role of family processes in linking economic problems to self-derogation, transgression proneness, and other aspects of maladjustment (Silbereisen et al., 1990).

Noncollege youth are especially adversely affected by unemployment (Kieselbach, 1987). In some regions of Britain, for instance, one-third of all school leavers have had to anticipate long-term unemployment (Roberts, 1984). Because adequate work environments provide opportunities for learning, iniative, social contact, and self-reliance (Greenberger & Steinberg, 1981; Jahoda, 1979), the negative impact of unemployment on mental health is not surprising (McPherson & Hall, 1983; Warr, Banks, & Ullah, 1985) and is more severe among adolescents high in job commitment (Jackson, Stafford, Banks, & Warr, 1983).

The effect of poverty in non-Western nations, as measured by their gross national products (GNPs), was examined by Offer and colleagues (1988); that research revealed that the emotional tone or mood of adolescents from ten countries was positively related to national income. Impulse control and body image seemed particularly poor in low-GNP countries. Adolescents from poorer families also reported more psychological problems (Venkata Rami Reddy, 1979), were in poorer health, and performed worse on intelligence tests (Misra et al., 1982).

7. CONCLUDING COMMENT

This sampling of research on adolescence cannot do justice to the large and varied body of extant work. However, in the present review we have attempted not only to aid understanding of adolescence, but also to illuminate development in general. Because there are so many changes during adolescence, and these changes require effective coping on the part of the individual, the processes involved are likely to be ones he or she will need to use to respond to challenges throughout life. Furthermore, we could hypothesize that adolescence differs from earlier years in the nature of the challenges encountered and in the capacity of an individual to respond effectively to challenge. If this hypothesis is correct, adolescence will be the first phase of life requiring, and presumably stimulating, mature patterns of functioning that persist throughout life. Conversely, failure to cope effectively with the challenges of adolescence may represent deficiencies in an individual that bode ill for subsequent development. Continued research on the biological, psychological, and social factors that affect the developmental course over adolescence will surely inform future knowledge on these questions. Cross-national research is particularly needed to distinguish generality from specificity in particular results.

REFERENCES

Adelson, J. (Ed.). (1980). *Handbook of adolescent psychology*. New York: Wiley.

Adelson, J., & Doehrman, M. J. (1980). The psychodynamic approach to adolescence. In J. Adelson (Ed.), *Handbook of adolescent psychology* (pp. 99–116). New York: Wiley.

Akinboye, J. O. (1984). Secondary sexual characteristics and normal puberty in Nigerian and Zimbabwian adolescents. *Adolescence, 19*, 483–492.

Anderson, E. R., Hetherington, E. M., & Clingempeel, W. G. (1986). *Pubertal status and its influence on the adaptation to remarriage*. Paper presented at the Society for Research in Adolescence, Madison, WI.

Anthony, K. H. (1985). The shopping mall: A teenage hangout. *Adolescence, 20*, 307–312.

Antonovsky, H., & Sagy, S. (1986). The development of a sense of coherence and its impact on responses to stress situations. *Journal of Social Psychology, 126*, 213–235.

Aries, P. (1962). *Centuries of childhood: A social history on family life*. (R. Baldick, Trans.). New York: Random House.

Attie, I., Brooks-Gunn, J., & Petersen, A. C. (1987). A developmental perspective on eating disorders and eating problems. In M. Lewis & S. M. Miller (Eds.), *Handbook of developmental psychopathy*. New York: Plenum.

Bachman, J. G., Green, S., & Wirtanen, I. D. (1971). *Youth in transition: Dropping out—Problem or symptom* (Vol. 3). Ann Arbor, MI: Institute for Social Research.

Bachman, J. G., Johnston, L. D., & O'Malley, P. M. (1981). *Monitoring the future: Questionnaire responses from the nation's high school seniors*. Ann Arbor: Institute for Social Research.

Baltes, P. B., Reese, H. W., & Lipsitt, L. P. (1980). Life-span developmental psychology. *Annual Review of Psychology, 31*, 65–110.

Bandura, A. (1964). The stormy decade: Fact or fiction? *Psychology in the Schools, 1*, 224–231.

Bandura, A. (1982). Self-efficacy mechanism in human agency. *American Psychologist, 37*, 122–147.

Bandura, A. (1987). Self-regulation of motivation and action through goal systems. In V. Hamilton, G. H. Bower, & N. H. Fryda (Eds.), *Cognition, maturation, and affect: A cognitive science view*. Dordrecht: Martinus Nijhoff.

Baumrind, D. (1985). Familial antecedents of adolescent drug use: A developmental perspective. In C. L. Jones & R. J. Battjes (Eds.), *Etiology of drug abuse: Implications for prevention* (NIDA Research Monograph No. 56) (pp. 13–44). Rockville, MD: National Institute on Drug Abuse.

Baumrind, D., & Moselle (1985). A developmental perspective on adolescent drug abuse. *Advances in Alcohol and Substances Abuse, 4*(3–4), 41–67. Berkeley: University of California Institute of Human Development.

Bayer, L. M., & Bayley, N. (1959). *Growth diagnosis*. Chicago: University of Chicago Press.

Bayley, N. (1949). Consistency and variability in the growth of intelligence from birth to eighteen years. *Journal of Genetic Psychology, 75*, 165–196.

Bengtson, V. L. (1975). Generation and family effects in value socialization. *American Sociological Review, 40*, 358–371.

Bigelow, B. J., & La Gaipa, J. J. (1975). Children's written descriptions of friendship. *Developmental Psychology, 11*, 857–858.

Block, J. H., & Block, J. (1980). The role of ego-control and ego-resiliency in the organization of behavior. In W. A. Collins (Ed.), *The Minnesota Symposia in Child Psychology: Vol. 14. The development of cognition, affect, and social relations* (pp. 39–101). Hillsdale, NJ: Erlbaum.

Block, J. H., Block, J., & Gjerde, P. F. (1986). The personality of children prior to divorce: A prospective study. *Child Development, 57*, 827–840.

Block, J. H., & Gjerde, P. F. (1990). Depressive symptomatology in late adolescence: A longitudinal perspective on personality antecedents. In J. E. Rolf, A. Masten, D. Cicchetti, K. H. Nuechterlein, & S. Weintraub (Eds.), *Risk and protective factors in the development of psychopathology*. New York: Cambridge University Press.

Blood, L., & D'Angelo, R. (1974). A progress report on value issues in conflict between runaways and their parents. *Journal of Marriage and the Family, 36*, 486–491.

Blos, P. (1962). *On adolescence: A psychoanalytic interpretation*. New York: Free Press.

Blos, P. (1970). *The young adolescent*. New York: Free Press.

Blyth, D. A., Simmons, R. G., Bulcroft, R., Felt, D., VanCleave, E. F., & Bush, D. M. (1981). The effects of physical development on self-image and satisfaction with body-image for early adolescent males. In R. G. Simmons (Ed.), *Research in community and mental health* (Vol. 2, pp. 43–73). Greenwich, CT: JAI.

Bolger, N., Caspu, A., Downey, G., & Moorehouse, M. (Eds.). (1988). Persons in context: Developmental processes. New York: Cambridge University Press.

Brandstaeder, J., Krampen, G., & Greve, W. (1987). Personal control over development: Effects on the perception and emotional evaluation of personal development in adulthood. *International Journal of Behavioral Development, 10*, 99–120.

Brim, O. G., & Kagan, J. (1980). *Constancy and change in human development.* Cambridge, MA: Harvard University Press.

Bronfenbrenner, U. (1979). *The ecology of human development: Experiments by nature and design.* Cambridge, MA: Harvard University Press.

Bronfenbrenner, U. (1989). Ecological systems theory. In R. Vasta (Ed.), *Six theories of child development: Revised formulations and current issues,* Annals of Child Development, Vol. 6 (pp. 187–249). Greenwich, CT: JAI.

Brooks-Gunn, J. (1983). *Psychological functioning and pubertal status: The effects of different maturational indices.* Paper presented at the annual meeting of the American Psychological Association, Anaheim, CA.

Brooks-Gunn, J., & Petersen, A. C. (Eds.). (1983). *Girls at puberty: Biological and psychosocial perspectives.* New York: Plenum.

Brooks-Gunn, J., & Petersen, A. C. (1984). Problems in studying and defining pubertal events. *Journal of Youth and Adolescence, 13*, 181–196.

Brooks-Gunn, J., & Warren, M. P. (1985). Effects of delayed menarche in different contexts: Dance and nondance students. *Journal of Youth and Adolescence, 14*, 285–300.

Brooks-Gunn, J., & Warren, M. P. (1987). *Biological contributions to affective expression in young adolescent girls.* Paper presented at the Biennial Meeting of the Society for Research in Child Development, Baltimore.

Camarena, P. M., Sarigiani, P. A., & Petersen, A. C. (1990). Gender-specific pathways to intimacy in early adolescence. *Journal of Youth and Adolescence, 12*, 19–32.

Caplow, T., & Bahr, H. M. (1979). Half a century of change in adolescent attitudes: Replication of a Middletown survey by the Lynds. *Public Opinion Quarterly, 1*, 17.

Cashmore, J. A., & Goodnow, J. J. (1985). Agreement between generations: A two-process approach. *Child Development, 56*, 493–501.

Chiam, H. (1987). Change in self-concept during adolescence. *Adolescence, 22*, 69–76.

Chilman, C. S. (1968). Families in development at mid-stage of the family life cycle. *Family Coordinator, 17*, 297–331.

Cicchetti, D. (1984). The emergence of developmental psychopathology. *Child Development, 55*, 1–7.

Clarke, A. M., & Clarke, A. D. B. (Eds.). (1976). *Early experience: Myth and evidence.* New York: Free Press.

Coleman, J. C. (1974). *Relationships in adolescence.* London: Routledge & Kegan Paul.

Coleman, J. C. (1980). Friendship and peer group in adolescence. In J. Adelson (Ed.), *Handbook of adolescent psychology* (pp. 408–431). New York: Wiley.

Comite, F., Prescovitz, O. H., Sonis, W. A., Hench, K., McNemar, A., Klein, R. P.,

Loriaux, D. L., & Cutler, G. B., Jr. (1987). Premature adolescence: Neuroendocrine and psychosocial studies. In R. M. Lerner & T. T. Foch (Eds.), *Biological-psychosocial interactions in early adolescence* (pp. 155–172). Hillsdale, NJ: Erlbaum.

Conger, J. J., & Petersen, A. C. (1984). *Adolescence and youth* (3rd ed.). New York: Harper & Row.

Connell, J. P., & Furman, W. (1984). The study of transitions: Conceptual and methodological considerations. In R. Emde & R. Harmon (Eds.), *Continuities and discontinuities in development* (pp. 153–173). New York: Plenum.

Cooper, C., Grotevant, H., & Condon, S. (1983). Individuality and connectedness in the family as a context for adolescent identity formation and role-taking skills. In H. Grotevant & C. Cooper (Eds.), *Adolescent development in the family* (pp. 43–60). San Francisco: Jossey-Bass.

Crockett, L. J., Losoff, M., & Petersen, A. C. (1984). Perceptions of the peer group and friendship in early adolescence. *Journal of Early Adolescence, 4*, 155–181.

Crockett, L. J., & Petersen, A. C. (1987). Pubertal status and psychosocial development: Findings from the Early Adolescence Study. In R. M. Lerner & T. T. Foch (Eds.), *Biological-psychosocial interactions in early adolescence* (pp. 173–188). Hillsdale, NJ: Erlbaum.

Csikszentmihalyi, M., & Larson, R. (1984). *Being adolescent*. New York: Basic Books.

Damon, W., & Hart, D. (1982). The development of self-understanding from infancy through adolescence. *Child Development, 53*, 841–864.

Das, V. (1979). Reflections on the social construction of adulthood. In S. Kakar (Ed.), *Identity and adulthood* (pp. 89–104). Delhi, India: Oxford University Press.

Davis, D. J., Cahan, S., Bashi, J. (1977). Birth order and intellectual development: The confluence model in light of cross-cultural evidence. *Science, 196*, 1470–1472.

Deutsches Institut für Wirtschaftsforschung. (1988). *Wochenbericht 32/88* [Weekly Report]. Berlin: Duncker & Humbolt.

Dhammi, R., Sathyavathi, K., & Murthy, H. N. (1978). Perception of parents by modern youths. *Indian Journal of Clinical Psychology, 5*, 123–129.

D'Hondt, W., & Vandeweile, M. (1983). Attitudes of Sengalese school-going adolescents towards tobacco smoking. *Journal of Youth and Adolescence, 12*, 333–353.

D'Hondt, W., & Vandeweile, M. (1984). Use of drugs among Senegalese school-going adolescents. *Journal of Youth and Adolescence, 13*, 253–266.

Diallo, N. (1982). *A Dakar childhood*. Harlow, U.K.: Lougman Group.

Dornbusch, S. M., Carlsmith, J. M., Bushwall, S. J., Ritter, P. L., Leiderman, H., Hastorf, A. H., & Gross, R. T. (1985). Single parents, extended households, and the control of adolescents. *Child Development, 56*, 326–341.

Douvan, E., & Adelson, J. (1966). *The adolescent experience*. New York: Wiley.

Dulit, E. (1972). Adolescent thinking a la Piaget: The formal stage. *Journal of Youth and Adolescence, 1*, 281–301.

Dunphy, D. C. (1963). The social structure of urban adolescent peer groups. *Sociometry, 26*, 230–246.

duToit, B. M. (1987). Menarche and sexuality among a sample of black South African schoolgirls. *Social Science and Medicine, 24*, 561–571.

Ebata, A. T. (1987). *A longitudinal study of psychological distress during early adolescence*. Unpublished doctoral dissertation. Penn State University, State College, PA.

Eccles, J., Midgley, C., & Adler, T. F. (1984). Grade-related changes in the school environment: Effects on achievement motivation. In J. G. Nicholls (Ed.), *The development of achievement motivation: Advances in motivation and achievement* (Vol. 3, pp. 283–331). Greenwich, CT: JAI.

Edelstein, W., Keller, M., & Wahlen, K. (1984). Structure and content in social cognition: Conceptual and empirical analyses. *Child Development, 55*, 1514–1526.

Eichorn, D. H. (1975). Asychronizations in adolescent development. In J. E. Dragastin & G. H. Elder, Jr. (Eds.), *Adolescence in the life cycle: Psychological change and social context*. Washington, DC: Hemisphere.

Eichorn, D. H., Mussen, P. H., Clausen, N., Haan, M. P., & Honzik, M. P. (1981). Overview. In D. H. Eichorn, J. A. Clausen, N. Haan, M. P. Honzik, & P. H. Mussen (Eds.), *Present and past in middle life* (pp. 411–434). New York: Academic.

Elder, G. H., Jr. (1974). *Children of the great depression: Social change in life experience*. Chicago: University of Chicago Press.

Elder, G. H., Jr., & Caspi, A. (1988). Human development and social change: An emerging perspective on the life course. In N. Bolger, A. Caspi, G. Downes, & M. Moorehouse (Eds.), *Persons in context: Developmental processes* (pp. 77–113). Cambridge, MA: Cambridge University Press.

Erikson, E. H. (1968). *Identity: Youth and crisis*. New York: Norton.

Eveleth, P. B., & Tanner, J. M. (1976). *Worldwide variation in human growth*. Cambridge: Cambridge University Press.

Faiman, C., & Winter, J. S. D. (1974). Gonadotropins and sex hormone patterns in puberty: Clinical data. In M. M. Grumbach, G. D. Grave, & F. E. Mayer (Eds.), *Control of the onset of puberty* (pp. 32–55). New York: Wiley.

Farrington, D. P. (1986). Age and crime. In M. Tony & N. Morris (Eds.), *Crime and justice: An annual review of research* (pp. 189–250). Chicago: University of Chicago Press.

Faust, M. S. (1983). Alternative constructions of adolescent growth. In J. Brooks-Gunn & A. C. Petersen (Eds.), *Girls at puberty: Biological and psychosocial perspectives* (pp. 105–126). New York: Plenum.

Featherman, D. L., & Petersen, T. (1986). Markers of aging: Modeling the clocks that time us. *Research on Aging, 8*, 339–365.

Felsman, J. K., & Vaillant, G. E. (1987). Resilient children as adults: A 40-year study. In E. J. Anthony & B. J. Cohler (Eds.), *The invulnerable child* (pp. 289–314). London: Guilford Press.

Fend, H., & Schroer, S. (1985). The formation of self-concept in the context of educational systems. *International Journal of Behavioral Development, 8*, 423–444.

Fillmore, K. M., Golding, J. M., Leino, E. V., Ager, C. R., & Ferrer, H. (1991). *Aggregate-level predictors of group-level drinking consistency: A cross-study longitudinal analysis from the collaborative alcohol-related longitudinal project*. Paper presented at the 36th International Institute on the Prevention and Treatment of Alcoholism, Stockholm.

Frankenhaeuser, M. (1983). The sympathetic-adrenal and pituitary-adrenal response to challenge: Comparison between the sexes. In T. M. Dembroski, T. H. Schmidt, & G. Bluemchen (Eds.), *Biobehavioral bases of coronary heart disease* (pp. 91–105). Basel: Karger.

Freud, A. (1958). *Adolescence: Psychoanalytic study of the child* (Vol. 13). New York: Academic Press.

Friedrich, W., & Mueller, H. (Eds.). (1985). *Zur Psychologie der 12-bis 15-jaehrigen* [On the psychology of the 12-to-15-year-old]. Berlin: VEB Deutscher verlag der Wissenschaften.

Furstenberg, F. F., Jr., Brooks-Gunn, J., & Morgan, S. P. (1987). *Adolescent mothers in later life*. New York: Cambridge University Press.

Galambos, N. L., & Silbereisen, R. K. (1987). Substance use in West German youth: A longitudinal study of adolescents' use of alcohol and tobacco. *Journal of Adolescent Research, 2*, 161–174.

Garner, D. M., & Garfinkel, P. E. (1980). Socio-cultural factors in the development of anorexia nervosa. *Psychology and Medicine, 10*, 647–656.

Goodnow, J. J. (1988). Children, families, and communities: Ways of viewing their relationship to each other. In N. Bolger, A. Caspi, G. Downey, & M. Moorehouse (Eds.), *Persons in context: Developmental processes* (pp. 50–76). Cambridge: Cambridge University Press.

Gottlieb, D., & Chafetz, J. S. (1977). Dynamics of familial generational conflict and reconciliation. *Youth and Society, 9*, 213–224.

Gottman, J., & Mettetal, G. (1987). Speculations about social and affective development: Friendship and acquaintanceship through adolescence. In J. M. Gottman & J. Parker (Eds.), *Conversations of friends* (pp. 192–237). New York: Cambridge University Press.

Gove, W. R., & Herb, T. R. (1974). Stress and mental illness among the young: A comparison of the sexes. *Social Forces, 53*, 256–265.

Grant Foundation. (1988). *The forgotten half: Pathways to success for America's youth and young families*. Washington, DC: The William T. Grant Commission on Work, Family and Citizenship.

Grave, G. D. (1974). Introduction. In M. M. Grumbach, G. D. Grave, & F. E. Mayer (Eds.), *Control of the onset of puberty* (pp. xxiii-xxiv). New York: Wiley.

Green, L. W., & Horton, D. (1982) Adolescent health: Issues and challenges. In J. Coates, A. C. Petersen, & C. Perry (Eds.), *Promoting adolescent health: A dialog on research and practice* (pp. 23–43). New York: Academic Press.

Greenberger, E., & Steinberg, L. (1981). The workplace as a context for the socialization of youth. *Journal of Youth and Adolescence, 10*, 185–210.

Grinker, R. R., Sr., Grinker, R. R., Jr., & Timberlake, I. (1962). Mentally healthy young males (homoclites). *Archives of General Psychiatry, 6*, 311–318.

Grotevant, H., & Cooper, C. (1985). Patterns of interaction in family relationships and the development of identity exploration in adolescence. *Child Development, 56*, 415–428.

Grumbach, M. M., Grave, G. D., & Mayer, F. E. (Eds.). (1974). *Control of the onset of puberty*. New York: Wiley

Gupta, D., Attanasio, A., & Raaf, S. (1975). Plasma estrogen and androgen concentrations in children during adolescence. *Journal of Clinical Endocrinology and Metabolism, 40*, 636–643.

Hall, G. S. (1904). *Adolescence: Its psychology and its relation to physiology, anthropology, sociology, sex, crime, religion, and education* (Vols. 1, 2). New York: Appleton-Century-Crofts.

Hamburg, B. A. (1974). Early adolescence: A specific and stressful stage of the life cycle. In G. V. Coelho & J. E. Adams (Eds.), *Coping and adaptation* (pp. 101–124). New York: Basic Books.

Haq, M. (1984). Age at menarche and the related issue: A pilot study on urban school girls. *Journal of Youth and Adolescence, 13,* 559–567.

Hartup, W. W. (1983). Peer relations. In E. M. Hetherington (Ed.), *Handbook of child psychology: Vol. 4. Socialization, personality and social development* (pp. 103–196). New York: Wiley.

Hauser, S. T., Powers, S. I. Noam, G. G., Jacobson, A. M., Weiss, B., & Follansbee, D. J. (1984). Familial contexts of adolescent ego development. *Child Development, 55,* 195–213.

Hill, J. (1980). The family. In M. Johnson (Ed.), *Toward adolescence: The middle school years* (pp. 32–55). Chicago: University of Chicago Press.

Hill, J., Holmbeck, G., Marlow, L., Green, T., & Lynch, M. (1985a). Menarcheal status and parent-child relations in families of seventh-grade girls. *Journal of Youth and Adolescence, 14,* 301–316.

Hill, J., Holmbeck, G., Marlow, L., Green, T., & Lynch, M. (1985b). Pubertal status and parent-child relations in families of seventh-grade boys. *Journal of Early Adolescence, 5,* 31–44.

Himmelweit, H. T., & Turner, C. F. (1982). Social and psychological antecedents of depression: A longitudinal study from adolescence to early adulthood of a nonclinical population. In P. B. Baltes & O. G. Brim, Jr., *Life-span development and behavior* (Vol. 4, pp. 315–344). New York: Academic Press.

Holmberg, M. B. (1985). Longitudinal studies of drug abuse in a fifteen-year-old population. 1. Drug career. *Acta Psychiatrica Scandinavia, 71,* 67–79.

Huang, Y., Yang, Z., Liu, Z., & Yao, P. (1985). A study of the development of the ability for logical inference in Chinese school pupils and students. *Information on Psychological Sciences, 6,* 26–33.

Hurrelmann, K. (1988). *Social structure and personality development.* Cambridge: Cambridge University Press.

Hurrelmann, K., Engel, U., Holler, B., & Nordlohne, E. (1988). Failure in school, family conflicts, and psychosomatic disorders. *Journal of Adolescence, 25,* 205–215.

Hurrelmann, K., Rosewitz, B., & Wolf, H. K. (1985). *Lebensphase Jugend* [The youth phase of life]. Munich: Juventa.

Inhelder, B., & Piaget, J. (1958). *The growth of logical thinking from childhood to adolescence.* New York: Basic Books.

Jackson, Stafford, Banks, & Warr (1983). Unemployment and psychological distress in young people: The moderating role of employment committment. *Journal of Applied Psychology, 68* (3), 525–535.

Jacobs, J. (1971). *Adolescent suicide.* New York: Wiley.

Jahoda, M. (1979). The impact of unemployment in the 1930s and the 1970s. *Bulletin of the British Psychological Society, 32,* 309–314.

Jahoda, M., Lazarsfeld, P. F., & Zeisel, H. (1933). *Die Arbeitslosen von Marienthal: Ein soziographischer Versuch* [The unemployed of Marienthal: A sociographic investigation]. Frankfurt am Main: Suhrkamp.

Jessor, R., & Jessor, S. L. (1977). *Problem behavior and psychological development.* New York: Academic.

Jogawar, V. V. (1982). Development of self-concept during adolescence. *Asian Journal of Psychology and Education, 9,* 3–7.

Johnston, L. D., O'Malley, P. M., & Bachman, J. G. (1986). *Drug use among American high school students, college students, and other young adults.* U. S. Department of Health and Human Services, Rockville, MD: National Institute on Drug Abuse.

Kandel, D. B., & Adler, J. E. S. (1981). The epidemiology of adolescent drug use in France and Israel. *American Journal of the Public Health, 66,* 256–265.

Kandel, D. B., & Davies, M. (1982). Epidemiology of depressive mood in adolescents. *Archives of General Psychiatry, 39,* 1205–1212.

Kandel, D. B., Davies, M., Karus, D., & Yamaguchi, K. (1986). The consequences in young adulthood of adolescent drug involvement: An overview. *Archive of General Psychiatry, 43,* 746–754.

Kandel, D. B., Kessler, R., & Margulies, R. (1978). Adolescent initiation into stages of drug use: A developmental analysis. In D. B. Kandel (Ed.), *Longitudinal research on drug use: Empirical findings and methodological issues.* Washington, DC: Hemisphere-Wiley.

Kandel, D. B., & Lesser, G. S. (1972). *Youth in two worlds.* San Francisco: Jossey-Bass.

Kaplan, H. B. (1980). *Deviant behavior in defense of self.* New York: Academic.

Kaplan, S. L., Hong, G. K., & Weinhold, C. (1984). Epidemiology of depressive symptomology in adolescents. *Journal of the American Academy of Child Psychiatry, 23,* 91–98.

Kaye, K. (1985). Toward a developmental psychology of the family. In L. L'Abate (Ed.), *The handbook of family psychology and therapy* (Vol. 1, pp. 38–72). Homewood, IL: Dorsey.

Keating, D. P. (1987). Structuralism, deconstruction, reconstruction: The limits of logical reasoning. In W. F. Overton (Ed.), *Reasoning, necessity, and logic: Developmental perspectives* (pp. 299–319). Hillsdale, NJ: Erlbaum.

Keating, D. P., & Clark, L. V. (1980). Development of physical and social reasoning in adolescence. *Developmental Psychology, 16,* 23–30.

Kestenberg, J. (1968). Phase of adolescence with suggestions for correlation of psychic and hormonal organizations: Part III. Puberty growth, differentiation, and consolidation. *Journal of the American Academy of Child Psychiatry, 6,* 577–614.

Kieselbach, T. (1987). *Bremer Beiträge zür Psychologie* [Bremen Contributions to Psychology]. *Vol. 20 Youth unemployment—Health consequences and recommendations for psychosocial interventions.* Bremen: University of Bremen.

Kirmil-Gray, K., Eagleston, J. R., Gibson, E., & Thorensen, C. E. (1984). Sleep disturbance in adolescents: Sleep quality, sleep habits, beliefs about sleep, and daytime functioning. *Journal of Adolescence, 13,* 375–384.

Kitahara, M. (1983). Female puberty rites: Reconsideration and speculation. *Adolescence, 18,* 957–964.

Kohen-Raz, R. (1974). Physiological maturation and mental growth at preadolescence and puberty. *Journal of Child Psychology and Psychiatry, 15,* 199–213.

Kolvin, I., Miller, F. J. W., Fleeting, M., & Kolvin, P. A. (1988). Risk/protective factors for offending with particular reference to deprivation. In M. Rutter (Ed.), *Studies of psychosocial risk: The power of longitudinal data* (pp. 77–95). Cambridge: Cambridge University Press.

Kox, W., Meeus, W., & 't Hart, H. (1991). Religious conversion of adolescents: Testing the Lofland and Stark model of religious conversion. *Sociological Analysis, 52*, 227–240.

Largo, R. H., & Prader, A. (1983). Pubertal development in Swiss girls. *Helvetia Paediatrica Acta, 38*, 229–243.

Larson, R., Csikszentmihalyi, M., & Graef, R. (1980). Mood variability and the psychosocial adjustment of adolescents. *Journal of Youth and Adolescence, 9*, 469–490.

Lerner, R. M., (1981). Adolescent development: Scientific study in the 1980s. *Youth and Society, 12*, 251–275.

Lerner, R. M. (1984). *On the nature of human plasticity*. New York: Cambridge University Press.

Lerner, R., Karson, M., Meisels, M., Knapp, J. R. (1975). Actual and perceived attitudes of late adolescents: The phenomenon of the generation gaps. *Journal of Genetic Psychology, 126*, 197–207.

Lerner, R., & Spanier, G. B. (1978). A dynamic interactional view of child and family development. In R. Lerner & G. Spanier (Eds.), *Child influences on marital and family interaction: A life-span perspective*. New York: Academic.

Linn, M., & Peterson, A. C. (1985). Facts and assumptions about the nature of sex differences. In S. S. Klein (Ed.), *Handbook for achieving sex equity through education* (pp. 53–77). Baltimore: Johns Hopkins University Press.

Lipsitz, J. (1977). *Growing up forgotten: A review of research and programs concerning early adolescence*. Lexington, MA: Heath.

Loesel, F., Bliesener, T., & Kaeferl, P. (1989). On the concept of "invulnerability": Evaluation and first results of the Bielefeld project. In M. Brambring, F. Loesel, & H. Showronek (Eds.), *Children at risk: Assessment and longitudinal research* (pp. 187–227). Berlin: de Gruyter.

Lynd, R. S., & Lynd, H. M. (1929). *Middletown: A study in contemporary American culture*. New York: Harcourt-Brace.

Maccoby, E., & Martin, J. (1983). Socialization in the context of the family: Parent-child interaction. In E. Hetherington (Ed.), *Handbook of child psychology* (Vol. 4, 4th ed., pp. 1–102). New York: Wiley.

Madhavan, S. (1965). Age at menarche of South Indian girls. *Indian Journal of Medical Research, 53*, 669–673.

Magnusson, D. (1987). *Individual development in an interactional perspective* (Vol. 1). Hillsdale, NJ: Erlbaum.

Magnusson, D. (1988). *Individual development from an interactional perspective: A longitudinal study*. (Vol. 1). Hillsdale, NJ: Erlbaum.

Magnusson, D., Stattin, H., & Allen, V. L. (1985). Biological maturation and social development: A longitudinal study of some adjustment processes from mid-adolescence to adulthood. *Journal of Youth and Adolescence, 14*, 267–283.

Malina, R. M. (1985). Growth and physical performance of Latin American children and youth: Socio-economic and nutritional contrasts. *Collegian Antropologicum, 9*, 9–31.

Mallik, N. B., Ghosh, K. K., & Chattopadhyay, P. K. (1986). Hormonal and psychological changes in adolescent boys. *Journal of Psychological Researches, 30*, 165–169.

Marshall, W. A., & Tanner, J. M. (1969). Variations in the pattern of pubertal changes in girls. *Archives of Diseases in Childhood, 44*, 291–303.

Marshall, W. A., & Tanner, J. M. (1970). Variations in the pattern of pubertal changes in boys. *Archives of Diseases in Childhood, 45*, 13–23

Martorano, S. C. (1977). A developmental analysis of performance on Piaget's formal operations tasks. *Developmental Psychology, 13*, 666–672.

McClure, G. M. G. (1988). Adolescent mental health in China. *Journal of Adolescence, 11*, 1–10.

McCubbin, H. I., Needle, R. H., & Wilson, M. (1985). Adolescent health risk behaviors: Family stress and adolescent coping as critical factors. *Family Relations, 34*, 51–62.

McKenry, P. C., Walters, L. H., & Johnson, C. (1979). Adolescent pregnancy: A review of the literature. *Family Coordinator, 28*, 16–28.

McPherson, A., & Hall, W. (1983). Psychiatric impairment, physical health and work values among unemployed and apprenticed young men. *Australian and New Zealand Journal of Psychiatry, 17*, 335–340.

Melikian, C. H. (1981). *Jassim: A study in the psychosocial development of a young man in Qatar.* New York: Longman.

Meyer-Bahlberg, H. F. L., Ehrhardt, A. A., Bell, J. J., Cohen, S. F., Healey, J. M., Feldman, J. F., Morishima, A., Baker, S. W., & New, M. I. (1985). Idiopathic precocious puberty in girls: Psychosexual development. *Journal of Youth and Adolescence, 14*, 339–353.

Mikesell, J., & Sörensen, S. (1989). *Family typology as a predictor of adolescent self-image.* Paper presented at the Biennial Meeting of the Society for Research in Child Development, Kansas City.

Misra, R. S., et al. (1982). An exploration of health and mental status of children. *Child Psychiatry Quarterly, 15*, 50–55.

Montemayor, R. (1983). Parents and adolescents in conflict: All families some of the time and some families most of the time. *Journal of Early Adolescence, 3*, 83–103.

Morales, B. A., & Atilano, V. J. (1977). *A survey of drug dependence in the student population of Barranquilla.* Ministry of Public Health, Division of Mental Health, Bogota.

Munroe, R. L., & Munroe, R. H. (1983). Birth order and intellectual performance in East Africa. *Journal of Cross-Cultural Psychology, 14*, 3–16.

Neugarten, B. L. (1979). Time, age, and life-cycle. *American Journal of Psychiatry, 136*, 887–894.

Newcombe, N., & Dubas, J. S. (1987). Individual differences in cognitive ability: Are they related to timing of puberty? In R. M. Lerner & T. T. Foch (Eds.), *Biological-pschosocial interactions in early adolescence* (pp. 249–302). Hillsdale, NJ: Erlbaum.

Noack, P., & Silbereisen, R. K. (1988). Adolescent development and choice of leisure settings. *Children's Environments Quarterly, 5*, 25–33.

Nottelmann, E. D., Susman, E. J., Inoff-Germain, G., Cutler, G. B., Jr., Loriaux, D. L., & Chrousos, G. P. (1987). Developmental processes in early adolescence: Relations between adolescent adjustment problems and chronological age, pubertal stage, and puberty-related serum hormone levels. *Journal of Pediatrics, 110*, 473–480.

Offer, D., & Offer, J. (1975). *From teenage to young manhood: Psychological study.* New York: Basic Books.

Offer, D., Ostrov, E., Howard, K., & Atkinson, R. (1988). *The teenage world: The adolescents' self-image in ten countries.* New York: Plenum.

Olweus, D. (1979). Stability of aggressive reaction patterns in males: A review. *Psychological Bulletin, 86*, 852–75.

Palmonari, A., Pombeni, M. L., Kirchler, E. (1989). Peergroups and evolution of the self-esteem in adolescence. *European Journal of Psychology of Education, 4*, 3–15.

Papini, D., & Datan, N. (1983). *Transition into adolescence: An interactionist perspective.* Paper persented at the Biennial Meeting of the Society for Research in Child Development, Detroit.

Petersen, A. C. (1982). Developmental issues in adolescent health. In T. J. Coates, A. C. Petersen, & A. C. Perry (Eds.), *Promoting adolescent health: A dialog on research and practice* (pp. 61–72). New York: Academic Press.

Petersen, A. C. (1983). Pubertal change and cognition. In J. Brooks-Gunn & A. C. Petersen (Eds.), *Girls at puberty: Biological and psychosocial perspectives* (pp. 179–198). New York: Plenum.

Petersen, A. C. (1988). Adolescent development. *Annual Review of Psychology, 39*, 583–607.

Petersen, A. C., & Crockett, L. J. (1985). Pubertal timing and grade effects on adjustment. *Journal of Youth and Adolescence, 14*, 191–206.

Petersen, A. C., & Ebata, A. T. (1987). Developmental transitions and adolescent problem behavior: Implications for prevention and intervention. In K. Hurrelmann (Ed.), *Social prevention and intervention.* New York: de Gruyter.

Petersen, A. C., Ebata, A. T., & Graber, J. A. (1987). *Coping with adolescence: The functions and dysfunctions of poor achievement.* Paper presented at the Biennial Meeting of the Society for Research in Child Development, Baltimore.

Petersen, A. C., Ebata, A. T., & Sarigiani, P. (1987). *Who expresses depressive affect in adolescence?* Paper presented at the Biennial Meeting of the Society for Research in Child Development, Baltimore.

Peterson, A. C., & Hamburg, B. A. (1986). Adolescence: A developmental approach to problems and psychopathology. *Behavior Therapy, 17*, 480–499.

Peterson, C., & Seligman, M. E. (1984). Causal explanations as a risk factor for depression: Theory and evidence. *Psychological Review, 91*, 347–374.

Petersen, A. C., & Taylor, B. (1980). The biological approach to adolescence: Biological change and psychosocial adaptation. In J. Adelson (Ed.), *Handbook of adolescent psychology* (pp. 117–155). New York: Wiley.

Poole, M. E., Cooney, G. H., & Cheong, A. C. S. (1986). Adolescent perceptions of family cohesiveness, autonomy, and independence in Australia and Singapore. *Journal of Comparative Family Studies, 17*, 311–332.

Projektgruppe Tudrop (1984). *Heroinabhängigkeit unbetreuter Jugendlicher* [Heroin addiction in youth without families]. Weinheim: Beltz.

Pulkkinen, L. (1982). Self-control and continuity from childhood to late adolescence. *Life-span Development and Behavior, 4*, 63–105.

Pulkkinen, L. (1983). Youthful smoking and drinking in longitudinal perspective. *Journal of Youth and Adolescence, 12*, 253–283.

Pulkkinen, L. (in press). Social development: Predictive validity of an impulse control model for social behavior from childhood to adulthood. *International Journal of Behavioral Development*.

Rao, V. N., Channabasavanna, S. M., & Parthasarathy, R. (1982). Family situations of disturbed adolescents. *Child Psychiatry Quarterly, 15*, 113–118.

Remschmidt, H. (1989). Developmental psychopathology as a theoretical framework for child and adolescence psychiatry. In M. H. Schmidt & H. Remschmidt (Eds.), *Needs and prospects of child and adolescent psychiatry* (pp. 3–24). Bern: Huber.

Roberts, K. (1984). Problems and initiatives in youth unemployment. *Journal of Community and Health Care, 62*, 320–326.

Rolf, J. E., Master, A., Cicchetto, D., Nuecchterlein, K. H., & Weintraub, S. (Eds.). (1987). *Risk and protective factors in the devlopment of psychopathology*. Cambridge: Cambridge University Press.

Rosenthal, D. A., Efklides, A., & Demetriou, A. (1988). Parental criticism and young adolescent self-disclosure: A cross-cultural study. *Journal of Youth and Adolescence, 17*, 25–39.

Rutter, M. (1980). *Changing youth in a changing society: Patterns of adolescent development and disorder*. Cambridge, MA: Harvard University Press.

Rutter, M. (1986). The developmental psychopathology of depression: Issues and perspectives. In M. Rutter, C. Izard, & P. Read (Eds.), *Depression in young people: Developmental and clinical perspectives* (pp. 3–30). New York: Guilford.

Rutter, M. (1987). Continuities and discontinuities from infancy. In J. Osofsky (Ed.), *Handbook of infant development* (Vol. 3, pp. 1256–1296). New York: Wiley.

Rutter, M., Graham, P., Chadwick, O., & Yule, W. (1976). Adolescent turmoil: Fact or fiction? *Journal of Child Psychology and Psychiatry, 17*, 35–56.

Sandhu, T. S. (1984). In Punjabi U, Patiala, India. *Asian Journal of Psychology and Education, 13*, 39–44.

Santrock, J. W. (1987). *Adolescence: An introduction* (3rd ed.). Dubuque, IA: William C. Brown.

Savin-Williams, R. C., Small, S. A., & Zeldin, R. S. (1981). Dominance and altruism among adolescent males: A comparison of ethological and psychological methods. *Ethology and Sociobiology, 2*, 167–176.

Schneewind, K. A. (1987). The analysis of family and parent-child relations in a systems-oriented perspective. *Family Perspective, 21:* 337–353.

Schulenberg, J. E., Asp, C. E., & Petersen, A. C. (1984) School from the young adolescent's perspective: A descriptive report. *Journal of Early Adolescence, 4*, 107–130.

Seligman, M. E. P., & Peterson, C. (1986). A learned helplessness perspective on childhood depression: Theory and research. In M. Rutter, C. Izard, & P. Read (Eds.), *Depression in young people: Developmental and clinical perspectives* (pp. 223–249). New York: Guilford Press.

Semmer, N. K., Dwyer, J. H., Lippert, P., Fuchs, R., Cleary, P., & Schindler, A. (1987). Adolescent smoking from a functional perspective: The Berlin-Bremen Study. *European Journal of Psychology of Education, 2*, 387–402.

Shellow, R., Schamp, J., Liebow, E., & Unger, E. (1967). Suburban runaways of the 1960s. *Monographs of the Society for Research in Child Development, 32* (Serial No. 111).

Shulman, S., Seiffge-Krenke, I., & Samet, N. (1987). Adolescent coping as a function of perceived family climate. *Journal of Adolescent Research, 2*, 367–381.

Shuttleworth, F. K. (1939). The physical and mental growth of girls and boys age six to nineteen in relation to age at maximum growth. *Monographs of the Society for Research in Child Development, 4* (Serial No. 22).

Sieber, M., & Angst, J. (1981). *Drogen, Alkohol und Tabakkonsum: Ein Beitrag zur Epidemiologie und Aetiologie bei jungen Erwachsenen* [Drugs, alcohol and tobacco use: A contribution to epidemiology and etiology among young adults]. Bern: Huber.

Silbereisen, R. K., Noack, P., & Eyferth, K. (1986). Place for development: Adolescents, leisure settings, and developmental tasks. In R. K. Silbereisen, K. Eyferth, & G. Rudinger (Eds.), *Development as action in context* (pp. 87–108). New York: Springer-Verlag.

Silbereisen, R. K., Noack, P., & von Eye, A. (1992). Adolescents' development of romantic friendship and change in favorite leisure contexts. *Journal of Adolescent Research, 7*, 80–93.

Silbereisen, R. K., & Reitzle, M. (1992). On the constructive role of problem behavior in adolescence: Further evidence on alcohol use. In L. P. Lipsitt & L. L. Mitnick (Eds.), *Self-regulatory behavior and risk taking: Causes and consequences* (pp. 199–217). Norwood, NJ: Ablex.

Silbereisen, R. K., Walper, S., & Albrecht, H. T. (1990). Families experiencing income loss and economic hardship: Antecedents of adolescents' problem behavior. In V. C. McLoyd & C. Flanagan (Eds.), *Risk and protective factors in children and adolescents' response to economic crises and deprivation* (New directions for child development, pp. 27–47). San Francisco: Jossey-Bass.

Simmons, R., & Blyth, D. A. (1987). *Moving to adolescence: The impact of pubertal change and school content.* New York: Aldine.

Simmons, R., Blyth, D. A., & McKinney, K. L. (1983). The social psychological effects of puberty on white females. In J. Brooks-Gunn & A. C. Petersen (Eds.), *Girls at puberty: Biological and psychosocial perspectives* (pp. 229–272). New York: Plenum.

Simmons, R., Blyth, D. A., VanCleave, E., & Bush, D. (1979). Entry into early adolescence: The impact of school structure, puberty, and early dating on self-esteem. *American Sociological Review, 4*, 948–967.

Simmons, R., Rosenberg, M. F., & Rosenberg, M. C. (1973). Disturbance in the self-image at adolescence. *American Sociological Review, 38*, 553–568.

Singh, A. (1984). The girls who ran away from home. *Child Psychiatry Quarterly, 17*, 1–8.

Singh, L., & Ahuja, S. (1979). Age at menarche among the Gujar girls of Punjab. *Acta Medica Auxologica, 11*, 53–55.

Singh, R. A., & Singh, N. (1986). Effects of sex on adolescents' perception of maternal and paternal behavior. *Indian Psychological Review, 30*, 37–41.

Smetana, J. G. (1987). Adolescent-parent conflict: Reasoning about hypothetical and actual family conflict. In M. R. Gunnar (Ed.), *21st Minnesota Symposium on Child Psychology*. Hillsdale, NJ: Erlbaum.

Soueif, M. I., El-Sayed, A. M., Darweesh, Z. A., Hannourah, M., & Yunis, F. A. (1988). *Drug abuse in Egypt: Extent and patterns among students in Greater Cairo*. Cairo: National Centre for Social and Criminological Research.

Statisches Bundesamt. (1987). *Statisches Jahrbuch* [Statistical yearbook]. Stuttgart: Kohlhammer.

Steinberg, L. D. (1981). Transformations in family relations at puberty. *Developmental Psychology, 7*, 833–840.

Steinberg, L. D. (1985). *Adolescence*. New York: Knopf.

Steinberg, L. D., & Hill, J. P. (1978). Patterns of family interaction as a function of age, the onset of puberty, and formal thinking. *Developmental Psychology, 14*, 683–684.

Sudha, B. G., & Tirth, L. V. (1986). Effect of parental career and marriage expectation on the problems of rural and urban adolescent girls in relation to their religion and socioeconomic status. *Indian Psychological Review, 30*, 9–17.

Suomi, S. (1987). *Individual differences in Rhesus monkey behavior and adrenocortical responses to social challenge: Correlations with measures of heart rate variability*. Paper presented at the Biennial Meeting of the Society for Research in Child Development, Baltimore.

Susman, E. J., Nottelmann, E. D., Dorn, L. D., Gold, P. W., & Chrousos, G. P. (1987). *Coping with uncertainty: Biological behavioral and developmental perspectives*. Hillsdale, NJ: Erlbaum.

Tanner, J. M. (1962). *Growth at adolescence*. Springfield, IL: Thomas.

Tanner, J. M. (1974). Sequence and tempo in the somatic changes in puberty. In M. M. Grumbach, G. D. Grave, & F. E. Mayer (Eds.), *Control of the onset of puberty* (pp. 448–470). New York: Wiley.

Teck-Hong, O. (1986). Inhalant abuse in Singapore. *International Journal of Addictions, 21*, 955–960.

Teichmann, M., Rahav, G., & Barnea, Z. (1987). Alcohol and psychoactive drug use among Israeli adolescents: An epidemiological and demographic investigation. *International Journal of Addictions, 22*, 81–92.

Turner, R. J. (1980). *Social support as a contingency in psychological well-being*. Paper presented at the meeting of the American Sociological Association, New York.

Uchtenhagen, A., & Zimmer-Hoefler, D. (1987). Psychosocial development following therapeutic and legal interventions in opiate dependence. A Swiss national study. *European Journal of Psychology of Education, 2*, 443–458.

Udry, J. R., Billy, J. O. G., Morris, N., Groff, T., & Raj, M. (1985). Serum androgenic hormones motivate sexual behavior in adolescent boys. *Fertility and Sterility, 43*, 90–94.

Udry, J. R., Talbert, L. M., & Morris, N. M. (1986). Biosocial foundations for adolescent female sexuality. *Demography, 23*, 217–230.

Ullman, C. (1982). Cognitive and emotional antecedents of religiousconversion. *Journal of Personality and Social Psychology, 43*,183–192.

UNESCO (Ed.). (1981). *Youth, tradition and development in Africa*. Regional Meeting on Youth in Africa, Nairobi, Kenya, December 1979. Nautes, France: UNESCO Press.

United Nations Population Division. (1976). *Population by sex and age for regions and countries, 1950–2000, as assessed in 1973: Medium variant.* New York: United Nations, Department of Economic and Social Affairs.

U.S. Bureau of the Census. (1982). *Projections of the population of the United States.* (Current Population Reports, Series P-25,No. 992). Washington, DC: U. S. Government Printing Office.

Vandewiele, M. (1981). Wolof adolescents' perception of their parents. *Journal of Psychology, 109,* 173–177.

Vandewiele, M., & D'Hondt, W. (1983). How conformist Senegalese adolescents consider themselves to be. *Journal of Adolescence, 6,* 87–92.

Van Hasselt, V. B., & Hersen, M. (Eds.). (1987). *Handbook for adolescent psychology.* New York: Pergamon.

Van Vliet, W. (1983). Exploring the fourth environment. *Environment and Behavior, 15,* 567–588.

Venkata Rami Reddy, A. (1979). Do the rich and the poor differ in the level of their adjustment? *Indian Psychological Review, 18,* 58–64.

Visser, D. (1987). The relationship of parental attitudes and expectations to children's mathematics achievement behavior. *Journal of Early Adolescence, 7,* 1–12.

von Eye, A., & Brandtstaedter, J. (1988). Evaluating developmental hypotheses using statement calculus and nonparametric statistics. In P. B. Baltes, D. L. Featherman, & R. M. Lerner (Eds.), *Life-span development and behavior* (Vol. 8, pp. 61–97). Hillsdale, NJ: Erlbaum.

Waber, D. P. (1976). Sex differences in cognition: A function of maturation rate? *Science, 192,* 572–574.

Waber, D. P. (1977). Sex differences in mental abilities, hemispheric lateralization, and rate of physical growth at adolescence. *Developmental Psychology, 13,* 29–38.

Wadkar, A. J., Gore, S. D., & Palsane, M. (1986). *Journal of Human Development, 22,* 14–20.

Warr, P. B., Banks, M. H., & Ullah, P. (1985). The experience of unemployment among black and white urban teenagers. *British Journal of Psychology, 76,* 75–87.

Weeks, S. G. (1973). Youth and the transition to adult status: Uganda. *Journal of Youth and Adolescence, 2,* 259–270.

Weiner, I. B. (1980). Psychopathology in adolescence. In J. Adelson (Ed.), *Handbook of adolescent psychology* (pp. 447–471). New York: Wiley.

Weiner, I. B., & DelGaudio, A. (1976). Psychopathology in adolescence. *Archives of General Psychiatry, 33,* 187–193.

Weissman, M. M., & Klerman, G. L. (1977). Sex differences and the epidemiology of depression. *Archives of General Psychiatry, 34,* 98–111.

West, D. J. (1982). *Delinquency: Its roots, careers and prospects.* London: Heinemann.

Wohlwill, J. F. (1973). *The study of behavioral development.* New York: Academic Press.

Yamaguchi, K., & Kandel, D. B. (1985). On the resolution of the role of incompatibility: A life event history analysis of family roles and marijuana use. *American Journal of Sociology, 90,* 1284–1325.

Youniss, J., & Smollar, J. (1985). *Adolescent relations with mothers, fathers, and friends.* Chicago: University of Chicago Press.

Zakin, D. F., Blyth, D. A., & Simmons, R. G. (1984). Physical attractiveness as a mediator of the impact of early pubertal changes for girls. *Journal of Youth and Adolescence, 13*, 439–450.

Zank, S. (1988). *Zur Entwicklung des Lösungsmittelschnuffelns bei Jugendlichen und jungen Erwachsenen* [On the development of solvent sniffing among youth and young adults]. Berlin: Berlin Verlag.

2

The Social World of Adolescents:
A Sociological Perspective

Klaus Hurrelmann

Adolescence as a phase of the human life course is a historically shaped social "product" that is in a state of constant change. In this introductory section, I first describe the historical emergence of the life phase of adolescence. I then discuss the essential structural changes in this life phase over the past decades. A central topic will be the recent changes within the process of social integration that have occurred as a result of shifts in educational and occupational opportunities. I postulate that this structural change in the phase of adolescence can be interpreted as a process of restructuring of the phase of life called adolescence. Finally, I discuss implications for a social policy for adolescents.

1. THE HISTORICAL DIFFERENTIATION OF THE PHASE OF ADOLESCENCE

As the study of social history has shown, adolescence has been identified as a specific and independent phase of the human life course since the second half of the last century. The emergence of the phase of adolescence was closely linked to economic, political, and cultural changes evoked by the industrialization process and the accompanying establishment of a compulsory school system (Gillis, 1974).

Among the mostly rural families of preindustrial society, young and old people lived together under one roof and shared many of the same tasks and activities in their daily routines. The child was something like a miniature of the adult (Aries, 1975). Because of industrialization and the beginnings of the process of urbanization, the behavioral domains and action spheres of children and adults were driven further apart. Work outside the family became more and more the norm. As a consequence, new forms of family life arose.

The factory system moved work out of the home, leading adults to build social relationships around the workplace and separating children and adults during their daily routines. Within urban regions, this process was accompanied and accelerated by a new social and pedagogical definition of the role of children: They were no longer seen as small adults, but as human beings in an independent phase of development that made special behavioral demands, which were no longer identical with those made on adults.

This social separation of the generations was supported by the establishment of a common school system in the second half of the 19th century. Education, primarily understood as a preparation for occupational demands, was increasingly taken over by organized and purposefully built organizations. This process accelerated the separation of a specific social world for young people. Through the decades, this dynamic process spread into more sectors of daily life, including leisure time and the use of media. Soon the transition to adulthood was delayed beyond the end of puberty, at first among middle-class youth. This delay led to the rise of a new phase within the human life course that became separate from the others: the phase of adolescence.

1.1. The Emergence of the Phase of Adolescence

The phase of adolescence emerged at a time when the complexity of job qualifications, which were mainly determined by technological needs, had reached a level that demanded certain skills, attitudes, and requirements. Simultaneously, this stage of societal development saw the emergence of opportunities to grant the younger generation what was considered to be a necessary period for the development of maturity. Technological development and the spread of societal welfare systems reduced the need to exploit human working potential. At the same time, moral and pedagogical ideas on the necessity and appropriateness of a suitable development of society's young members gained strength.

Gradually, at first within the middle class, the phase of adolescence grew into an independent phase. The right to the full practice of an adult occupation and the connected privilege of becoming self-reliant were bound to the completion of certain stages of education and training. And professional maturity was generally seen as the requirement for attaining the right of marriage. Because all societies were interested in providing a sheltered upbringing and appropriate education for their offspring, and the family possessed a virtual monopoly on these activities, the right of marriage was given to men and women only if it seemed that they had learned enough about the culture of the society and if, in addition, it could be assumed that their material situation guaranteed the security of their own children.

In accordance with this, adolescence was first of all a historical product of the bourgeois middle class. The middle class was wealthy enough to support an extended time of preparation for career life. It also propagated the idealistic picture of adolescence as a psychosocial moratorium on the way to maturity, providing protection from the various burdens of adult life. As industrialization advanced, the young members of the working class and of rural families also entered the phase of adolescence step by step.

At least since the 1950s and 1960s, adolescence has been a common cultural good in the societies of the industrialized West. It is no longer only in the possession of the bourgeois male groups of the population. Because economic conditions and living conditions, which are closely linked, still show considerable variation, the phase of adolescence still has several class- and sex-specific features.

As was mentioned, for all adolescents the social differentiation of the phase of adolescence was realized by extending general compulsory school attendance over the past 100 years. Today, in most industrial societies, the typical minimum of 10 years of compulsory school attendance guarantees a certain period of adolescence to the young members of all social strata. Many years of the period of adolescence are defined by school attendance. Class- and sex-specific differences are no longer mainly expressed by the single fact of school attendance but by the kind of school attended and the long-term prospects for career and life opportunities that are connected with the type and quality of certificates and diplomas attained.

The age at which individuals enter careers has shifted considerably, partly as a result of extended school attendance. At the same time, the entry into a social relationship based on marriage, which is a clear indicator of successful social separation from the family of origin, takes place earlier in life. In Germany, for example, at the turn of the century the average marrying age of the total group of men was 28 years and for women, it was 26; as the 20th century approached its end, men were about 26 years old and women, about 23 (Jugendwerk der Deutschen Shell, 1981). At the time of this writing, the average age of entry into the world of occupation and gainful employment stood at about 20 years of age; it might have been 15 to 16 at the birth of the 20th century. Thus, these two transitional points in the life course have moved closer to each other.

The same evidence is given in an American study by Modell, Furstenberg, and Hershberg (1977), who used Philadelphia census data to make direct comparisons between youth cohorts in 1870 and 1970. They focused on five elements of the transition to adulthood: exit from school, entrance to the workforce, departure from the family of origin, marriage, and the establishment of a household. They determined the distribution of ages in young people making these five transitions. They found clear evidence that formal schooling had been extended by 1970 and that employment began earlier in 1870. They also found that on the average, the five transitions occurred in closer proximity to one another and were completed in a shorter period of time in 1970 than in 1870. Delayed marriage was more common in 1870. Young people continued to live with their parents longer, and it was common for young married couples to live with parents for several years before establishing their own residence.

What occurred as the 20th century progressed, therefore, was not simply a prolongation of youth, but a change in the pattern of transition and in the importance of different elements of this transition. No longer were the family transitions the predominant consequential ones. Today school departure and workforce entry are far more important in shaping the subsequent career than a century ago. And today the familial transitions do not take as long as was once the case. In the 19th century, the family was a unique and powerful institution. In the 20th, it was one of the many in and out of which individuals had to thread their way (Modell et al., 1977, p. 29).

2. STRUCTURAL CHANGES IN THE PROCESS OF SCHOOL-TO-WORK TRANSITION

The decision regarding which position in the social structure a member of a society will occupy when he or she becomes an adult (that is, how the positioning and placement on the central societal dimensions of power, influence, property, and prestige take place) is "programmed" at the age of adolescence. The process of integration into adult society is also always a process of social selection for certain status positions (Engel, 1987; Persell, 1977).

Today's industrial societies are achievement-oriented in such a way that an individual's economic achievement typically decides position in the social structure rather than—as was the case in preindustrial societies—his or her social background. For this reason, the main social organizations that determine the process of individuals' integration are no longer their families but the educational and occupational institutions that were specifically established to educate and train the individual capacities of the young members of society. The educational system dominates the qualification of the offspring of society for occupations and their selection according to different levels of prestige and qualification. The final decision about the status attained takes place within the occupational system, but the predecision in the form of presenting school-leaving certificates of different qualities is made within the educational system (cf. Engel, 1989; Poole, 1989; Roberts & Parsell, 1989).

This is not to say that the family of origin has no influence on the process of socialization. But the form and shape of this influence has changed considerably within one century. The nuclear family influences its offspring's scholastic abilities in educational institutions by supporting or prompting them. This is an indirect control of the process of status attainment; compared to former times, there has been a decrease in the possibilities of direct control.

2.1. Educational Opportunities and Prospects

Because of the great importance granted to the structuring of the process of status attainment, I shall now specify the educational and occupational prospects of adolescents more precisely.

For the "educational market" alone, the opportunity structure has improved continuously over the past three decades. The Federal Republic of Germany can serve as a fairly typical example for most of the Western industrial nations. Here the infrastructural weight of the educational system has been reinforced considerably in the last three to four decades. More and more adolescents from all age groups remain in full-time and part-time educational institutions for a longer period of time.

Table 1 gives an impression of the extent of the educational expansion that has occurred during the past decades. As can be seen, school attendance has become the dominant activity of adolescents far into the age group of 19-year-olds. Attendance at full-time secondary schools and vocational schools has increased considerably during the last two and a half decades.

Schooling in Germany is compulsory from age 6 to 18. Students must attend school full-time for 10 years in most states and then at least part-time during vocational training for an additional 2 to 3 years. As Table 1 shows, the percentage of those leaving school after compulsory education who go on to full-time vocational schools (trade and technical schools, such as the Berufsfachschule, Fachoberschule, and Handelsschule) for 1 to 3 years of further study is rising. Others who leave general school at this point pass directly into vocational training in the "dual system." Under this system, they sign on with a firm and are trained in accordance with the vocational legislation applying to a particular trade. They learn on-the-job four days a week and spend one day a week at part-time vocational school (Berufsschule). The classroom time is divided into one-third general studies and two-thirds trade-oriented studies over a period of between 2 and 3.5 years. Students must take a state-approved examination upon completion of their apprenticeships at the age of about 18 years. Students in secondary schools also have to take their final examination (Abitur) at about 18 or 19 years.

Higher education in Germany has also grown tremendously. Over 250,000 new college places were created between 1970 and 1985. The abolition of student fees and the provision of government grants have made the acquisition of a college education a goal for many young people who, in the past, would not have thought it possible. In the early 1950s, only 6 percent of each age group attended institutions of higher learning, compared to 22 percent in 1980. The average length of study at universities increased to 6.5 years, and at polytechnical schools it was 3.8 years (Bundesminister für Bildung und Wissenschaft, 1987). Since young men had to serve almost 2 years in the army or in obligatory

Table 1. Population Percentages of German Adolescents by School Type

Age in Years	Year	Total	Full-Time General Schools		Part-Time Vocational Schools		Full-Time Vocational Schools	
			Males	Females	Males	Females	Males	Females
16	1960	93%	23%	18%	71%	65%	3%	6%
	1970	95	29	23	63	58	7	10
	1980	97	47	49	43	33	8	16
	1984	99	57	57	35	25	7	16
17	1960	66	16	11	52	43	2	6
	1970	84	18	13	63	58	7	9
	1980	89	26	27	58	45	8	16
	1984	91	28	29	56	40	11	19
18	1960	32	11	7	24	14	3	5
	1970	47	13	9	40	19	5	8
	1980	70	19	19	49	34	7	12
	1984	78	22	23	53	37	8	14
19	1960	17	7	4	11	5	3	4
	1970	21	7	3	15	6	4	6
	1980	41	10	8	29	19	7	6
	1984	49	10	9	34	25	6	12
20	1960	7	3	1	5	1	2	3
	1970	10	4	1	6	2	3	4
	1980	19	3	2	13	8	4	8
	1984	25	3	2	17	15	5	10
21	1960	3	0	0	2	0	2	2
	1970	3	0	0	2	0	2	2
	1980	9	0	0	8	4	3	4
	1984	13	0	0	8	8	3	6
22	1960	1	0	0	0	0	2	1
	1970	2	0	0	0	0	2	1
	1980	5	0	0	3	1	3	3
	1984	4	0	0	0	0	3	4

Note: Taken from Bundesminister für Bildung und Wissenschaft (1987, p. 24).

civil service, the average age at which they completed a university education was about 27; young women completed that education at about age 25.

The educational attainment of the disadvantaged groups of adolescents who come from families of low socioeconomic status improved over the three decades preceding this writing in Germany. In grammar schools, for example, the share of these adolescents doubled between 1950 and 1980, going from 5 percent to 10 percent. Working-class adolescents succeeded in increasing their representation in the realm of high-prestige education. But the share of working-class adolescents was still significantly below their share in the general population (about 40 percent). The higher the level of the educational institution, the smaller the percentage of working-class youngsters it contained.

In those three decades, working-class adolescents generally were not able to make any basic improvements in their relative starting positions for entrance into the employment system. They were not the only ones who were able to increase their participation in education; adolescents from the families of white-collar workers, public officials, and the self-employed did the same. In these classes as well, the general expansion in education led to a further increase in the proportion of adolescents who completed secondary school education up to the university entrance level. For this reason, there was hardly any change in the class distribution of students in such schools.

Despite the fact that the opportunity structure of the educational system was objectively more favorable than before, competition for an attractive starting position in the vocational placement process increased considerably. To retain the social status of their families of origin, adolescents had to obtain qualifications that were higher than those of their parents. Differences in starting conditions still characterize the race for the highest qualifications. Adolescents from the middle and upper classes received more effective support—both material and nonmaterial—when adopting and persevering in an optimization strategy in the education market (Persell, 1977).

Following the period of education in school, most German adolescents pass through a specific phase of vocational training. This phase extends the process of educational qualification with a period that produces the marketable skills of the future adult member of society that can actually be offered in the labor market. The period of vocational training is a significant step on the path to one of the key roles of the adult status, namely, employment. It represents a first release from school as an obligatory and enforced institution of education and thus guides the adolescent into the process of directly productive, qualified work. The transfer from school to vocational training therefore calls for an important occupational decision and is a decisive crossroads in determining the situation and quality of the adolescent's future life (cf. King, 1989; Wallace, 1989).

Access to desirable apprenticeships is competitive. Training institutions can select applicants they consider to be suitable from the now very large group of highly qualified school leavers. A high-quality school education and a good school-leaving certificate qualify as a reference indicating a willingness to adapt and commit to vocational training. School leavers without certificates are forced out of the qualified business, managerial, and technical professions and have to take up manual vocations.

These dislocation processes give adolescents a bitter foretaste of the reality of the labor market that awaits them after the completion of vocational training. Even those among them who successfully complete an apprenticeship are no longer certain of being accepted into the labor market.

Higher education has also come up against the pressure of contractive trends in the labor market. Since the 1980s, a university degree no longer guarantees entrance into correspondingly high professional positions. Partially as a reaction to this situation, in Germany there has been a continuous decline in the proportion of students who enter university immediately after successfully completing grammar school (Gymnasium). In 1950, practically 100 percent did so; by 1985, that number was approximately 70 percent. The proportion of adolescents with university entrance qualifications who entered business training as apprentices increased and was roughly two in ten in 1985.

University training also shows clear inequalities in opportunity structures (cf. Weidmann, 1989). Government service has been a traditional labor market for university graduates (teachers, judges, doctors, etc.), but this sector has dramatically narrowed in Germany since the mid-1970s, and competition among groups of adolescents with differing social privileges has grown in the university sector. Here, the same patterns can be found as in the general schools: Various optimization strategies, such as double degrees and supplementary courses, are embarked upon and, depending on an individual's material and nonmaterial starting position, maintained with varying degrees of success.

2.2. Placement in the Labor Market

The placement process comes to an at least preliminary close with the first permanent position in the employment system that is taken up after completion of the educational and vocational qualification process. A consistent extension can be seen in the lines of structural inequality in placement that I reported for the school and training sector. This inequality is reinforced by the contractive trends in the labor market in most Western European countries. Increasing productivity and redundancies due to advances in technology have led to a sinking demand for manpower. The dislocation race thus continues with unappeased ferocity in this section of the placement process as well, with the result being that a growing minority of adolescents find no entrance into the employment system.

The expansion of the educational system can partially be seen as a reaction to this process of contraction in the employment system. The largely state-controlled educational system in Western European countries has become a safety net for the overspill of applicants for entrance into the employment system. By lengthening compulsory education, successfully encouraging adolescents to obtain university entrance qualifications, and expanding full-time vocational schools and vocational education institutions, it has been possible to withhold an increasing proportion of 16- to 18-year-olds from the employment system, so that today large proportions of adolescents in this age group are retained in the educational system.

The employed quota, which represents the proportion of employed persons within the same age group in the residential population of a state, correspond-

Table 2. Employed Quotas of German Adolescents as Population Percentages

	1957		1974		1980	
Age	Males %	Females %	Males %	Females %	Males %	Females %
15–20	81	76	57	53	49	41
21–25	92	76	81	68	82	71
26–30	97	52	91	56	90	63
31–35	97	45	97	50	97	56

Note: Taken from Baethge, Schomburg, and Voskamp (1983).

ingly sank in the adolescent age group. Baethge, Schomburg, and Voskamp (1983) computed West German figures for previous decades on the basis of available statistical data. As Table 2 shows, the employed quotas in the group of 15- to 20-year-old adolescents sank by over 30 percent between 1957 and 1980. Even in the 21- to 25-year-old age group there were decreases of 10 percent for males and over 4 percent for females. These figures show that employment was no longer a typical structural feature for people under 20 in the 1980s.

The considerable sex-specific differences in the trends of the employed quotas are conspicuous in this table. Although female adolescents under 20 have moved out of employed life more strongly than males during the interval covered, this trend is inverted in the higher age groups. The employment behavior of women approaches that of men, or at least the differences in the employment behavior of the sexes have become lower in all age groups. It would appear that young women, and especially those over the age of 25, increasingly strive to earn their own living through employment.

As these figures show, the entrance into the employment system, and thus the transfer to a major subrole of the adult status, has shifted into the third decade of life for the majority. At the same time, the problems of starting professional life have become continuously greater: A growing minority of adolescents of both sexes, but particularly female and working-class adolescents, are pushed to the extreme margins of the employment system and into unemployment. The exact number of unemployed adolescents is difficult to ascertain because the official statistics of the unemployment offices are very selective. Germany, for example, only records those adolescents who definitely register as unemployed at the labor office and thus excludes all those who have not formally registered for some reason or other. Among those who are not registered but could possibly be regarded as additional unemployed are adolescents who help out in their families, casual workers, and those attending vocational courses. The number of unrecorded cases can therefore be estimated as considerable.

Nevertheless, I will look at the official statistics to obtain a picture of the extent of unemployment. They show that since the 1970s, adolescents have made

Table 3.   Participation of Adolescents in the U.S. Labor Force (percentage of adolescents employed)

Age	1960		1975		1980	
	M %	F %	M %	F %	M %	F %
16–17	46	29	49	40	50	44
18–19	69	51	71	58	71	62
20–24	88	46	85	64	86	69

Note. Taken from U.S. Department of Commerce, Bureau of the Census, Statistical Abstract, 1984, p. 407.

up a disproportionately high share of the unemployed in Germany. This trend has continued to rise: In the mid-1980s, the quota of 15- to 20-year-olds was almost 10 percent (despite the prolongation of placement in the training system described above), and almost 20 percent in 21- to 25-year-olds. Female and working-class adolescents were particularly highly represented among the unemployed.

The trends in Western Europe are somewhat different from those in the United States. In the latter, the participation of adolescents under 25 in the labor force markedly increased and did not decrease between 1960 and 1980, as can be seen from Table 3.

These figures reflect the different political strategies for the labor market in Europe and the United States. However, the situation for the 1980s was very similar, in spite of the different genesis: Only a minority of those under 18 years of age were full-time members of the labor force. The proportion of adolescents who were forced into extremely unfavorable sectors of the labor market increased. The surplus of labor led to the growth of an area with unattractive terms of employment. A sort of two-class system is formed: Alongside the relatively privileged sector enjoying normal terms of employment with long-term work contracts and the opportunity to take advantage of professional advancement through in-service training, an underprivileged sector develops in which employment is provided on the basis of short-term arrangements such as work contracts, freelance contracts, and subcontracts. This sector offers only uncertain employment and shades into the area of nonlegal work. Unemployment benefits or social security are unknown, and there is no permanence in such vocational activity.

Having more flexible material needs and social roles than adults, adolescents more often find themselves in this insecure section of the labor market and, as a result, experience higher unemployment than adults. As it would seem that the contractive trend in the labor market will continue, unfavorable conditions of vocational placement must be anticipated for growing minorities of adolescents.

The transition from school to occupation and gainful employment is taking place later in life. At the same time, it has also changed qualitatively: Paths that were once clear have grown increasingly hard to negotiate; "waiting-loops," "detours," and transitional employment that is outside of individuals' training and occupations are increasing; and links between education, training, and occupation, which had previously been relatively calculable in Western European countries, have become more open and less reliable. The equation "more education equals better career and life chances" becomes less and less true; yet at the same time less education and less training normally result in career disadvantages.

The consequences for the adolescent socialization process are obvious: Gainful employment, which until the beginning of the 20th century was, at least in Europe, typical for the largest proportion of adolescents, has been replaced by scholastic learning or systematic training off-the-job. The experience of being immediately useful to society, of behaving according to the economic norms of rationality, and of being responsible for personal material livelihood can only arrive relatively late in life. School does provide many intellectual and social stimulations, but it is an area that allows only marginal experiences of responsibility and solidarity and, instead, encourages a strong individualistic moral of competition and favors mainly abstract and theoretical learning (cf. Baethge, 1989). The fact of not being forced to work within the employment sector offers young people a high degree of individual freedom in the use of time, the selection of communication forms and partners, and the arrangement of everyday life, particularly in the world of media and consumption. As long as young people attend full-time schools, colleges, or universities, however, they are not seen as being really adult, regardless of their actual age.

3. STRUCTURAL CHANGES IN FAMILY AND PEER AFFILIATIONS

Adolescence is a stage of preparation not only for the transition to work, but also for the status-relevant process of choosing a partner and possibly getting married. The choice of a partner may also change an individual's social position from that of his or her family of origin. As today this choice is guided by an individual process of reciprocal affection, the family of origin has little opportunity for direct intervention but depends on providing indirect guidance through the arrangement of social contacts. Personal decisions are channeled by the objectively given possibilities. Social conventions, demographic conditions, and other factors constitute a "market for marriages" with rules and opportunities that affect all persons. Typically, adolescents today postpone the formal choice of a marriage partner, but they start partner relations very early (Hurrelmann, Rosewitz, & Wolf, 1985).

The family's situation as a central institution for adolescents' socialization has changed considerably because of the economic, educational, and cultural processes mentioned above. Today, families are relatively small units with only a few members; they are increasingly households of one or two persons. They have become social systems that are highly susceptible to disturbance, mainly because of the rising instability of matrimony, the social heart of the family's relationships. Some 20 percent of all West German households in 1985 were single-parent households. In the United States the percentage was even higher. Obviously, single-parent families and stepfamilies are more likely to have problematic internal interactions and detrimental consequences for the socialization of young people.

Family relationships in adolescence are of high emotional and social importance. At the same time, one of the developmental tasks at the age of adolescence is to become emotionally, socially, and economically detached from just the important reference group that the family represents. Today this process of becoming detached is structurally very complex: Because of the long-term economic dependence on parents that results from prolonged scholastic and vocational education, it takes place later in life than a generation ago. However, today's adolescents develop a lifestyle that is typically independent from their parents', especially within the area of leisure time and consumption (cf. du Bois-Reymond, 1989; Neubauer & Melzer, 1989). Young people tend to move earlier into communities with peers or partners of the other sex. Some figures for young people living with parents in parental homes in West Germany are illustrative: 18- to 20-year-olds, 92 percent in 1964, 75 percent in 1981; 21- to 24-year-olds, 78 percent in 1964, 45 percent in 1981 (Jugendwerk der Deutschen Shell, 1981). As the process of becoming detached takes place in the different domains at different times, relations with an individual's family of origin are complicated. The family's importance as an economic support and also as an institution that adolescents consult for career decisions is very high, whereas its role as a social institution shaping the actual cultural lifestyle of adolescents is small.

During the separation process, families negotiate the transition from a primarily unilateral relationship between parents and children to a condition more like a mutual coalition during the children's late adolescence. Adolescents beyond the age of 13 or 14 spend significantly more leisure time with peers than with parents or alone, but overall (leisure time plus work time), they spend equal amounts of time with parents and peers. The data reveal that parents' and peers' activities mainly center around the completion of a variety of social and household activities, whereas peer time is spent in entertainment, playing games, and talking (Beck, 1987; Biddle, Bank, & Marlin, 1980).

There is evidence that the influence of parents and peers upon adolescents varies according to types of activities and topics of conversation. In all industrial countries, parents' influence seems to prevail in future-oriented domains, such as choice of school and career plans (cf. Baker & Stevenson, 1989; Dronkers, 1989; Matsuda, 1989; Meeus, 1989); peers' influence centers around current events and activities. Daily friendship interactions take up a substantial portion of adolescents' leisure time. Adolescents report spending more time talking to peers than on any other activity and describe themselves as most happy when so engaged (cf. Bø, 1989; Hamilton & Darling, 1989; Hendry, 1989).

Comparative historical studies conducted in West Germany showed that at the stage of adolescence the meaning of the peer group as a significant social reference group had increased. In a comparative study, Allerbeck and Hoag (1985) were able to show that the status of peer relations had risen over the previous 20 years. Evidently, the social network of peers was denser. The authors noted that membership in a group of friends (a "clique") was reported by 16 percent of adolescents in 1962 and by 57 percent in 1983. The status of the peer group appears to increase as a function of adolescents' social detachment from their parents. In this difficult time of separation, the peer group can take over the functions of stabilizing the adolescent socially and psychologically until a new modus of relations between parents and adolescents has been found (Blyth, Hill, & Thiel, 1982).

Obviously, the peer group's influence on the organization of consumption and leisure-time activities in adolescence is of outstanding importance. Peer groups set standards in the field of consumption and, while doing so, very often set effective standards for adolescents' behavior. Parts of peer groups sometimes create their own youth culture, which makes the development of a personal, independent lifestyle possible. Peer groups offer opportunities of equal participation to their members, which family or school do not provide to the same extent. Peer groups are an important medium in which adolescents are able to experience self-determination (Heitmeyer & Möller, 1989; Rapoport, 1989).

Today's adolescents live a life of their own ideas within the areas of friends, partners, media, and consumption. Nowadays, they often have more than adequate financial resources at their disposal: The majority of adolescents live in material wealth. They are able to realize many of their wishes in the consumption and leisure field, wishes that their parents would never have thought of and could never have realized. But adolescents are living their lives under circumstances of economic dependence rather than circumstances of independence based on their own active, gainful employment. This social position allows for a wide spectrum of personal development and offers a high level of autonomy, spontaneity, creativity, and individuality. Most adolescents enjoy this latitude for decisions, alternatives, and individual shaping of everyday life in a highly imaginative manner. In Germany, most studies have reported a self-confident way of organizing life beyond the adults' paths among adolescents when they are dealing with fashion and dress, taste in music, leisure-time activities, language usage, and political articulation. Adolescents are obviously able to develop forms of sensory, aesthetic, emotional, interactive, and communicative experience.

However, adolescents develop their spontaneity and individuality in a social context that is insecure and unstable. The social position "being adolescent" is always temporary and never concrete and permanently secure. Neither parents, teachers, apprenticeship trainers, nor friends can reassure adolescents that opportunities for individualization will become reality. The occupational future is hardly calculable for adolescents. Reliable future perspectives for the realization of life plans do not exist.

4. IS SOCIETY FACING A RESTRUCTURING OF THE PHASE OF ADOLESCENCE?

Assessments of the changes in the structure of the life situation in adolescence and its individual and societal significance are controversial. Some authors have pointed out that the liberation from gainful employment that has taken place since the 1950s has for the first time also granted a notably large scope for self-exploration and self-definition to previously underprivileged groups of adolescents. The broad scope for self-experience and self-examination and the development of a personal lifestyle in the area of leisure time and consumption that was traditionally only available for male adolescents from the middle classes has been enlarged by this general liberation and is now also accessible to female adolescents and those from the working and lower classes (Jugendwerk der Deutschen Shell, 1981).

Other authors have pointed out that the high level of autonomy of action that is now granted to adolescents and even to children in the area of leisure time and consumption has made their behavior, orientation patterns, and lifestyles similar to and even the same as those of adults. As, in addition, children, adolescents, and adults, regardless of their social situation and their psychological maturity, are addressed and influenced in the same way by the entertainment media, the life and development space that is typical for adolescence disappears according to this concept. Therefore, the idea and the reality of the phase of adolescence are drawing apart.

Doubts should be cast on such sweeping interpretations. The same applies to widespread fears that the far-reaching removal of work-related forms of life from the phase of adolescence would lead to the development of value and interest orientations that are foreign to work and career, making it impossible for adolescents to develop suitable orientations in occupational life. In this context, attention is often drawn to the increasing orientation of adolescents toward post-materialistic and even hedonistic values. This concept links the orientation toward pleasure and immediate gratification to a strong orientation toward the consumption and leisure-time sector and suggests that the latter encourages attitudes and life designs that are alien to work and achievement (Inglehart, 1977). Such schematic estimations of the effects of the change in the structure of the phase of adolescence are superficial and unproductive. They concentrate on only one manifestation of adolescent behavior in each case and render it absolute.

Doing so leads to an overinterpretation of secondary aspects that can only be analyzed and interpreted meaningfully from a holistic perspective.

The phenotype of the adolescent phase since the 1980s is characterized by deep contradictions that are difficult to comprehend in a closed interpretation. My analysis has shown that, for at least the majority of individuals, the predominant characteristic of adolescent life is extended school attendance with institution-specific demands on social and achievement behavior and deep biographical significance for placement in the social structure of society. The phase of adolescence is first and foremost a phase of schooling, and because of the hard battle for a favorable starting position in the placement process, a phase of direct coping with life-relevant tasks and problems (cf. Coleman, 1989).

Besides the educational sector, with its demands that essentially refer to the employment sector, other sectors of activity open their doors to adolescents. In these sectors, adolescents also have to follow institution- and system-specific behavioral norms, but a comparatively higher degree of self-determination is possible. Young people have a relatively large scope for self-determined behavior in the field of leisure time and consumption, in the use of basic commodities and consumer goods, including luxury goods, in the field of direct social relationships with peers of both sexes, and in the field of political and religious activity. Early in their lives, they discover an opportunity structure that provides them with broad opportunities for development and freedom and a favorable position as a group in the nonmaterial privilege structure.

However, it should be noted that this collective, relatively broad latitude for development and self-determination is partially only an illusion created by the unwritten norms and behavioral demands applying to the leisure-time and consumption sectors that are, to some extent, controlled by commercial interests. It is also often overlooked how much the opportunity to exploit this freedom is influenced by the social situation arising from an adolescent's particular social class.

4.1. Internal Changes in the Structure of Adolescence

Although the phase of adolescence in modern industrial societies has gone through fundamental change from a historical perspective, the constitutive elements for the definition and delimitation of adolescence as an independent phase of life have not lost their meaning. Researchers can talk about a restructuring, a change in the structure of the phase of adolescence, and when they consider the traditional middle-class conception of adolescence, perhaps even about a dismantling of the classical phase of adolescence, but they cannot talk about its disappearance.

Even if adolescents (have to) meet behavioral demands that are similar or even equal to those of adulthood in some activity sectors, and even if those demands shape their actual behavior, it does not mean that the phase of adolescence should no longer be assigned an independent status in the human biography. I have characterized the imbalance between independence and dependence, between self-determination and determination by others that is still predominant today as a constitutive element of the phase of adolescence.

Nevertheless, scholars have to ask whether the prolonging of school attendance and the deferral of beginning work as well as the accompanying adoption of the leisure-time and consumption sphere have led to such radical changes in the internal structure of the phase of adolescence that they can talk about the existence of a postadolescent phase. In some respects, the classical phase of adolescence is receiving a social extension. A new, socially regulated age group is arising between adolescence and adulthood. That is, increasingly more adolescents do not enter adulthood after their adolescent phase as students; instead, they become independent from a social, moral, intellectual, political, erotic, and sexual, or, to put it shortly, a sociocultural perspective, yet they do this without developing the economic independence predicted in the historical model of adolescence (Jugendwerk der Deutschen Shell, 1981, p. 100–101; cf. Gaiser & Müller, 1989; Palazzo, 1989).

Without doubt, the extent to which gainful employment is postponed has led to the development of an internally structured life stage of postadolescence that helps young people to cope with and overcome the contradiction between the personal needs for autonomy that increase with age and the economic impediments to the realization of this autonomy. Adolescents discover a life space that is, though economically insecure, socioculturally reliable and that offers dependable social commitments and value orientations. It is characterized by early departure from the parental home, flexible commitments in unconventional forms of living arrangements, and provisional cohabitation with a steady partner without the legal formalities of family life (Jugendwerk der Deutschen Shell, 1981, p. 105).

However, from a sociostructural perspective, there is nothing historically new about the lack of autonomy or partial autonomy in some areas of action combined with complete autonomy in other areas presented here. Such a status inconsistency is characteristic of and constitutive for the phase of adolescence as a whole and particularly for the final phase of adolescence. It is far more the specific expression that this status inconsistency achieves today that is historically new: In broad strata of adolescence, autonomy in the employment sector is only reached biographically late, yet in contrast to former times, autonomy comes earlier in the political, ethical, intimate, cultural, and consumption-oriented fields of action.

This constellation differs from the structure that was typical two or three generations ago. It is questionable whether this specific manifestation of status inconsistency forms the basis for an autonomous and homogeneous lifestyle at the end of the phase of adolescence that takes a consistent form for all adolescents over the age of 18. The social content and societal definition of the different life constellations of postadolescence is very heterogeneous. Scholars cannot talk about a homogeneous life phase of postadolescence. Care should also be taken with an attribution of maturity or majority. A reliable basis for complete autonomy of action and the development of a self-identity can only be considered as given if self-responsibility is achieved in all personally and socially significant areas of action, and therefore also in the area of employment. Sociocultural majority can therefore only be a partial majority that has to be made complete by economic majority.

4.2. Characteristic Structural Features of the Change in the Phase of Adolescence

There can be no doubt that the adolescent phase has undergone fundamental structural change. However, historical and systematic analysis has produced no certain indications for an imminent disappearance of adolescence as an independent phase of life in the human biography. The process of the historical segregation of the adolescent phase of life is not annulled because adolescents and adults are confronted with the same demands and show the same forms of action and behavior in a few everyday fields of action. Instead, it is necessary to take a differentiated perspective and assume that social institutions and organizations are in a process of segregation that is running parallel to the continuing trend in a process of segregation of life phases. This institutional process of differentiation runs at right angles to the process of increasing segregation of life phases and has its own particular influences on the manifestations of the segregation of life phases. It affects the life conditions of all members of society, regardless of their age.

The manifestations of adolescent behavior that are the subject of the present debate on adolescence can only be explained if an interaction between these two independent processes is assumed.

As with the segregation of life phases, the historical origins of this institutional segregation lie in the preindustrial family unit. During the course of industrialization, the societal functional areas of economics, social control, religion, and education that were originally interlinked and restricted to the family unit, as well as more recent functions such as emotional stabilization, entertainment, and information, have, over a period of time that extends to the present day, been transferred to institutions and organizations that each specialize in one of these tasks. The family retains some essential functions, but it is now only one societal subinstitution among many.

Each of the subinstitutions and suborganizations, such as company, church, law, school, commodity market, and so forth, is constructed according to system-specific rules and procedures and sets specific demands that differ from those of the other systems and can rarely be transferred from one system to another. They form self-contained and separated areas of life with specific action and behavior demands.

This institutional segmentation creates similar or equal life conditions for the members of all phases of life. At the same time, a certain bandwidth of special institutions develops; for adolescents, for example, schools, vocational training centers, universities, and children's homes. These extrafamilial authorities of education and socialization take over essential tasks in supporting the process of individuation and integration. The everyday activity of adolescents is decisively characterized by an adjustment to the specific institutions that are standard for their age group. Each of the institutions imposes demands within the framework of its own system-specific conditions and acts according to the patterns of its own functional structures.

In addition to these institutions of education and socialization, which to some extent also include peer groups, other institutionalized areas of activity also involve adolescents. With the exception of the employment system, there are very few sectors in present-day societies to which adolescents do not have access. Particularly in the political, ethical, and cultural and consumption-oriented areas of activity and communication (including the mass media), they are frequently as involved as adults in the functional procedures of the institutions, organizations, and media. To some extent, this statement applies for children as well.

This approach can be used to explain the specific profile of the forms of activity and behavior that can be found in adolescents today. Because of the institutional segmentation that has occurred, adolescents have to find their own path of individual development and social integration in the separated activity sectors of education, consumption, politics, information, partnership, and so forth. In many areas, they succeed in coping with these action demands in ways that are similar to those used by adults. Adolescents encounter broad freedoms of action that present them with many personal possibilities at an early stage in their development. In other areas, they are excluded from such scope for development.

Therefore, at different times and in different situations, adolescents achieve the degree of autonomy and responsibility that is characteristic of adult status in different behavioral sectors. They have to cope permanently with a double inconsistency of action demands: On the one hand, there are the inconsistent demands of the different behavioral sectors, each with its own specific structure and form; on the other hand, there are the demands that result from the degree of inclusion and autonomy that is reached in each of the different sectors. Thus, the transfer to the adult status breaks down into a loosely interconnected sequence of single "status passages," each of which follows different social and temporal patterns. The relationships between the different demands of the status passages are tense and even contradictory. To a large extent, each adolescent has to cope alone with these status transfers.

In the end, each adolescent has to bear alone the burdens and the responsibility of coordinating divergent action demands with a broad variety of options and the necessary decision steps that accompany them. No single societal institution actively assists in this coordination; the entire network of support that is formed by the interplay of the different institutions and organizations in which they are embedded is important for adolescents.

A differentiated sociological analysis must accordingly lead to the conclusion that although the adolescent phase is undergoing fundamental processes of structural change that derive from constellations in society as a whole, it remains an independent phase of life as understood in my original definition. It is and remains typical of the structure of adolescence to have in each case a historically specific constellation of "status inconsistency." The particular extent of this status inconsistency can lead to internal substructurings of the phase of adolescence. Such substructurings must not be interpreted ad hoc as indicating the disappearance or severance of the phase of adolescence. The postponement of the transfer to the employment system, which can be observed among all adolescents in the last decades, is by itself not enough to create, for example, a homogeneous life situation of postadolescence. It is far more the case that there remains a considerable breadth of variation in the configuration of the phase of adolescence that depends on specific constellations of living conditions and status inconsistencies, on the social network of support, and on individual forms of processing reality.

5. IMPLICATIONS FOR SOCIAL SUPPORT STRATEGIES IN ADOLESCENCE

I believe that the findings reported in this chapter underscore the value of taking a broad ecological and socialization approach to understanding both the normal and deviant development and behavior of adolescents (Bronfenbrenner, 1979). One of the key implications of the reported studies is the importance of interactions with parents, peers, teachers, and other significant partners for the prevention of adolescent involvement in deviant behavior. The findings reported strongly suggest that the maintenance of frequent, constructive interactions with significant others, including parents and other significant adults, is very important not only in childhood but also in adolescence.

From all reports, it becomes obvious that measures to improve adolescents' personal well-being and self-esteem, and measures for improving their material and ecological living conditions and integration into the social network, are of evident significance for the whole process of successful or unsuccessful socialization (Hurrelmann, 1988; Hurrelmann, Kaufmann, & Lösel, 1987).

What does this mean for the most important agencies of socialization that have been mentioned in this chapter?

1. Regarding the family area: The more stable and dependable the relationships between parents and children before the latter enter the phase of adolescence, the better are the starting positions for their further personality development during the age of adolescence. All policies concerned with families must aim to guarantee a minimum amount of economic security and cultural stimulation within the family, as these provide the basis for later satisfactory relationships between parents and adolescents. The erosion of the family as an educational authority at the stage of adolescence makes this task more and more difficult. Parents find themselves in the precarious situation of forcing their children's scholastic and vocational careers, pushing them into individual competition, but without being able to assure them that these efforts will lead to an acceptable life perspective.

2. Regarding the peer group and leisure domains: the great dilemma is that adolescents have a lot of freedom within the social and financial area but are without a real challenge to and satisfaction of their needs and interests. The mass media offer only a superficial fulfillment and a pretense of adventure and experience to them. There is a lack of serious personal challenges that would allow them to try out their personal physical power and psychological competences and thus test their personal possibilities and the limitations of behavior. Tentative confrontation or experimentation with law and order is likely to bring the immediate intervention of police or control authorities. Today's highly civilized and rationalized society has largely filled in and leveled out opportunities for such confrontation. The only plausible alternative is to reactivate these opportunities artificially by creating new activities in sports clubs, scout groups, travel groups, and social work groups, while recognizing the problem that today's adolescents only start using these institutionalized offers in a very hesitant way.

3. A key role is taken by the occupational sector. Even in our so-called leisure-time society, this sector constitutes the main area for defining self and prestige. Our society pushes adolescents into enormous difficulties by not giving them a guarantee of future gainful employment after they have successfully finished school. By doing this, the society destroys an essential, minimal calculability of the future on which adolescents at their specific life phase are dependent. Taking up an occupation—in addition to getting married and establishing one's own family—has for a long time been the decisive symbolic step toward adulthood. If the ability to take this step is not guaranteed, society takes away the adolescent's social basis for becoming adult.

4. What can the specific role of schools be in this endeavor? Schools have been, as has been shown, strongly affected by the structural changes in the life phase of adolescence. As a necessary consequence of this fact, the position of school in adolescents' everyday lives has to be rethought.

The schools' potential to provide social support should be strengthened. If school, besides being an institution providing knowledge and intellectual training, also becomes a social platform, an encouraging part of adolescents' everyday lives, then it is available for experiences that are important for personal development in many dimensions. A good school in this sense is a society's unsurpassable contribution to youth policies. The school has to offer working and training opportunities with different learning situations for adolescents that they will find meaningful and important. A good school with a pleasant climate can be a social area with a preventive influence on antisocial behavior and health impairment (Hurrelmann, 1987).

At school, many hours are spent on social communication among students and between students and teachers. The schools' potential for social support has to be carefully analyzed. It is helpful to imagine school as just one social institution among others within the entire social network of adolescents. School as a social institution dominates a large sector of adolescents' social world and has a formative influence on all main sectors of the life course. For this reason, school is one of the most important institutions responsible for the competent and healthy development of adolescents. Because adolescents are obliged to attend school for many years, school makes contact with practically all members of an age cohort, and it is therefore an ideal and institutionally unique location for supportive measures (Hamilton, 1984).

It should be noted that the consequences of the heavy emphasis on school during adolescence are ambiguous: On the one hand, the extension of school time deprives adolescents of an important field of social experience. Later entry into employment prevents full material independence. Opportunities for earning money, for self-determination, and for leading a life that is relatively independent of the family of origin are no doubt restricted because of the prevailing state of dependence. In many respects, employment is a prerequisite for the acquisition of independence in other areas, offering more than just a material basis in view of its substantial psychological and social implications for adolescents and their social environment. Both publicly and privately, the phase of adolescence is mainly defined and interpreted as a process of transition into working life and the economic system.

On the other hand, the extension of school time offers access to good educational opportunities and large measures of independence and autonomy in a number of action fields, such as leisure, entertainment, consumption, politics, information, and sexual relations. All of this enables adolescents to choose and try out new and individual paths leading toward optimal growth and social integration. It is the task of schools to offer help to adolescents that will enable them to cope with this situation.

Any form of psychosocial and psychosomatic health impairment and antisocial behavior has to be interpreted as an individual way of coping with life stress in adolescence. Therefore, intervention measures have to take directly into account the psychosocial functions that drug abuse, delinquent behavior, and psychosomatic symptoms possess for adolescents. It is no use developing highly specialized intervention technologies. Society can only provide support and help that is politically, psychologically, pedagogically, and socially effective if the whole life situation of adolescence is considered. Developing advisory services, treatment, and therapy designed to treat single symptoms within the psychosocial and psychosomatic domain is necessary, but society must not spend all its energy on this curing of symptoms. Those seeking to intervene have to concentrate on the real starting positions for the appearance of the symptoms, which have complex structural origins. In the face of the many facets of this problem, combination and coordination of the activities provided in family and youth work, schools and youth advisory services, public health departments and hospitals, and welfare offices and employment agencies is needed, along with the setting up of accessible institutions to which parents and adolescents can turn for advice in their neighborhoods.

REFERENCES

Allerbeck, K. R., & Hoag, W. J. (1985). *Jugend ohne Zukunft* [Youth without a future]. Munich/Zurich: Piper.

Baethge, M. (1989). Individualization as hope and disaster: A socioeconomic perspective. In K. Hurrelmann & U. Engel (Eds.), *The social world of adolescents* (pp. 27–41). Berlin: de Gruyter.

Baethge, M., Schomburg, H., & Voskamp, K. (1983). *Jugend und Krise* [Youth and crisis]. Frankfurt: Campus.

Baker, D. P., & Stevenson, D. L. (1989). Parents' management of adolescents' schooling: An international comparison. In K. Hurrelmann & U. Engel (Eds.), *The social world of adolescents* (pp. 339–350). Berlin: de Gruyter.

Beck, S. (1987). Research issues. In V. B. Hasselt & M. Hersen (Eds.), *Handbook of adolescent psychology* (pp. 227–241). Elmsford, NY: Pergamon Press.

Biddle, B., Bank, B. J., & Marlin, M. M. (1980). Parental and peer influence on adolescents. *Social Forces, 58,* 1057–1079.

Blyth, D. A., Hill, J. P., & Thiel, K. S. (1982). Early adolescents' significant others. *Journal of Youth and Adolescence, 11,* 425–450.

Bø, I. (1989). The significant people in the social networks of adolescents. In K. Hurrelmann & U. Engel (Eds.), *The social world of adolescents* (pp. 141–165). Berlin: de Gruyter.

Bronfenbrenner, U. (1979). *The ecology of human development: Experiments by nature and design.* Cambridge, MA: Harvard University Press.

Bundesminister für Bildung und Wissenschaft. (1987). *Grund- und Strukturdaten* [Basic and structural data]. Bad Honnef, Germany: Bock.

Coleman, J. C. (1989). The focal theory of adolescence: A psychological perspective. In K. Hurrelmann & U. Engel (Eds.), *The social world of adolescents* (pp. 43–56). Berlin: de Gruyter.

Dronkers, J. (1989). Working mothers and the educational achievements of their children. In K. Hurrelmann & U. Engel (Eds.), *The social world of adolescents* (pp. 185–198). Berlin: de Gruyter.

du Bois-Reymond, M. (1989). School and family in the lifeworld of youngsters. In K. Hurrelmann & U. Engel (Eds.), *The social world of adolescents* (pp. 213–228). Berlin: de Gruyter.

Engel, U. (1987). Youth, mobility and social integration. In O. Hazekamp (Ed.), *Youth research in Europe*. Amsterdam: Free University Press.

Engel, U. (1989). Uncertain career prospects and problem behavior in adolescence. In K. Hurrelmann & U. Engel (Eds.), *The social world of adolescents* (pp. 393–403). Berlin: de Gruyter.

Gaiser, W., & Muller, H. U. (1989). The importance of peer groups in different regional contexts and biographical stages. In K. Hurrelmann & U. Engel (Eds.), *The social world of adolescents* (pp. 279–296). Berlin: de Gruyter.

Gillis, J. R. (1974). *Youth and history: Tradition and change in European age relations 1770-present*. New York: Academic Press.

Hamilton, S. F. (1984). The secondary school in the ecology of adolescent development. In E. W. Gordon (Ed.), *Review of research in education* (pp. 227–258). New York: American Educational Research Association.

Hamilton, S. F., & Darling, N. (1989). Mentors in adolescents' lives. In K. Hurrelmann & U. Engel (Eds.), *The social world of adolescents* (pp. 121–139). Berlin: de Gruyter.

Heitmeyer, W., & Moller, K. (1989). Milieu attachment and erosion as problems of individual socialization. In K. Hurrelmann & U. Engel (Eds.), *The social world of adolescents* (pp. 297–319). Berlin: de Gruyter.

Hendry, L. B. (1989). The influence of adults and peers on adolescents' lifestyles and leisure-styles. In K. Hurrelmann & U. Engel (Eds.), *The social world of adolescents* (pp. 245–263). Berlin: de Gruyter.

Hurrelmann, K. (1987). The importance of school in the life course. *Journal of Adolescent Research, 2*, 111–125.

Hurrelmann, K. (1988). *Social structure and personality development*. New York: Cambridge University Press.

Hurrelmann, K., Kaufmann, F. X., & Lösel, F. (Eds.). (1987). *Social intervention: Potential and constraints*. Berlin/New York: de Gruyter.

Hurrelmann, K., Rosewitz, B., & Wolf, H. K. (1985). *Lebensphase Jugend* [The youth phase of life]. Weinheim/Munich: Juventa.

Inglehart, R. (1977). The silent revolution. Princeton, New Jersey: Princeton University Press.

Jugendwerk der Deutschen Shell (Ed.). (1981). *Jugend '81. Lebensentwürfe, Alltagskulturen, Zukunftsbilder* [Youth '81, life plans, everyday culture, views of the future]. Opladen, Germany: Leske.

King, A. J. C. (1989). Changing sex roles, lifestyles and attitudes in an urban society. In K. Hurrelmann & U. Engel (Eds.), *The social world of adolescents* (pp. 265–275). Berlin: de Gruyter.

Matsuda, S. (1989). Significant partners in childhood and adolescence. In K. Hurrelmann & U. Engel (Eds.), *The social world of adolescents* (pp. 199–209). Berlin: de Gruyter.

Meeus, W. (1989). Parental and peer support in adolescence. In K. Hurrelmann & U. Engel (Eds.), *The social world of adolescents* (pp. 167–183). Berlin: de Gruyter.

Modell, J., Furstenberg, F. F., & Hershberg, T. (1977): Social change and transitions to adulthood in historical perspective. *Journal of Family History, 1*, 7–32.

Neubauer, G., & Melzer, W. (1989). The role of school, family, and peer group in the sexual development of the adolescent. In K. Hurrelman & U. Engel (Eds.), *The social world of adolescents* (pp. 321–336). Berlin: de Gruyter.

Palazzo, D. (1989). The lifeworld of young people: A systems-theoretical perspective. In K. Hurrelmann & U. Engel (Eds.), *The social world of adolescents* (pp. 57–64). Berlin: de Gruyter.

Persell, C. H. (1977): *Education and inequality*. New York: Free Press.

Poole, M. E. (1989). Adolescent transitions: A life-course perspective. In K. Hurrelmann & U. Engel (Eds.), *The social world of adolesents* (pp. 65–85). Berlin: de Gruyter.

Rapoport, T. (1989). Experimentation and control in family, school, and youth movement. In K. Hurrelmann & U. Engel (Eds.), *The social world of adolescents* (pp. 229–244). Berlin: de Gruyter.

Roberts, K., & Parsell, G. (1989). Recent changes in the pathways from school to work. In K. Hurrelman & U. Engel (Eds.), *The social world of adolescents* (pp. 369–391). Berlin: de Gruyter.

Wallace, C. (1989). Social reproduction and school leavers: A longitudinal perspective. In K. Hurrelmann & U. Engel (Eds.), *The social world of adolescents* (pp. 351–367). Berlin: de Gruyter.

Weidman, J. C. (1989). The world of higher education: A socialization-theoretical perspective. In K. Hurrelmann & U. Engel (Eds.), *The social world of adolescents* (pp. 87–105). Berlin: de Gruyter.

3

Social Psychology and the Study of Youth

Willem Doise

It was in 1904 that Stanley Hall published a book, *Adolescence,* with the rather lengthy subtitle "Its psychology and its relations to physiology, anthropology, sociology, sex, crime, religion and education." This enumeration of scientific disciplines to which the psychological approach should be related, together with the evocation of sex and crime, and of the highly institutionalized domains of religion and education, offers a strange mixture. It is an indication of the polyphonic nature of youth psychology at its very beginning. And still today, the psychology of youth remains a kind of joint venture in which different voices concur—voices that express basic scientific concerns—as well as anxious voices about AIDS, drugs, and unemployment and voices that question educational, economical, and political institutions.

However, if the general impression I retain from studies on youth or adolescence is not precisely one of perfect harmony, it is not one of cacophony either. The psychology of youth, perhaps more than other branches of the discipline, illustrates that scientific and societal concerns are not necessarily antagonistic. After all, the association of terms in the subtitle of the book of youth psychology's founding father probably did not sound strange when the book was first published, and today it still could be a subtitle for many edited books on the psychology of adolescence. Of course, the ambitions of scholars at the beginning of the century were much broader in scope than those of most scholars today. The frontiers between disciplines and subdisciplines were not so tight as they are today, and the social relevance of research was not necessarily considered to be a threat to its objectivity. Scholars are presently more interested in the study of specific processes of psychic life, but their transformation in adolescents is evidently linked to changes in social positions and to important societal challenges. That is probably the reason why youth psychologists more often than other psychologists try to put their findings in a broader framework. Even when they deal with specific issues, they are not prevented from seeing the forest for the trees.

In this contribution, I will try to illustrate this assertion. In the first part, I will show that the study of detailed social psychological processes, in line with the general evolution of psychological research toward more specificity, is nevertheless highly relevant socially. Processes of dissonance reduction, sociocognitive conflict, social comparison, and social attribution are, to use a well-known image, the bricks and mortar of social life. In the second part, I will deal more directly with analyses that start from a societal perspective in order to study adolescents' identity and political socialization. But this broad dichotomy is artificial and does not do justice to the variety and sophistication of much research on adolescence. Therefore, I will mention in the third part some approaches that I consider typical of more recent research on adolescents that incorporate in their operational models the intricacy of the links between psychological and societal variables.

1. SOCIETAL RELEVANCE OF SOCIOPSYCHOLOGICAL PROCESSES

The dissonance reduction process is studied at the level of the individual: the definition of dissonance involves only the presence of incompatible cognitions for an individual. But incompatibility in itself is already socially defined, and much of the traditional research on dissonance is research on forced compliance, severity and initiation, intensity of threat, and so on. The least one can say is that not only are the incompatible cognitions produced socially, but that also the degree of their incompatibility is socially defined. I will not deal here with various reinterpretations of the dissonance effect in terms of maintenance of self-image or group image or in terms of the intervention of an ideology of the consistent rational individual (cf. Poitou, 1974), but will limit myself to drawing your attention to a recent reinterpretation of dissonance theory by Joule and Beauvois (1987), two French social psychologists. The main point of their conception bears on the central function of behavioral commitment in generating dissonance. According to Joule and Beauvois (1987), only cognitions directly linked to an individual's awareness of his or her behavioral commitment are relevant for defining the intensity of dissonance in a given situation. An important way of reducing dissonance is therefore to generate new behavior that is consistent with previous actions. Of course, the authors make the link with well-studied effects such as the foot-in-the-door effect and the low-ball effect. They obtained interesting results in the domain of smoking abstinence by asking people to abstain for a short time and then, once the subjects had complied with the first request, immediately asking them to abstain for a longer period. Offering the subjects the possibility of committing themselves for a longer period is in fact offering them a cognition consonant with their previous commitment. These authors actually applied their ideas in AIDS prevention campaigns. Beauvois and Joule (1981) considered dissonance reduction an important process in ideological rationalization. It is reasonable to assume that for adolescents, forced compliance situations abound and therefore, this period of life offers numerous occasions to elaborate rationalizations of the kind postulated by dissonance theory. The French sociologist Wieviorka, who certainly cannot be accused of psychological reductionism, found a plausible explanation in dissonance theory for the psychological functioning of terrorists who recur to violent actions in order to rationalize their commitments. Wieviorka (1988) wrote that dissonance theory "is compatible with a sociology of action, as this theory investigates at its own level psychological mechanisms in a much better way than other approaches that reduce the explanation of violent acts to projections of personality or to psychological dysfunctioning, when they do not simply limit themselves to naturalizing individual or collective violence in considering them to be caused by instinct or aggressive drives" (p. 109).

The investigations of my team at Geneva on the social development of the intellect afford another important explanation for cognitive conflict that is socially produced. Such conflict is considered to be an important motor of cognitive progress. A special instance of such sociocognitive conflict occurs when the incorrect cognitive solutions of a task involving specific objects contradict the social norms mediated through the use of these objects. Such conflicts were studied in, for instance, tasks involving conservation of liquids. Children of a certain age usually think that equal amounts of liquid contained in two equal glasses do not remain equal when they are poured into unequal glasses. The setting changes drastically when this apparent inequality contradicts a norm of equal sharing; in such a "socially marked" situation children acquire conservations of equality and generalize their new skill to tasks that are less socially relevant. For more examples and more complete theoretical justification of these results, allow me to refer to Doise and Mugny (1984) and to De Paolis, Doise, and Mugny (1987). But other authors, not necessarily using the same theoretical premises, have stressed the constructive role of cognitive conflicts that are socially produced in educational settings; Johnson and Johnson (1979) are an example. But here let me quote a Swiss educational psychologist, Oser, who described the main characteristics of interactional situations that should promote and stimulate moral development through sociocognitive conflict as follows:

1. Presentation of the subjective truth completely and exhaustively (competence) as conceived by the participants in the conflict; 2. absence of an authority presenting an outside or observer's point of view of the "right" answer; 3. creation of a disequilibrium by presenting different arguments and different opinions to stimulate development of moral judgment on increasingly complex grounds; 4. interaction among students (discussants) coordinated in such a way that everyone reacts openly and fairly to one another's point of view (positive climate and transactional discourse); 5. linking of the principles of discourse to the principles of justice. (1986, p. 922)

These characteristics are homologous to the ones I have described in my work with Gabriel Mugny on the social development of the intellect. They are: confrontation and coordination of viewpoints, avoidance of compliance, sociocognitive conflict, articulation of organizing social principles with more abstract cognitive principles (for the social construction of the intellect) or with fundamental principles of justice (for social construction of ethics). And interestingly enough, these conditions are also homologous to some of those that, according to Janis (1982), should prevent "groupthink" from exerting its often disastrous effects in collective political decision making.

In fact, more than a century ago, Cattaneo (1864) stressed the importance of conflict in furthering cognitive growth. But other pioneers who also wished to depart from the idealistic philosophy of a general mind have joined Baldwin (1897) in stressing the role of imitation in the appropriation of a cultural heritage; Bandura's (1977) theory of social learning is part of that tradition. Since the beginning of scientific psychology, two kinds of social processes have been invoked to account for cognitive development: conflict is supposed to explain the genesis of new coordinations, and imitation has to explain the appropriation of existing societal products. It is my opinion that the research on sociocognitive conflict and social marking not only continues the study of conflictual innovative and imitative adaptive processes but articulates empirically the study of both processes. But again, it would be too simplistic to divide into two classes the social psychological processes intervening in individual development. On which side of this dichotomy should one locate the individuation and deindividuation processes studied by Monteil (1989)? Let me briefly describe some of his experiments.

In a first experiment, two groups of secondary school pupils with a big difference in academic status, of which they were aware, listened to a biology lesson in two different conditions: anonymity and individuation. In the first condition, the pupils were informed that nobody among them would be asked questions during the lesson; in the second condition, they were told that everybody would be asked questions. Furthermore, half of the pupils were not reminded of their academic status, whereas the other half were. In fact, no questions were asked during the lesson, but all pupils answered ten questions of a posttest bearing on the content of the course, and their responses were evaluated by four independent judges. Subjects who had not been explicitly reminded of their academic status performed as usual, without differences attributable to the anonymity or individuation condition: good pupils performed better than bad pupils in both conditions. Results were very different when the subjects were reminded of their academic status: anonymity made bad pupils perform as well as good students, but individuation made them perform very differently, the good ones performing much better in this condition than the bad ones.

In a second experiment, only good pupils participated, but half of them were told that they had succeeded or failed on a previous task. Here academic status was experimentally manipulated and made salient for all subjects. Anonymity and individuation were also introduced, as in the previous experiment. As predicted, subjects in the anonymity condition performed equally well on the post-test whether high or low academic status was ascribed to them, but in the individuation condition, subjects in the failure condition performed much worse than subjects in the success condition. A third experiment using the same procedures as the second one but tasks in four different areas, ranking from those with high academic prestige (mathematics or biology) to those with low prestige (history and geography or manual and technical education), showed that the interaction effect between a status of success and failure on the one hand, and anonymity and individuation on the other, was much stronger for areas with high academic prestige than for those with low academic prestige.

To conclude this brief report on Monteil's research: individuation, perhaps through anticipated visibility, enhances the differences between individuals in relation with the status positions they have been afforded, even when these differences are to be expressed on dimensions of cognitive functioning.

I have detailed these experiments because they offer a nice illustration of the paradoxical links between individual autonomy and social interdependence. The experiments of Monteil are operationalizations of important ideas developed by Emile Durkheim in the foreword to his famous book, *The Division of Labor in Society.* Almost 100 years ago, the sociologist wrote:

> As to the question which gave rise to this work, it is that of the relations between the individual personality and social solidarity. What explains the fact that, while becoming more autonomous, the individual becomes more closely dependent on society? How can he simultaneously be more personally developed and more socially dependent? For it is undeniable that these two developments, however contradictory they may seem, are equally in evidence. That is the problem which we have set ourselves. What has seemed to us to resolve this apparent antinomy is a transformation of social solidarity due to the steadily growing development of the division of labor. (Durkheim, 1902, pp. xliii–xliv)

Perhaps scholars still cannot truly explain the paradox, but at least it is known for sure that social comparison processes can intervene in pupils' performances at school for the better or worse, depending on circumstances.

Since the publication of Schachter's (1959) work, *The Psychology of Affiliation,* the importance of social comparison processes for making meaning of affective states has often been evidenced. More generally, such processes are considered to be important whenever individuals share a common fate, which is often the case for individuals belonging to the same group or category (Rabbie & Horwitz, 1969). This relationship suggests a social psychological reason for the importance of peer reference groups during adolescence: there are so many new things adolescents have to make sense of that they no longer share with their parents. Once such a categorical differentiation between peers and the parental generation has been triggered, a spiral of more reciprocal differentiation is often put into motion. And many parents know that their children prefer peers when the children build meaning systems in many different areas. Muzafer and Carolyn Sherif's 1964 study, *Reference Groups,* remains a classic in the field, and since its appearance the interest in identification with peer groups has grown in intensity (Allerbeck & Hoag, 1985). Youth centrism, as studied by Meeus (1989), is an important manifestation of this peer group bias, and his data show that this centrism is relatively independent of other centrisms such as authoritarianism and sexism, although it is related to ethnocentrism and to academic status; pupils of lower-status school streams are more youth-centered than others. Meeus measured this new form of centrism "in terms of a 25 item scale [assessing] (1) aversion to parents and a marked orientation toward peers; (2) a critical attitude regarding adult institutions (family, state) and their representatives (parents, teachers, police, politicians); (3) a generation gap; and (4) reliance on the ability of youth to resist the 'adult world'" (1989, p. 169).

Results on the scale are negatively related to the support adolescents receive, or should I say accept, from their parents in the life spheres of school, social relationships, and leisure time. But the differentiation of these life spheres remains important in specifying the influence of parental support. In findings reported by Youniss and Smollar (1985), Dutch parents were more important than peers in the context of school performance.

To conclude this far-from-exhaustive list of classic social psychological research paradigms, let me also mention attribution, or locus of control, studies. It is generally assumed that internal attribution, or internal control, is also developmentally determined, with children becoming aware as they mature that an internal locus of control is generally more valued than an external one (cf. Dubois, 1987). In a certain sense, children are gradually led to believe that they should act as if they were responsible for their own fates, and according to LePoultier (1986, 1990), it is also part of the job of social workers to instill such ideas into the minds of the persons they attend to. In Brussels, Van Overwalle, Segebarth, and Goldchstein (1989) tried to do that with students who had failed their exams, noting that they tried "to teach university students to make more adaptive causal ascriptions for their examination failures, and in doing this, increase their subsequent examination performance" (p. 75). Results showed that such attribution training was in itself effective and that classic study skills training did not add anything to the effects. Studying individuals at the other end of the life scale, Schulz (1976) addressed the effects of effective control and predictability on "the psychological and physical well-being of the institutionalized aged." And even if this proposition may hurt the feelings of youth researchers committed to youth centrism, it is perhaps possible to learn from research with aged people who are at times confronted with marginalization not entirely different from that experienced by adolescents.

2. A SOCIETAL PERSPECTIVE

In introducing this second part, allow me to state that adolescents are not just individual beings or social groups, but also sources of social representations. Not only do they construct their own representations of the social world—other categories of their social environment construct representations of them. These representations have an important characteristic: they are predominantly negative in evaluative terms. This is evidenced, for instance, in a study by Claes (reported in *Le Journal de Geneve,* July 13, 1991) on articles dealing with adolescents in the French-language newspapers of Montreal. Maassen and De Goede (1986) offered questionnaire results showing that in the Netherlands younger people both received less favorable ratings from adults than older people, and tended to describe older people in slightly more favorable terms than their own age group.

Generational discrimination is a reciprocal affair, according to the data of this Dutch study, adults being at least as group-centered, if not more so, than younger respondents.

The most consistent investigation of social representations of youth was carried out by Marie-Jose Chombart de Lauwe (1984). Although her research was more centered on the representations of childhood in, for instance, literature or printed and filmed images, I nevertheless think that her main assumption remains applicable to social representations of adolescence. She considered the notion of dominance to be indispensable for explaining adults' representations of children. As regards the characteristics of these representations, she asserted:

> The representation of each member of a dominated category is effected by reference to the model of the dominant category, according to two processes: a scaled-down identification (i.e. resembling the dominant model but with less developed characteristics) or inversion (i.e. with attributes that are contrary to those of the dominant model). The discourse of the dominant category over the dominated one betrays the values of a society. It is doubly interesting to analyze this discourse, because, on the one hand, the attributes which characterize the model of the dominant category are those which are valued by society at large, and, on the other hand, the representations of the dominated are vested either with negative attributes, or with attributes which are valued in a compensatory world of fantasy, through a mode of thinking which is mythical in nature. (Chombart de Lauwe, 1984, p. 188)

A notable characteristic of the representation of childhood is the oppositional system "genuine child" versus "oppressive society":

> The two poles are not represented on an equal footing, their presence is more or less important. At times, society appears as a blur, all the narrative aiming at the enhancement of the small idealized child. Conversely, in other narratives, society becomes the focus of attention. It has destructive effects on the genuine child who

becomes its victim. The authors analyze the procedures whereby society integrates and transforms the genuine child according to its own rules. In some cases, he only exists as a point of reference, thus appearing as a lost ideal. The relation between the two ways of existing is established through the diverse situations and reactions of the child. The confrontation can take place at a distance, as if the two worlds were only looking at each other or, on the contrary, it can be very violent. (Chombart de Lauwe, 1984, p. 195)

I think the last pattern is present more often than others in scholars' representations of adolescents.

Social representations deal with beliefs, opinions, and stereotypes that correspond to specific social relationships. They intervene in the thought that precedes scientific activity, presenting commonsense truths that orient the construction of hypotheses to be investigated. The research on the psychology of sex differences very convincingly illustrates the fact that social sciences often reformulate commonsense knowledge in a more sophisticated way. Social representations also transform the products of scientific investigation, as for instance, when psychoanalysis becomes part of popular knowledge. Moscovici (1961) described processes of ojectification (for instance, complexes become entities that can be taken away by an experienced psychoanalyst) and of anchoring new information in preexisting frames of knowledge (for instance, psychoanalytic treatment is considered to be a kind of confession to a new kind of priest, a belief that also results in a transformation of current beliefs about confession and the psychoanalytic conception of transference). Therefore, scientific activity is intimately related to social representations, which also intervene in scientific activity itself (Doise, 1987). I think that this is the case with Erikson's (1977) description of the relationships between individuals and industrial society and with the theme of the unkept promise that Bakan expressed as early as the beginning of the 1970s:

> The profoundly pervasive metaphor of appropriate behavior in adolescence as a form of capital investment for the realization of returns in the future necessarily falters in cogency as the likelihood of such returns declines. The problems of order in the schools, juvenile delinquency, and other forms of expressive alienation cannot readily be solved by making small changes in the schools. . . . It would appear that the schools cannot promise much because the society cannot promise much. (Bakan, 1972, p. 84)

It is not my intention to challenge such interpretations, which abound in the scientific literature on adolescence, as they are certainly true to the extent that they express the relationships between the authors and the groups they study in a given societal context.

My present concern is not a polemic one; it is to draw attention to the fact that investigating social categories also means investigating society. In other words, it is difficult to theorize on adolescence without theorizing on its relationship with contemporary society. This difficulty is of course evident for studies of the political socialization of adolescents; however, it is less so for studies of their identity.

Firstly, I will show that studies of social identity necessarily have to take into account the intervention of very strong and general social norms. This is not to deny that important differences exist between subgroups of adolescents, differences about which they are aware, as was shown by a whole series of studies carried out in northern Italy by Palmonari, Pombeni, and Kirchler (1989) in naturalistic settings on more than 3,000 adolescents. For example, an important distinction agreed upon by adolescents is the one between informal groups (that is, common interest groups without adult leadership) and formal groups (groups with a clear goal to be attained under the supervision of an adult). The first ones often meet at street corners, parks, or coffee shops, the latter in meeting places provided by sports clubs and religious, political, or humanitarian organizations. An important finding is that members of formal groups often perceive informal groups as their out-groups, and members of informal groups often perceive formal groups as their out-groups. Research has shown that adolescents make many other distinctions between groups, such as distinctions related to gender in numerous studies and differences between immigrants and Swiss in a Genevan school population (Doise & Lorenzi-Cioldi, 1990).

In Tajfel's and Turner's (1979) theory of social identity, making such differentiations is considered to be important for constructing a positive self-concept. And that may be so.

But let us look at some results bearing on self-images. One cannot miss the striking similarity in the self-images held by members of different groups. The three sources of data I will describe refer to very different settings and methods of data gathering and analysis. First are the data on members of informal and formal groups by Palmonari and colleagues (1989): they are average results on five-point scales that are grouped according to high loadings on four different factors resulting from a principal component analysis. The second study (Ravaud, Beaufils, & Paicheler, 1986) bears on self-images and group images of physically handicapped and nonhandicapped pupils of a French secondary school specially conceived to admit both groups. The third study (Doise & Lorenzi-Cioldi, 1990) bears on second-generation immigrants and Swiss pupils in Genevan secondary schools who were asked to describe themselves, their friends, and Swiss and foreigners in general. All these studies converge in showing important similarities in the self-images of members of different groups, notwithstanding the clear distinctions that the same subjects make between the different groups they belong to. To these studies I could add data related to sex differences obtained by Nakbi (1990; Nakbi & Arnal-Duchemin, 1987), who found that the self-images of boys and girls differed only slightly, whereas the images of own gender and other gender were very different. Cowan and Hoffman (1986) and Inoff, Halverson, and Pizzigati (1983) also reported data on younger children who seemed to adhere to conventional gender stereotypes but ascribed similar positive traits to themselves independent of the traits' sexual connotation.

One could conclude that this absence of important overall differences in the self-images of members of different categories reflects a high intracategory variation in these images. At least for the Genevan results noted, this is apparently not the case; self-images are highly stereotypical, sometimes more so than the images of relevant in-groups or out-groups: for members of the same groups, between-subjects variation on scales related to selves is less important than between-subjects variation on the same scales related to groups. These striking similarities in self-descriptions within and across groups can be explained in terms of general societal norms. Group stereotypes do not seem to be very important in shaping self-images, but general norms are very important in defining what an individual should be in contemporary society. This conclusion is in line with current speculations on androgyny favoring the notion of a person who finds his or her identity in personal characteristics that are considered to be independent of group characteristics.

Let me finish these remarks on current identity research with a reference to a Dutch investigation. In a nationwide sample, Maykel Verkuyten (1990) found very small but significant differences (accounting for about 1 percent of the variance) between Dutch adolescents and adolescents from the Turkish minority group. A standardized multiple regression analysis with global self-esteem as the dependent variable, and the five components of the self-concept as independent variables, was carried out for the two groups. For both, body image had the greatest impact on global self-esteem, and evaluation of ethnic identity, one of the lowest. There were no differences between the Turkish and Dutch adolescents on the impact of these two components as there was hardly any difference on the other components. Verkuyten concluded that ethnic identity, although important, is not a decisive criterion in the self-concept of adolescents. Body image has probably more impact related to the physical changes that occur during puberty. But the similarity of the fabric of global self-esteem in two ethnic groups occupying distinct positions in the same society is also an indication of the existence of similar patterns of norms weighting in an equal way the particular components of the self-concept in different subgroups of society. Furthermore, this similarity of patterns suggests that some values characteristic of contemporary industrial society transcend cultural barriers, perhaps through the homogenizing effect of the school system.

A series of Dutch studies directly investigated issues related to the political socialization of youth. One question tackled by such authors as Hagendoorn and Janssen (1986) and Meeus (1988) has to do with an alleged increase in conservative attitudes among the younger generations. The model of Middendorp (1979), which Meeus adopted, distinguishes two domains in which conservative and progressive standpoints are to be defined before conservatism is measured:

In the socio-economic domain, the conservative standpoint advocates freedom of enterprise and opposes government restrictions, while the progressive standpoint rejects freedom of enterprise on the assumption that it leads to social inequality. In the non-economic domain, conservatism is opposed to individual freedom and maintains that the individual should be subjected to traditional values and authority. Here the progressive view is a liberal one; it holds that individuals should, to a large extent, be free to work out their values and morals. (Meeus, 1988, p. 102)

Taking this distinction into account, Meeus constructed appropriate scales and obtained two independent dimensions, one related to economic conservatism and the other to cultural conservatism. He detected meaningful links with education level, parental occupation, and value orientations and concluded that the present adolescent generation may be characterized as combining economic conservatism and cultural progressiveness.

Raaijmakers (1988) investigated a related issue, designing several scales in order to measure aspects of work ethic attitudes, authoritarianism, ethnocentrism, racism, youth centrism, anomie, traditional family values, and sexism. Cultural conservatism as an independent dimension was indeed found to be linked to traditional work ethic attitudes, and comparison with other studies did not allow the conclusion that adolescents would be more conservative on such a dimension than adults, as they have consistently been found to have less conservative values than adults. Differences in the work ethic attitudes of specific categories of adolescents also seemed unrelated to their chances in the job market. The adolescents seemed to participate in the general systematic shift of the Dutch population toward more liberal attitudes, and they even seemed to be more advanced in this change.

French findings obtained by Percheron and Chiche (1991) also depict the 17–37 age group as more tolerant of change in the domain of religion and family, and less condemning of black market labor practices, abortion, and cohabitation of unmarried couples. These data fit in with the progressive outlook of younger Dutch people, another indication that a change in values is occurring across societies (cf. Stoetzel, 1983).

This general change does not prevent a fraction of adolescents from manifesting the intolerant attitudes usually described as ethnocentrism and sexism. A psychodynamic interpretation was proposed by Adorno and his colleagues (Adorno, Frenkel-Brunswik, Levinson, & Sanford, 1950), who attributed the origin of aggressive drives that exteriorize themselves in the detraction of weaker targets to the authoritarian educational practices of parents. Vollebergh (1989) expressed doubts about such an interpretation and reported data on significant differences between pupils from more and less prestigious educational streams and between boys and girls, with the first-mentioned group in each contrast more often being authoritarian, ethnocentric, or sexist.

Furthermore, more consistent patterns of high correlations between the different syndromes appeared for pupils from the more prestigious stream, but the correlations were rather low for girls of the lower stream. All these data are very difficult to explain in terms of a psychodynamic interpretation. Vollebergh proposed a model of political intolerance of minorities as an organizing principle of the interindividual differences related to these various syndromes. Indeed, her data are intriguing, particularly her report of the absence of significant differences in authoritarianism, ethnocentrism, and racism between boys and girls who did not develop political party preferences and of the presence of differences when party preferences did exist, the boys being more authoritarian than the girls. However, a consistent, significant difference in sexism and antifeminism existed before and after the appearance of party preferences. The process would then be a two-step one: firstly, sexist boys will be attracted by political parties, and secondly, once they are involved in politics a generalization of their intolerance takes place. For females, the same process is less likely to occur, so their more tolerant attitudes persist.

3. ARTICULATION OF ANALYSES

The characteristics of the investigations just reported can now be more carefully compared to the characteristics of those reported in the first part of this article. The research on social identity and political socialization is, in fact, research on social representations. In practical terms that means that the researchers assume, at least implicitly, that individuals live in a symbolic environment that consists of a structured set of beliefs, attitudes, and stereotypes. Individuals share these beliefs to a greater or lesser extent, or perhaps it is better to say that they take personal stands toward common reference points. That is the reason I try to avoid the terms "common" and "consensual" to characterize these shared beliefs and attitudes. Only stereotypes are by definition consensual, but empirically they also allow for a lot of variance. Paradoxically, the self, often assumed to be an important source of particularity and interindividual differences, can turn out to be an object of the most consensual definitions.

The research traditions cited in the first part also cannot do without studying social representations. But they do it in a more indirect way. Their objects of study are more often processes than contents, but processes that are in fact transformational devices of social representations.

But how far does this distinction between processes and general values or beliefs bring the study of adolescence? Not very far, and fortunately social psychological analyses are not limited to these two kinds of approaches. An important concept is to be added in order to account more exhaustively for the explanation offered by many social psychologists: the notion of articulation between different levels of analysis. The distinction between societal values on the one hand and specific psychosocial processes on the other, although useful, remains too crude to permit a grasp of the subtleties and complexity of most of the sociopsychological research on youth. What is important is the analysis of the intertwining of variables of different natures in explaining adolescents' behavior; in other words, it is the use of situational and positional analyses that links the study of processes and of general values or beliefs.

Let us, for instance, look at the role of motivation in explaining school performance. By definition, at a commonsense as well as at a psychological level, motivation is an important factor in explaining individual achievement. In a very detailed study, Anne-Marie Fontaine (1990) proposed a general theoretical model articulating educational practices and cognitive factors. The latter included social stereotypes regarding differences in the competences of members of social groups, the importance of scholastic achievement, and so on. It is impossible here to go into greater detail, but allow me to present some illustrations of her findings on, for instance, the link between the locus of control of mothers and the level of motivation of their children. Locus of control was internal when a mother believed that a child was responsible for what happened to it and that the mother could also determine its fate. Generally, the relation with motivation of the children was expected to be positive, and this was the case for most of the subgroups (defined by the sex of the children, socioeconomic status of the family, and rural or urban background). However, there were important exceptions: the link was negative for boys of a lower economic status and for girls of a higher one. The general interpretation was the following: the more children succeed, the more their self-image is gratified by an internal control explanation and the greater will be their motivation. But failures occur often in the lower classes, and for boys especially, those failures are a threat to their self-images, at least when the explanation offered is in terms of internal control. A way of protecting themselves from this threat is to recur to explanations in terms of external control; this would explain the fact that the less internal control was invoked, the better the boys of the lower classes remained motivated. A more or less similar explanation was invoked for the girls of higher classes.

Another example taken from the same study bears on the links between the level of expectation of success on a task and motivation. As expected, a positive relationship was generally found, except for rural girls, the explanation being that as the objects of multiple negative stereotypes, they entertained very low levels of expectations. The lower these expectations were, the more easily they were fulfilled, and the less anxious were the girls, who therefore remained relatively more motivated.

Such explanations require intricate methods of data analysis, such as multiple regression analysis, path analysis, LISREL procedures, and so on. Social developmental psychologists are now using more and more data analysis methods such as these for the testing of hypotheses on time-lagged effects. An example of the use of such methods figures in Silbereisen and Noack's (1988) chapter on the constructive role of problem behavior in adolescence; they investigated links between leisure time orientations, self-esteem, and drinking or smoking behavior. A general theoretical path model presented by Stattin and Magnusson (1989) integrates the role of self-concept and peer networks as variables mediating between biological maturation and transition behaviors during adolescence.

I could, of course, mention many more examples of articulations of analyses in studies of different aspects of adolescence. But such studies abound now. Sometimes the epithet "socioecological" is used for characterizing these studies, and they indeed appear more concerned with investigating concrete social phenomena in their natural settings than do the studies described in the two previous sections. A closer inspection shows that this difference is only a superficial characteristic; at a theoretical level, processes are invoked of the type described in the beginning of this chapter, just as the intervention of more or less shared social meanings is also postulated.

But how to bridge the gap between the study of specific processes and the recourse to general values and beliefs? In a previous study (Doise, 1986), I showed that combining different levels of explanation is a common characteristic of research in social psychology. Four levels of explanation characterize social psychological studies. A first level is confined to the study of psychological or intraindividual processes that are supposed to account for the manner in which an individual organizes his or her experience of the social environment. Research on the treatment of complex information, on cognitive balance, and on categorization processes exemplifies this kind of approach. A second level of explanation is concerned with interindividual and intrasituational processes; many experiments using game matrixes, communication networks, and interindividual processes are representative of this type. The studies reported in the first section of this chapter mainly involve analyses based on intraindividual and interindividual processes. A third kind of explanation uses differences in social position or social status as intervening variables to account for variations in the actualization of intra- and interindividual processes. As far as their societal position and status are considered, individuals are no longer considered to be interchangeable. Studies of social identity, gender, and marginalization typically resort to explanations of this kind. Finally, as was also shown in the second section of this chapter, sociopsychological analyses are sometimes also explicitly based on the general conceptions or social representations that individuals adhere to.

The relevance of these distinctions was shown for studies of cognitive development, social influence, and intergroup relations. These three areas deal respectively with intraindividual, interindividual, and positional dynamics. But in each of these fields, analyses of other levels were necessary to account more exhaustively for the functioning of processes analyzed at a given level.

Let us consider the study of intergroup relations, whose relevance for the study of adolescence has already been mentioned. There is no doubt that intergroup studies are concerned with the statuses and roles groups and categories of individuals occupy in society, and therefore, those studies ask for analyses intended to obtain the third type of explanation noted above, which I henceforth call "level three analyses." But cognitive processes that organize individuals' perceptions of intergroup situations and interindividual dynamics that characterize such situations also have been studied.

For the first studies, the explanatory approach used by Tajfel (1981; Tajfel & Wilkes, 1963; Tajfel, Sheikh, & Gardner, 1964) was originated in research on the accentuation of contrasts in quantitative judgments (Tajfel, 1959), and that approach has been proved very useful for better understanding intergroup differentiation processes. Current trends analyzing social differentiation processes derive from prototypicality theory. A prototype (cf. Rosch, 1975, 1978) is defined in terms of the differences among other elements of its membership category fully represented by the prototype, as well as in terms of differences with elements of another category. The main novelty is that the prototypical categorization model explicitly states that degrees of category membership are possible. In this sense, prototypical categorization can deal with processes that simultaneously account for both within-category singularization and between-category differentiation.

But not less important are models bearing on the structuring of interdependency relations between individuals, as was shown by the Sherifs' (1964) experiments on negative interdependency (competition) and positive interdependency (superordinate goals) between groups and by Rabbie's experiments on common fate (Rabbie & Horwitz, 1969) and behavioral interaction models (Rabbie, Schot, & Visser, 1989).

Given the importance of level one and two analyses, it remains true that one can hardly think of research on intergroup relations that does not also directly involve level four analyses. Indeed, processes of categorical differentiation, of cooperative and competitive interaction along group lines, and of intergroup comparison in terms of status and position all presuppose the intervention of general beliefs and values, of representations diffused in a society that determine the dimensions on which groups are defined in relation to one another.

Some such social representations, for instance, bear on the nature of relationships within and between groups (cf. Lorenzi-Cioldi, 1988; Lorenzi-Cioldi & Doise, 1990). *Aggregate* groups are considered to be groups comprising individuals who define themselves primarily by holistic features that distinguish their group from other groups as such and cause in-group members to feel similar to each other. According to such an intergroup representation, between-group differentiation and within-group differentiation are inversely related. On the contrary, *collection* groups are constituted by individuals perceiving themselves as distinct from one another and considered to be typical, even before their insertion into a group. Within-group differentiation and between-group differentiation can go together or covary in such a system of representations (cf. Deschamps, 1984).

In a series of studies, Lorenzi-Cioldi demonstrated that experimental variations of relationships between groups in terms of relative power, positive or negative interdependency, and interindividual similarities or differences produced consistent effects in the way group members actualized an aggregate or collection type of group membership. Clémence and Doise (1989) also investigated different patterns of relationships between within-group and between-group differentiations and found that the so-called covariation pattern was often found.

Such results showing that between-group differentiation can be combined with within-group differentiation or homogenization according to respective group status require articulation of analyses. Analyses at different levels certainly have their own legitimacy, but more exhaustive explanations have to combine different explanations. In the social sciences, no theory or model fully describes all the conditions necessary to actualize the dynamics described by one model. Other explanations are always necessary; a hypothesis only has meaning through its implicit—and preferably explicit—articulation with other hypotheses. In this sense, I adhere to a "contextualist" view of knowledge:

> An adequate understanding of either a phenomenon or a theory requires that it be investigated through a program of research planned to reveal the wide range of circumstances that affect the phenomenon and the rich set of implicit assumptions that limit the theory, thus making explicit the contexts in which one or another relationship obtains. (McGuire, 1983, p. 22)

At a theoretical level, implicit assumptions become hypotheses or theoretical conjectures when they are invoked to specify the conditions under which processes will hold or explain modifications in the dynamics described by a model:

> Adding multiple independent variables, each uniquely predicted by a different theory to produce an interaction effect, helps the researcher to appreciate that explanation is not a zero-sum game: however firmly one believes in Boyle's Law, one need not reject Charles' Law. A diverse set of theorized processes may be operative with wide variation from situation to situation in the proportion of common variance contributed by each of the mediators. . . . A research design that includes interaction variables each suggested by a different theory is an example of the heuristic value of the contextualist approach. (McGuire, 1983, p. 27)

To conclude, in referring to intergroup studies in the above paragraphs I did not abandon the area of youth studies. In fact, all the research referred to investigated intergroup representations and behaviors of adolescents. From a theoretical point of view, it can be argued that a serious challenge for adolescents is to define their intergroup relations, amongst themselves as well as in relation with older people. Social psychology's contribution to the study of adolescence consists in the descriptions of specific processes and in the study of societal values that intervene in such aspects of their identity construction. But processes and values do not really deal with adolescents as such; they only do so when the particular situations and positions of adolescents in a network of societal relationships are linked to the study of processes and values.

REFERENCES

Adorno, T. W., Frenkel-Brunswik, E., Levinson, D. J., & Sanford, N. R. (1950). *The authoritarian personality.* New York: Norton.

Allerbeck, K. R., & Hoag, W. (1985). *Jugend ohne Zukunft* [Youth without a future] Munchen: Piper Verlag.

Bakan, D. (1972). Adolescence in America: From idea to social fact. In J. Kagan & R. Coles (Eds.), *Twelve to sixteen: Early adolescence* (pp. 73–89). New York: Norton.

Baldwin, J. M. (1897). *Le developpement mental chez l'enfant et dans la race.* [Race and the mental development of children]. Paris: Felix Alcan.

Bandura, A. (1977). *Social learning theory.* Englewood Cliffs, NJ: Prentice-Hall.

Beauvois, J. L., & Joule, R. V. (1981). *Soumission et ideologies. Psychosociologie de la rationalisation* [Submission and ideologies]. Paris: Presses Universitaires de France.

Cattaneo, C. (1964). Dell'antitesi come metodo di psicologia sociale [About antithesis as methods in social psychology]. *Il Politecnico,20,* 262–270.

Chombart de Lauwe, M. J. (1984). Changes in the representation of the child in the course of social transmission. In R. M. Farr & S. Moscovici (Eds.), *Social representations* (pp. 185–209). Cambridge: Cambridge University Press.

Clémence, A., & Doise, W. (1989). Categorisation sociale et comportement de discrimination dans une tache d'allocation d'argent a soi et aux autres membres de l'intra et du hors-groupe [Social categorization and discriminatory behavior in a task of money allocation to oneself and to other in-group and out-group members]. In J. L. Beauvois, R. V. Joule, & J. M. Monteil (Eds.), *Perspectives cognitives et conduites sociales: Part 2, Representations et processus socio-cognitifs.* Cousset, Switzerland: Delval.

Cowan, G., & Hoffman, C. D. (1986). Gender stereotyping in young children: Evidence to support a concept-learning approach. *Sex Roles, 14,* 211–224.

De Paolis, P., Doise, W., & Mugny, G. (1987). Social marking in cognitive operations. In W. Doise & S. Moscovici (Eds.), *Current issues in European social psychology* (pp. 1–45). Cambridge: Cambridge University Press.

Deschamps, J. C. (1984). Identite sociale et differentiations categorielles [Social identity and categorical differentiation]. *Cahiers de Psychologie Cognitive, 4,* 449–474.

Doise, W. (1984). Social representations, inter-group experiments and levels of analysis. In R. M. Farr & S. Moscovici (Eds.), *Social representations* (pp. 255–268). Cambridge: Cambridge University Press.

Doise, W. (1986). *Levels of explanation in social psychology.* Cambridge: Cambridge University Press.

Doise, W. (1987). Pratiques scientifiques et representations sociales: Que faire de la psychologie de Piaget? [Scientific practice and social representations: How does

80 Willem Doise

Piaget's psychology apply?] *Cahiers du Centre de Recherche Interdisciplinaire de Vaucresson, 3*, 89–108.

Doise, W., & Lorenzi-Cioldi, F. (1990). L'Identite comme representation sociale [Identity as social representation]. In S. Aebischer, J. P. Deconchy, & E. M. Lipiansky (Eds.), *Ideologies et representations sociales* (pp. 273–286). Cousset, Switzerland: Delval.

Doise, W., & Mugny, G. (1984). *The social development of the intellect*. Oxford: Pergamon Press.

Dubois, N. (1987). *La psychologie du controle* [The psychology of control]. Grenoble: Presses Universitaires de Grenoble.

Durkheim, E. (1902). *De la division du travail social* (2nd ed.). [About the division of social work]. Paris: Alcan.

Erikson, E. (1977). *Childhood and society*. London: Paladin.

Fontaine, A. M. (1990). *Motivation pour la reussite scolaire* [Motivation for academic success]. Porto, Portugal: Instituto Nacional de Investigacao Cientifica, Centro de Psicologia da Universidade do Porto.

Hagendoorn, A., & Janssen, J. (1986). Right-wing views among Dutch secondary school pupils. *The Netherlands' Journal of Sociology, 22*, 87–96.

Hall, G. S. (1904). *Adolescence*. New York: Appleton.

Inoff, G., Halverson, C. F., & Pizzigati, K. A. L. (1983). The influence of sex-role standards on children's self- and peer-attributions. *Sex Roles, 9*, 1205–1222.

Janis, I. L. (1982). *Victims of groupthink*. Boston: Houghton Mifflin.

Johnson, D., & Johnson, R. (1979). Conflict in the classroom. *Review of Educational Research, 49*, 51–61.

Joule, R. V. & Beauvois, J. L. (1987). *Petit traite de manipulation a l'usage des honnetes gens* [Small manipulation trait for honest people]. Grenoble: Presses Universitaires de Grenoble.

LePoultier, F. (1986). *Travail social, inadaptation sociale et processus cognitifs* [Social work, social maladaptation and cognitive processes]. Vanves: Centre Technique National d'Etudes et de Recherches sur les Handicaps et les Inadaptations.

LePoultier, F. (1990). *Recherches evaluatives en travail social* [Evaluative research and social work]. Grenoble: Presses Universitaires de Grenoble.

Lorenzi-Cioldi, F. (1988). *Individus dominants et groupes domines. Images masculines et feminines* [Dominant individuals and dominant groups: Masculine and feminine images]. Grenoble: Presses Universitaires de Grenoble.

Lorenzi-Cioldi, F., & Doise, W. (1990). Levels of analysis and social identity. In D. Abrams & M. A. Hogg (Eds.), *Social identity theory* (pp. 71–88). London: Harvester.

Maassen, G., de Goede, M. (1986). Beelden over jongeren en jeugdwerklozen [Images of youngsters and unemployed youth]. In M. Matthijssen, W. Meeus, & F. van Wel (Eds.), *Beelden van jeugd* [Images of youth](pp. 187–206). Groningen, the Netherlands: Wolters-Noordhoff.

McGuire, W. J. (1983). A contextualist theory of knowledge: Its implications for innovation and reform in psychological research. In L. Berkowitz (Ed.), *Advances in experimental social psychology, vol. 16* (pp. 1–47). New York: Academic.

Meeus, W. (1988). Adolescent conservatism: A two-dimensional concept. In J. Hazekamp, W. Meeus, & Y. te Poel (Eds.), *European contributions to youth research* (pp. 101–115). Amsterdam: Free University Press.

Meeus, W. (1989). Parental and peer support in adolescence. In K. Hurrelmann & U. Engel (Eds.), *The social world of adolescents* (pp. 167–183). Berlin: Walter de Gruyter.

Middendorp, C. (1979). *Ontzuiling, politisering en restauratie in Nederland* [Removal of traditional religious and socio-political barriers, politicizing and restoration in the Netherlands]. Meppel: Boom.

Monteil, J. M. (1989). *Eduquer et former. Perspectives psychosociales* [Educating and training: Psychosocial perspectives]. Grenoble: Presses Universitaires de Grenoble.

Moscovici, S. (1961). *La psychanalyse, son image et son public* [Psychoanalysis, its image and the public]. Paris: Presses Universitaires de France.

Nakbi, J. L. (1990). Evolution de l'identite psychosociale feminine et masculine de l'enfance a l'age adulte [The evolution of feminine and masculine psychosocial identity from infancy to adulthood]. *Psychologie Francaise, 35,* 43–49.

Nakbi, J. L. & Arnal-Duchemin, M. J. (1987). Dynamique des representations chez les femmes et les hommes [The dynamic of representations in men and women]. *Les Cahiers de Psychologie Sociale, 34,* 1–9.

Oser, F. K. (1986). Moral education and values education: The moral discourse perspective. In M. C. Wittrock (Ed.), *Handbook of research on teaching* (3rd ed.). New York: Macmillan.

Palmonari, A., Pombeni, M. L. & Kirchler, E. (1989). Peergroups and evolution of the self system in adolescence. *European Journal of Psychology of Education, 4,* 3–15.

Percheron, A., & Chiche, J. (1991). Age, morale et politique: Ordre et desordre des ages [Age, morals, and politics: The order and disorder of ages]. In A. Percheron & R. Remond (Eds.), *Age et politique* (pp. 151–201). Paris: Economica.

Poitou, J. P. (1974). *La dissonance cognitive* [Cognitive dissonance]. Paris: Armand Colin.

Raaijmakers, Q. (1988). The work ethic of Dutch adolescents. In J. Hazekamp, W. Meeus, & Y. te Poel (Eds.), *European contributions to youth research* (pp. 117–130). Amsterdam: Free University Press.

Rabbie, J. M., & Horwitz, M. (1969). Arousal of ingroup-outgroup bias by a chance win or loss. *Journal of Personality and Social Psychology, 13,* 269–277.

Rabbie, J. M., Schot, J. C., & Visser, L. (1989). Social identity theory: A conceptual and empirical critique from the perspective of a behavioral interaction model. *European Journal of Social Psychology, 19,* 171–202.

Ravaud, J. F., Beaufils, B., & Paicheler, H. (1986). Handicap et integration scolaire [Disabilities and educational mainstreaming]. *Sciences Sociales et Sante, 4,* 167–184.

Rosch, E. (1975). Cognitive representations of semantic categories. *Journal of Experimental Psychology: General, 104,* 192–233.

Rosch, E. (1978). Principles of categorization. In E. Rosch & B. B. Lloyd (Eds.), *Cognition and categorization.* Hillsdale, NJ: Erlbaum.

Schachter, S. (1959). *The psychology of affiliation.* Stanford: Stanford University Press.

Schulz, R. (1976). The effects of control and predictability on the psychological and physical well-being of the institutionalized aged. *Journal of Personality and Social Psychology, 33*, 563–573.

Sherif, M., & Sherif, C. W. (1964). *Reference groups*. Chicago: Henry Regnery Company.

Silbereisen, R. K., & Noack, P. (1988). On the constructive role of problem behavior in adolescence. In N. Bolger, A. Caspi, G. Downey, & M. Moorehouse (Eds.), *Persons in context: Developmental processes* (pp. 152–180). Cambridge: Cambridge University Press.

Stattin, H., & Magnusson, D. (1989). Social transition in adolescence: A biosocial perspective. In A. de Ribaupierre (Ed.), *Transition mechanisms in child development* (pp. 147–190). Cambridge: Cambridge University Press.

Stoetzel, J. (1983). *Les valeurs du temps present: Une enquete europeenne* [The values of the present time: A European inquiry]. Paris: Presses Universitaires de France.

Tajfel, H. (1959). Quantitative judgement is social perception. *British Journal of Psychology, 50*, 16–29.

Tajfel, H. (1981). *Human groups and social categories: Studies in social psychology*. Cambridge: Cambridge University Press.

Tajfel, H. and Turner, J. C. (1979). An integrative theory of intergroup conflict. In W. G. Austin and S. Worchel (Eds.), *The social psychology of intergroup relations*. Monterrey, CA: Brooks/Cole.

Tajfel, H., Sheikh, A. A., & Gardner, R. C. (1964). Content of stereotypes and the inference of similarity between members of stereotyped groups. *Acta Psychologica, 22*, 191–201.

Tajfel, H., & Wilkes, A. L. (1963). Classification and quantitative judgment. *British Journal of Psychology, 54*, 101–114.

Van Overwalle, F., Segebarth, K., & Goldchstein, M. (1989). Improving performance of freshmen through attributional testimonies from fellow students. *British Journal of Educational Psychology, 59*, 75–85.

Verkuyten, M. (1990). Self-esteem and the evaluation of ethnic identity among Turkish and Dutch adolescents in the Netherlands. *The Journal of Social Psychology, 130*, 285–297.

Vollebergh, W. (1989). Politische Interesse und politische Intoleranz bei Heranwachsenden [Political interest and political intolerance among youth]. In B. Claussen (Ed.), *Politische Sozialisation jugendlicher in Ost und West* (pp. 238–252). Darmstadt: May & Co.

Wieviorka, M. (1988). *Societes et terrorisme*. [Societies and terrorism]. Paris: Fayard.

Youniss, J., & Smollar, J. (1985). *Adolescent relations with mothers, fathers, and friends*. Chicago: University of Chicago Press.

4

Toward a Psychosocial Analysis of Adolescent Identity: An Evaluation of the Epigenetic Theory (Erikson) and the Identity Status Model (Marcia)

Wim Meeus

Few social-scientific concepts lodge themselves in popular speech, and it can be taken as a measure of a concept's importance if it does do so. Evidently, a concept like that touches the everyday thinking of people, and they recognize its relevance. Identity is such a concept. Most people use it and can describe it one way or another. In more formal terms, people have a social representation of the concept "identity."

An important, if not major, "inventor" of the identity concept is the psychologist Erikson. His *Identity: Youth and Crisis* (1968) was highly instrumental in establishing the concept. In this and other publications, Erikson connected identity formation and adolescence, viewing development of an identity as the major developmental task of the adolescent period.

The identity status model designed by Marcia (1964, 1966) is unknown among the general public. Nevertheless, it is the foremost research-oriented elaboration of identity development in adolescence. To date, more than a hundred research publications (articles and dissertations) have appeared dealing with this model (Coté & Levine, 1988).

In Dutch youth research conducted since World War II, the theme of identity development in adolescence has continually occupied a significant place. According to Abma (1986), some 10 percent of all research relates to this theme. However, only a small percentage of the Dutch researchers in this domain have made use of Marcia's identity status model. Almost all of them do refer to Erikson.

In this chapter, I discuss Erikson's identity theory and Marcia's identity status model. In both cases, I look at the major theoretical aspects, after which I evaluate their empirical validity. With respect to the identity status model, an alternative theoretical interpretation is offered. Referring to empirical studies, I will show that the import of a given identity status differs per social environment.

1. ERIKSON

1.1. Foundations

Some authors (e.g., Gottschalch, 1985; Roazen, 1976) have supposed that Erikson's interest in identity formation has much to do with the course of his own life. Shortly after his birth, his Danish father and German-Jewish mother divorced. His stepfather was a German Jew. Erikson was considered a Jew by his schoolmates and sometimes pestered, but owing to his Germanic looks, Jewish children tended to look upon him as non-Jewish. Early childhood thus already faced Erikson with the question, Who am I? The question continued to haunt him, as when, for instance, he received no recognition as a psychoanalyst in the United States because he was not a medical doctor.

Academically speaking, too, Erikson had a plural identity. He was a trained psychoanalyst and was himself analyzed by Anna Freud, and he had engaged in anthropological research, among the Sioux and elsewhere.

Erikson is considered an ego-psychologist. His work is markedly psychoanalytic. Erikson's four phases of individual development (see Figure 1) are evident reformulations of the first four phases of psychosexual development as described by Freud: the oral, anal, and phallic phases, and the latency period. Like Freud, Erikson assumed that individual development takes its course according to the principle of the organism's biological maturation. Individual development has a basic scheme: it occurs epigenetically (Erikson, 1968, p. 92).

The major difference between classical psychoanalysis and Erikson concerns the meaning of the social in individual development. Erikson held that the insertion of the individual into a variety of social roles works out positively for personality development. That is to say, he rejected Freud's idea that social insertion suppresses the essential impulses of the id and, if sublimation fails or defense mechanisms function poorly, leads to all kinds of disturbances in personality development.

Erikson, then, ascribed two principles to the development of the individual: biological maturation and insertion into cultural and social institutions. The ego is crucial to this development since it must harmonize the two processes. If the ego is successful, the development of the individual is achieved. It comes down to this: Will the ego be able "to integrate the timetable of the organism with the structure of social institutions?" (Erikson, 1959).

1.2. Erikson's Theory of Phases
in Personality Development

At the core of Erikson's work lies the theory of phased development. The theory has the following features:

1. It is a theory concerning the development of a person throughout the course of life; it deals with childhood, adolescence, adulthood, and old age. In the decade in which Erikson formulated his theory—the 1950s—this scope was exceptional. Developmental psychologists used to emphasize childhood, implicitly or explicitly assuming that the development of the individual takes shape then. Erikson rejected this assumption, asserting that development takes a lifetime.
2. The total life course can be divided into eight phases that occur in a fixed order. In each of them the ego must resolve a core conflict of individual development. The solution will or will not result in expanded ego-strength and the addition of vital power.
3. This theory of development is a conditional one. Every phase has to be traversed satisfactorily before the next one can be embarked upon by a healthy individual. Thus, Erikson's theory features a cumulative moment. All it takes for development to stagnate is that a single phase not be left behind successfully. Erikson called this situation "foreclosed" development.
4. Development intends a healthy person. Erikson, borrowing from Marde Jahoda, wrote that "a healthy personality *actively masters* his environment, shows a certain *unity of personality,* and is able to *perceive* the world and himself *correctly*" (1968, p. 92).

Erikson represented his theory in the so-called epigenetic chart (Figure 1). The chart has a vertical axis (cells I,5–V,5), a horizontal axis (cells V,1–V,8), and a diagonal. The diagonal represents the eight life phases and their typical core conflicts. The vertical axis indicates how the first four phases contribute to the identity conflict of phase 5. Let me illustrate with an example. The core conflict in the first period (cell I,1) concerns the issue of trust or mistrust. This conflict is resolved in either mutual recognition or autistic isolation (cell I,5). Mutual recognition creates the basis for positive identity development, whereas isolation renders such development impossible since it poses an early block to development (foreclosure) and leads to confused identity. Cell V,1 shows how the solution of the core conflict in phase 1 returns in the core conflict of phase 5. If the conflict in the first phase has resulted in trust, phase 5 will embrace this result as a positive aspect of identity, namely, a clear temporal perspective. But if phase 1 leads to distrust, the fifth phase will incorporate this result as a negative aspect of identity, namely, time confusion.

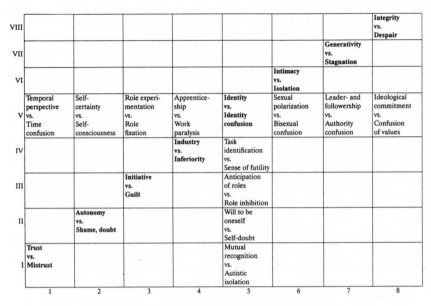

	1	2	3	4	5	6	7	8
VIII								Integrity vs. Despair
VII							Generativity vs. Stagnation	
VI						Intimacy vs. Isolation		
V	Temporal perspective vs. Time confusion	Self-certainty vs. Self-consciousness	Role experimentation vs. Role fixation	Apprenticeship vs. Work paralysis	Identity vs. Identity confusion	Sexual polarization vs. Bisexual confusion	Leader- and followership vs. Authority confusion	Ideological commitment vs. Confusion of values
IV				Industry vs. Inferiority	Task identification vs. Sense of futility			
III			Initiative vs. Guilt		Anticipation of roles vs. Role inhibition			
II		Autonomy vs. Shame, doubt			Will to be oneself vs. Self-doubt			
I	Trust vs. Mistrust				Mutual recognition vs. Autistic isolation			

Figure 1. Erikson's Epigenetic Diagram.

The central developmental task in adolescence is the achievement of identity. How do the prior four phases contribute to accomplishing this task?

(1) Trust versus mistrust. This phase covers the first year of a person's life. To have its needs satisfied, a child is utterly dependent upon its mother. The development of a healthy personality is conditional upon the trust the child learns to have in its immediate nurturer, and this trust in turn can occur only if the child's needs are consistently satisfied. If this is not the case, the child will fail to develop a positive attitude toward others and in later years will lack the vital power of "hope."

(2) Autonomy versus shame and doubt. This period encompasses the second and third years of life. Toilet training (note the relevance of Freud's anal phase) confronts the child with its first experience of autonomy: it learns to control its physical functions. This awareness of independence can be developed only if the child continually experiences its capacity to make choices. Those who nurture the child must therefore allow the child sufficient leeway to explore, help it in difficult moments, and shield it from dangerous situations. If these conditions are met, the child will develop the vital strength of "willpower." A negative development expresses itself in self-doubt, shame, or both.

(3) Initiative versus guilt. In the course of the fourth and fifth year, the child distances itself to a greater degree from its parents and orients itself increasingly

to the outside world (penetration of the environment, comparable to Freud's phallic phase); it learns to take the initiative. It is in this phase that conscience is developed and that parental prohibitions are internalized in the child's awareness of normativity. If parents are too strict, or if they punish too liberally, the child will develop too rigid a conscience, so that initiative is inhibited by feelings of guilt. These feelings, in turn, lead to a negative self-perception and to passivity. The difference between shame (phase 2) and guilt (phase 3) is that guilt implies an internalized negative self-judgment and shame is a momentary feeling. If the development is normal, the child will achieve the vital power of "purposiveness," a positive attitude toward future roles.

(4) Industry versus inferiority. This period comprises roughly the years in which the child is an elementary school pupil. The child has to learn to *work,* to appropriate for himself the "tools of technology" (the three Rs—reading, writing, and arithmetic). There are many reasons why children may have difficulty in doing so; their parents may have prepared them insufficiently for school life, or maybe they find that at school there is a kind of pecking order, a hierarchy of good to bad, perhaps determined by race or parental social status. Acquiring skills, then, is a continuous competition marked with the fear of falling short, with a feeling of inferiority. If the development runs a positive course, the child will gain the vital power of "competence": the feeling of having the ability to perform well.

(5) Identity versus identity confusion. The fifth period is the time of adolescence, which poses the problem of identity versus identity confusion. The adolescent reviews his or her life, has to decide who he or she shall be, and is therefore confronted with choices and decisions regarding occupation, relationships, sexuality, and politics. Once again, the question arises as to how the previous four phases contribute to the formation of identity.

In phase 1, the child develops trust or mistrust, confidence or suspicion. In identity formation, this development returns as temporal perspective—the capacity to place one's own future in the proper perspective—or else as time confusion. In the second phase, the child develops a feeling of self-confidence (autonomy) or self-doubt. During identity formation, this development comes back in the guise of self-assurance or shyness. In phase 3, the child gains an attitude of initiative or develops feelings of guilt regarding its own shortcomings. In identity formation, this development leads to experimenting with a variety of social roles or else to role fixation. In phase 4, the child learns skills or fails to do so. During the formation of an identity, this development expresses itself in the desire to learn or in passivity.

A positive completion of the fifth phase is necessary if an individual is to enter the sixth phase, the phase of engaging in intimate relationships, with a positive prognosis.

1.3. Empirical Research

Erikson's integral theory has not been researched empirically very much. There are two reasons for this lack. (1) Researching Erikson's theory requires a complex and hence costly apparatus. Investigators need longitudinal studies that trace people from the year they are born to the time of their demise, so that measurements can be taken in each of the eight phases. Following such a procedure would be the only way to investigate whether prior development influences later phases. A researcher needs a lot of money for this kind of study and will undertake it only if he or she is confident of the theory's empirical evidential value. It is probable that both money and confidence have been lacking. (2) A fair amount of research has, however, been inspired by Erikson's theory. But the studies have tended to concentrate on phase 5, identity formation, primarily because relatively reliable empirical instruments have been developed to chart this phase (see below).

In the remainder of this section, I discuss some research into Erikson's theory. My criterion for including research was that it should cover at least two phases or deal with the effects of age within a single phase. The research can be arranged under three headings.

The Phasing.   Ciaccio (1971, p. 306) analyzed stories told by 5-, 8-, and 11-year-olds, obtained via a projection test. He expected that the stories of the youngest group would relate mostly to autonomy (phase 2), that those of the 8-year-olds would primarily concern initiative (phase 3), and that the last group's would center on skills (phase 4). These expectations were mostly fulfilled. The 5-year-olds talked mostly about phases 2 and 3, the median group about phase 3, and the older children about phase 4. Ciaccio took these findings as support for Erikson's thesis that identity development is phased, with each phase involving a theme of its own. At the same time, it turned out that for each of the three groups the same core conflict, autonomy, had been resolved least: In the two older groups, a large number of respondents had solved the basic conflicts encountered in phase 3 or 4 or both, but not the conflict associated with phase 2. It appears, then, that a positive completion of an earlier phase (phase 2) is not a prerequisite for the solution of core conflicts in subsequent phases. Review articles by Marcia (1980) and Waterman (1985) indicate that this result is representative of research into Erikson's theory. None of the studies have been able to demonstrate convincingly that development in earlier phases is determinative for later phases.

Identity Development: Age Effects.   Some research has been done on identity development among secondary school pupils and university students. Most of these studies are designed cross-sectionally; that is, comparisons are made between groups of young people of different ages. Waterman's review (1982) of these studies shows that in general there is no identity development during the secondary school period, but it does occur among university students. The development described by Erikson for phase 5, then, comes to fruition in late adolescence.

Identity and Intimacy. According to Erikson, identity is presupposed in the initiation of intimate relationships. Matteson (1982) reviewed studies on this topic, discussing women and men separately. Regarding development among women, two conclusions are of note. (1) Most studies indicate that among girls intimacy is developed more strongly than identity. Hence, in a general sense identity is no precondition for intimacy; rather, the opposite seems more likely. (2) Identity development is domain-specific; that is to say, people may develop a strong identity in one domain, say, politics, but in another domain—for example, career—they do not do so. Against this background, Hodgson and Fischer (1979) sought to determine identity in the five domains: occupation, politics, religion, sex role, and sex orientation. Their study confirmed earlier results, indicating a generally strong identity (that is, strongly developed in all domains) does not lead to a higher score in intimacy. But women who had a strong identity in one of the domains scored higher on intimacy.

Various studies (Matteson, 1982) have revealed that for men development of an occupational identity is most important. There are no indications that among men occupational identity is a precondition for intimacy. The most plausible interpretation of the research results is that identity and intimacy have a parallel development.

These studies lead me to conclude as follows: (1) There is relatively strong support for Erikson's assumption that people mature positively in a number of aspects of personality, such as trust and autonomy (Constantinople, 1969; Marcia, 1982; Waterman, 1982). (2) There is little or no support for Erikson's thesis that completion of one phase is a prerequisite for positive growth in the next phase. In Ciaccio's (1971) study, autonomy did not prove a precondition for initiative and skill. Matteson's review showed that identity does not necessarily precede intimacy.

The first conclusion means that Erikson did identify a number of important aspects of personality development. The second conclusion suggests that there is scant support for the phasing proposed by Erikson. Aspects of personality do not necessarily develop in the order he assumed. Erikson's work, then, cannot be considered as having provided researchers with an adequate developmental theory.

Erikson's work is important, especially because he brought into view the social dimension of individual development. In doing so, he opened the way to an interdisciplinary theory of socialization in which individual and social aspects of individual development are interrelated. At the same time, it should be noted that Erikson looked at the social dimension in an undifferentiated way. For example, his theory postulates no effects of social class on personality.

2. MARCIA'S IDENTITY STATUS MODEL

As noted, Erikson's work has been especially conducive to research and theory regarding the theme of the fifth phase, identity development. Marcia's theory of identity status has been the most influential of these theories.

2.1. Identity Statuses

Marcia (1980, p. 159) defined identity as an "ego-structure": an internal, self-constructed, and dynamic organization of aspirations, skills, beliefs, and individual experiences. Following Erikson, he looked upon adolescence as the period in which youngsters experience an identity crisis that they resolve by making choices regarding their futures in a number of life domains. "Crisis" and "choice" are the core variables in Marcia's identity status model. These variables make it possible to distribute adolescents over four identity statuses, as Table 1 shows.

In the status "identity diffusion," the adolescent has not yet made a choice regarding a specific developmental task and may not have experienced a crisis in that domain. In the identity status "foreclosure," the adolescent has made a choice without having experienced a crisis. In the status "moratorium," the adolescent is in a state of crisis and has made no choice or, at best, made an unclear one. In the status "identity achievement," the adolescent has resolved the crisis and made a choice.

Designing his model, Marcia took his cue from the polarity identity/identity diffusion in phase 5 of Erikson's epigenetic model (Marcia, 1964). He added the statuses moratorium and foreclosure; these terms, too, are derived from Erikson. Initially, Marcia assumed that the four identity statuses could be arranged in a linear order, with identity diffusion the unhealthy pole and identity achievement the healthy pole. Eventually Marcia (1980, p. 161) reconsidered and emphasized that each of the four identity statuses implied degrees of health and lack of health. In the status foreclosure, for instance, a person may appear steadfast or rigid, and a person in the status moratorium may seem flexible or fickle. In spite of Marcia's stance on this, the literature frequently describes identity achievement and moratorium as healthy statuses and foreclosure and identity diffusion as

Table 1.   Marcia's Identity Status Model

Variables	Identity Diffusion	Foreclosure	Moratorium	Identity Achievement
Crisis	Yes or no	No	Actual	Yes, past
Choice	No	Yes	Unclear	Yes

unhealthy. In the present text, I conform to this convention until I present an alternative interpretation of the identity status model.

Marcia's approach can hardly be called a theory; what it amounts to is an operationalization of Erikson's concept of identity (and identity crisis). As operationalization, Marcia's model has been very successful and has been used in many studies. I turn to these at this point.

2.2. The Validity of the Identity Status Model: Empirical Research

Table 2 shows how identity statuses are related to personality characteristics, to the behavior of young people in various life domains, and to relationships. The table, which is based on a secondary analysis of the studies discussed in the review articles by Marcia (1980) and by Waterman (1982, 1985), allows some general conclusions: (1) No relationship obtains between formal intellectual skills (i.e., measured as the traits intelligence and formal operations) and identity. (2) In 10 of the remaining 14 traits, domains, and relationships, identity statuses can be divided into two groups: one group comprises identity achievement and moratorium; foreclosure and identity diffusion belong to the second group.

Of the four variables to which this division does not apply, there are three (authoritarianism, school performance, and doubt regarding cooperation and competition) in which one identity status is different from the other three; in cognitive complexity,[1] the identity statuses can be grouped into three.

The bipartition in identity statuses becomes more pronounced at the level of the average ranking for five of the six subcategories. The exception is that the division does not occur in the average ranking for the subcategory cognition. Thus, on the level of the three broad categories (personality traits, life domains, and relationships), the bipartition does apply. I conclude that the identity statuses identity achievement and moratorium are quite similar, as are the identity statuses foreclosure and identity diffusion.

Identity Achievement and Moratorium. Identity achievers possess a positive self-image, are cognitively flexible and independent, adhere to noble moral principles, and reject authoritarianism. They perform well at school, are fairly liberal regarding the use of drugs, and score high on cultural participation. Their engagement in relationships runs smoothly. Identity achievers, then, are prototypes of healthy development. The moratorium group differs from the identity achievers on the following points: they have greater fears, their cognitive flexibility is lower, and they are more uncertain about cooperation and competition; their school performance is not as good and they are less satisfied with their schools; and their attitudes toward the use of drugs is more positive. Like the identity achievers, they have positive self-images, and their relationships are

Table 2. Identity Statuses in Relation to Personality Traits and Life Domains[a]

Variables	Number of Studies	Identity Statuses			
		(1) Identity Achievement	(2) Moratorium	(3) Foreclosure	(4) Identity Diffusion
		PERSONALITY TRAITS			
General					
Fear	5	2	1	4	3
Self-esteem	5	1.5	1.5	3.5	3.5
Autonomy	7	1.5	1.5	4	3
Average ranking		**1.66**	**1.33**	**3.83**	**3.17**
Cognition					
Intelligence	6	2.5	2.5	2.5	2.5
Formal operations	3	2.5	2.5	2.5	2.5
Cognitive flexibility and independence	6	1	2	4	3
Cognitive complexity	4	2.5	2.5	4	1
Average ranking		**2.13**	**2.38**	**3.25**	**2.25**
Moral reasoning and authoritarianism					
Moral reasoning	5	1.5	1.5	3.5	3.5
Authoritarianism low	10	2	2	4	2
Average ranking		**1.75**	**1.75**	**3.75**	**2.75**

LIFE DOMAINS

School					
Dissatisfaction with school	2	2.5	1	4	2.5
School performance	2	1	3	3	3
Average ranking		**1.75**	**2**	**3.5**	**2.75**
Leisure Time					
Use of drugs	2	2	1	4	3
Participation in culture	1	1	2	3.5	3.5
Average ranking		**1.5**	**1.5**	**3.75**	**3.25**
RELATIONSHIPS					
Insecurity Regarding Cooperation and competition	1	3	1	3	3
Intimate relationships	2	1.5	1.5	3	4
Social skills	2	1	2	3.5	3.5
Average ranking		**1.83**	**1.5**	**3.16**	**3.5**

[a]The relationships are expressed hierarchically; a "1" means that the trait is closely linked to the status, a "4" means that this is not the case.

satisfying. Basically the "moratoria" evince positive development, flanked by a large measure of uncertainty regarding the future. This observation accords rather well with Marcia's definition of moratorium as a situation of crisis.

Foreclosure and Identity Diffusion. "Foreclosers" display a combination of conventionality and rigidity. They are very satisfied about school, reject the use of drugs, and tend to be authoritarian. They are sure of themselves but show no autonomy, cognitive flexibility, or independence. Their self-esteem is low and their relationships are not trouble-free. This picture, too, fits well with Marcia's description of foreclosure. Youngsters with this identity status experience no crisis and prefer a conventional way of life. But the question is if they develop an identity of their own: Foreclosers show little self-esteem and their social skills are mediocre.

Identity diffusers have low self-esteem and few satisfying relationships. In these characteristics, they are similar to foreclosers. But they are somewhat less conventional and rigid than the latter. They take a more independent stance, displaying autonomy, cognitive flexibility, and independence, and are less authoritarian, more critical of school, and slightly more liberal with respect to drugs. They have not explicitly chosen a conventional way of life, and they show no strong personal or social identity. Marcia's description of identity diffusion as characteristic of people who may or may not be in crisis, but have made no choices, once again seems to capture the salient features adequately.

My general conclusion is that the identity status model possesses an acceptable degree of validity.

The identity status model is a developmental model and rests on two assumptions: crises pass, and at some point youngsters make decisions or choices regarding the various life domains. The combination of overcoming crises and making choices leads to self-identity.

For a model of this sort, research over time is crucial. Is it the case that in the course of time a person develops from the "lower" to the "higher" identity statuses? The question has been researched to a limited degree in a number of cross-sectional and longitudinal studies. One important cross-sectional study was conducted by Meilman (1977). He compared identity development among five groups of boys, aged 12, 15, 18, 21, and 24 years. The identity status of the 12-year-olds was mostly foreclosure or identity diffusion, and the young men of 21 years had reached identity achievement. The transition from foreclosure and identity diffusion to identity achievement generally took place between the ages of 18 and 21. Offer, Marcus, and Offer (1970) found that at the ages of 19 and 20, adolescents were frequently moratoria in the process of solving identity crises. These results have been confirmed in a number of other studies (Waterman, 1985).

To determine with certainty that intrapersonal development really does show a transition from lower to higher identity statuses, longitudinal studies that trace the same persons over a long period are needed. There are but a few such studies. Table 3 summarizes them.

Table 3. Longitudinal Studies of Identity Development

Study	Type of Respondents	Interval in Years	Identity Statuses [a]											
			A1	A2	A(s)	M1	M2	M(s)	F1	F2	F(s)	D1	D2	D(s)
Waterman, Geary, & Waterman, 1974	Students	4	12	42	59	13	1	9	39	23	44	35	34	50
Waterman & Goldman, 1976	Students	4	20	34	54	14	7	0	28	23	46	39	35	67
Adams & Fitch, 1982	Students	1	17	29	68	34	40	50	40	26	61	9	5	42
Fitch & Adams, 1983	Students	1	17	23	69	27	45	67	46	24	47	5	10	25
Kroger & Haslett, 1988	Students	2	20	47	80	31	20	26	28	24	52	20	8	33

[a] A = identity achievement, M = moratorium, F = foreclosure, and D = identity diffusion; 1 = first measurement, 2 = second measurement, and (s) = stability of the status.

The studies present a fairly consistent picture. (1) In each of the studies, the number of identity achievers increases over time; in three of the five studies, the number of moratoria diminishes; in all the studies, the number of foreclosers decreases and the number of identity diffusers remains the same or diminishes. (2) After identity status, stability is an issue: to what degree did people retain the same identity status over time? In every study, identity achievement is more stable than the others; in three of the five studies, moratorium is the least stable status; and foreclosure and identity diffusion occupy the middle ground in this respect.

Both the cross-sectional and the longitudinal studies show that youngsters go through a development from lower to higher identity statuses. This finding lends support to Marcia's assumption of progressive identity development. The data on identity status stability, too, support Marcia. A high level of identity development should lead to stability, because the identity crisis has passed. Identity achievement proves the most stable identity status. Marcia suggested that moratorium is the identity status in which the young person experiences much crisis, and the studies show that this status is the least stable.

2.4. Identity Development among Women

In the large majority of studies (Waterman, 1985), the distribution of males and females over the various identity statuses is the same. In their relationship to premarital sex, however, males and females vary; in this connection, the identity status of the greater part of the girls is moratorium or identity achievement; for most boys, it is foreclosure. As I understand it, this result indicates that although boys' view of premarital sex is self-evident, girls tend to reflect on the issue consciously before they determine their attitude.

In section 2.2, I showed that the identity statuses could be divided into two kinds: a high level of identity development (identity achievement and moratorium) and a low level (foreclosure and identity diffusion). But most studies (Marcia, 1980; Waterman, 1985) indicate that girls and boys are dissimilar with respect to this order of higher and lower. For boys, the above arrangement is valid, but for girls foreclosure and moratorium are inverted. In their case, identity achievement and foreclosure stand for a high level of identity development and moratorium and identity diffusion for a low level. How can this difference be explained?

Many researchers concerned with this issue have concentrated on the significance of foreclosure for females. As I have shown in section 2.2, those whose status is foreclosure are typically traditional and conventional. In the case of girls, then, foreclosure indicates a choice of the traditional woman's role. Evidently, this choice confers a strong identity on women. Josselson (1987) supported this interpretation. For her unique study, she interviewed women in 1973 and again in 1983. The foreclosure women indeed displayed a more conventional pattern of life than others did. To the former, their families came first; they maintained little contact with contemporaries and, even though these American, academic women all held jobs at which they were reasonably successful, their work did not conflict with their families: work was unreservedly subordinate. Tradition, too, can make for strong self-identity.

But a description of the identity status foreclosure among women does not solve the problem. The question remains why this interpretation would not hold for men. Why does an attitude of traditionalism not result in a strong identity for men?

To answer the question, a closer look at the crisis concept in Marcia's model is in order. The term "crisis" refers to two things: (1) assessment of a number of choices, and (2) a situation of serious psychological disturbance resulting from inability to choose. This second aspect in particular seems empirically untraceable; most boys do not experience a period of severe crisis (Offer, 1969). For this reason, some researchers have replaced the term crisis with "exploration" (Bosma, 1985; Grotevant & Cooper, 1986). This terminological change implies that in Marcia's model, strong identity results from both choice and the degree to which available choices are assessed or explored.

This substitution allows one to say that the two wholesome identity statuses for boys (identity achievement and moratorium) are marked by a high level of exploration, and for girls, the two wholesome statuses (identity achievement and foreclosure) are marked by the presence of alternatives (choices). That is to say, for boys the healthy and unhealthy identity statuses are distinguished by the criterion exploration, but for girls this criterion is choice. The question just asked can now be answered. A traditional attitude precludes the need for exploration: tradition determines behavior. In view of the negative relation between tradition and exploration, a traditional attitude—and hence the identity status foreclosure—cannot confer a strong identity on males. But for girls this argument does not apply, because for them the relation between making choices and tradition is not a negative one. On the contrary, they may choose a traditional identity. In this analysis, then, the relation between identity statuses and social patterns emerges. The classical woman's role of nurturer and mother is rather unequivocal and socially valued. It is a respectable choice and confers on girls a positive identity. The male role is far more differentiated and flexible. The male occupational role encompasses a continually changing plurality of types of occupations in a differentiated status hierarchy. To explore this complex field is a precondition for a positive identity. This argument implies that for girls who do not opt for the traditional woman's role, the hierarchy of lower and higher identity statuses will be similar to the one for boys.[2]

3. THE THEORETICAL SIGNIFICANCE OF
THE IDENTITY STATUS MODEL

The preceding sections showed that the identity status model stands up well under empirical testing. The validity of the model is high, development from one identity status to another displays a pattern that fits the model well, and the differences in identity development between men and women can be interpreted within the model's framework. Does this mean that the identity status model can be understood as a theory of identity development? I shall now argue that this is not the case and try to indicate what the significance of the model actually is.

3.1. Is the Identity Status Model a Theory of Identity Development?

This question has two aspects: (1) Does identity development necessarily mean transition from the lower to the higher identity statuses? and (2) Does the model imply that development is completed once the status identity achievement is reached? Waterman (1982) drew a model of identity development in relation to the four statuses.

A person in the status identity diffusion can (1) transfer to moratorium by weighing a number of alternative choices (D → M), (2) transfer to foreclosure to opt for the first realistic alternative perceived (D → F), or (3) not transfer (D → D).

A person in the status foreclosure can (1) transfer to moratorium by reconsidering the earlier choice and weigh new alternatives (F → M), (2) remain in foreclosure (F → F), or (3) retreat to the status identity diffusion if the previous choice is abandoned and not replaced with a new one (F → D).

A person in the status moratorium can move into identity achievement by making a clear and decisive choice (M → A) or transfer to identity diffusion by no longer searching for viable alternatives (M → D). Waterman held that an

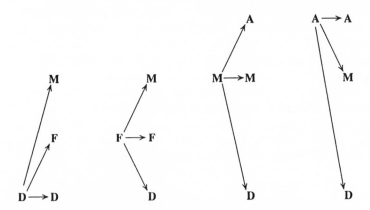

Figure 2. Sequential patterns in identity development according to Waterman, adjusted at one point. "A" stands for Identity Achievement, M = Moratorium, F = Foreclosure, and D = Identity Diffusion.

individual cannot remain in the status moratorium for long because an identity crisis cannot last. But I replaced the term crisis by exploration (see the previous section); it is very possible that a person will continue to explore a variety of alternatives at length (M → M).

A person in the status identity achievement can (1) remain there (A → A), (2) transfer to moratorium if earlier choices are reconsidered (A → M), or (3) fall back into identity diffusion if earlier choices are not maintained and new ones are not sought (A → D).

Waterman (1982, p. 343) stated that his model is descriptive and cannot be understood as a theory of individual development because almost no transition from one status to another is consistent with the model; in other words, the model is insufficiently specific to be taken as such a theory. The reason for this non-specificity is that an identity status is identified in terms of only two features: exploration and choice. If one of these alters, the identity status changes as well. But the model does not specify when—that is, in which identity status—one of these features will not change. The identity construct is not defined extensively in Marcia's model, which led Coté and Levine (1988) to speak of "construct under-representation." Hence, the identity status model is not a theory of individual development.

A first conclusion can be drawn. If the identity status model is not a theory of individual development, then it contains no *theoretical* criteria to distinguish between lower and higher statuses. The continuum from lower to higher identity statuses initially assumed by Marcia cannot be upheld in theoretical argument. Marcia (1980) and Waterman (1988) have admitted this limitation.

A second conclusion is that the status identity achievement need not be seen as the terminal point of identity development. Even a well-argued choice can at some point lose its value. This is why the term exploration is a more adequate one than crisis to define an identity status. Crisis emphasizes the process charac-ter of identity development too much; a stable identity is produced and the crisis left behind. In contrast, exploration is a process term; it refers to incessant scouting and repeated appropriation of (the same or another) identity.

3.2. An Alternative Interpretation of the Identity Status Model

But if the identity status model is not a theory of individual development, then what is it? As I see it, an identity status refers to a combination of (1) *psychologi-cal principles* of individual development, and (2) the *environment-specific validi-ty* of these principles. Let me elaborate on this.

The psychological principles of the identity status model are exploration and choice (see section 2.4). Young people must scout their environment and at some point determine their attitude to this environment, or choose a way of behaving.

The extensiveness of the exploration process and the presence or absence of a fixed behavioral pattern define whether or not an individual's identity is positive. In the identity status model, then, exploration and choice—in other words, the principle of argued choice—is a positive norm.

When he designed the model, Marcia assumed that this normativity was universally valid. Many authors (e.g., Coté & Levine, 1988) have criticized this assumption. Cultures and social environments often contain a limited number of alternatives regarding occupation and private life, so that there is no need for exploration. The environment-specific validity of the principle of argued choice is then absent.

This means that identity statuses can have two meanings. If the environment-specific validity of the principle of argued choice is present, one meaning prevails, and if it is absent, the other does so. That is to say, in the first case the identity statuses can be arranged on a continuum in which identity achievement and moratorium are healthy statuses and foreclosure and identity diffusion are less healthy. If the opportunity to explore and choose is there, not making use of it would indeed point to a relatively low level of identity development.

If, however, the principle of argued choice has no environment-specific validity, the identity statuses identity achievement and moratorium will not occur. After all, identity achievement stands for choice after exploration, and the status moratorium implies a process of argued choice. In this case foreclosure indicates respectability: the person's identity is determined without questioning his or her environment. Identity diffusion refers to a nonconscious or unreflective attitude. This person feels no need to define his or her identity or to question the environment. I represent this constellation in Table 4.

The table shows that foreclosure and identity diffusion can have two meanings. In one case, they stand for a low level of identity development and in the other, for respectability or an unreflected (nonconscious) identity. In this second case, foreclosure and identity diffusion cannot be defined as low-level identities; rather, they are forms of identity appropriate to or at least functional in a specific environment.

3.3. Is This Alternative Interpretation Empirically Valid?

To check the empirical validity of this interpretation, I matched it against (1) the found division in identity statuses, (2) the results of longitudinal research in identity development, and (3) the differences in identity development found between men and women.

1. The low identity statuses in the division are characterized by conventionality (especially foreclosure) and by a low score on a number of indicators for

a positive identity (autonomy, self-esteem, and social skills). This picture accords well with the two meanings that foreclosure and identity diffusion can have in my interpretation of the identity status model. On the one hand, these statuses can stand for a low level of identity development; on the other hand, they may refer to a functional, conventional type of identity development.

2. Longitudinal studies reveal that during adolescence identity development is progressive, a process of transition from lower to higher identity statuses. At the same time, many of the youngsters who have been studied were still in foreclosure or identity diffusion when the second measurement was taken. Once again, these results fit the interpretation. For some young people, the principle of argued choice applies: they develop from the lower to the higher identity statuses. Youngsters for whom the principle does not apply remain at the self-evident terminus of the development, foreclosure or identity diffusion.

3. The differences in the identity development of men and women were analyzed above with the help of the concepts exploration and choice. I noted that for men, the principle separating the higher and lower identity statuses is exploration; for women, the principle is choice. In terms of my alternative interpretation, this difference means that the principle of argued choice holds for men more than for women. Accordingly, the number of women who define their identity conventionally is greater than the number of men who do so. Consequently, for more women foreclosure is a functional identity status. For women to whom the principle of argued choice does apply, identity achievement is obviously the highest identity status. In other words, regarding the total group of women, identity achievement and foreclosure stand respectively for the highest and the most functional level of identity development. For most men, the principle of argued choice does apply, which means that for them foreclosure is not a functional identity status, but identity achievement and moratorium are.

The conclusion is that the alternative interpretation of the identity status model is empirically valid.

3.4. Marcia and Erikson

To end this section, I comment on Marcia's and Erikson's work. As section 2 described, Erikson was sensitive to the social aspects of personality development. It also appeared that he took little notice of variations within the social realm. For example, his theory does not accommodate the influence of the effects of social class or environment.

Marcia's position regarding the social aspect of identity development is somewhat comparable. Implicitly, his is a psychosocial theory. A person has a strong identity if his or her attitude to the environment is stable—that is, if the individual has chosen a stable stance relative to that environment. Since for Marcia, too, the environment consisted of social institutions, he looked upon social integration as a precondition of identity development. To this point, he and Erikson are alike. The difference lies in the way Marcia and Erikson use the concepts of moratorium, identity diffusion, identity achievement, and foreclosure. Let me limit myself to moratorium. For Erikson, it is an umbrella concept: moratorium refers to the way in which adolescence takes shape in modern Western societies as well as to the actual choice behavior of young people and their cognitive and motivational assessment of alternatives. Marcia restricts moratorium to the last point only: this identity status refers to individual evaluation of alternatives. Marcia thus emphasizes the psychological aspect of moratorium.

Finally, an important similarity is that both Marcia and Erikson take little account of the influences of social class and social environment on identity development. The conceptualizations of the authors contain no reference to these influences. The alternative interpretation of the identity status model demonstrates that this is an omission. Empirical research in identity development can be interpreted more adequately if the influence of the social environment is taken into consideration.

4. SUMMARY

In this chapter my focus was on Erikson's epigenetic theory of development and Marcia's model of the identity statuses. Erikson's work counts as the most important source of theoretical inspiration for the study of identity, and the model offered by Marcia is the most important and most frequently empirically tested model in adolescent psychology.

The merit of Erikson's theory is that he described a number of aspects of human identity development. Research has shown that people do indeed go through a progressive development related to these aspects. But as a theory of development, Erikson's approach is inadequate. It has proved impossible to demonstrate that completion of an earlier developmental phase is a prerequisite for positive development in a later phase.

A comparable shortcoming applies to Marcia's identity status model, in which the definition of the identity concept is not broad enough to provide a theory of identity development. The model does have great validity. The alternative interpretation shows that the model can be interpreted in two ways: (1) as a continuum on which the four identity statuses indicate a high or a low level of identity development, and (2) as a typology of two functional identity statuses in a conventional environment. The validity of this alternative interpretation needs to be determined in further research. The question of whether identity statuses have environment-specific significance can be answered only if more study is made of identity development in distinct social classes. In addition, there is a decided need for longitudinal research into identity development. Such research alone can indicate the conditions under which the identity status model can represent a continuum from low to high identity development.

NOTES

1.   Cognitive complexity can be defined as the capacity to distinguish many aspects of an object (differentiation) and to group these aspects again in one or more concepts (integration).

2.   This analysis contains a normative element, namely that exploration of distinct roles should be valued more than exploration of just one role. It is of course possible that a single exploration is more intense than a plural exploration. In this analysis, however, the operative power of the norm is assumed.

REFERENCES

Abma, R. (1986). Cultuur en tegencultuur in het Nederlands jeugdonderzoek [Culture and counterculture in Dutch youth research]. In M. Matthijssen, W. Meeus, & F. van Wel (Eds.), *Beelden van jeugd* [Images of young people] (pp. 209–228). Groningen: Wolters-Noordhoff.

Adams, G., & Fitch, S. (1982). Ego stage and identity status development: A cross-sequential analysis. *Journal of Personality and Social Psychology, 43*, 574–583.

Bosma, H. (1985). *Identity development in adolescence.* Dissertation, University of the Netherlands, Groningen.

Ciaccio, N. (1971). A test of Erikson's theory of ego epigenesis. *Developmental Psychology, 4*, 306–311.

Constantinople, A. (1969). An Eriksonian measure of personality development in college students. *Developmental Psychology, 1*, 357–372.

Coté, J., & Levine, G. (1988). A critical examination of the ego identity status paradigm. *Developmental Review, 8*, 147–185.

Erikson, E. (1959). *Young man Luther: A study in psychoanalysis.* London: Faber.

Erikson, E. (1968). *Identity: Youth and crisis.* New York: Norton.

Fitch, S., & Adams, G. (1983). Ego identity and intimacy status: Replication and extension. *Developmental Psychology, 19*, 839–845.

Gottschalch, W. (1985). *Sociologie van het zelf* [Sociology of the self]. Meppel, the Netherlands: Boom.

Grotevant, H., & Cooper, C. (1986). Individuation in family relationships. *Human Development, 29*, 82–100.

Hodgson, J., & Fischer, J. (1979). Sex differences in identity and intimacy development in college youth. *Journal of Youth and Adolescence, 8*, 37–50.

Josselson, R. (1987). *Finding herself. Pathways to identity development in women.* San Francisco: Jossey-Bass.

Kroger, J., & Haslett, S. (1988). Separation-individuation and ego identity status in late adolescence: A two-year longitudinal study. *Journal of Youth and Adolescence, 17,* 59–79.

Marcia, J. (1964). *Determination and construct validation of ego identity status.* Doctoral dissertation, Ohio State University, Columbus.

Marcia, J. (1966). Development and validation of ego-identity status. *Journal of Personality and Social Psychology, 3,* 551–558.

Marcia, J. (1980). Identity in adolescence. In J. Adelson (Ed.), *Handbook of adolescence psychology* (pp. 159–187). New York: Wiley.

Matteson, D. (1982). Van identiteit naar intimiteit: Geen eenrichtingsverkeer [From identity to intimacy: No one-way traffic]. In H. Bosma & T. Graafsma (Eds.), *De ontwikkeling van identiteit in de adolescentie* [Identity development in adolescence] (pp. 65–83). Nijmegen: Dekker & Van de Vegt.

Meilman, P. (1977). *Crisis and commitment in adolescence: A developmental study of ego identity status.* Doctoral dissertation, University of North Carolina, Chapel Hill.

Offer, D. (1969). *The psychological world of the teenager.* New York: Basic Books.

Offer, D., Marcus, D., & Offer, J. (1970). A longitudinal study of normal adolescent boys. *American Journal of Psychiatry, 126,* 917–924.

Roazen, P. (1976). *Erik H. Erikson.* New York: Free Press.

Waterman, A. (1982). Identity development from adolescence to adulthood: An extension of theory and a review of research. *Developmental Psychology, 18,* 341–358.

Waterman, A. (1985). Identity in the context of adolescent psychology. In A. Waterman (Ed.), *Identity in adolescence: Processes and contents* (pp. 5–24). San Francisco: Jossey-Bass.

Waterman, A. (1988). Identity status theory and Erikson's theory: Communualities and differences. *Developmental Review, 8,* 185–208.

Waterman, A., & Goldman, J. (1976). A longitudinal study of ego identity development at a liberal arts college. *Journal of Youth and Adolescence, 5,* 361–369.

Waterman, A., Geary, P., & Waterman, C. (1974). Longitudinal study of changes in ego identity status from freshman to the senior year at college. *Developmental Psychology, 10,* 387–392.

II

SOCIAL NETWORKS AND SOCIAL SUPPORT

The selections in Part II offer a relatively positive view, focusing on the human relations in which adolescents are embedded, both those with peers and those with parents and other adults. A brief description of Chapters 5–9 follows.

The Significant People in the Social Networks of Adolescents

Comparing adolescents' social networks in a small town and a city in Norway confirms the expectation that those in smaller communities interact with each other more often and interact with more people than their urban peers. Bø's findings also counter the claim that adolescents interact primarily with each other, showing instead quite diverse networks, especially for girls in the small town. He calls attention to differences in methods of mapping social networks that confound comparisons across studies.

Social Support during Adolescence: Methodological and Theoretical Considerations

Beginning with a useful brief review of the literature on social support, the authors, Cauce, Mason, Gonzales, Hiraga, and Liu, examine the relationship between support and attachment. Their evidence that they are both aspects of the same phenomenon suggests a life course sequence beginning with maternal and other familial attachments and then moving outward to incorporate peers and other social network members in relations patterned after the initial ones. Methodological issues include the question of whether it is useful to differentiate among components of support, whether the type of support or the source is more important, and whether support should be summed from multiple sources or analyzed as a function of a set of dyads.

Social Support in the Relationships between
Older Adolescents and Adults

The exploratory study reported here by Gottlieb and Sylvestre examines the processes through which social relations with unrelated adults become supportive to adolescents. It identifies many barriers to the establishment of such relationships. Theoretically, it provides an interesting contrast to the preceding chapter by emphasizing the embeddedness of social support in social relations and by treating it as an aspect of ordinary interactions rather than a response to stressful situations.

The Roles of Parents and Peers in the Sexual
and Relational Socialization of Adolescents

Parents and peers are frequently portrayed as competing over the values and choices of adolescents, especially regarding sexual behavior. The authors du Bois-Reymond and Ravesloot found peers to be confidants about sexual matters, but not active supporters. Many parents see themselves as more open than their sons and daughters see them as being, probably because parents compare themselves with their own parents rather than with what their children would prefer.

Mentors in Adolescents' Lives

The ideal relationship between an adolescent and an unrelated adult is captured by the word "mentor," which connotes both caring and advice. This study by Hamilton and Darling found that older adolescents are more likely to report having mentors than younger adolescents and that males are more likely to do so than females. Unrelated adult mentors did not appear to compensate for the absence of "mentoring" parents. In the context of this volume, one question implicitly posed by this chapter is whether institutional arrangements in other countries make mentoring relationships between adolescents and unrelated adults more likely to develop than they are in the United States.

5

The Significant People in the Social Networks of Adolescents

Inge Bø

Important spheres of life, like family, work, local environment, learning, and leisure, need to be connected to maximize the potential for individuals' socialization (Bronfenbrenner, 1977, 1979). The substance of these links is *relations between people*. According to social observers, these previously intertwined areas are, as a result of urbanization and industrialization, being split into segregated life domains. Thus, people are becoming alienated—and also age-stratified—in relation to each other (Handlin & Handlin, 1971). In particular, it is maintained that adolescents have been cut off from the adult world and abandoned to both age-segregated peer groups and exploitive commercial interests (Bronfenbrenner, 1973; Coleman, 1974; Condry & Siman, 1974; Montemayor & Van Komen, 1980).

Several scholars have expressed concern about this situation and argued that the alleged isolation of adolescents may lead to a host of detrimental consequences. For example, it has been suggested that the main cause of the impaired well-being of so many young people in terms of mental health, social behavior, and academic performance, is a breakdown of the social ecology in which they live (Bronfenbrenner, 1973, 1974, 1979; Coleman, 1974; Magnussen, 1983). At the same time, researchers have become increasingly aware that pivotal to this ecology are children's relationships with people of various ages and in various roles, particularly people outside the immediate family who are considered significant others, role models, mentors, and so forth (Erikson, 1968; Mead, 1952; Sherif & Sherif, 1964).

1. PREVIOUS RESEARCH

Systematic studies of children's and adolescents' social relationships date back to extensive mid-20th-century parent-child research, sociometric approaches inspired by Moreno, and (mostly) postwar research on friendship and peers. (For literature reviews, see Rubin [1980]; Epstein [1983]; Foot et al. [1980]; and Serafica and Blyth [1985]).

Age and role segregation are assumed to be widespread, and speculation about the nature and consequences of the composition and effects of adolescents' social worlds has a long history, but very few direct empirical attempts to describe adolescents' social relations have been accomplished (Blyth, Hill, & Thiel, 1982, p. 427; Montemayor & Van Komen, 1980). Research on adolescents' social relations has rather been limited to more fragmentary issues, like the relative influences of parents and peers, peer group popularity, status effects, and friendships, or to the effects of parental practices upon adolescent behavior (Blyth, Hill, & Thiel, 1982; Cooper & Ayers-Lopez, 1985; Serafica & Blyth, 1985; Tietjen, 1982). Research has focused largely on the direct effects of single environmental factors and personal categories on the developing person without taking into account the total setting in which both physical factors and persons are embedded, thus neglecting "aspects of the environment beyond the immediate situation containing the subject" (Bronfenbrenner, 1977, p. 514). Accordingly, proposed preventive and remedial measures have to a great extent been atomistic—that is, they have been isolated actions aimed at isolated problems, taking into focus one problem at a time (Bronfenbrenner, 1974, 1979).

During the 1960s and 1970s, a number of investigations (reviewed by Galbo [1984, 1986]) were also carried out regarding the persons whom young people rated as significant in their lives. According to Galbo's review, most of these studies may have limitations in terms of depth, breadth, and methodology. For example, they have tended to be based on survey instruments and, occasionally, structured interviews (as distinct from in-depth ones). Also, they have largely been restricted to important adults, sometimes even to a limited number of people. Often these relationships were putative, that is, determined as significant by the researchers before the study started rather than left to the free choice and perception of the subjects. No attempt has been made to assess the meanings and implications of various adolescent responses. Finally, many of the studies are now obsolete, given that youth's values and lifestyles have changed considerably during past decades (Galbo, 1984, p. 957).

Certainly, these and other previous studies have identified a number of important aspects and functions of adolescents' social relationships. But despite the large amount of data generated, the studies, whether taken separately or together, do not provide a satisfying and comprehensive picture of young people's social worlds. Adolescents' relations with children (e.g., siblings), extended family members, coaches, adults in youth-serving agencies, and other "caretakers" (other than parents) for the most part have been ignored in empirical studies (Blyth, Hill, & Thiel, 1982). There also has been a tendency to overlook the importance of adolescents' own determination of salience and to ignore the connections between adolescents' significant people and the larger social environment.

More holistic approaches to the study of social landscapes have since been introduced to meet these shortcomings. One key to conceiving this situation is the use of social network concepts: Adolescents live within a network of relations and experience their social worlds with a variety of persons comprising their networks. These are the persons with whom the adolescents' knowledge of social reality is "co-constructed."

Since the late 1960s, there has been extensive interest in the assessment of social networks in general; more recently, there has also been interest in the social networks of young parents and the social ties of preschool and young elementary school children (Cochran & Brassard, 1979; Cochran, Gunnarson, Gräbe, & Lewis, 1984; Feiring & Lewis, 1981; Gunnarsson, 1985; Tietjen, 1982; Tiller, 1980). Despite this work and the research on whom teenagers rate as significant adults or role models, only recently have researchers begun to apply network analysis in empirical studies of adolescents' social relations that are based on more open-ended approaches and particularly directed at those perceived as significant others.

Garbarino, Burston, Raber, Russell, and Crouter (1978) used network analysis in a three-year longitudinal study to map the people preadolescents listed as important in their lives during the transition to adolescence (core family members were omitted). The work showed that during this period, an individual's social world is increasingly made up of peers. In-depth analysis was, however, restricted to the top 10 most significant relationships. Further support for age segregation during adolescence was provided by a naturalistic study (observations) conducted by Montemayor and Van Komen (1980). This study showed that adolescents were most often observed with peer friends, next with adults, and least frequently with children.

The project of Blyth and his colleagues (1982) is a very extensive study of youth's social networks. These investigators invited more than 2,400 students in the seventh to tenth grades to identify the significant people in their lives, using a modified social network approach. They found that the single most frequent type of significant other listed was nonrelated peers of the same sex (about 31 percent of the total). Other-sex young people were more likely to be listed as significant others by older adolescents. Nonkin peers of both genders made up only approximately 40 percent of all significant others listed by both males and females. However, this percentage rose to 57 when teenage siblings and teenage extended family members were also included.

In an exploratory study, Galbo (1983) asked 31 mid-teen males and females to list their most significant adults. He found that parents were the adults most frequently chosen, though some youths selected no parents at all. Nonkin adults were preferred over kin at a ratio of nearly two to one. Male subjects chose an average 4.79 significant adults, and females chose an average 4.47. Boys tended to prefer male adults, whereas girls chose females. Girls chose fewer adults overall than the boys chose.

Another interesting network approach to understanding parts of adolescents' social landscapes is the "whom-to-turn-to" technique. Using an instrument developed in Czechoslovakia by Jurosky, Asne Gardsjord (1972) assessed the "social proximity" of 318 Norwegian students aged 14 to 18. These youths responded to questions about whom they would turn to for advice or support in various kinds of daily-life situations, with whom they would share their joys and sorrows, and so forth. Altogether, 25 person categories and 21 issues/situations were prelisted. Gardsjord's main findings suggest that (1) as a whole, across all the issues, parents exceeded all other person categories in importance, with best friend and other peers rated second and third, and (2) to whom youths go depends to a certain extent on the seriousness and context of the issue at stake: the more important the issue, the more they sought their parents.

Klagholz (1987) reported a similar network study of 223 adolescents aged 15 and 18 from rural and urban locations. She found that social network size and diversity varied significantly by sex and location. Boys and rural students had smaller and less diverse networks than girls and urban students. Regarding choice of person, the overall pattern was—as opposed to Gardsjord's findings—that *peers* were the most frequent choice and mothers the second. Klagholz's data also showed that person preferences varied not only by issue (as in the case of the Norwegian study) but also by sex and place of residence: Girls chose peers more frequently than boys, whereas boys chose parents and unrelated adults more often than girls. Rural students, particularly boys, relied on their parents, especially fathers, more than urban students. Urban adolescents rarely chose fathers at all and instead chose peers, siblings, and unrelated adults more frequently.

So far, the cited network studies have largely been descriptive in design. It is generally agreed that personal networks might be looked upon as social capital, that is, as a resource needed to promote cognitive development as well as social skills and mental health (Cochran & Brassard, 1979; Epstein, 1983; Galbo, 1986; Garbarino et al. (1978). Recent years have also seen analytical research considering relations between aspects of adolescents' social networks and behavior. For example, Blyth and Traeger (1985) and Coates (1985) looked at connections between young people's self-esteem/self-concept and their personal networks. Vondra and Garbarino (1985) examined such relations with respect to adolescent psychological adjustment, whereas Fischer, Sollie, and Morrow (1986), in a short-term longitudinal study, focused on the possible effects of social network variables on self-esteem and social competence. Also, Klagholz (1987) related social network variables to behavior, in her case to "social understanding."

The broad descriptive network study directed by Blyth, referred to above, has also been supplemented with an analytical part: Blyth, Durant, and Moosbrugger (1985) and Foster-Clark and Blyth (1987) analyzed how the different sets of significant others, including both peers and adults, operated for groups of moderate-to-heavy regular marijuana users and nonusers. Their focus was on the quality rather than the quantity of the relationships with others; for example, frequency of contact and the perceived intimacy and quality of relationships were included in their analytic model.

Although Blyth and Traeger, Vondra and Garbarino, and Fischer and colleagues failed to identify clear and substantial relationships between network characteristics and psychological outcomes, Coates and Klagholz revealed complex sets of relationships between both quantitative and qualitative measures of network features and self-concept (Coates) and societal understanding (Klagholz). The Blyth teams found that drug users were also much more oriented to older youth than were those adolescents not involved with drugs; this was particularly the case for junior high school boys. Also, the type of leisure contexts from which the adolescents derived peer intimacy appeared to be related to both their own drug use and the tendency to have drug-using friends: the stronger the involvement in adult-supervised activities, the lower the drug use and the greater the tendency to have nonusing friends: The study also showed that the patterns of mediational effects were rather intricate.

Although most of these studies suffer from methodological shortcomings—for instance, they fail to control for socioeconomic status (SES) and other social structure factors—these lines of research show considerable promise.

2. RESEARCH QUESTIONS AND METHODS
OF THE NORWEGIAN STUDIES

The objective of the present study was to examine who are the significant people in the lives of teenaged Norwegians. With Bronfenbrenner's conception of the ecology of human development, stressing the importance of a phenomenological orientation, as the guiding theoretical perspective, I used social network analysis as the central approach. This chapter has primarily this double focus: (1) to present a technique of mapping young people's social world, and (2) to present a picture of who it is that 15- to 16-year-olds rate as important people in their lives.

A subordinate purpose was to illustrate by examples how aspects of the personal networks of the young people studied related to their behavior.[1]

2.1. Research Questions

The presentation of results will concentrate on the following questions: (1) How many people do youngsters at this age perceive as significant? (2) Which age groups do the significant ones belong to? (3) To whom do adolescents feel most strongly attached? (4) To what extent do parents know their offsprings' networks? (5) With whom do adolescents most frequently interact? (6) In which roles do adolescents know their salient network members? (7) Which SES factors contribute the most to their social networks? (8) What connections can be found between their networks and school-related variables?

Whereas the first six questions are descriptive, the last two are analytic.

2.2. Settings

The research reported here actually includes two studies. The main study was conducted in the oil-boom city of Stavanger, on the southwest coast of Norway; the area's population was about 200,000 at the time of the study. The other one, originally a pilot study succeeding two prepilots, was done in a nearby fjord village of about 5,000 inhabitants, labeled here by the pseudonym Fjordvik.[2]

2.3. The Sample

In Fjordvik, 82 students—37 girls and 45 boys—belonging to the village junior high school's catchment area participated in the study. This group comprised practically all the 15- to 16-year-olds in the village. The Stavanger sample consisted of 92 sixteen-year-old boys attending the ninth grade classes in two junior high schools selected because they could provide a cross section of Stavanger youth.[3]

2.4. Measures

As was pointed out, researchers have been slow to adopt the network paradigm for understanding the social world of adolescents. Because, to my knowledge, both empirical studies and measures were lacking, I approached the problem in an exploratory manner. Three main instruments were developed: the Network Interview Form (NIF), the Background, Attitudes, and Behaviors Questionnaire (BAB), and the School Rating Scale (SRS).

The Network Interview Form was developed via two prepilots and finally tested in the Fjordvik study. When interviewing people about their social networks, a researcher confronts the following methodological issues (Blyth, 1982): (1) how to define social network—in the present case, how to delimit significant others; (2) how to operationalize the definition; and (3) how to help the respondents identify the relevant contact persons.

These issues are related, and they are also crucial in terms of what kind of data a researcher receives. In the prepilots, much effort was therefore invested in testing all three issues.

Concerning the first issue, in the final two studies five criteria were selected. The respondents were asked to identify people (1) who had significance for them and/or for whom they felt important, (2) whose names they knew, (3) who knew their names, (4) with whom they did something, and (5) with whom they were in regular contact.

The criteria were thoroughly explained; examples given included friends of the family, relatives, friends from school and other settings, neighbors, teachers, and club leaders. Probes also mentioned people of different ages, the possibility of telephone and letter contact, and the fact that a contact person did not have to be liked to have significance for the adolescent.[4]

Concerning the second and third issues, the problem was to word the instructions and the network interviews in such a way that they listed network members who fit the stated criteria. It was vital that the respondents not only included as significant others the most salient persons—those whom they recalled immediately—but also more hidden ones, whom they would recognize on the basis of the eliciting words and who made a difference in their lives. Another problem was to prevent the network interview from becoming a memory test. As far as can be seen, much of the previous network research might have stumbled into pitfalls of these kinds.

To accommodate these demands, a network interview form was constructed in which several kinds of information were gathered for each network member, including sex, age, length of time known, perceived importance of the relationship, and role or roles occupied (sister, mother, neighbor, friend, and so forth). This procedure yielded maps of relations with adults, youths, and children living both inside and outside the respondents' nuclear and extended families.

The Background, Attitudes, and Behaviors Questionnaire contained many different measures, from which only selected data are included in this report: measures of (1) SES variables, (2) time spent in direct contact with parents and with peers, and (3) the extent to which respondents wanted contact with adults and the elderly.

The School Rating Scale had several sections. The main section consisted of two parallel Likert-type rating scales, which were completed separately by two teachers. These scales contained a large number of items with content relating to personality characteristics and various kinds of school behavior such as motivation, general conduct, discipline, absenteeism, and so forth. Another section of the SRS provided space for the fall-term grades in four core subjects taken from school records. Factor analysis was used to derive new indexes.

2.5. Variable List

The following indicators were selected for use in the analytic part of the research: family's socioeconomic status (family's SES) is an index combining the father's (mother's) number of years of schooling with a score representing the prestige of his (or her) occupation (r = .61). School achievement is an index composed of grades in four theoretical subjects (Cronbach's α = .92). School adaptation combines 10 ratings including discipline, general conduct, class conduct, "social risk," and disruptive behavior (α = .94). Personality traits provides ratings of six personality characteristics, including diligence, independence, emotionality, and helpfulness (α = .88). The Neighborhood Milieu Index is a composite score created by combining separate ratings of members of the school staff, the city police department, and the department of social services. These individuals rated the 18 residential areas in which the respondents lived along a five-point scale according to their general perceptions of the areas as having more or fewer problems than other areas (rank correlations between raters were .52, .53, and .61).

2.6. Data Collection

The study was explained to all the students collectively prior to data collection. The BAB was administered to the students in groups of 10 to 15 in their classrooms. In another setting, an orientation to the network interview was given to all the participants.

Students were then called from the classroom in pairs and given an hour of detailed instruction and an interview by a trained data collector. During this hour, the students completed interview protocols for 10 to 30 of their network members under the auspices of the collector. To get away from a snapshot approach and to make sure that important network contacts beyond those the students could name "off the top of their heads" were included, the data collector gave the students blank network forms to take home and complete during the next 10 to 14 days. On the day an individual delivered the forms, he or she was debriefed extensively for another hour by the original interviewer. In the debriefing session, the network forms and the questionnaires were checked for missing information. A set of additional probes asked the students about their networks to make sure that significant relationships had not been overlooked.

The School Rating Scale and the Neighborhood Milieu Measure, completed by the groups of school and staff members, police, and social welfare personnel, were administered during site visits.

3. RESULTS: THE SIGNIFICANT PEOPLE IN THE SOCIAL NETWORK

3.1. Network Size

Network size refers to the number of contacts in a person's social network. As previously indicated, the size and other properties of an individual's social net-

Table 1. Number of Contacts in the Social Networks
of Adolescents

		Network Contacts	
Sample	n	Number	Mean
Prepilots[a]	20	3,175	159
Fjordvik girls	37	2,748	74
Fjordvik boys	45	2,925	65
Fjordvik total	82	5,673	69
Stavanger[b]	92	4,709	51

[a] Ten girls and 10 boys.
[b] Boys only.

work depend on the phrasing of the definition and operationalization of network. To give an idea of the effect a difference in phrasing can make, I include data from the prepilots in Table 1. In this study, the first item (the one on significance) in the network definition was skipped (see note 4).

The means are all surprisingly high compared to those in the small amount of network research on teenagers that is known. The figures demonstrate that young Norwegians in their mid-teens relate to quite a few people. The prepilot data suggest that the number of acquaintances increases substantially if the nonimportant, looser ties are also calculated. Other data (not shown) suggest that the range is large, from an extreme of 409 network contacts for a well-adjusted 15-year-old girl in the first prepilot to the contrasting extreme of 3 for an isolated boy in Fjordvik.

The table also indicates that the youths in the rural village incorporated a substantially larger number of people in their groups of significant others than the Stavanger youths; the respective means were 69 and 51. This discrepancy probably has to do with density; people in Fjordvik were interconnected, with "everybody knowing everybody" to a larger extent than the people in the more metropolitan Stavanger.

A comparison between the two genders in Fjordvik (only boys were studied in Stavanger) indicates that the girls had a larger circle of significant people than the boys; respective means were 74 and 65. Fjordvik boys listed more male than female contacts: means were 40 male contacts and 25 female contacts. However, the girls in Fjordvik included males and females equally in their networks, an average of 37 each.

3.2. To Which Age Groups Do Network Members Belong?

The mean ages of the network members in the two samples is 25.8 (Fjordvik) and 27.3 (Stavanger), with standard deviations of 3.1 and 5.1, respectively. In

Table 2.   Adolescents' Social Network Members[a]

Age	Fjordvik Girls (n = 37)	Fjordvik Boys (n = 45)	Fjordvik Total (n = 82)	Stavanger (n = 92)
0–6	3.1	1.9	2.4	1.3
7–12	4.1	3.5	3.8	3.0
13–17	30.0	29.3	29.7	24.0
18–24	6.6	4.8	5.5	4.0
25–39	14.3	10.6	12.2	7.8
40–64	13.3	12.5	12.9	8.4
65+	2.6	2.0	2.3	2.6
Total	74.3	65.0	69.2	51.2

[a] Means are shown.

the Stavanger group, the mean age in the "youngest" network was only 17.5 years, whereas the mean in the "oldest" network was 48 years. (The boy with the oldest network reported only adults.) The Fjordvik girls' networks were a bit older than the boys'. The distribution is shown in Table 2. The table confirms the expectation that the largest age group in the adolescents' social networks is made up of peers. The data point to the interesting fact, however, that a *majority* of their significant network members does *not* belong to the peer group. The Fjordvik females tended to incorporate into their circles of significant people slightly more adults than the male students.

3.3. Zone Assignment

By zone, I mean the degree of importance an individual network member has for the anchoring person. Zone placement might therefore be looked upon as a measure of intimacy. The primary network (zone 1) contains contacts rated by the students as the most intimate, whereas those next in terms of emotional ties and importance constitute zone 2 (the secondary network). The third zone (the tertiary network) is made up of those people perceived to be less important than both zone 1 and zone 2 members but still felt to have significance. The social network members' distribution in zones shows that about one in four (Stavanger) and one in five (Fjordvik) network members are assigned to the primary zone. In average numbers, each Stavanger youth is surrounded by 13 intimate relationships, and each Fjordvik youth by 15.

A natural question in this connection is to which age groups the respondents felt emotionally closest. The Stavanger data show that 80 percent of all the children and 75 percent of all the adults 25 years and older are placed in zones 1 or 2. In contrast to this, 85 percent of the peers are placed in zone 2 or 3. The tendency is evident: these 16-year-olds were more emotionally tied to the children and adults in their networks than to the peers. Peers are significantly under-represented in their intimate zone.

3.4. Network Overlap

In this study, network overlap referred to the degree to which a mother and/or a father knew (by name and otherwise) their child's network contacts. Mother *and* father were reported to know a mean of as many as two-thirds of all the network members. As expected, network overlap was more common in the village. The average mother knew the most—in Fjordvik, she knew 95 of the contacts in addition to those the father also knew. That Fjordvik is a more interconnected community than the Stavanger neighborhoods is shown by the fact that only 17 percent of the students' significant others in this town were unknown to both mother and father. The corresponding figure in Stavanger is 27 percent.

Turning to another vantage point reinforces the fact that peers are underrepresented among youths' significant others: Of all the contacts simultaneously reported as known by their parents and as zone 1 people—the VIPs in the students' lives—only 25 percent belonged to the peer group ($M = 2.3$), whereas the rest ($M = 7$) belonged to the other age groups. As many as 30 percent ($M = 2.7$) of these VIPs were uncles, teachers, coaches, and so forth, aged between 25 and 55 years; 20 percent were older.

3.5. Contact Frequency

Table 3 shows how often the students had contact with their network members.

According to the table, the subjects "touch base" with about half of their network contacts "daily," defined as at least four days a week. These contacts are primarily members of the core family, friends, and schoolmates. If we add those contacts whom they meet "weekly" (at least every two weeks), most of whom are

Table 3.   Frequency of Contact[a]

Frequency	Fjordvik Girls (n = 37)	Fjordvik Boys (n = 45)	Fjordvik Total (n = 82)	Stavanger (n = 92)
Daily	49%	58%	54%	49%
Weekly	24	17	20	21
Monthly	10	9	10	13
2–5 months	7	5	6	8
6 months +	8	8	8	10

[a] Figures are percentages.

club friends, sport chums, coaches, and so forth, we approach three-quarters of the total networks.

Which age groups do they most regularly interact with? Splitting the various age groupings on frequency of contact, as was done for the Stavanger sample, showed that of all the network members the studied adolescents encountered daily, 70 percent were peers (13- to 17-year-olds), about 20 percent were adults over the age of 25, and 6 percent were children under the age of 7. This pattern indicates that a normal (working) day for a teenager is filled with exchanges with peers in the various arenas outside home—school, sports, street corners, and so forth.

Data from the BAB questionnaire also confirm that the mid-teen group spent much time interacting with their peers, but also that the amount of time spent with their parents, in particular with their mothers during working days, was notably greater. The subjects reported spending similar amounts of time with peers and parents during the weekends.

When asked how often they communicated with adults other than their parents and with people older than 60 years, the respondents gave answers indicating a surprisingly high frequency of contact. In Fjordvik, for example, half of the students touched base with the elderly at least once a week. In Stavanger, the corresponding figure was 28 percent. Only 6 to 7 percent of the students in the two locations reported no contact with this age group.

3.6. Relationships

How were the subjects related to their network contacts, that is, in which roles did they know them?

Taken as a whole, relatives dominated the networks of significant people: 38 to 40 percent of the total network members belonged to either the nuclear or the extended family. Next in size came schoolmates, own friends, and neighbors. Other large groups were the family's common friends, hobby friends, teachers, and so forth. But here role multiplexity becomes a consideration: Network connections whom the respondents knew in two or more roles were counted in all roles (Table 4).

3.7. Socioeconomic Level and Network Size

An individual's network is not formed in a social, cultural, or economic vacuum. I attempted to trace links between a series of demographic conditions on the one hand (like the quality of a neighborhood and length of residence) and characteristics of a youth's social networks on the other. Table 5 is restricted to the connections between family socioeconomic characteristics and network size.

Table 4.   Network Contacts by Role Categories[a]

Categories	Fjordvik (n = 82)	Stavanger (n = 92)
Core family: parents and siblings	7%	8%
"Near" family: aunts, uncles, cousins, grandparents	30	24
"Remote" family: other kin members	3	6
Family's common friends, parents'workmates, etc.	8	12
Own friends (minus pure sport and school friends)	16	30
Own friends' family members and friends of friends	3	5
School and workmates	29	28
Neighbors, vacation neighbors, clerks, postmen, etc.	12	13
People known through hobbies, sports, clubs, etc.	8	16
Teachers, school staff, coaches, leaders, etc.	13	6

[a]Percentages are shown. It should be borne in mind that a relationship can be "multiplex"—a respondent might know the same person in two or more roles, for instance, as uncle, neighbor, and coach. Thus, columns sum to more than 100.

Father's work prestige turned out to be the strongest of the single SES variables.[5] It appears likely that the higher the parents' job prestige and education, the more people their offspring are exposed to, and the more they are trained in network-building skills.

3.8. Connections between Networks and School Variables

The analytic model consists of three variable groups: *background variables* are family's SES and the Neighborhood Milieu Index; *process variables* are social network variables, including time spent with parents and peers; and *effect variables* are school achievement, school adaptation, and personality traits.

Table 5.   Network Size and Five Measures of Family's Socioeconomic Level[a]

	Occupation[b]		Education[c]		Income[d]		SES[e]	SES[f]
	F	M	F	M	F	M	F	F+M
Network Size	.37	.10	.24	.15	.15	.21	.36	.31

[a]F = father, M = mother. Pearson correlations are shown. For r's $\geq$ .19, $p <$ .05; r's $\geq$ .25, $p <$ .01; r's $\geq$ .32 $p <$ .001.
[b]Measured by a Norwegian version of Treiman's *Occupational Prestige in Comparative Perspective.*
[c]Six-level scale.
[d]Taxable income offered by the taxation authorities.
[e]Sum of father's occupational prestige score and educational level.
[f]Sum of father's and mother's prestige scores and educational levels.

Table 6.   Relationships of Background and Network Variables with Outcomes[a]

Variables[b]	School Achievement		School Adaptation		Personality Traits	
	A	B	A	B	A	B
Background						
Family's SES	.49	—	.27	—	.43	—
Neighborhood Milieu Index	.28	—	.37	—	.30	—
Network						
Size of network	.50	.36	.53	.45	.56	.45
Size of peer network	.45	.33	.46	.40	.50	.40
Size of adult network	.43	.33	.49	.39	.48	.39
Mutiplexity	−.32	−.32	−.42	−.36	−.17	−.10
Frequency	−.24	−.09	−.25	−.10	−.13	−.05
Zone	−.10	−.17	−.25	−.32	−.14	−.20
Overlap	−.29	−.27	−.17	−.20	−.24	−.27
Time with parents	.25	.10	.36	.26	.30	.17
Time with peers	−.26	−.14	−.28	−.18	−.28	−.16

[a] "A" columns contain Pearson correlations generated without controlling for the two background variables. "B" columns are correlations computed with controls. For r's ≥ .19, p < .05; r's ≥ .25; p < .01; r's ≥ .32, p < .01.

[b] High scores on outcome variables are positive. For example, a high Neighborhood Milieu Index score indicates few social problems; a high school adaptation score means positive behavior as perceived by the school.

Multiplexity gives the mean measure of the strength/weakness dimension of an individual's social network. The larger the mean, the stronger the ties between anchor person and network. See Table 4, note "a."

The scores for contact frequency, network zone, and overlap have been made linear by weighting. For example, a network person to whom "daily exchange" was ascribed was weighted highest, and a person seen only once a year was weighted lowest.

Columns labeled "A" in Table 6 show some of the relationships found: In accordance with my expectations, family's socioeconomic level contributes to school-related behavior. It is also interesting to see how the other ecological background factor—neighborhood quality—connects with the outcome variables, particularly school adaptation. The two clusters of network variables (variables 3–5 and 6–9, "B" columns in Table 6) also relate quite extensively to the chosen school indexes, but in opposite directions.

Size appears to have strong positive effects in itself (see below). The data also suggest that there is no difference in the predictive powers of the size of peer and the size of adult groups. (Other data, not shown, indicate that the size of the network group "younger than 13 years" contributes to the same extent as the size of these other age groups.)

Multiplexity, frequency, zone, and overlap, however, all show a consistently negative correlation with the outcome variables. This result means that the stronger the ties, the more frequent the exchange, the greater the intimacy, and the

Table 7.   Results of Stepwise Regression Analysis

Variables	School Achievement			School Adaptation			Personality Traits		
	Beta	F[a]	R²	Beta	F[a]	R²	Beta	F[a]	R²
Family's SES	.39	18.6	11	.14	—	—	.19	4.0	2
Network size	.30	10.2	25	.43	23.2	28	.41	18.0	31
Overlap	−.17	3.7	—	−.11	2.6	—	−.24	7.0	4
Multiplexity	−.29	10.3	7	−.21	4.1	3	.02	—	—
Zone	−.01	—	—	−.26	5.9	9	−.06	—	—
Time with parents	.10	—	—	.18	4.0	—	.22	6.1	7
Time with peers	−.16	3.4	—	−.13	—	—	−.14	—	—

[a] $F = 4.0, p < .05; F = 2.6, p < .10$. Only variables whose coefficients are significant at the .1 level are included in the table.

higher the degree of density, the *poorer* the school behavior. The relationships between time spent with parents and peers on the one side, and behavior on the other side, have opposite directions: the more time spent with peers, the more negative the school ratings; the more time spent with parents, the better the ratings.

There are, however, a number of interesting correlations between all the variables used (not shown), for example, between the two demographic variables (.19), and between the demographic variables and network variables. Since the demographic variables enter the arena temporally prior to the networks, this relationship might include causal links. Thus, the demographic factors may influence behavior both directly and indirectly, via the networks. In the model, therefore, the demographic factors are perceived as independent variables, whereas the network measures are seen as process variables.

Because of the danger of attributing to one variable predictive power that may in fact be more appropriately assigned to other variables with which variance is shared, it makes sense to partial out some of the shared variance before attempting to interpret these relationships. This process was undertaken with first- and second-order partial correlation procedures, as shown in Table 6. Partialing out family's SES, the correlation between neighborhood on one side and the network and behavioral variables on the other leads to slight decreases (the mean drop across all process variables is .06). When the neighborhood risk factor is controlled for, the same picture emerges (a mean drop of .05). These findings mean that both family's SES and neighborhood quality contribute separately and weakly to the network characteristics, parent and peer involvement, and the school behavior outcome.

The next relationships of interest are those between the intermediate social processes—time with parents and peers and network involvement—and the various clusters of school outcome variables when both background variables are controlled. (Compare the A and B columns in Table 6.) The emerging pattern shows an overall drop in the correlation coefficients (the mean is about .09), with the exception of zone and overlap. Thus, when the effect of the background variables (SES and neighborhood) is withdrawn, there is still a relatively strong connection between the network indicators and school-related behaviors.

Finally, multiple regression analysis was also utilized. The two background and the nine process variables were put into the model simultaneously (see Table 7).

In every case, the R^2 shown is the amount (percentage) of variance explained when all other variables are controlled. The overall picture is that the network indexes, particularly size, overlap, multiplexity, and time with parents, appear to be the best predictors of school-related behavior for the 16-year-old boys. Family's SES is also a relatively strong contributor, especially to school performance, and the milieu index and the sizes of the peer and adult groups are expelled as nonsignificant from the pool of possible predictors. Please note from the beta coefficients that some relationships are negative.

4. DISCUSSION

There are many myths about teenagers in contemporary societies. According to one of these, their contact networks are not only meager, but also "kinship-alienated" and strongly peer-centered. This chapter attempts to shed light on certain aspects of adolescents' social landscape. It also provides examples of how demographic and social network variables directly and indirectly connect to adolescents' school behavior.

Referring to my first research question, the data document that the mean number of network members in the pilot and main studies turned out to be 69 and 51, respectively, with a huge range. Young Norwegians—at least those in urban and semiurban areas—know, appreciate, and exchange with a surprisingly *heterogeneous* array of people and report the members of that array as being of significance to them. The contrast in terms of size between the networks of the prepilot group (Stavanger youth) and the two other groups is probably the result of the different criteria sets used in network definition, whereas the distinction between the Fjordvik and Stavanger groups relates to the degree to which people are interconnected at the two sites.

The other conclusion to be drawn is that definition, operationalization, and choice of data collection technique are of crucial importance when mapping out people's social networks. This conclusion relates to the determination of both size and other characteristics and also to the problem of finding the point of balance between not making the network listing interview a test of immediate recall and the other extreme of pressing the respondents to include people who do not meet the criteria.

These issues make comparisons with other studies problematic. It might seem as if both Blyth and colleagues (1982) and, to a certain extent, Coates (1985) used eliciting techniques similar to the ones utilized in the present study. Blyth's research team found a mean of 15.6 persons in the suburban neighborhoods they studied, whereas Coates reported 29.1. Garbarino's team (1978) found means of 16.8 (rural area), 12.2 (city) and 11.1 (suburban), with nuclear family members excluded. Galbo, in his 1983 study, reported averages of 4.79 for boys and 4.47 for girls, but he asked for significant adults only.

The Americans, however, based their network interviews on the snapshot technique, which differs from my combination interview-supervision-logbook technique. In addition, two of the teams had other built-in limitations in their approaches. These methodological distinctions are probably of vital importance and might explain the reported differences between the sizes of the networks of American and Norwegian youth. Those differences might also reflect genuine differences between young people's social landscapes and lives in the two countries.

The data from Fjordvik indicate that girls maintain more contacts than boys and also that they have more heterogeneous networks. The girls included more children and more members of the other sex in their networks which are also a bit older than the boys'. All this probably mirrors attitudinal and cultural differences between the sexes, including girls' stronger sociability and higher level of maturity at the ages studied.

Findings also suggest that villages the size of Fjordvik (population 5,000) encourage the formation of larger networks than big city areas. Network density, as measured by the degree of parents' overlap, is also larger. This tendency might be curvilinear, with small cities and towns providing the best environment for network formation and conditions becoming less favorable when cities grow larger and villages smaller. Table 3 also shows a tendency on the part of the Fjordvik students to "push" their significant network members toward the outer circles. Again, this tendency might suggest that adolescents living in dense villages of this size know and appreciate many people, but also that they are less selective than young persons living in larger cities. An alternative interpretation would be that in some way, everybody is more intimate in a village, so it makes sense not to seek individual intimacy.

Turning to the second question, it seems to be a common aspect of both the American and Norwegian studies that the young subjects include people of many ages and roles but that peers are the single dominating group. In the present study, however, most of the peers were rated as secondary and tertiary network members (question 3), and the most intimate zone of the networks was made up of core family, some selected extended family members, and a close friend or two. No one in these samples excluded their parents or stepparents from the primary zone. These tendencies seem very consistent with the findings of Gardsjord (1972), Blyth and colleagues (1982), and Galbo (1983): Core family members—and especially parents—are rated as surprisingly important to young people of this age group. While respondents in Gardsjord's and Blyth's studies gave increasing salience to peer friends with increased age, at no point did peers overtake parents as the most significant people in the lives of these teenagers. In addition to these people, youngsters appreciated contact and exchange with teachers, leaders, coaches, neighbors, salespeople at local stores, and so forth (cf. Galbo, 1986; Blyth, Hill, & Thiel, 1982; Serafica & Blyth, 1985).

It is also evident (question 4) that even in "metropolitan" Stavanger the social networks of parents and their offspring substantially overlap. In line with this, data from the questionnaire indicate that there was extensive exchange between friends of Norwegian adolescents and their parents. Likewise, the respondents also seemed to spend a considerable amount of time in their home settings in contact with their parents. Between 30 and 50 percent of the students reported weekly contact with elderly persons, and half of them also expressed a wish for more contact with adults; only one girl living in Fjordvik wanted less contact with adults. These findings correspond fairly well with results of a study conducted in a suburb of Stavanger. Among girls and among individuals of both genders living in single-parent households, a substantial *increase* in the wish for closer contact with adults was found in youths between the ages of 13 and 14 and 15 and 16 (Hauboff et al., 1988).

Taken together with research focusing on adolescents' norm orientation, preferences, standards, indications of to whom they would turn for advice or comfort, and so forth, the results from this study call into question stereotypes maintaining that adolescents in general live in a separate world—a teenage culture—detached from adult society (Anderson, 1982; Befring, 1972; Bø & Boyesen, 1984; Brittain, 1963; Henricson, 1973). The present study confirms that people of various ages and roles are rated as important by adolescents and that they feel a stronger emotional connection to adults and children, particularly to kin, than to peers. I also recognize, as did Blyth and his colleagues (1982), that frequency of contact does not necessarily relate to the level of importance, the quality, or the intimacy of interaction.

The implications of diverse networks for identity formation are not clear because I did not look at identity. Diversity should also be balanced against the effect of contact frequency. Both my and the American studies demonstrate that adolescents have much more frequent exchanges with their peer groups than with other groups, and also that friends are seen in more settings than any other age group (except parents and siblings). These are interactions and situations that undoubtedly expose the adolescents to relatively strong conformity pressure.

This high level of contact with peers may account for the differences that have been found among data on young people's social worlds collected by observation, questionnaires, and interviews: Studies employing direct observation (Montemajor & van Komen, 1980) tend to find adolescents associating mainly with peers, but those that ask adolescents to list significant others or use a "whom-to-turn-to" approach show a much more differentiated picture of the adolescents' social world. If literature reviews as a whole offer partly a blurred and partly a complex picture of this world, it might be because adolescents' perceptions of who is a significant contact are situational, as are the contacts' influences on the youths' self-concepts, attitudes, and behavior. In other words, network perceptions and effects depend—as phenomena in the psychosocial world always do—on the ecology surrounding the subjects: macrostructures, SES, ethnicity, nationality, and so forth.

So, from an ecological point of view, in order to construct the correct picture of adolescents' social landscape, researchers need a more comprehensive approach (Serafica & Blyth, 1985, p. 274). For example, researchers need simultaneous studies of whom youth rate as significant others, whom they turn to for advice, comfort, sharing feelings, exchanging goods, and so forth, and with whom they actually associate in their daily interactions in the various arenas in which they live their lives. Assessment of changes in their relationships with significant agents over time, both as a function of age and of contextual factors such as ecologically contrasting environments (Garbarino, Burston, Raber, Russell, & Crouter, 1978), is also needed.

Given that an individual's personal network contains rich potential for growth and well-being, it is also important to disentangle the links connecting aspects of the network with formation of the self, with attitudes, and with behavior. This chapter points to one possible approach to such research questions, also illustrating some connections to school-related behavior. These findings suggest that both demographic factors, like SES and neighborhood quality, and social network factors exert influence. Partialing out the demographics, the network factors in themselves appear to correlate quite highly with all three outcome indexes. In the regression analysis, total network size emerged as the most powerful single factor. Likewise, partial analyses (not all shown) indicate that the sizes of the network subgroups (i.e., the quantitative aspects of the networks), such as different age and[6] kin groups, zones, and so forth, all correlate significantly, but not equally strongly, with school variables. For example, the Pearson correlation coefficient between size of primary zone and school adaptation is .23, and the coefficient between size of tertiary zone and the same outcome variable is .45, when the two background variables are controlled. This tendency might confirm the importance, emphasized by so many scholars, of exposing children to an array of significant others representing heterogeneous roles, ages, occupations, lifestyles, and so forth, because such encounters stimulate identity and nourish development (Brim, 1965; Bronfenbrenner, 1979; Coser, 1982).

Blyth and his team underscored the positive connections between qualitative network features and drug-related indicators. With this point as background, it might seem as remarkable that in the present study the more qualitative aspects of the networks—multiplexity, frequency, zone, and overlap—correlate *negatively* with the school variables. This relationship might mean that a personal network distinguished by a (too) high degree of "strandedness", closure, density, intimacy, and contact frequency is a less fertile seedbed for personal growth than a more open, unstranded, and heterogeneous network. If this is a correct interpretation, it confirms Granovetter's (1973) theory of "the strength of weak ties." I hypothesize, however, that further analyses will indicate that both types of networks, both strong and weak ties, are needed to stimulate growth. Perhaps sparse, uniplex relations have the strongest potential for the development of instrumental-cognitive skills, whereas dense, multiplex relations have the strongest potential for the development of emotional-expressive social skills.

When focusing on the relationship between social networks on the one side and behavior and personality on the other, one is confronted with the problem of causality. With the exception of the two background variables, the influences between network and behavior are probably reciprocal. Thus, being well-adjusted to school standards and in addition a high achiever in school might well develop sociability, friendship, and popularity and produce a big network as a result, which in turn stimulates growth.

More research is needed before conclusions can be reached on these questions. I believe that the network interview technique used in the present study has proved to be a promising way of getting a better, bird's-eye perspective of adolescents' social landscape, of tracing the links along which influences flow between individuals and their significant network members, and also of unraveling the substance of these influences.

ACKNOWLEDGMENT

Acknowledgements are expressed to Dale Blyth and Moncrieff Cochran, Cornell University, Ithaca, New York, for sharing their considerable competence in network research. Appreciation is also conveyed to the Norwegian Ministry of Cultural and Scientific Affairs, the Norwegian Ministry of Consumer Affairs and Government Administration, the Norwegian Research Council for Science and Humanities, and Högskolesenteret i Rogland for their support of this research.

NOTES

1.   The study presented in this chapter is part of a more comprehensive project, the main focus of which is to trace the possible links between aspects of young people's social networks and selected behavioral variables such as self-reported attitudes, crime, alcohol consumption, school achievement, and teacher-reported social behavior. The data from this section are still under analysis (Cochran & Bø, 1988).

2.   For several reasons, the Stavanger sample was limited to boys: First, the pilot study had shown very little variation in the girls' antisocial behavior as reported by the girls

themselves and their teachers. Second, financial limitations restricted the overall size of the sample. The arguments for including some data from the pilot study here are based on the following: (1) The approach was the same as for the main study, except for some insignificant changes in the layout of the interview form. (2) The study was carried out without any difficulties. (3) The study offered the opportunity to make comparisons between Fjordvik and Stavanger. (4) The pilot study also includes girls, and the main study does not.

3. Of the total number of students in the classes (90 in Fjordvik and 97 in Stavanger), 8 in the pilot study and 5 in the main study did not join in—some because of absenteeism (4 and 1, respectively) and some because of refusal, either their own (2 and 3) or their parents' (2 and 1). Data from the school protocols suggest that the 5 decliners in the Stavanger study were slight underachievers. Otherwise, no information (grades and teachers' ratings) indicated that the attrition groups deviated from the two achieved samples.

4. In the prepilot studies, the first item in the definition (on the significance of the person) was omitted—partly out of curiosity about the possible maximum number of acquaintances with whom young people in their mid-teens had some kind of interaction.

5. The combination of father's work prestige and educational level was chosen because of high intercorrelation and because this combination appeared to exceed other SES combinations in predictive power (when tested in a correlation matrix). Of the 92 Stavanger boys, 9 lived in single-mother families. In these cases, mother's SES was used. Thus, the factor is called family's SES.

6. New, promising approaches to the study of relationships between a broader ecological context and adolescents' development and contranormative attitudes have been undertaken in Berlin, directed by Silbereisen. These studies (to a certain degree inspired by Elder's 1974 study of the Great Depression) include macrostructures, SES variables, leisure settings, and more in their analytic models (Silbereisen, Noack, & Eyferth, 1986; Walper & Silbereisen, 1987).

REFERENCES

Andersson, B.-E. (1982). *Generation efter generation. Om tonarskultur, ungdomsrevolt och generationmotsatningar*. [Generation after generation. On teenage culture, youth rebellion and generational conflict.] Malmo: Liber Forlag.

Befring, E. (1972). *Ungdom i et bysamfunn. En sosialpeddogogisk studie av Oslo-ungdom*. [Adolescents in an urban society. A social pedagogical study of Oslo youth]. Oslo: Universitetsforlaget.

Blyth, D. A. (1982). Mapping the social world of adolescents: Issues, techniques, and problems. In F. C. Serafica (Ed.), *Social-cognitive development in context* (pp. 240–272). New York: Guildford Press.

Blyth, D. A., Hill, J. P., & Thiel, K. P. (1982). Early adolescents' significant others: Grade and gender differences in perceived relationships with familial and nonfamilial adults and young people. *Journal of Youth and Adolescence, 11*, 425–450.

Blyth, D., Durant, D., & Moosbrugger, L. (1985). *Perceived intimacy in the social relationships of drug and non-drug-using adolescents*. Paper presented at the Society for Research in Child Development Biennial Meeting, Toronto.

Blyth, D., & Traeger, C. (1985). *The impact of quality, frequency of perceived other relationships on early adolescents' self-esteem.* Paper presented at Social Connections from Crib to College, City College of New York.

Bø, I., & Boyesen, M. (1984). *Pa jakt etter "ungdomskulturen." En sosialpssykologisk studie av holdninger og normoppfatninger hos 15-aringer i en fjordkommune pa Vestlandet* [Searching for the "Youth Culture." A social psychological study on attitudes and norm perceptions among 15-year-olds in a Western Norwegian fjord township]. Arbeidspapiere [Working Papers]. Stavanger: Rogalund University Center no. 10.

Brim, O. G., Jr. (1965). Adolescent personality as self-other systems. *Journal of Marriage and the Family, 27*, 156–162.

Brittain, C. V. (1963). Adolescent choices and parent-peer–cross-pressures. *American Sociological Review, 28*, 358–391.

Bronfenbrenner, U. (1973). *Two worlds of childhood: US and U.S.S.R.* New York: Pocket Books.

Bronfenbrenner, U. (1974). Developmental research and public policy. In J. M. Romanyshyn (Ed.), *Social science and social welfare* (pp. 159–182). New York: Council on Social Work and Education.

Bronfenbrenner, U. (1977). Toward an experimental ecology of human development. *American Psychologist, 32*, 513–531.

Bronfenbrenner, U. (1979). *The ecology of human development. Experiments by nature and design.* Cambridge: Harvard University Press.

Bronfenbrenner, U. (1980). On making human beings human. *Character, 2*, 1–7.

Coates, D. L. (1985): Relationship between self-concept measures and social network characteristics for black adolescents. *Journal of Early Adolescence, 5*(3), 267–283.

Cochran, M., & Bø, I. (1989) The social networks, family involvement, and pro- and antisocial behavior of adolescent males in Norway. *Journal of Youth and Adolescence, 4*, 377–398.

Cochran, M., & Brassard, J. A. (1979). Child development and personal social networks. *Child Development, 50*, 601–616.

Cochran, M., Gannarson, L., Gräbe, S., & Lewis, J. (1984). *The social support networks of mothers with young children: A cross-national comparison.* Research Bulletin 25, Department of Education Research, University of Gothenburg.

Coleman, J. S. (1974). *Youth: Transitions to adulthood.* Chicago: University of Chicago Press.

Condry, J. C., & Siman, B. (1974). Characteristics of peer- and adult-oriented children. *Journal of Marriage and the Family, 65*, 543–554.

Cooper, C. R., & Ayers-Lopez, S. (1985). Family and peer systems in early adolescence: New models of the role of relationships in development. *Journal of Early Adolescence, 5*(1), 9–21.

Coser, R. L. (1975). The complexity of roles as seedbed of individual autonomy. In L. Coser (Ed.), *The idea of social structure: Essays in honor of Robert Merton* (pp. 237–263). New York: Harcourt Brace Janovich.

Elder, G. H., Jr. (1974). *Children of the great depression.* Chicago: University of Chicago Press.

Epstein, J. L. (1983). Examining theories of adolescent friendships. In J. L. Epstein & N.

L. Karweit (Eds.), *Friends in school: Patterns of selection and influence in secondary schools* (pp. 39–62). New York: Academic Press.

Erikson, E. H. (1968). *Identity: Youth and crisis*. New York: Norton.

Feiring, C., & Lewis, M. (1981). *The social networks of three year old children*. Paper presented at the Society for Research in Child Development, Boston.

Fischer, C. S., Jackson, R. M., Stueve, C. A., Gerson, K., Jones, L. M., & Baldassare, M. (1977). *Networks and places. Social relations in the urban setting*. New York: Free Press.

Fischer, J. L., Sollie, D. L., & Morrow, K. B. (1986). Social networks in male and female adolescents. *Journal of Adolescent Research, 6*(1), 1–14.

Foot, H. C., Chapman, A. J., & Smith, J. R. (Eds.). (1980). *Friendships and social relations in children*. New York: Wiley.

Foster-Clark, F. S., & Blyth, D. (1987). *Predicting adolescents' drug use: The role of personal and social network characteristics*. Paper presented at the Biennial Meeting of the Society for Research in Child Development, Baltimore.

Galbo, J. J. (1983). Adolescents' perceptions of significant adults. *Adolescence, 70*, 417–427.

Galbo, J. J. (1984). Adolescents' perceptions of significant adults: A review of the literature. *Adolescence, 76*, 951–970.

Galbo, J. J. (1986). Adolescents' perceptions of significant adults: Implications for the family, the school, and youth serving agencies. *Children and Youth Service Review, 8*, 37–51.

Garbarino, J., Burston, N., Raber, S., Russell, R., & Crouter, A. (1978). The social maps of children approaching adolescence: Studying the ecology of youth development. *Journal of Youth and Adolescence, 7*, 417–418.

Garbarino, J., & Associates (1985). *Adolescent development: An ecological perspective*. Columbus: Merrill.

Gardsjord, Å. (1972). *Ungdom og sosial naerket. Hovedoppgave i sykologi* [Adolescents and social proximity]. Master's thesis, University of Oslo, Norway. (Klausul).

Granovetter, M. S. (1973). The strength of weak ties. *American Journal of Sociology, 78*, 1360–1380.

Gunnarsson, L. (1985). Sociala natverk, familiestod och utvecking. [Social networks, family support and development. In I. Bø (Ed.), *Barn i miljo. Oppvekst i en utviklingsokologisk sammenheng* [Children in their environment. Childrearing in a human ecological context] (pp. 110–133). Oslo: Cappelen.

Handlin, O., & Handlin, M. F. (1971). *Facing life: Youth and the family in American history*. Boston: Little, Brown.

Hauboff, A. L., et al. (1988). *Ungdoms behov for voksenkontakt. Kandidatoppgave* [Adolescents' need for adult contact]. Stavanger: Hogskolesenteret i Rogaland.

Henricson, M. (1973). *Tonaringar och normer. En undersokning av tonoringars normklimat* [Teenagers and norms. A study of teenagers' norm structure]. SO-report, April. Stockholm: Utbildningsforlaget.

Klagholz, D. D. (1987). *Adolescent social networks and social understanding*. Paper presented at the Biennial Meeting of the Society for Research in Child Development, Baltimore.

Magnussen, F. (1983). *Om a bli voksen* [On becoming an adult]. Oslo: Universitetesforlaget.

Mead, G. H. (1952). *Mind, self and society from the standpoint of a social behaviorist.* Chicago: University of Chicago Press.

Montemayor, R., & van Komen, R. (1980). Age segregation of adolescents in and out of school. *Journal of Youth and Adolescence, 9,* 371–381.

Rubin, Z. (1980). *Children's friendships.* Cambridge: Harvard University Press.

Serafica, F. C., & Blyth, D. (1985). Continuities and changes in the study of friendship and peer group during early adolescence. *Journal of Early Adolescence, 5*(3), 267– 283.

Silbereisen, R. K., Noack, P., & Eyferth, K. (1986). Place for development: Adolescents, leisure settings, and developmental tasks. In R. K. Silbereisen, K. Eyferth, & G. Rudinger (Eds.), *Development as action in context* (pp. 87–107). Berlin: Springer-Verlag.

Sherif, M., & Sherif, C. (1964). *Reference groups: Exploration into conformity and deviance of adolescents.* New York: Harper & Row.

Tietjen, A. M. (1982). The social networks of preadolescent children in Sweden. *International Journal of Behavioral Development, 5,* 111–130. North-Holland Publishing.

Tiller, P. O. (1980). *Barns: "sosiale landskap." Delrapport fra prosjektet "Sosial endring og oppveksmiljo"* [Children's "social landscape." Preliminary report from the project "Social Change and Growing-up Conditions"]. INAS report 80:1. Oslo: Institut for anvendt socialivintenskapelig forskning [Institute for Applied Social Research].

Vondra, J., & Garbarino, J. (1985). *Social influences on adolescent behavioral problems.* Paper prepared for Social Connections from Crib to College: Studies of the Social Networks of Children, Adolescents, and College Students, City College of New York.

Walper, S. U., & Silbereisen, R. K. (1987). *Economic loss, strained family relationships and adolescents' contranormative attitudes.* Paper presented at the Biennial Meeting of the Society for Research in Child Development, Baltimore.

6

Social Support during Adolescence: Methodological and Theoretical Considerations

Ana Mari Cauce, Craig Mason, Nancy Gonzales,
Yumi Hiraga, and Gloria Liu

Although there is little support for the once popular notion that adolescence is inevitably characterized by extreme turmoil or "Sturm und Drang," it is still considered to be a pivotal developmental period (Elliot & Feldman, 1990). Research indicates that life stress steadily increases throughout childhood and into early adolescence (Coddington, 1972a, 1972b). Adolescence is also marked by an increase in negative emotions, probably a result of hormonal changes (Brooks-Gunn & Reiter, 1990). Rates of suicide, depression, conduct disorders, eating disorders, and substance use also increase during this period, making it a time of heightened risk (Adams & Gullotta, 1989). Yet, although some adolescents experience much uncertainty and unhappiness, others easily navigate through this normative life transition and remain happy and confident about themselves and their abilities. Part of what distinguishes the first group from the second may be the second group's sense of involvement in a stable set of relationships that form a safety net of support, love, and caring.

Over the last decade, few areas of research have appeared as promising as that on social support and social support networks. Hundreds of studies conducted with adults suggest that social support enhances both physical and psychological well-being and acts as a buffer against the negative effects of life stress. In contrast, research is only now beginning to address whether supportive relationships with parents, friends, teachers, grandparents, and important others affect childrens' and adolescents' social and emotional development.

Problems of definition and measurement have made it especially difficult to conduct this type of research. Thus, we begin this chapter with a selective review of the social support literature as it relates to the assessment and conceptualization of support. This review reflects the fact that most of the relevant research has been conducted with adult populations, but we cite studies conducted with child or adolescent populations whenever doing so is relevant and possible. Then we draw upon data collected as part of a larger study to examine the relationship and adjustment correlates of social support during adolescence. We hope that this examination will help illuminate what social support measures measure.

1. CRITICAL DIMENSIONS IN SOCIAL SUPPORT ASSESSMENT

1.1. Distinctions between Types of Support

The social support construct is multidimensional, and it has been conceptualized and assessed in many ways. Distinctions between the key conceptual and assessment approaches were identified by Barrera (1986) in a typology that has become widely accepted. Drawing upon his typology, we distinguish between three broad categories of support measures: those based upon a *social network* framework that gauges social connections, those that assess *received* or *enacted support,* and those that assess *perceived support.*

Social Networks and Connections. The social network literature has a long and rich history in anthropology and sociology. Social network analysis, which does not rest on the assumption that networks are supportive, has been used to study phenomena ranging from attendance at working parties in Tanzania to the behavior of married couples in Britain (Barnes, 1972; Mitchell, 1969). A true social network approach analyzes the arrangement of relationships among a network's members. These relationships can be viewed as separate strands that form a fabric or mesh. In a personal social network, an individual is the anchor point from which strands emanate to all other members. The structural characteristics of networks most frequently measured are size and density. Size indicates the number of persons in the network and density indicates how tightly the mesh is interwoven.

Anthropologists and sociologists have typically been less concerned with size and more concerned with density. Persons in dense networks are more likely to have stable and highly committed opinions and attitudes (Lauman, 1973); dense networks encapsulate individuals within groups that may provide them support but may also prevent them from making new connections and isolate them from other channels of information (Granovetter, 1973; Horwitz, 1977; Wolf, 1966). Although there is no "social network theory" (Mitchell, 1969), social network analysis has suggested that neither size nor density is necessarily related to social support. When an attempt is made to link such measures to psychological adjustment, researchers typically find that high density can either help or hurt (Hirsch, 1980; Vaux & Harrison, 1985). After reviewing the social network literature, Cauce (1986) suggested that the best indicator of whether a social network is supportive is the degree to which it includes reciprocal, intense, and multidimensional relationships (see Mitchell [1969] for a full definition of these terms). In an examination of the friendship networks of African American adolescents, she found that a measure of perceived support from friends was moderately correlated ($r = .42$) with the number of reciprocated best friendships, which are generally considered intense and multidimensional. However, the type of network assessment used in that study was only made possible by use of sociometric techniques and by limiting the focus to classroom friendship networks. The methodology is not adaptable to the study of larger social networks.

The more typical studies that cast themselves in the social network rubric (see Feiring and Lewis [1989] and Furman and Buhrmester [1985, 1992] for examples) have gauged support obtained from a broader range of relationship categories. Still, they only assessed a relatively small number of relationship categories. Some justification does exist for assessing a limited portion of a social network. House and Kahn (1985) noted that to assess social support, one need only examine a relatively small set of relationships (5 to 10). When social networks are conceptualized as concentric circles surrounding an individual, those in the inner circle can be seen as providing the individual with the most support (Antonucci, 1986; Levitt, 1991).

Most so-called social network studies of social support have limited themselves to an assessment of those social network providers closest to a focal individual and have focused on egocentric rather than sociocentric networks (Klovdahl, 1985). In fact, although some noteworthy exceptions exist, virtually all social network measures that social support researchers have used with children or adolescents diverge from measures derived using traditional social network analysis in three additional ways: (1) they focus almost exclusively on the social support provided to the anchor individual rather than on other types of exchange or on support provided by the anchor individual to network members, (2) they generally ignore relationships between one network member and another that do not involve the anchor person, and (3) they rely almost exclusively on information provided by the anchor individual and rarely obtain additional information from another network member or an outside observer.

Because of these dramatic differences between traditional social network methods and those used by most social support researchers, we believe it would be preferable to consistently refer to these quasi-network support measures as measures of personal social support networks. It is also worth noting that we could find no consistent and appreciable difference between most of the social network measures used by social support researchers and the measures most typically called perceived support measures.

Received or Enacted Support. Measures that focus on received or enacted support assess the frequency of the supportive transactions an individual has engaged in, usually as the recipient. For example, a scale assessing received support might include questions like this item from the Social Relations Questionnaire (Blyth, Hill, & Thiel, 1982): "During the past month, which of these people (previously listed) actually gave you some important advice?"

At first glance, such questions appear to provide a relatively straightforward and objective measure of the social support construct. However, a closer examination reveals two key problems with these measures. First, received support is generally confounded with the need for support (Coyne, Ellard, & Smith, 1990). People are most apt to give support when they think others are stressed or distressed and in need of support. In fact, received support has often been related positively to stress and related negatively to desirable outcomes (Barrera, 1981; Belle, 1982). "Reserve" buffering effects have also been noted (Husiani, Neff, Newbrough, & Moore, 1982).

The second problem with received or enacted support measures is their assumption that social support is some objective entity that is given to others in specific and observable transactions (Albrecht & Adelman, 1987). Such transactions would also, presumably, be verifiable. Unfortunately, the research evidence does not support these benign assumptions. The providers and receivers involved in presumably the same transactions differ substantially as to the quantity or quality of support given or gotten (Antonucci & Israel, 1986; Dunkel-Schetter & Bennett, 1990; Kessler, Price, & Wortman, 1985). As the anthropologist Jacobson (1987) stated, the same set of activities can be seen as "mothering" or "smothering." This formulation led him to regard social support as a "symbolic activity" (cf. Albrect & Adelman, 1987). He further noted that a "cognitive revolution" was taking place in research on social support.

Perceived Support.   Most researchers now acknowledge that individuals' assessments of their social support are based on their interpretation of supportive transactions and the personal meanings they attach to them. This fact is explicitly acknowledged in the rationales underlying perceived support measures, which generally ask individuals to assess who or how much support they think would be available to them if needed. They might also be asked to rate whether they are satisfied with the available support.

Individuals are assumed to make their assessments of support in part on the basis of how much support they have received from others in the recent past. However, in contrast to conceptualizations of received support, it is typically believed that assessments of perceived support are also influenced by more long-standing personality traits, concurrent stresses, and coping abilities (see Heller and Swindle [1983] for a fuller discussion).

Irwin and Barbara Sarason, along with their colleagues, pursued an intriguing line of research that explored the antecedents of perceived support. Drawing from Bowlby's attachment theory (Bretherton, 1992), they argued that, at least by early adulthood, people are predisposed to interpret potentially supportive transactions in specific ways. They suggested that perceptions of support have the stability of a personality characteristic, which they called a sense of social support or a sense of acceptance (Sarason, Pierce, & Sarason, 1990). These researchers conducted a persuasive series of studies, albeit mostly with college student samples, to bolster their arguments (see Sarason, Sarason, and Pierce [1990] for an overview).

Our own conceptualization of perceived support is in substantial agreement with this perspective. Like the Sarasons and their colleagues, we believe that, over the course of development, a person's past history of help-seeking and help-receipt increasingly comes to influence his or her assessment of whether help will be forthcoming in the future. We also think that people who feel confident that others can be counted on (i.e., those "secure" in their attachments) will be less distressed and behave more competently. But we are not entirely convinced that the attachment construct, as reified in the "strange situation,"[1] is the only or best theoretical anchor for these facts. We also suspect that cultural and contextual factors play a more central role in determining the meaning and form of help-seeking behaviors than they are typically given in most attachment research.

Although it has not always been clear what perceived support is, research findings provide a strong practical rationale for using this type of measure. Studies with both children (Cotterell, 1992; Dubow & Ullman, 1989) and adults (Kessler & McLeod, 1985; Wethington & Kessler, 1986) have suggested that measures of perceived support are more potent predictors of adjustment than are measures of received support and simple network size, alone or in combination.

Distinctions within Support Types. Any of the three types of support measures can be further subdivided. The most common way in which this is done in adult studies is along functional lines. Cohen and Wills (1985) described the main functions of support networks as the provision of emotional support, informational support or advice, social companionship, and instrumental support or material aid. Other researchers have suggested different typologies of support (e.g., Furman & Buhrmester, 1985; House, 1981), but they also primarily identify the various functions or contents of supportive interactions.

These typologies have led to the development of different social support measures, each defining support in a slightly different manner. Nonetheless, there is evidence that such fine-grained distinctions among support functions add little to the sensitivity of measures for adult populations (cf. Sarason, Shearin, Pierce, & Sarason, 1987). Studies of children have also suggested that, when factor-analyzed, most descriptions of supportive behaviors load on a single factor (Berndt & Perry, 1986; Dubow & Ullman, 1989) or are so highly correlated that they can be combined into one scale (Furman & Buhrmester, 1992).

In research on children and adolescents, the critical distinction has been between sources or providers of support rather than between support functions (Cauce, Reid, Landesman, & Gonzales, 1990; Cauce & Srebnik, 1989). A sophisticated study conducted by Wolchik and colleagues (1989) suggested that children make distinctions among groups of providers in their personal social support networks that account for considerably more of the variance in their support than do distinctions among support functions. A study of first grade children also suggested that when the relationship between support and adjustment was examined, distinctions among support providers were most important (Cauce et al., 1990). In fact, when a pure functional model was used, no relationships between support and adjustment were found.

A series of studies conducted by Cauce and her colleagues has suggested that three provider "support systems" (see Cauce and Srebnik [1990] for a fuller discussion of this term) can be readily identified. Two of these, the family and friend systems, consist of informal support providers. The third is a formal system that consists largely of school employees for youthful samples. Various studies have suggested that these distinctions among support providers have implications for how support may relate to adjustment (Barrera & Chassin, 1993; Barrera & Garrison-Jones, 1992; Cauce, Ptacek, Mason, & Smith, 1992).

We believe that it is especially important to make distinctions among support providers during the adolescent years, when relationships are being redefined and renegotiated. One of the defining features of adolescence is the movement toward independence from parents and increasing reliance upon friends. Research examining developmental changes in social support networks consistently suggests that support from friends increases dramatically in the period from middle childhood to adolescence; support from teachers decreases and support from parents remains somewhat more stable (Cauce et al., 1990; Furman & Buhrmester, 1992).

It is also worth noting that some measures represent a truly global approach, in which no distinctions whatsoever are made among providers or functions. Perhaps the best example of this is support *satisfaction* as measured by the widely used Social Support Questionnaire (Sarason, Sarason, & Shearin, 1986). This global measure, which cuts across providers and functions, has been found to be correlated with retrospective accounts of family relationships and a host of personality variables and adjustment indexes in college students.

1.2. Summary

Different strategies have been used in the assessment of social support. However, it is often difficult to match the purported strategy (or its theoretical underpinnings) to the actual assessment device. Social network and received support measures are as apt to be based on an individual's perception of support as are perceived support measures. Measures that purport to assess social networks sometimes assess dyadic relationships. Theory-based distinctions between support functions collapse under close scrutiny. One way to get a handle on the support construct is to examine its correlates; when theory fails to clarify, it's worth giving crass empiricism a try.

2. CORRELATES OF PERCEIVED SUPPORT DURING ADOLESCENCE

This section is organized around two basic questions: How is perceived support related to other measures of relationship quality? And how is perceived support related to various indexes of psychological adjustment and competence? The data used to examine these questions were drawn from a larger prospective study of ecological and family correlates of adolescent adjustment.

2.1. Study Participants and Procedures

Participants in the study were 144 African American adolescents (91 female, 53 male) and at least one primary caregiver per adolescent. All the adolescents were in the seventh or eighth grade, and their average age was about 13.5 years. Income level varied considerably among the families. A few more than 40 percent were lower-income families, but close to 20 percent were solidly middle-class or above. Most of the mothers had completed high school, and 11 percent had completed college. About half of the adolescents were living in homes headed by single women.

In most cases, the adolescents and caregivers were interviewed in their homes and completed questionnaires there, although occasionally they elected to complete them in our laboratory. The measures we examine here fall into two main categories: those related to relationships and those related to psychological outcomes.

2.2. Relationship Measures

Perceived Social Support. This construct was measured using the Social Support Rating Scale-Revised (SSRS-R; Cauce et al., 1992), which was designed to measure perceived support among adolescents. The SSRS-R includes questions about emotional support and help and guidance. It yields four key subscales: family support, friend support, school support, and support satisfaction. A series of studies conducted with varied adolescent populations has suggested that the scale is a highly reliable and valid measure of support.[2] Given the importance that has been attributed to the African American extended family, a measure of extended family support consisting of support from grandparents, aunts or uncles, and cousins was also constructed. For purposes of comparison, we also constructed single-provider subscales for mother, best friend, teacher, and grandparent.

Network Orientation. A scale measuring help seeking was constructed from answers to two items. The first asked, "In general, when the occasion arises, are you the type of person who turns to others for caring and emotional support?" The same question was also asked in terms of help and guidance and answers.

Attachment.   The Inventory of Parent and Peer Attachment (IPPA; Armsden & Greenberg, 1987), which is based on the tenets of attachment theory, assesses self-reported attachment as it is manifested during adolescence. The IPPA yields separate subscales for attachment to mother, father, and peers. High scores indicate more trust and communication in a relationship and less alienation.

Parental Warmth and Restrictiveness.   The Child-Rearing Practices Report (CRPR; Block, 1965) was administered to mothers to assess their perceived levels of warmth and restrictiveness. These two dimensions of parenting style were derived from a factor-analytic study conducted by Rickel and Biasatti (1982). A sample item from the warmth scale is "My child and I have warm, intimate times together." An item indicating restrictiveness is "I expect a great deal of my child." It is worth noting that the restrictiveness scale does not simply represent appropriate levels of parental monitoring, but rather suggests that the parents are overly controlling, as does the item "I instruct my child not to get dirty when s/he is playing."

Family Cohesion.   The family cohesion subscale of the Family Environment Scale, Short Form (FES; Moos & Moos, 1981) was completed by adolescents. This scale assesses the degree of family closeness and the perceived support that family members give to each other.

2.3. Adjustment Indexes

Adolescents' perceptions of their own competence were assessed via the global self-worth, social competence, school competence, and romantic competence subscales of the Self-Perception Profile for Adolescents (PSCS; Harter, 1989). The PSCS is a widely used questionnaire that was specifically constructed to avoid a socially desirable response set. Depression was gauged via the Child Depression Inventory (Kovacs, 1981), one of the most widely used inventories for this purpose. In total, these measures examine a relatively broad cross section of areas of psychological adjustment and competence.

2.4. Analytic Strategy

After presenting support profiles, we report analyses consisting of simple correlations evaluated with two-tailed significance tests. First, we examine support as defined through the "support system" model (Caplan, 1974; Cauce & Srebnik, 1990). In the second set of analyses, a single person within each system, such as an adolescent's mother or best friend, was used to represent a key individual within that system. This approach yields subscales more similar to those found in measures that focus on specific dyadic relationships, such as My Family and Friends (Reid, Landesman, Treder, & Jaccard, 1989) and the Network Relationships Inventory (Furman & Buhrmester, 1992). Finally, satisfaction with support is examined.

2.5. Perceived Support Profiles

Figure 1 presents the means for support ratings separately by gender. As this figure indicates, the ratings were highest for support from mothers, followed by best friends, fathers, regular friends (e.g., peers), and grandparents. At the lower end of the spectrum were classmates and adult school personnel. This pattern of results is remarkably similar to that found for adolescents in the two studies using the Networks of Relationships Inventory, a much longer measure. However, the general lack of gender differences, particularly in terms of best friend support, contrasts with the results of those studies.

However, they were conducted with very homogeneous samples of white, middle-class youth predominantly in two-parent families; other studies of peer relationships among African American youth have also failed to yield gender differences in friendships (Cauce, 1986; Hirsch & Dubois, 1992). This pattern points out the need to replicate findings across diverse samples.

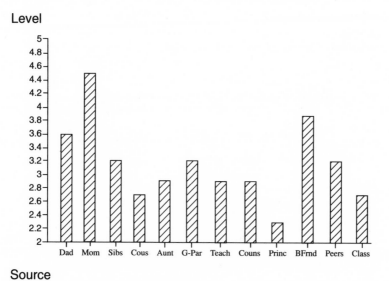

Figure 1. Mean Level of Social Support.

2.6. Perceived Support and Relationship Qualities

As noted previously, Sarason and colleagues (1987) suggested that perceived support "may be a counterpart in adult life to the attachment experience in childhood described by Bowlby." More recently, Cotterell (1992) suggested the same may be the case during adolescence. However, the results of his investigation with Australian youth yielded mixed results. Corresponding indexes of attachment and support were uniformly correlated among females, but not among males. Given the inconclusiveness of these findings, we reexamined the issue here. We also examined the correlations between social support and other variables that an attachment perspective would suggest it should be related to. These include maternal warmth and restrictiveness, family cohesion, and an adolescent's network orientation.

If perceived support in adolescence is a manifestation of attachment, or functions like it, we would expect perceived support to be highly correlated with attachment measures, with maternal reports of warmth, and with family cohesion. We would also expect those with higher levels of perceived support to be more willing to turn to others for help if it were needed. But we would expect support to be negatively related to maternal restrictiveness or "overcontrol."

Table 1 reports the results of these analyses. For the sake of simplicity, genders were combined; an examination of the results for males and females separately suggested that relationships between support and attachment within each gender were similar, and formal tests yielded no significant differences. As Table 1 indicates, in keeping with an attachment perspective on support, corresponding measures of support and attachment, such as mother attachment and perceived mother support, were at least moderately correlated. More modest correlations

Table 1. Correlations between Perceived Support and Relationship Indexes

	Warmth	Restrictiveness	Mother	Father	Peer	Family Cohesion	Turns to
Family	−.07	−.06	.35	.50	.18	.22	.28
Friend	−.01	.02	.18	−.02	.50	.11	.25
School	−.06	.16	.19	.15	.19	.08	.22
Extended	−.09	.22	.23	.22	.19	.09	.16
Mother	−.02	−.14	.44	.19	.27	.26	.21
Best friend	−.01	−.04	.25	.06	.57	.12	.26
Teacher	.01	.09	.22	.19	.13	.10	.23
Grandparent	−.06	.20	.05	.17	.15	.07	.04
Satisfaction	−.08	−.02	.42	.28	.49	.38	.43

also existed between measures that had no direct correspondence. For example, both general friend support and best friend support were related to mother attachment. This finding is also consistent with an attachment perspective, since the first attachment relationship, usually with the mother, is seen as providing a foundation for subsequent attachments. The mother attachment and friend attachment subscales, as measured by the IPPA, are also modestly to moderately intercorrelated.

Support satisfaction was also found to be consistently and moderately correlated with all indexes of attachment. The sense of comfort people feel with the amount of support available to them, which is what satisfaction indicates, may be the most direct indicator of general security within relationships. Also consistent with an attachment perspective are the positive correlations between most support indexes and the "turns to" network orientation index. This sense of knowing that help is available when needed and that one can access such support may, in fact, lead to more autonomous coping and problem solving (Holler & Hurrelmann, 1990).

Contrary to expectations, maternal self-reports of warmth and restrictiveness were generally unrelated to support. This finding stands in contrast to results with college students indicating that their levels of perceived support were related to recollections of their mothers' parenting styles (Sarason, Shearin, Pierce, & Sarason, 1987). However, the measure of parenting used here was completed by the mothers, not the adolescents. When the adolescents themselves reported on their families' cohesion, a construct similar to warmth, we did find the variable to be positively correlated with perceived support.

A more unexpected result was the mildly positive association between maternal restrictiveness and extended family/grandparent support. This association suggests that adolescents in overly restrictive homes may compensate by depending upon or turning to kin. This finding is worthy of further investigation, given the important role that extended family members play in African American families (Wilson, 1989).

2.7. Perceived Support and Adjustment

It is well established that perceived social support is positively related to wellbeing among adults. However, the question is far from resolved for children and adolescents, partly because few studies have been conducted, and partly because their results have been less than straightforward. A review of research on children by Wolchik and colleagues (1989) suggested that support from family members and other adults was usually positively related to adjustment. In contrast, support from peers was often unrelated or negatively related to indexes of adjustment.

Results from several studies by Cauce and her colleagues suggest an even more complicated picture of peer support. She has suggested that whereas friend support will generally be negatively related to distress, it will only be positively related to specific areas of adjustment or competence if a youth's peer group values the behaviors entailed (cf. Cauce, 1986). For example, within some peer subcultures, doing well in school is not viewed positively (cf. Fordham & Ogbu, 1986). So, for members of that subculture or social niche, Cauce would predict that peer support would be negatively related to school competence. Presenting a similar argument, Cotterell (1992) suggested that peer support will influence academic adjustment only "under those circumstances where adolescent psychological well-being is associated with the level of attachment to friends, rather than to parents" (p. 39).

Attachment theory suggests that children who are securely attached more readily engage in exploratory behavior (Ainsworth, 1982), which, by adolescence, we expect to translate into greater self-confidence and competence. So, if perceived support is like attachment, it should be negatively related to distress and positively related to perceived competence. But attachment theory would not lead us to make specific predictions about differential relationships between attachments to different types of figures (e.g., family vs. friends) and adjustment.

Table 2 presents the results of our correlational analyses. Once again, results are presented together for the two genders, since there were no significant differences between them. These findings do not lend themselves to a parsimonious summary. The general pattern of relationships between family (or maternal) support and adjustment was not as strong or pervasive as expected. Nonetheless, both measures were correlated, in the expected direction, with depression and school competence, two important adjustment indexes for this age group.

Correlates of school and extended family support were even more circum-

Table 2.   Correlations between Perceived Support and Adjustment Indexes

			Competence			Problem
	Depression	*Self-Worth*	*Social*	*School*	*Romantic*	*Behavior*
Family	−.18	.09	.05	.18	.17	.13
Friend	−.25	.26	.40	.30	.37	.11
School	−.10	.08	.13	.12	.24	.05
Extended	−.08	.17	.25	.13	.34	.06
Mother	−.20	.17	.10	.21	.13	.01
Best friend	−.26	.15	.31	.21	.34	.07
Teacher	−.16	.12	.08	.24	.21	−.05
Grandparent	−.05	.22	.23	.14	.24	.01
Satisfaction	−.46	.31	.22	.28	.22	−.06

scribed. Support from school personnel and from extended family members, rated both by the "system" and the dyadic measures, were related to romantic competence. This pattern suggests that it is when adolescents feel supported by those outside of the nuclear family that they are more confident about their attractiveness to potential romantic partners.

Support from extended family members was also related to more general social competence and to self-worth, underscoring the importance of kinship networks, at least for African American youth. Not surprisingly, support from teachers was related to school competence. However, this effect was diffused when the full school system was examined. No other relationships between school or extended family support and adjustment were found.

In contrast, both indexes of friend support were negatively related to distress and positively related to all areas of adjustment. Although this pattern contrasts with the findings reported in Wolchik et al.'s review, it is consistent with several studies that have focused exclusively on adolescents (Burke & Weir, 1978; Hirsch & Dubois, 1992; Newcomb & Bentler, 1988) and further confirms the important role of peers during this age.

The positive relationship between peer or best friend support and school competence is in keeping with Cotterell's hypothesis, since support from peers was generally more related to adjustment indexes than support from parents. To examine the role of peer group values as a determining factor in this relationship, we conducted a hierarchical regression analysis using preliminary data collected in the second year of the larger study. In this prospective analysis, school competence at Wave 2 served as the dependent variable. Wave 1 school competence was entered into the first step of the equation, followed by the adolescents' reports of their peer support and their assessments of whether their friends valued school. In the third step, the interaction between the two was entered. Results indicated that 45 percent of the variance in school competence was accounted for by the main effects of earlier school competence, peer group support, and peer group values. Nonetheless, even when these variables were controlled, there was a trend toward significance for the two-way interaction between peer support and peer group values ($F_{4, 108} = 3.20, p < .08$). In keeping with Cauce's hypothesis, the nature of this trend was that those adolescents who reported both high levels of peer support and friends who valued school also reported the highest levels of school competence. Those high in peer support who reported that their friends did not value school reported the lowest levels of school competence. Thus, it may be important to know more about the peer group culture of an adolescent, or a group of adolescents, before predicting how peer support will be related to value-laden indexes of adjustment.

Perhaps the most striking finding is the relatively strong and consistent correlation between adjustment and global support satisfaction. This relationship provides the strongest support for an attachment perspective. As mentioned previously, asking people to assess whether they think others would provide them with support if it were needed is very similar to assessing how secure they feel about their relationships.

2.8. Summary

This study had three interrelated purposes. The first was simply to confirm the importance of social support during adolescence. The second was to examine methodological issues related to the assessment of social support in the focal age group. The third was to explore the nature of social support during adolescence.

Results confirmed the importance of social support during adolescence. In general, relationships between perceived support and adjustment existed for this age group. Nonetheless, this relationship was sometimes quite weak, and it varied by the provider system examined. The relatively weak and inconsistent pattern of relationships between family support and adjustment calls into question previous findings suggesting that support from family members is more central to adjustment than support from peers (cf. Barrera & Garrison-Jones, 1992; Cauce et al., 1992). Further research is needed to clarify these discrepancies, which may be due to the different characteristics of the samples examined.

On the most practical level, no clear advantage emerged for either of the two scoring strategies compared; one of these was based on a support system model, the other, on a dyadic relationship model. We continue to prefer the system model, both because it better captures what was originally meant by social support (e.g., Caplan, 1974) and because multiple-item measures demonstrate more stability than single-item measures. For those who prefer to examine dyadic relationships, the SSRS-S scale format can be used. We would be most prone to examine dyads when studying family support. For example, we plan to examine whether adolescents perceive fathers who visit regularly but do not live with them as less supportive than live-in fathers.

However, it is important to note that one problem with examining a full dyadic relationship model is that it requires generating a relatively large number of correlations. For example, to examine the relationship between support and four indexes of adjustment, a dyadic model would require 36 correlations, as opposed to the 12 a systems model would require; thus, the dyadic analysis substantially increases the possibility of a Type II error. An alternative might be to examine the finer-grained dyadic model only if significant effects emerge at the systems level. Thus, if a relationship emerges between family support and depression, one would then examine the degree to which mother, father, or sibling support accounted for the effect. Although this is an extremely conservative strategy, we believe it makes the most sense unless there is a theoretical basis for expecting an effect to be relationship-specific.

The index that demonstrates the clearest advantage over the others is the measure of support satisfaction. This global assessment demonstrated the strongest and most consistent relationships with adjustment and competence. It would be tempting to simply use this index as a two-item measure of perceived support. But it is important to remember that these questions were asked after the adolescents had rated support from all other providers first. The fact that participants engaged in these ratings may have led them to a more informed assessment of their support satisfaction. We do not, at this time, recommend using satisfaction as a stand-alone indicator of perceived support.

3. THEORETICAL CONSIDERATIONS

On a theoretical level, the results presented here should prove encouraging to those who posit that perceived support represents an extension of early childhood attachment. Social support was originally conceptualized as a set of social resources that lay outside the person and were accessed through interindividual relationships. It was not viewed primarily as an intraindividual difference variable like attachment.[3] Yet the results obtained here, which are consistent with those summarized in Sarason, Sarason, and Pierce (1990), suggest that this is the case.

The similarity between social support and attachment may be in part an artifact of the way in which researchers typically measure support. By measuring support via an individual's perceptions, we ensure that we tap intraindividual factors. The methodology for assessing social resources in a less cognitively dependent manner exists (see Klovdahl [1985], Liebow [1989], and other articles in the journal *Social Networks*), but it is extremely time-consuming and largely ethnographic.

Reliance on an individual's perceptions as the basis for assessing support is not unique to perceived support measures. As mentioned previously, almost all studies of social support, regardless of whether they purport to measure social networks, received support, or perceived support, depend exclusively on one individual's perceptions of support. These perceptions appear to incorporate some systematic biases. For example, some sources of support are typically overlooked.

Nestmann and Niepel (1994) found that adults often fail to mention their children as members of their social networks. Nonetheless, most children, except for the very young, do provide their parents with at least some forms of support almost daily. There are many other providers whom people routinely overlook when asked to name their network members or to assess who would provide them with support. Many people, especially those who are upper middle class in status, routinely receive large amounts of tangible, and probably emotional, support from paid helpers such as secretaries, baby-sitters, maids, and house-keepers, but the recipients rarely mention such support. Their lives would proba-bly be much more stressful without this support, which is why they purchase it to begin with. Yet most people perceive that their support comes from "communal" rather than exchange-based relationships (Clark and Mills, cited in Coyne et al. [1990]).

The perceptual tendency to gloss over exchange-based relationships, or the precise nature of exchanges in any one relationship, ensures that self-report social support instruments essentially capture the degree to which an individual is involved in relationships believed to be characterized by acceptance, open com-munication, and love (Sarason et al., 1986). Self-reported attachment assesses the degree to which people characterize their relationships in terms of trust, open communication, and the absence of alienation. Thus, strong empirical associa-tions between the two measures should not be surprising, since they essentially "pull for" the same psychological construct. At this point, we believe it is largely a matter of personal preference whether one calls that construct perceived sup-port or self-reported attachment. The frameworks undergirding the two labels lead to remarkably similar predictions. An attachment framework suggests that a secure attachment should lead to healthy adaptation; a social support framework suggests that high levels of social support should lead to good coping. Both frameworks also suggest that this association should be especially strong when an individual is stressed or distressed. Attachment is prototypically assessed in the "strange situation" in which a toddler is stressed by a separation from mother; social support was originally conceptualized as serving to buffer the ill effects of life stress.

In sum, when it comes to adolescents' and young adults' perceptions of their close relationships, it seems that some core construct consistently emerges. No matter what conceptual framework structures the bow, or what methodological arrow is used, you hit the same bull's-eye.

In attempting to assess social resources, we may have instead stumbled upon a construct or mechanism underlying important developmental continuities in how people cognitively construct (or reconstruct) their social worlds. This is an excit-ing prospect. Perhaps this construct is best described as a working model that evolves from the attachment experience within a first meaningful relationship. It may also be a social or relationship script that is culturally grounded and de-veloped as young children learn to distinguish among different types of rela-tionships. Or it could be some combination of these or something altogether different. Myriad hypotheses are plausible. Longitudinal research drawing upon observational methodologies, ethnographic and qualitative techniques, and self-reports is clearly needed to clarify the nature of this construct across the life span.

So what do social support measures measure? We still don't know, but what-ever it is, it seems to be important.

NOTES

1.   In the "strange situation," a widely used test of attachment, a toddler is stressed by separation from his or her mother.

2.   Some of the data presented here come from the third SSRS-R validity study (Cauce et al., 1992). There are some minor differences between the correlations presented here and those in that study because slightly different methods were employed in coding. For the correlational analyses presented here, in all cases we coded the amount of support from a provider as zero if no such provider was reported; for example, if an adolescent had no sibling, he or she received a rating of zero for sibling support. In the other study, except for father support, we coded absent sources of support as missing data. Compelling arguments can be made for both approaches, but results suggest that the differences are relatively inconsequential when a support system approach is used.

3.   Attachment as operationally defined in the "strange situation" is clearly an inter-individual variable but, later in life, attachment is conceptualized in terms of "working models," an intraindividual construct.

REFERENCES

Adams, G., & Gullota, T. (1989). *Adolescent life experiences*. Belmont, CA: Wadsworth.

Ainsworth, M. D. S. (1982). Attachment: Retrospect and prospect. In C. M. Parkes & J. Stevenson-Hinde (Eds.), *The place of attachments in human behavior* (pp. 3–30). New York: Basic Books.

Albrecht, T. L., & Adelman, M. B. (1987). Communicating social support: A theoretical perspective. In T. L. Albrecht & M. B. Adelman (Eds.), *Communicating social support* (pp.18–38). Beverly Hills, CA: Sage.

Antonucci, T. C. (1986). Social support networks: A hierarchical mapping technique. *Generations* (Summer), 10–12.

Antonucci, T. C., & Israel, B. A. (1986). Veridicality of social support: A comparison of principal and network members' responses. *Journal of Consulting and Clinical Psychology, 54*, 432–437.

Armsden, G. C., & Greenburg, M. T. (1987). The Inventory of Parent and Peer Attachment: Individual differences and their relationship to psychological well-being in adolescence. *Journal of Youth and Adolescence, 18*, 427–454.

Barnes, J. A. (1972). *Social networks*. Reading, MA: Addison-Wesley.

Barrera, M., Jr. (1981). Social supports in the adjustment of pregnant adolescents: Assessment issues. In B. H. Gottlieb (Ed.), *Social networks and social support* (pp.69–96). Beverly Hills, CA: Sage.

Barrera, M., Jr. (1986). Distinctions between social support concepts, measures, and models. *American Journal of Community Psychology, 14*, 413–445.

Barrera, M., Jr., & Chassin, L. (1993). Effects of social support and conflict on adolescent children of alcoholic and nonalcoholic fathers. *Journal of Personality and Social Psychology, 64*, 602–612.

Barrera, M., Jr., & Garrison-Jones, C. (1992). Family and peer social support as specific correlates of adolescent depressive symptoms. *Journal of Abnormal Child Psychology, 20,* 1–16.

Belle, D. (1982). Social ties and social support. In D. Belle (Ed.), *Lives in stress: Women and depression* (pp. 133–144). Beverly Hills, CA: Sage.

Berndt, T. J., & Perry, T. B. (1986). Children's perceptions of friendships as supportive relationships. *Developmental Psychology, 22,* 640–648.

Block, J. H. (1965). *The childrearing practices report.* Berkeley, CA: Institute of Human Development, University of California.

Blyth, D. A., Hill, J. P., & Theil, K. S. (1982). Early adolescents' significant others: Grade and gender differences in perceived relationships with familial and non-familial adults and young people. *Journal of Youth and Adolescence, 11,* 425–450.

Bretherton, I. (1992). The origins of attachment theory: John Bowlby and Mary Ainsworth. *Developmental Psychology, 28,* 759–775.

Brooks-Gunn, J., & Reiter, E. O. (1990). The role of pubertal processes. In S. S. Feldman & G. R. Elliot (Eds.), *At the threshold: The developing adolescent* (pp.16–53). Cambridge, MA: Harvard University Press.

Burke, R. J., & Weir, T. (1978). Benefits to adolescents of informal helping relationships with their parents and peers. *Psychological Reports, 42,* 1175–1184.

Caplan, G. (1974). *Support systems and community mental health.* New York: Behavioral Publication.

Cauce, A. M. (1986). Social networks and social competence: Exploring the effects of early adolescent friendships. *American Journal of Community Psychology, 14,* 607–628.

Cauce, A. M., Ptacek, J. T., Mason, C., & Smith, R. E. (1992). *The Social Support Rating Scale-Revised: Three studies on development and validation.* University of Washington, Seattle.

Cauce, A. M., Reid, M., Landesman, S., & Gonzales, N. (1990). Social support in young children: Measurement, structure, and behavioral impact. In B. R. Sarason, I. G. Sarason, & G. R. Pierce (Eds.), *Social support: An interactional view* (pp. 64–95). New York: Wiley.

Cauce, A. M., & Srebnik, D. (1989). Peer social networks and social support: A focus for preventive efforts. In L. A. Bond & B. Compas (Eds.), *Primary prevention and promotion in the schools* (pp. 235–254). Newbury Park, CA: Sage.

Cauce, A. M., & Srebnik, D. S. (1990). Returning to social support systems: A morphological analysis of social networks. *American Journal of Community Psychology, 18,* 609–616.

Coddington, R. D. (1972a). The significance of life events as etiologic factors in the diseases of children: 1. *Journal of Psychosomatic Research, 16,* 7–18.

Coddington, R. D. (1972b). The significance of life events as etiologic factors in the diseases of children: 2. *Journal of Psychosomatic Research, 16,* 205–213.

Cohen, S., & Wills, T. A. (1985). Stress, social support, and the buffering hypothesis. *Psychological Bulletin, 98,* 310–357.

Cotterell, J. L. (1992). The relation of attachments and supports to adolescent well-being and school adjustment. *Journal of Adolescent Research, 7,* 28–42.

Coyne, J. C., Ellard, J. H., & Smith, D. A. F. (1990). Social support, interdependence, and the dilemmas of helping. In B. R. Sarason, I. G. Sarason, & G. R. Pierce (Eds.), *Social support: An interactional view* (pp. 129–149). New York: Wiley.

Dubow, E. F., & Ullman, D. G. (1989). Assessing social support in elementary school children: The survey of children's social support. *Journal of Child Clinical Psychology, 18,* 52–64.

Dunkel-Schetter, C., & Bennett, T. L. (1990). Differentiating the cognitive and behavioral aspects of social support. In B. R. Sarason, I. G. Sarason, & G. R. Pierce (Eds.), *Social support: An interactional view* (pp. 267–296). New York: Wiley.

Elliot, G. R., & Feldman, S. S. (1990). Capturing the adolescent experience. In S. S. Feldman & G. R. Elliot (Eds.), *At the threshold: The developing adolescent* (pp. 1–14). Cambridge, MA: Harvard University Press.

Feiring, L., & Lewis, M. (1989). The social networks of girls and boys from early through middle childhood. In D. Belle (Ed.), *Children's social networks and social supports* (pp. 119–150). New York: Wiley.

Fordham, S., & Ogbu, J. U. (1986). Black students' school success: Coping with the "burden of acting white." *Urban Review, 18,* 176–206.

Furman, W., & Buhrmester, D. (1985). Children's perceptions of the personal relationships in their social networks. *Developmental Psychology, 21,* 1014–1024.

Furman, W., & Buhrmester, D. (1992). Age and sex differences in perceptions of networks of personal relationships. *Child Development, 63,* 103–115.

Granovetter, M. S. (1973). The strength of weak ties. *American Journal of Sociology, 78,* 1360–1380.

Harter, S. (1989). *Manual for the Self-Perception Profile for Adolescents.* Denver: University of Denver.

Heller, K., & Swindle, R. W. (1983). Social networks, perceived support, and coping with stress. In R. D. Felner, L. A. Jason, J. Moritsugu, & S. Farber (Eds.), *Preventive psychology: Theory, research, and practice in community intervention* (pp. 87–100). New York: Pergamon.

Hirsch, B. J. (1980). Natural support systems and coping with major life changes. *American Journal of Community Psychology, 8,* 159–172.

Hirsch, B. J., & Dubois, D. L. (1992). The relation of peer social support and psychological symptomatology during the transition of junior high school: A two year longitudinal analysis. *American Journal of Community Psychology, 20,* 333–347.

Holler, B., & Hurrelmann, K. (1990). The role of parent and peer contacts for adolescents' state of health. In K. Hurrelmann & F. Lösel (Eds.), *Health hazards in adolescence* (pp. 409–432). Berlin: de Gruyter.

Horwitz, A. (1977). Social networks and pathways to psychiatric treatment. *Social Forces, 56*(1), 86–105.

House, J. S. (1981). *Work stress and social support.* Reading, MA: Addison-Wesley.

House, J. S., & Kahn, R. L. (1985). Measures and concepts of social support. In S. Cohen & S. L. Syme (Eds.), *Social support and health* (pp. 83–108). Orlando, FL: Academic Press.

Husiani, B. A., Neff, J. A., Newbrough, J. R., & Moore, M. C. (1982). The stress-buffering role of social support and personal competence among the rural married. *Journal of Community Psychology, 10,* 409–426.

Jacobson, D. (1987). The cultural context of social support and social networks. *Medical Anthropology Quarterly, 1*(1), 42–67.

Kessler, R. C., & McLeod, J. (1985). Social support and mental health in community samples. In S. Cohen & L. Syme (Eds.), *Social support and health* (pp. 219–240). New York: Academic Press.

Kessler, R. C., Price, R. H., & Wortman, C. B. (1985). Social factors in psychopathology: Stress, social support, and coping processes. *Annual Review of Psychology, 36,* 531–572.

Klovdahl, A. S. (1985). Social networks and the spread of infectious disease: The AIDS example. *Social Science & Medicine, 21,* 1203–1216.

Kovacs, M. (1981). Rating scales to assess depression in school aged children. *Acta Paedpsychiatrica, 46,* 305–315.

Laumann, E. O. (1973). *Bonds of pluralism: The forms and substance of urban social networks.* New York: Wiley.

Levitt, M. J. (1991). Attachment and close relationships: A life span perspective. In J. L. Gerwitz & W. F. Kurtines (Eds.), *Intersections with attachment* (pp. 183–205). Hillsdale, NJ: Erlbaum.

Liebow, E. B. (1989). Category or community? Measuring urban Indian social cohesion with network sampling. *Journal of Ethnic Studies, 16,* 67–100.

Mitchell, J. C. (1969). *Social networks in urban situations.* Manchester: Manchester University Press.

Moos, R. H., & Moos, B. S. (1981). *Family Environment Scale manual.* Palo Alto, CA: Consulting Psychologists Press.

Nestmann, F., & Niepel (1994). Social support in single-parent families: Children as sources of support. In F. Nestmann & K. Hurrelmann (Eds.), Social networks and social support in childhood and adolescence (pp. 323–346). Berlin: de Gruyter.

Newcomb, M. S., & Bentler, P. M. (1988). Impact of adolescent drug use and social support on problems of young adults: A longitudinal study. *Journal of Abnormal Psychology, 97,* 64–75.

Reid, M., Landesman, S., Treder, R., & Jaccard, J. (1989). My Family and Friends: Six to twelve year old children's perceptions of social support. *Child Development, 60,* 896–910.

Rickel, A. U., & Biasatti, L. R. (1982). Modification of the Block Child Rearing Practices Report. *Journal of Clinical Psychology, 39,* 129–134.

Sarason, B. R., Pierce, G. R., & Sarason, I. G. (1990). Social support: The sense of acceptance and the role of relationships. In B. R. Sarason, I. G. Sarason, & G. R. Pierce (1990). *Social support: An interactional view* (pp. 97–128). New York: Wiley.

Sarason, B. R., Sarason, I. G., & Pierce, G. R. (1990). *Social support: An interactional view.* New York: Wiley.

Sarason, B. R., Shearin, E. N., Pierce, G. R., Sarason, I. G. (1987). Interrelationships among social support measures: Theoretical and practical implications. *Journal of Personality and Social Psychology, 52,* 813–832.

Sarason, I. G., Sarason, B. R., & Shearin, E. N. (1986). Assessing social support: The Social Support Questionnaire. *Journal of Personality and Social Psychology, 50,* 845–855.

Vaux, A., & Harrison, D. (1985). Support network characteristics associated with support satisfaction and perceived support. *American Journal of Community Psychology*, *13*, 245–267.

Wethington, E., & Kessler, R. C. (1986). Perceived support, received support, and adjustment to stressful life events. *Journal of Health and Social Behavior*, *27*, 78–89.

Wilson, M. N. (1989). Child development in the context of the Black extended family. *American Psychologist*, *44*, 380–385.

Wolchik, S. A., Beals, J., & Sandler, I. N. (1989). Mapping children's support networks. In D. Belle (Ed.), *Children's social networks and social supports* (pp. 191–220). New York: Wiley.

Wolf, E. F. (1966). Kinship, friendship, and patron-client relations in complex societies. In M. Banton (Ed.), *The social anthropology of complex societies*. London: Tavistock.

7

Social Support in the Relationships between Older Adolescents and Adults

Benjamin H. Gottlieb and John C. Sylvestre

This chapter presents and illustrates a perspective on the study of social support that differs from that underlying the usual purposes and methods of past research on the topic. Rather than examining a particular set of behaviors that are defined a priori as supportive, we focus on the ways in which supportive meaning is derived from the conduct of personal relationships. In addition, whereas past research has concentrated on social support's role in the stress process, we are primarily concerned with the ways in which social support arises in the ordinary conduct of personal relationships. In short, we spotlight how personal relationships take on their supportive character, rather than treating these relationships as the vessels through which supportive resources are conveyed. Accordingly, we do not regard support as a commodity that is extracted from people's social ties but as an aspect of the process of conducting human relationships. Our purpose, then, is to understand how interpersonal processes may communicate support within the context of a particular relationship under study. In addition, we wish to learn how the broader social influences impinging on particular relationships affect the supportive meaning of these relationships.

The chapter begins by contrasting our approach and purpose with those of past investigations. Next, we discuss how the study of personal relationships may contribute to knowledge of social support among an underresearched group, namely, older adolescents. This discussion is followed by a brief review of the literature on the subject of resilience. Because this body of research suggests that the risk of psychological harm to youths in this age group may be reduced by their relationships with adults other than family members, we chose to launch an inquiry on youths' relationships with such adults. The remainder of the chapter presents selected findings from this qualitative study. Specifically, the findings address several factors that constrain and spur the formation of personal relationships with adults, the factors that make particular adults more attractive as relationship partners to particular youths, and the relationship processes and events that convey closeness and support to the youths. Our overall purpose is to

appreciate, from the perspective of youths themselves, how their everyday interactions with particular adults, filtered through their own understanding of the
social world, bring supportive meaning to these relationships.

1. A RELATIONSHIP PERSPECTIVE ON SOCIAL SUPPORT

Our reading of the vast literature on social support among adults has led us to
make two general observations about the ways in which it has been conceptualized and measured empirically. These observations are presented below and
contrasted with the relationship perspective proposed in this chapter.

1.1. Supportive Meaning Arises from Interactions
in Personal Relationships

The first observation is that social support has been defined and measured
rather narrowly as a commodity of exchange, as a personal trait, and as a
cognitive process. As a result, the contextual and interactional character of the
construct has been occluded. We propose that social support should be investigated as negotiated interactions in personally valued, socially embedded
relationships.

It is instructive to recall that when Cassel (1974), Caplan (1974), and Cobb
(1976) introduced the ideas that launched the study of social support, they were
primarily concerned with the health-protective functions of people's natural social ties. They maintained that members of a social network provided feedback
about one another's role performance and worth, that they shared one another's
burdens, and that they provided companionship, advice, emotional support, and
practical assistance. However, these three authors placed their emphasis on the
capacity of a *special social unit* to communicate this information and aid. Its
special character derived from the network members' significance to the individual under study. In short, the network's supportive influence stemmed from the
significance the individual assigned to his or her relationships with its members.

However, when social support became the subject of numerous empirical
inquiries, the construct's grounding in the process of social interaction was
ignored. Instead, social support was conceptualized as a set of resources exchanged among the members of a network. Researchers concentrated almost
exclusively on the provisions relayed by the network, distinguishing among
emotional, tangible, and esteem support, and lost sight of the crucial fact that it
was the very existence of prior relationships that brought supportive meaning to
the interactions. With the development of measures of social support, these
supportive resources and the interactions thought to signify their provision were
further divorced from the relational and situational contexts that render social
interactions meaningful. The construct was conferred the status of a quantifiable

variable when it properly should have been seen as a dynamic social process subject to a complex set of contingencies.

A more recent and even narrower view of social support regards it as a relatively stable social cognition that reflects an amalgam of personality traits, personal beliefs, and self-perceptions. According to Sarason, Sarason, and Pierce (1990), a stable psychological perception of support originates in early childhood attachment experiences that lead to the development of "working models" of the self, significant others, and the ways others relate to the self. Secure childhood attachment fosters social schemata that enhance the capacity to experience emotional intimacy in adulthood and engender feelings of self-worth and self-efficacy. According to Sarason and colleagues (1990), "Over time, attachment patterns and perceptions of social support become the property of the individual" (p. 141). The implication of this claim is that a stable personal trait, not social interaction, is responsible for the much heralded stress-buffering effect of social support.

There is little doubt that individuals vary in their desire or need for support, in their skill in soliciting it from others, and in their perceptions of the availability of supportive others. However, the importance of social support lies in its social character, which draws attention to the interpersonal events that strengthen or undermine relationships and influence individuals' beliefs about these relationships and about themselves. It is these events, not a stable sense of support internalized through early childhood experiences, that shape the expression and experience of social support. Rather than positing the existence of a cognitive meaning system largely independent of these social events, a relationship approach examines the supportive meaning derived from social interactions occurring in the conduct of personal relationships.

In a given relationship, the sense of support can therefore fluctuate in accordance with a broad range of events that are affirming or disappointing. Further, a relationship approach takes into account how the social environment in which personal ties are embedded influences the kinds of support that are exchanged. Because a relationship approach focuses on interpersonal processes and the larger social ecology in which they are embedded, it reveals how social settings, relationships among network members, and broad social and cultural norms are implicated in the communication of support.

1.2. Support Is Communicated in the Routine Conduct of Personal Relationships

The second observation is that social support has been conceived in a utilitarian way, as explicit and remarkable expressions of aid and esteem that occur in exceptional circumstances marked by stress. This has diverted attention from the ways support is expressed in everyday interaction and derived through the shared meanings that develop from the normal conduct of relationships.

The investigation of social support had been unduly restricted to the remarkable attempts of network members to provide aid to an individual experiencing stress. Social support researchers have neglected the ways in which people conduct their relationships apart from the alarms of life's calamities and adversities. The stress and coping paradigm that has dominated inquiry on the subject of social support has neglected the fact that stress-related interactions in personal relationships constitute only a small part of the universe of potentially supportive communications.

It is important to acknowledge that, in most relationships, overt expressions of support are not common occurrences. In fact, according to Coyne, Ellard, and Smith (1990), explicitly supportive exchanges "represent the breakdown or inadequacy of shared meanings and routines of relationships under stress" and occur "when remedial work is needed" (p. 130). Leatham and Duck (1990) succinctly stated that "It may well be impossible to draw sharp lines around conduct within personal relationships and say, 'This is social support' and 'That is just normal relationship behavior'" (p. 2). In short, the occasions when support is actively solicited and when help is made salient do not faithfully represent the typical conduct of close relationships, and they do not encompass the range of interactions that have a supportive meaning to and an impact on the participants.

In contrast, a relationship perspective focuses on the ways interdependence is achieved and maintained through the ongoing commerce between two parties and how this interaction influences their sense of support. As the partners' experience in the relationship accumulates, they create a shared history, along with mutual understanding and expectations of one another, including expectations regarding the supportiveness of the other. A relationship perspective also provides insight into the study of explicit episodes of help given in crises and other stressful circumstances because it sets these episodes against a backdrop consisting of the regular conduct of the relationship. This backdrop forms the basis for the parties' expectations regarding both support and its consequences for the future of their relationship.

2. PERSONAL RELATIONSHIPS BETWEEN
ADOLESCENTS AND ADULTS

To illustrate a relationship perspective on social support, we will present selected findings from an exploratory study of youths' contact with adults other than their parents. However, we first address the reasons why we have focused on this particular topic.

2.1. Obstacles to the Development of Personal
Relationships between Adolescents and Adults

When children move into adolescence, their increased independence grants them the freedom to explore their surroundings, and they have greater opportunities than formerly to form relationships with a more diverse group of people. Whereas the social networks of children are more likely to be populated by adults who are known and approved by the children's parents, during adolescence youths experience fewer constraints on their choices for relationships. Presumably, they have the opportunity to form ties with a broader range of peers in a wider array of social contexts.

As adolescents gain autonomy, they also develop skills that allow for more sophisticated and varied kinds of interactions with adults. In fact, as they gain more varied social experience in a broader range of social roles, they practice new social skills in settings that are more heterogeneous in terms of the ages and roles of their occupants. They also gain a more complex understanding of the norms that operate in personal and role relationships and learn about the permeability of the boundary between the two.

However, several obstacles may inhibit the development of close personal relationships between older adolescents and the adults with whom they interact outside the home. First, many of the adults who come into regular contact with youths occupy such formal roles as teacher, coach, and job supervisor. These positions call for highly scripted behavior on the part of the adults who are sanctioned by parents or by the institutions of the community to mete out rewards and punishments. A second obstacle to the formation of more personal relationships between adolescents and adults stems from the typical ways in which their interaction is structured. In most academic, employment, and extracurricular activities, large groups of youths are instructed by adult leaders in settings in which opportunities for one-to-one dialogue are few. A study of the work settings in which adolescents are employed revealed little intergenerational contact. This may account for the finding that adults at work are among the last people chosen by adolescents as sources of help and support (Greenberger & Steinberg, 1981; Greenberger, Steinberg, Vaux, & McAuliffe, 1980).

Third, there are cultural restrictions on the formation of personal relationships between youths and unrelated adults. Adults may be reticent about intruding into the privacy of the family and stepping into quasi-parental roles with other people's children. The current climate of concern about the widespread incidence of sexual abuse and other forms of exploitation of youths is a further impediment. Young people are being educated to be wary of adults they do not know, and adults are being cautioned more strongly than ever before to consider the propriety of their contacts with youth.

2.2. Adults in the Social Networks of Adolescents

Despite these constraints on the development of personal relationships with adults, unrelated adults are nevertheless nominated as significant figures in adolescents' social networks. For example, in a study of 2,800 adolescents in the seventh through tenth grades, Blyth, Hill, and Thiel (1982) found that roughly

10 percent of all the significant adults noted were not relatives and that 60 percent of the males and 75 percent of the females listed at least one nonrelated adult as a significant other. Most of these adults were of the same gender as the respondent. Approximately half of the nonrelated adults were seen in the school, and 60 percent to 70 percent were seen in home settings. A majority of these adults were regularly contacted by phone, and almost half were seen daily.

Galbo (1983) studied youths in the same age group and found more nominations of significant ties with nonrelated adults than with related adults. Figures from religious settings were the most frequently mentioned nonrelated adults, and most of the adult nominees were under the age of 30. Interaction typically occurred in informal rather than institutional settings. Moreover, when Galbo (1983) asked the youths why they valued these relationships, they cited the adults' personal qualities, such as intelligence, open-mindedness, trustworthiness, and breadth of life experiences, as well as qualities of the relationships, such as friendliness, personal interest in the youth, willingness to spend time with the youth, and treatment of the youth as an equal.

Galbo's (1983) research is of special interest because he also inquired about the events or conditions that first led the youths to recognize the significance of these adults in their lives. The youths' responses fell into three categories: (1) during times of conflict, the adult helped a youth work through a personal problem, (2) the relationship arose as compensation for the absence of another adult, and (3) the youth's own maturation led to recognition of the capacity to relate more intimately with an adult.

It is noteworthy that neither the two studies cited above nor any other research on social support among adolescents (e.g., Gottlieb, 1991) has probed the interactions that actually occur in these valued relationships with adults. They have largely documented the fact that such relationships exist, that they arise in informal contexts, and that gender, socioeconomic, and ecological (e.g., urban vs. rural) variables are associated with the number and kind of these relationships. Moreover, these studies have not compared the significance of the adults who are nominated with that of other adults and peers. Are there unique aspects of the nominating adolescents' commerce with these adults that give these relationships special supportive meaning? Do these extrafamilial ties make a special contribution to the adolescents' maturation, preparing them for young adulthood? A growing body of literature on the subject of resilience suggests that these relationships may have both general and specific adaptive significance for youths experiencing stress.

2.3. Personal Relationships and Resilience

Recent interest in the subject of resilience stems from a diverse set of studies revealing that, under stressful conditions, some youths are able to adapt and even to achieve superior developmental outcomes. Garmezy's (1983) review of this research led him to identify three general protective factors that distinguish stress-resistant youths from those adversely affected by stress: (1) advantageous personality dispositions such as social responsiveness, (2) a cohesive and supportive family environment, and (3) the presence of external sources of support. Of these factors, the latter appears to be the least well documented and understood. Examples of external sources of support have included a supportive personal relationship with an adult; the presence of an adult with whom a youth closely identifies; participation in and commitment to activities that enable the youth to physically separate from the family and gain recognition, stability, and a sense of achievement; and participation in a supportive social agency (Beardslee & Podorefsky, 1988; Garmezy, 1983; Hetherington, 1989; Werner & Smith, 1982).

For example, in a study of youths whose parents had major affective disturbances, Beardslee and Podorefsky (1988) found that 16 of the 18 adolescents who showed healthy functioning described themselves as valuing close, confiding relationships and emphasized that these relationships were a central part of their lives. Nine individuals reported turning to someone outside their families during episodes of acute parental illness, and two of the nine nominated adults as significant in their lives. The majority of the youths were also deeply involved in academic, employment, and extracurricular pursuits. Beardslee and Podorefsky (1988) stated that the resilient youths' outside commitments and relationships allowed them to separate themselves from their parents' illnesses.

Hetherington (1989) also found that disengagement from the family contributed to resilience in the wake of parental divorce. She noted that "when disengagement from the family occurs, however, contact with an interested, supportive adult plays a particularly important role in buffering the child against the development of behavior problems" (p. 11). Specifically, about one-third of the adolescent children in her study became disengaged from their families following parental divorce and remarriage. The youths became involved in school activities and peer groups, "or, if they are fortunate, they attach themselves to a responsive adult or to the family of a friend" (Hetherington, 1989, p. 11).

Far greater precision is needed to document the processes implicated in the protection afforded by the resources external to the family. At this point, all researchers know is that there is something about youths' interaction with particular adults or their participation in adult-led social organizations, such as work, school, and athletic activities, that places them at an adaptive advantage. In either case, there are potential benefits to distressed youths from increasing and deepening their association with supportive adult figures. This observation, coupled with Rutter's (1987) conviction that resilience is achieved in part through a complex social process, not exclusively through the deployment of personal resources, further testifies to the desirability of promoting stable relationships with caring older figures.

Further headway might be made by inquiring about how relationships that prove vital during times of stress arise in the first place. It is unclear whether resilience is conferred by particular stress-related interactions or by the presence of a stable and warm relationship that serves as a refuge from stressful events but whose content may not include discussions of the youths' stressful experiences.

3. AN EXPLORATORY STUDY OF ADOLESCENTS' PERSONAL RELATIONSHIPS WITH ADULTS

To illustrate how understanding of social support can be advanced by examining the everyday conduct of personal relationships, we conducted an exploratory qualitative study of the relationships that older adolescents have formed with adults other than their parents. Rather than restrict our inquiry to explicit instances of support that occurred in such relationships, we probed the ways in which these relationships developed. We took this course because we wished to learn how intimacy and trust are created as youths' foundation for approaching older people for help. We were also interested in learning how youths experienced support in the normal course of their interactions, not only in those exceptional helping episodes that occur under stressful conditions. In short, our study centered on the support derived from youths' ongoing regular contact with particular adults. We begin by describing the participants' perceptions of the obstacles that prevent the formation of personal ties with adults and then consider how certain valued ties with adults were formed. Finally, we address the supportive meaning and developmental contribution of these ties to the youths.

The adolescents who were interviewed included 15 females and 5 males, all between the ages of 16 and 20, drawn from varied personal backgrounds. The respondents were recruited in several ways: 10 were contacted through a youth counseling center where they were receiving service; 6 were reached through a university subject pool; and the remainder were counselors at a children's summer camp or swim instructors at a community recreational facility. Of the 20 respondents, 5 were no longer living at home. Of these 5 youths, 2 were single mothers living alone with a child, 2 lived with older roommates, and 1 lived with the family of her boyfriend. Six respondents were interviewed two to three months after having moved away from home to a university, but they still maintained legal residence with their parents. Finally, 4 of these youths were no longer attending school, and of these, 3 were employed full-time.

The second author conducted semistructured interviews that began by asking the youths to list all persons except their parents who were older than themselves and with whom they had contact at least once a month. The respondents were then asked the following two questions: (1) "Of all the people we have listed here, who would you say are those people you've been able to get to know on a more personal basis?" and (2) "Of all the people on this list, who would you like to get to know better?"

The youths were then asked to describe why they wished to know some adults better and what had kept them from knowing these adults as well as they would have liked. The youths were also asked why they did not want to get to know certain adults better. They were then asked the following questions: (3) "Are there any people on this list who you particularly enjoy spending time with, either doing things together or just talking?" (4) "Are there any people on this list who you ever talked with about personal kinds of things? By personal things, I am thinking of important things that may have been going on in your life, or decisions you may have been trying to make, or problems with a relationship," and (5) "Has there ever been a time that you can remember when you were dealing with some kind of stress and someone on this list either became involved in some way or did or said something that made a difference for you?"

Up to three nominees were accepted for each of the preceding three questions. Finally, the respondents were also asked whether any of the adults on their lists "stands out above all others because you particularly value your contact with him or her."

Selectively, depending on the youths' ratings of the nominees, the interviewer used the following probes: Why a contact was valued, the forces constraining and spurring the relationship, how the youth typically spent time with the nominee, and how the time spent with the nominee was different from the time spent with peers or other people older than him- or herself.

Because of our interest in the ways that supportive meaning is gained through the normal conduct of personal relationships, the interviewer did not inquire directly about explicit instances of helping and support. Further, we asked about youths' contact with a variety of older others, not only with those nominees who were most valued, because we wanted to learn about relationships that the respondents had not judged to be supportive on conventional grounds but that nevertheless might prove to contribute to the youths' maturation. This choice was informed by the resilience literature, which suggests that relationships in achievement contexts, with role models, and with people who insulate a youth from stressful social spheres may be particularly protective. These valued figures might not have surfaced had we restricted our attention to relationships in which explicitly supportive interactions occurred.

3.1. Obstacles to Personal Relationships

There's no one who is a lot older that I would feel that close to. Like, I guess it's just the age difference again. And that's just something that society has placed on us. They've placed the big barrier between age groups. It's unfortunate.

Through their routine daily activities at school, at work, at home, and in their neighborhoods, the youths we interviewed came into contact with a wide variety of older people. However, they reported several reasons why only some of these adults were known on a more personal basis. These reasons pertained to the personal, interactional, and social constraints on the development of supportive cross-generational relationships.

First, status differences between youth and adults inhibited opportunities to form more personal relationships. Whether referring to adults who held positions of authority, such as teachers and work supervisors, or adults encountered in more informal settings, such as extracurricular activities, the youths felt that an "authority barrier" hampered open and relaxed communication. These adults expected the youths to respect and heed their elders, an expectation that precluded any possibility of forming more personal relationships. As one respondent observed:

> I think that's just something that people have grown up with . . . the father knows best theory . . . like the authoritative figure told the younger people what to do, and they could settle with that. And now people just think "Oh, those older people are going to tell me what to do. They're not going to be my friend."

Second, because interaction with many adults occurred in group settings in which the adults occupied rigid roles, there were few opportunities for informal or private dialogues. Indeed, some youths were reluctant to make claims on the adults' time and attention. For example, one youth expressed an interest in getting to know a pastor at church better but was reluctant to initiate contact with her because

> She and her husband are in charge of an entire congregation and because of her position, she's got to deal with everyone else too. . . . And I don't have any problems, necessarily, that I need her to deal with. I'd just like to know her better.

It is noteworthy that this respondent had also formed a judgment about the legitimate grounds for seeking out the pastor; she could do so only to secure help for a personal problem. More generally, adolescents may feel that in order to gain private access to certain adults, they must assume a subordinate or dependent posture, or at best take the role of learner, protégé, or trainee. All of those roles are inconsistent with the mutuality that is required for the development of personal relationships.

The respondents spoke of other barriers that prevented them from forming more personal relationships with adults, even when settings permitted informal interaction. For example, in explaining why she had not been able to reciprocate the friendly interest that one of her father's friends had shown in her on those occasions when he had visited her home, one female respondent stated:

> My Dad would probably look at it funny . . . like there's a breaking point for politeness. Like I wouldn't want my friends hanging out with my parents, you know, and I'm sure my parents wouldn't want me to sit down with their friends.

The youth's comments reveal a sense of both the impropriety and the risk of developing a relationship with an adult who has close ties to her parents. The impropriety may stem from her sense of presuming on a relationship that seems to be exclusive, and the risk may stem from the possibility that disclosures to adults who know other people in her network will become public. Another female respondent commented directly on the risk of impropriety that attended the formation of a personal relationship with a friend's mother. Although she wished to know the mother better, she observed:

> With the girlfriend that I hang around with I feel I may intrude or, uhm, because that's her Mum, not my Mum . . . sometimes I feel there's a little bit of jealousy there. So, that kind of tells me to go back, you know, just take a couple of steps back, don't get too close. . . . Because I had a friend do that to me . . . [I] don't want to step over my boundaries.

As for the risk of disclosing to an adult who knows other people in the youth's network, one respondent stated that she would not tell her aunt about problems at home because she feared the information would be relayed to her parents.

Generally, our respondents reported little disclosure to older relatives such as aunts, uncles, or grandparents. They were not only apprehensive that the information would be relayed to their parents, but also felt that the older relatives were unable to adjust to the youths' present level of maturity, adopting a style of communication that was established with them in their childhood. As one respondent observed:

> Well they forget that I'm not a kid anymore, and they're so used to treating me that way, but now it's like "Oh yeah, I forgot," you know? Or with my grandmother, for instance, she still buys me like little cars and stuff. She forgets I'm like 20 years old.

3.2. The Development and Course of Personal Relationships with Adults

Despite the perceived or actual constraints on the development of personal relationships between older adolescents and adults, all 20 respondents in our study reported regular contact with adults whom they knew on a personal basis. Further, all respondents identified adults with whom they enjoyed spending their time, and all but one identified adults to whom they spoke about personal issues. In addition, with the exception of two youths, all the respondents identified at least one older person to whom they had turned in a time of stress. In this section, we describe the factors that appear to have favored the development of more personal relationships with some adults.

Not surprisingly, the respondents had developed more personal relationships with people they had known longer. Therefore, older relatives (grandparents, aunts, uncles, siblings, cousins) were frequently nominated as valued figures. As one youth stated:

> I just feel comfortable with her and because I've known her for so long and we just, the way she used to be with me when I was a kid, just made me grow to make her my favorite aunt.

As mentioned earlier, few respondents reported disclosing personal problems to aunts, uncles, or grandparents or turning to them during times of stress. They valued these kin because they gained comfort, acceptance, or security from their contact with them. For example, one youth observed that the time she spent with her grandparents was

> just a lot different . . . just so laid back and stuff, you know? With friends, I feel that I have to kind of put on, not a show or anything but, friends are just so much different. But with my grandparents I can just act like myself, you know? I just really like being around them.

Why did our respondents value their personal relationships with these kin and yet not discuss personal matters with them? Perhaps routine, long-established patterns of interaction with them communicated warmth, esteem, and attachment. Even in the absence of disclosure and explicit help-seeking, these dependable routines may have safeguarded the youths' sense of worth, stability, and place. In the trajectory of a young person's life, these may have been the only figures other than parents with whom such comforting routines were sustained.

Similarly, teachers and coaches were more likely to have been nominated as adults whom the youths knew personally or to whom they spoke about personal matters if the adults had participated with the youths in extracurricular activities for a number of months. When asked about how she had formed a more personal relationship with a teacher who sponsored a school club in which she participated, one female respondent said:

> Uhm, well the fact that I was given the opportunity to actually meet her. I don't know if . . . maybe the other teachers are like that as well, but I've never been put in the position to actually meet them. But she was just there . . . happened to be in our club, so, I actually had the opportunity.

Repeated episodes of interaction with adults in informal dyadic or small group situations afforded respondents the opportunity to break the mold that constrained adult-adolescent relations and to communicate more personally about a broader range of topics. Our respondents were particularly drawn to adults at school who disclosed aspects of their personal lives to them. For example, referring to her soccer coach, one youth observed:

Yeah, he was really open about that too. You'd be talking and there would be something that he had done that related to that, like going on ski trips, or "Yeah I had a little nephew that did this and . . . " or "I went here on such and such a day and did this." So he was really open himself about that and letting you get to know the other side of him too, not just as a teacher and a coach.

Other respondents who nominated particular teachers as individuals whom they wished to know better, or with whom they enjoyed spending their time, recognized the limitations of these relationships. As one respondent observed:

I don't know how much more personal, like with the positions they're in. . . . Like a lot of them are teachers that I've had or, and I mean have been in contact in other ways too. But there's only so close I think you can get.

Another youth questioned the propriety of blurring the boundary between a personal and role relationship with a teacher:

Yeah, like they're great in school but, sometimes if you carry them outside of school you're not sure where they should lead? Like you're not sure it's right or proper or, should I know my teacher, know personal things about my teacher or not? Or is it bad? I don't know.

Extended periods of interaction were prerequisites, but not guarantees, of the development of more personal relationships with adults. In addition, the nominated adults had communicated a personal interest in the youths or revealed information about themselves that the youths considered to be private and personal. In short, the adults had to take the first step toward more personal relationships by making time to interact with the youths on a one-to-one basis, by letting down their guard about themselves, or by relaxing the requirements of the roles they had first assumed with the youths. Our respondents were sensitive to changes in the style of communication, as well as to those in its content. Examples were cited of instances in which adults cursed or smoked or drank alcohol in the youths' presence or in which teachers gossiped with them about others at school. These communications represented ways that the adults took the youths into their confidence, tacitly conveying the message that the youths could be trusted and had the maturity to deal with the adults on a more personal basis. Interestingly, there were few instances in which the youths themselves had taken initiatives that signaled their interest in forming more personal relationships with adults.

Personal relationships were more likely to arise when status differences concerning age and authority did not intrude on the interaction between youths and adults. This is clearly illustrated in the following quotations from two respondents:

But there's the odd adult you meet and you know that it's a friendship level. Like there's no hierarchy that you have to deal with. It's just like we're meeting each other on the same plane.

Some adults . . . they just accept you on a younger level . . . so when an adult can let down their guard and be themselves with you, that makes it very different. You can tell when people, especially adults, are not being themselves. You can tell when there's still that "I'm an adult barrier."

As relationships became more equitable, the adults were perceived to have a greater ability to adopt and validate the youths' perspectives, rather than judging their actions and attitudes. They were somehow able to suspend the authority normally vested in their roles and listen more closely than other adults. As one respondent observed about her aunt:

She doesn't stay at her own level. Sometimes she kind of comes down to my level and kind of relates to being a teenager and how *she* used to be and stuff and so I understand her better.

In contrast, most adults were reported as prone to making severe judgments that stifled the expression of feelings:

If you go like to a parent or another older person they'd be like "Oh well, I wouldn't have been doing that when I was that age." Like they couldn't get past the fact that "Well how come kids are doing that?" And you're like trying to finish your story type thing. . . . And you're like "Well no. That's not my point. My point is, like I'm feeling this way."

3.3. The Influence and Significance of Relationships with Adults

One of the observations about adolescence that has become virtually axiomatic is that it is a period when ties to family are loosened and when the peer group becomes ascendant. However, our interviews suggest that in late adolescence, as a joint function of the ecological transitions they undergo and their greater independence and mobility, some youth do form ties with adults removed from their family, neighborhood, and childhood friendship circles. From a structural perspective, these adults occupy a zone of the network that is set apart from all others. Because they do not communicate with other members of a youth's network, these adults are more trusted.

The greater latitude adolescents have in the choice of associates and in the structuring of their networks is accompanied by maturational changes that enable them to alter the quality of long-standing relationships. For example, ties to certain adults who were first introduced in childhood may be redefined through interactions that take place outside the family. Our respondents reported on several historic relationships that took on a new and more intimate character when it became possible for the respondents to interact with the adults on their own. For several respondents, these relationships offered asylum when conflict occurred in other spheres of the network.

For example, in one illustration of Rutter's (1983) ideas about the protective effect of one strong attachment outside the family, a 17-year-old respondent commented on the ways she could activate her relationship with her aunt when life at home became intolerable:

> Like when there was bad times with my Mom, she just said, come live with me, you know, and I lived with her, and when things were easier with my Mom, I went back to live with my Mom. Tammy was just there to make things easier, 'cause she can deal with it better.

The respondent also noted that she would confide in Tammy but not in her own friends because disclosures to friends "get back to you anyway." She continued, "But with Tammy, who is she gonna tell? Even if she does tell her friend, who is it going to get back to that's going to embarrass me?" Interestingly, however, this adult's position within the extended family network did cause conflict with the youth's mother:

> Yeah. It's made things, uhm, well with my Mom, my Mom feels that Tammy interferes. Even though she doesn't, it's me that makes her, you know, I get her involved. And then my Mom feels that she's just interfering, so, then my Mom doesn't talk to Tammy, even though they're sisters.

By comparison, another youth described her relationship with a woman for whom she had baby-sat and whom she considered a friend as well. Noting that she had initiated her relationship with this person independently, without her parents, she commented on its value to her during periods of conflict with her parents:

> Because, well when I really started getting to know Patty, that was when my Mom and I weren't that close. Or, like my parents and I weren't that close just because you aren't when you're that age. You know what I mean? Like, you tend to separate yourself from your parents. . . . Like 15. Around you know 14 or 15. And um, I could talk to her more about things that I couldn't with my parents.

A second value of a relationship that is set apart from the rest of an individual's network is that it offers a new vantage point for appraising relations with other network members. For example, one respondent was a teenage mother who had developed a close relationship with a female co-worker who was eight years her senior. She reported that, whereas her age-mates ignored or devalued her maternal responsibilities and financial obligations, her older friend just treats me like a normal person and she's there to talk to me about my other friends, saying, "Well Carrie, you have to look out for this. You have to look out for that." . . . you really have to be picky and choosy with your friends. Just helping me look at the things I'm vulnerable to.

In this instance, the adult encouraged the respondent to consider her choices regarding the childhood friends she would continue to associate with and those she might leave behind.

In other instances, adults became involved in discussions about social conflicts the youths were experiencing and, because they were untouched by the conflicts themselves, these adults were perceived as offering an unprejudiced hearing. Particularly among the youths in our sample who were seeing counselors, these removed figures were seen as expressing more objective views:

He is an impartial observer. He's someone who is not directly related to my family, or directly related to a close friend of mine. He's someone who's totally out in the middle of nowhere I can talk about anybody to.

In addition to helping the youths make more mature social choices, distance themselves from tensions in their networks, and consider alternative perspectives on these tensions, the adults also encouraged a greater measure of self-under-standing. They did so both indirectly, by sharing their own past experiences and the lessons they learned from them, and directly, by encouraging the youths to examine their own motives and psychological makeups. For example, one youth, who had formed an independent relationship with one of her mother's friends, stated that this adult had told her that "if I have a problem with some-body, then maybe I should take a look at myself because maybe the problem is with myself."

It would be misleading, however, to suggest that such perspectives could only be offered by individuals who were completely removed from the youths' net-works. Some youths attached great value to the adults' privileged knowledge of the youths' situation. Referring to one of her mother's friends, a person with whom she had independently struck up a friendship, one youth observed:

So she can relate to my Mom because, you know, my Mom talks to her and so she's got a pretty good idea about how my Mom feels too. So then she can give me feedback on my Mom, and why she may react the way she did.

As noted in the previous section, the adults with whom more personal relation-ships had been formed were generally more willing than other adults to disclose information about their own lives, both past and present. They talked about their own childhood difficulties and about consequential decisions they had faced. Occasionally, but more rarely, they revealed subjects that troubled them in their present lives. Such frank revelations signified to the youths that the adults believed the former had the capacity to listen and understand a relationship message that they found highly validating. These communications tacitly acknowledged a youth's worth as a target of disclosure, thereby offering concrete evidence of his or her maturity, trustworthiness, and attractiveness as a relationship partner. These revelations also seemed to satisfy a curiosity that many youths had about the adults they knew.

Several of the youths who were being counseled were particularly drawn to adults who were willing to share personal difficulties similar to the youths' that they had experienced in life. In commenting on her relationship with the husband of a co-worker, one respondent observed that he

> really helps me get to know that I'm not the only one that's out there and to know that I can go and talk to somebody who I know definitely has gone through those problems and he's willing to talk to me about them, you know. So to get to know him better just through talking and problem-solving and stuff like that, you know, it really helps.

The curiosity that other youths expressed about adults centered on other aspects of the adults' lives, including their travels, their education, and their occupations. For example, one youth said that he wanted to know more about his swim coach:

> To see how he juggled his time I guess, when he was in university. Like university and swimming and partying I guess, and just, you know, see how he did all that.

Another youth observed that she had acquired greater self-awareness from hearing about the life experiences that had shaped the character of the adult with whom she had forged a personal relationship:

> Well, it all builds on him as a person. Everything that he's been through, and everybody he's met have all built him up as a person, and it's interesting to take them apart, and see how each of them contributed to his life. Because there are a lot of people in my life who make me who I am. And make up a big part of me and it's interesting to see how those different people affect you and what your makeup is.

Our respondents were also particularly sensitive to the style of communication that adults adopted with them. When adults took the youths into their confidence, and when they did not censor the language they used, our respondents drew the inference that they were being treated as adults. For example, one respondent said:

> People are always very cautious around me, I found, because my mother was so like, making sure everything was nice and pretty for me type thing? But like now that I'm older I can actually talk on a more realistic level with them, type thing. They're not concerned about swearing in front of me because I'm too young.

The same respondent also expressed her pride in the fact that she had achieved the status of a conversation partner with an adult and no longer had to engage in the activities that she associated with childhood:

> Yeah. Like we'd go do the interesting things, like go watch movies and stuff but, you know, whenever you see a kid like you take them shopping or you take them. . . . But now we didn't have to go do a special thing. Like we could just talk, like regular adults talk, type thing.

These quotations suggest that there were certain manners and contents of speech that the respondents associated with adult behavior. When adults allowed them to interact in these ways, they bolstered the youths' sense of maturity. In short, these interactions admitted the youths to adult relationships.

Although, on the whole, communication with relatives had not caught up to the youths' current development, when relatives were able to shift to a more mature style of interaction, the effect on the youths' self-concepts was pronounced. For example, in the following quotation, one youth draws contrasts between the past and the present, and between her younger sister and herself, with respect to the ways her relatives communicate with her.

> You know, like I noticed that a lot more, especially this year, like the end of high school, going off to [university], it was more . . . I think they just started to treat me more as an, not even an adult, but you know a young adult than their niece or, you know, a kid. Like I have a younger sister and she's two years younger than I am. And even there's a difference there, just in the conversations. They'll talk to her about her boyfriend and talk to me about what I am going to do with my life.

In order to further explore how the support communicated in relationships with adults might differ from the support gained through interaction with peers, we asked respondents to contrast the two. One youth reported that talking with a teacher was different from talking to a peer because "She was, made you feel important. Like with your friend you're no more important than she is." Another youth described the differences in the following terms:

> Somebody like Heather [a peer] may only be able to see one side of it. Like my side. Whereas, uhm, Carrie [an older friend] would maybe be able to see my side, but also be able to relate to being on the other side. Like maybe I might want to talk to Mary [a peer] when I want reassurance. Like then I would talk to Julie [an older friend] too, knowing that Julie would give me feedback from the other side. . . .

Other youths said their friends did not take their problems seriously, offered unrealistic advice, or were not able to help because they were going through similar problems.

4. CONCLUSION

Our interviews shed light on some of the reasons why past studies have found that parents and peers, rather than adults outside the immediate family, compose the majority of adolescents' significant network members. Although they may have repeated contact with extended family members, teachers, coaches, clergy, and job associates, youths view few of these adults as available, appropriate, or willing partners for more personal relationships. Most of them are perceived as being too closely aligned with other network members, too constrained by the dictates of the roles they occupy, or too strongly conditioned to see the youths as children. At the same time, the settings in which interaction occurs and the stereotypes that both youths and adults bring to their interactions contain features that dim the prospects for personal relationships.

It is important to recognize, however, that the respondents' awareness of the diverse obstacles to the formation of personal relationships testifies to the emergence of a more complex understanding of the contingencies governing personal and impersonal relationships. That is, the considerations that led them to conclude that some older people were not appropriate or willing partners for closer relationships may also have served as guidelines for developing more personal and closer relationships with particular adults.

Closer and more personal relationships between adolescents and selected adults were marked by informality, spontaneity, acceptance, sustained interaction, willingness to break the rigid mold that characterized the majority of contacts with adults, and a measure of mutual disclosure. In addition, more personal ties were forged when adults took the initiative to relax the usual constraints imposed by age and authority disparities and when they adopted a style of communication that signaled that they felt the youths could be trusted and were capable of mature dialogue.

The interviews elicited a number of new insights about the supportive meaning of the youths' relationships with adults. Some relationships served as a refuge from conflict in other social spheres of the youths' lives, and others offered a new vantage point for appraising relations with peers. In addition, the youths' emergent maturity strivings were reinforced through relationships with adults who were willing to share their own experiences and who encouraged the respondents to examine their own motives and psychological makeups. Rather than making authoritative judgments about youths' behavior, these adults fostered greater self- and social understanding in the youths by engaging them in adult dialogue about their experiences.

Above all, our interviews underscore the fact that support can only be understood in terms of the context and character of relationships. These relationships, in turn, are products of the ways in which the social environment is structured, the ways in which social roles are defined, and the ways in which individuals engage one another. In the context of this study, the patterning of social roles and the opportunities afforded by the social environment severely constrain the formation of personal relationships between adolescents and older adults. However, the fact that selected personal relationships do arise between youths and adults testifies to the overriding influence of particular kinds of sustained and routine interactions that communicate mutual interest and investment. The support that resides in such a relationship cannot be further reduced but is itself an expression of the relationship's meaning to both parties.

REFERENCES

Beardslee, W. R., & Podorefsky, D. (1988). Resilient adolescents whose parents have serious affective and other psychiatric disorders: Importance of self-understanding and relationships. *American Journal of Psychiatry, 145*, 63–69.

Blyth, D. A., Hill, J. P., & Thiel, K. S. (1982). Early adolescents' significant others: Grade and gender differences in perceived relationships with familial and nonfamilial adults and young people. *Journal of Youth and Adolescence, 11*, 425–450.

Caplan, G. (1974). *Support systems and community mental health.* New York: Behavioral Publications.

Cassel, J. (1974). Psychosocial processes and "stress": Theoretical formulations. *International Journal of Health Services, 4*, 471–482.

Cobb, S. (1976). Social support as a moderator of life stress. *Psychosomatic Medicine, 38*, 300–314.

Coyne, J. C., Ellard, J. H., & Smith, D. A. F. (1990). Social support, interdependence, and the dilemmas of helping. In B. R. Sarason, I. G. Sarason, & G. R. Pierce (Eds.), *Social support: An interactionist view* (pp. 129–149). New York: Wiley.

Galbo, J. J. (1983). Adolescents' perceptions of significant adults. *Adolescence, 18*, 417–427.

Garmezy, N. (1983). Stressors of childhood. In N. Garmezy & M. Rutter (Eds.), *Stress, coping, and development in children* (pp. 43–84). New York: McGraw-Hill.

Gottlieb, B. H. (1991). Social support in adolescence. In M. E. Colten & S. Gore (Eds.), *Adolescent stress: Causes and consequences* (pp. 281–306). New York: de Gruyter.

Greenberger, E., & Steinberg, L. D. (1981). The workplace as a context for the socialization of youth. *Journal of Youth and Adolescence, 10*(3), 185–210.

Greenberger, E., Steinberg, L. D., Vaux, A., & McAuliffe, S. (1980). Adolescents who work: Effects of part-time employment on family and peer relations. *Journal of Youth and Adolescence, 9*(3), 189–202.

Hetherington, E. M. (1989). Coping with family transitions: Winners, losers, and survivors. *Child Development, 60*, 1–14.

Leatham, G., & Duck, S. (1990). Conversations with friends and the dynamics of social support. In S. Duck & R. Silver (Eds.), *Personal relationships and social support* (pp. 1–29). London: Sage.

Rutter, M. (1983). Stress, coping, and development: Some issues and some questions. In

N. Garmezy & M. Rutter (Eds.), *Stress, coping, and development in childhood* (pp. 1–42). New York: McGraw-Hill.

Rutter, M. (1987). Psychosocial resilience and protective mechanisms. *American Journal of Orthopsychiatry, 57,* 316–331.

Sarason, I. G., Sarason, B. R., & Pierce, G. R. (1990). Social support: The search for theory. *Journal of Social and Clinical Psychology, 9,* 133–147.

Werner, E. E., & Smith, R. S. (1982). *Vulnerable but invincible: A longitudinal study of resilient children and youth.* New York: McGraw-Hill.

8

The Roles of Parents and Peers in the Sexual and Relational Socialization of Adolescents

Manuela du Bois-Reymond and Janita Ravesloot

It is highly questionable whether one generation ago social researchers asked themselves in what ways young people sought and found supportive help among contemporaries and parents concerning sexuality. This topic is new and results from the various processes of pluralization and individualization that have taken place in industrialized countries during recent decades. These processes find their expression in a prolongation of the youth phase and a postponement of adulthood. Young people are exempted from immediate pressure to work and have time to enjoy their adolescence to the full. Cultural liberalization and secularization have resulted in changes in the parent-child relationship, which nowadays is typically characterized by relaxation, equality, openness, and negotiation. Moreover, the integration of sexuality into the youth phase is broadly accepted in the Netherlands and other countries (Fuchs-Heinritz, Kruger, & Ecarius, 1990; Ravesloot, 1992a).

Until the 1950s, the sexual development of adolescents was considered to be an autonomous biological process in which hormones and basic instincts drove changes in sexual behavior that led to sexual adulthood. The task of parents was to restrain any kind of sexual behavior or experimentation in their children until their marriage. Sexual education was characterized by strong restrictive moral codes and by restricted knowledge of sexual matters (du Bois-Reymond, 1992a). From the 1950s onward, scientists began to draw attention to social and individual differences in sexual development (Ford & Beach, 1952; Kinsey, Pomeroy, & Martin, 1948; Kinsey, Pomeroy, Martin, & Gebhard, 1953; Kooij, 1972). Today, attention is focused on the active role adolescents themselves play during their sexual maturation and their interaction with their surroundings. Sexual maturation is considered to be a process of social learning whose main goal is the acquisition of social and communicative skills that will enable young people to deal with their own sexuality as well as all kinds of questions that enlarge their horizons. Adolescents have to deal with the prevention of early pregnancy and sexually transmitted diseases, with sexual abuse and violence, and with limitations on sexual behavior. With the arrival of the acquired immune deficiency syndrome (AIDS), the necessity of having effective social skills at one's disposal has increased (Hurrelmann & Lösel, 1990; Oswald, Pforr, & Pippig, 1991; Rademakers, 1990).

In spite of the liberalized relationships between parents and their children and the acceptance of sexuality as a part of the youth phase, adolescents still receive insufficient sexual education and do not use contraceptives effectively (Neubauer & Melzer, 1989; Schmidt-Tannwald & Urze, 1983). One could conclude that parental sexual education is still failing; neither do peers replace parents as educators.

In this chapter, we focus on two aspects of the sexual socialization of adolescents. First, how important are peers as a supportive group with regard to sexuality?[1] Second, what role do parents play in the lives of their adolescent children as communication partners addressing sexuality?

1. METHODS

We will answer these questions with data from a longitudinal and intergenerational comparative research project.[2] The first aim of this project was to gain insight into the way in which young women and men from different social classes structured and experienced the transition to adulthood—going from school into the labor market, leaving the parental home, starting a sexual relationship—and how they prepared for and anticipated parenthood. The second aim was to gain insight into the changes in the youth phase that have occurred in the period since World War II by comparing different generations. We chose to take a qualitative approach to data analysis. The data gathered are based on semistructured interviews with 60 young men and 60 young women from different social strata conducted annually during the period 1988 to 1991.[3] Respondents were recruited from secondary schools in the city of Leiden. At the time of the first wave (1988), they were in the final year of secondary education, were 15 to 19 years old (birth cohort 1968–72), and were living in the city of Leiden or nearby. We also interviewed the parents of 60 boys and girls to gain insight into the way in which they guided their children through the transition to adulthood: How did they support their children? These parents (60 mothers and 60 fathers) were born between 1922 and 1953 and belonged to various social classes. All interviews were transcribed. Our variables were divided into categories shaped by the theoretical notions underlying the research and the interviews themselves. The interviews were coded to enable computer-assisted analysis. Because our sample was not statistically representative and most variables were on a nominal level, we used only the most basic statistics: frequencies and cross-tabulations.

2. RESULTS ON PEERS

Adolescence is a period of increasing independence from parents, and relationships with friends and peers have a specific function in this process of emancipation from home, although this process is not usually very dramatic as most values and norms that apply at home are not radically opposed to those of the youth culture (Sinnige, 1992; van der Linden, 1991). There is evidence that the influence of parents and peers upon adolescents varies according to types of activity, topics of conversation, and gender. In all Western countries, parents' influence and support seem to prevail mostly in future-oriented domains such as choice of school, education, career plans, and work ambitions, whereas peers' influence centers around current events and activities, such as spending leisure time (sports, going out), using alcohol and drugs, smoking, and delinquency. Concerning relationships, personal problems, and friendships, differences between parents' and peers' influences are hardly noticeable—although, on the whole, adolescents experience more social support from their mothers than from peers (Coleman, 1989; Meeus, 1990). Neubauer and Melzer (1989) found that adolescent girls most frequently talked about partnership and sexuality within cliques or with individual girlfriends and that adolescent boys mostly discussed those issues with male friends. These findings agree with those of the Shell Study (Fisher, Fuchs, and Zinnecker, 1985). We were also interested in the communication between adolescents and their peers and if and how they sought and found support, especially support focused on personal sexuality.

First, we asked the young men and women to specify their interlocutors: In particular, with whom did they communicate about themselves, about their own personal feelings, and about sorrows and secrets?[4] Table 1 shows their answers.

More than one-third of the respondents (47, 20 boys and 27 girls, independent of social class) shared their secrets, personal thoughts, and problems with close friends. Within this context, a close friend may be someone of the same or the other gender. Twenty-one adolescents (15 girls and 6 boys) mentioned their lovers as the main person they relied on.[5] Table 1 also shows that more than 50 percent of the respondents (68 adolescents) maintained confidential relationships with peers. This outcome is not surprising and is consistent with results of previous studies on this topic; van der Linden quoted an adolescent informant as follows: "A real friend is someone whom you can trust, who keeps secrets, whom you can rely on, upon whom you can depend because he/she is honest, trustworthy, who respects and appreciates you" (1991, p. 88).

If we now turn to the parents, the results suggest that fathers were much less involved than mothers: Only 4 respondents (2 boys, 2 girls) told us about confidential relationships with their fathers, whereas 21 (14 mostly lower-class girls and 7 boys) mentioned their mothers, and 4 considered both their parents interlocutors. As can be seen, communication between the female respondents was referred to more often as close, personal, and intimate. Girls were more strongly

Table 1.   Who Is Your Confidential Communication
            Partner?[a]

My father	4
My mother	21
Both my parents	4
My best friends	47
My relationship/partner	21
Nobody	16
Others	6

[a] All data contained in this table are in absolute numbers.
$N = 119$.

oriented toward their mothers than boys were. Neubauer and Melzer (1989) found the same outcome. We can thus still observe a traditional pattern of sex roles: Mothers more often have a relationship with their children characterized by emotional support and understanding, and fathers more often give practical support.

A relatively large number of respondents—3 girls and 13 boys, most of them from the lower and middle classes—did not communicate with anybody about themselves. At the time of the interviews, almost none of them (15 of 16) had a girl- or boyfriend. They were completely closed to the idea of exposing their emotions or personal experiences to others. But almost all of them shared their leisure time with friends of both genders—only two boys were "loners." It appears that these 13 boys enjoyed being with their friends but felt no need to become confidential. They regarded themselves as having no problems, functioned without any difficulty, and lived in their parents' homes without any conflict. Without attaching too much weight to social class as an explanatory factor, we might speculate that these (male) adolescents of the lower and middle classes were still attached to traditional youth culture and to youth values of being "sturdy" and behaving in a "manlike" way in the peer group, whereas boys of higher classes (and girls in general) preferred more individualized friendships.

In general, we can say that if adolescents communicate about themselves, they speak above all with their peers—close friends or lovers—or with their mothers. Fathers are not communication partners at a confidential level.

If peers are important partners with whom adolescents share problems and thoughts about themselves, in which areas do adolescents seek and find help from their peers? We asked them each year during the study. Table 2 shows the answers to this question.

Independent of social class, these young people attached importance to their peers as significant confidants for discussing problems concerning contacts with their contemporaries (love partners, best friends, and peer acquaintances). They discussed friendships with people of the same and the other gender, and they

Table 2. Areas in Which Respondents Seek and Find Help among
Their Peers[a]

	Research Years		
Areas	1988	1989	1990
For no problems at all	13	9	14
Concerning school/career	13	2	4
Concerning contacts/peers	53	94	55
Concerning sexuality	11	—	—
For all problems	30	13	45

[a] All data contained in this table are in absolute numbers. For 1988, $N = 120$;
1989, $N = 118$; 1990, $N = 118$.

talked about how to make advances: "Do you think he likes me?" or "Shall I ask
her for a date?" How can we explain the increase (from 53 to 94) in the number
of respondents mentioning peers as confidants from 1988 to 1989? Various
factors come into play here, but it is notable that in 1989 most of the respondents
went to a new school or to a university or started their first jobs. Consequently,
they met new peers and were confronted with unknown situations.

After their final exams in 1989, 65 adolescents were confronted with changes
in their peer groups. During that period, they were especially concerned about
their contacts and friendships with their peers. Once they got accustomed to their
new life situations and new friends, things stabilized.

Only a few adolescents (and the number decreases over the years) sought and
found help among contemporaries concerning education and career matters, even
when they were faced with their final exams and plans for the future, as was the
case in 1988! To our knowledge, youth research has not yet offered a satisfactory
explanation for this result. Du Bois-Reymond, Guit, and van Rooijen (1992)
suggested that this fact mirrors the feeling of young people that they (as an age
group) have no say in societal matters of education, or in political affairs, from
which they refrain as well.

About 10 percent of the respondents appeared not to be communicative about
any problem whatsoever. This group consisted of more boys than girls, and this
finding supports the view that girls are more likely and better able to speak about
their problems than boys are.

A considerable number of adolescents (independent of social class and gender)
told us they sought and found help among their contemporaries, whatever the
problem might be. These youngsters do not necessarily represent a group with
problems. Rather, the question captured the idea that they could count on their
peers if necessary. The reason for the lower figure in year 2 in the category "for
all problems" has been mentioned already—the transition to new life situations
after final exams.

Table 3.   Which Peers Make Demands concerning Sexuality?[a]

	Research Years		
Peers	*1988*	*1989*	*1990*
Nobody demands anything	54	67	77
Peer group	39	10	0
Close friend(s)	5	3	4
Steady relationship	21	40	39

[a] All data contained in this table are in absolute numbers. $N = 120$ for all years.

Concerning the life area of sexuality, we see some remarkable results. Almost none of the respondents sought or found help among their peers concerning this topic. Contrary to what might be expected, modern adolescents do not talk with their peers about their sexuality. Only 11 respondents (4 boys and 7 girls, independent of social class) were confidential on this topic. Could it be that most adolescents do not have any kind of problem or question concerning sexuality? Qualitative analyses counter this assumption: Almost 25 percent of the boys and girls felt uncertain about their own sexuality.[6] So the outcome arouses interest: Youngsters do talk about relationships and contacts with each other, but they hardly ever seek and find help concerning their own sexuality. Peers see each other as "company experts" rather than as "sex experts" (Ravesloot, 1992b).

According to Hurrelmann (1989, p. 16), peers set effective standards for adolescents' behavior. But it remains to be seen whether adolescents are aware of this function. We thus asked whether adolescents experienced an influence of their peers on their sexual behavior, and how many did so. The information we gathered on this point is shown in Table 3.

Most of the respondents—more boys than girls, independent of social class—did not feel any pressure from their peers to behave in a certain way. John, 16 years old, put it this way:

> I don't feel demands concerning sex, girlfriends . . . mainly smoking and drinking . . . that kind of behavior . . . you have to behave in the same way, otherwise you can be rejected, but that is not meant for having a girlfriend, no, it must happen to meet a nice girl . . . that's by coincidence for everyone and I don't think they really expect me to have a girlfriend or to have sex.

The number of respondents stating "nobody expects anything" increased over the years of the study; feelings of independence and autonomy became stronger as the adolescents grew older and turned to individualized love relationships.

A considerable group of 39 adolescents (more boys than girls, independent of social class) told us in the year of their final exams (1988) that they did feel a certain pressure from their peers. As can be seen, the number in this group decreased over the years. Within this group, an "old-fashioned," gender-specific difference can be seen. The male respondents mentioned pressure from their peer groups to experiment with heterosexual relationships. On the whole, the girls felt more pressure to behave decently and to "look after their good names"; their female friends, classmates, and sport mates cautioned against building up a bad reputation by experimenting too much with heterosexual relationships. As 18-year-old Monique put it, "My best friends do not allow me to date every boy . . . each week another one is not done . . . we think that's stupid . . . moreover . . . my friends are often jealous."

In contrast, with the decreasing demands of the peer group over the years, we noticed an increasing importance of the influence of the steady relationship. Young people negotiated about the use of contraceptives and about the limits of sexual behavior, and they communicated about sexual needs with their sexual partners. Girls with steady relationships were no longer confronted with such demands as "taking care of your good name," and boys with girlfriends no longer felt the pressure to demonstrate their "manliness." Adolescent friendships are usually based on comparable age, socioeconomic status, interests, and plans for the future (van der Linden, 1991), and young people seek and find peers with the same interests and value patterns. Thus, it is not surprising that hardly any of our respondents reported conflicts with peers concerning sexual behavior. There was one exception: during 1988, 4 boys, but 16 girls (independent of social class) had conflicts with their contemporaries about "manners and decent behavior." These girls were the same ones who felt they confronted demands from their peers concerning sex.

When describing friendship, the adolescents typically mentioned two features not commonly found in children's descriptions of friendship: First, friends must be loyal to each other and second, much importance is attached to the intimacy of friendships (Savin-Williams & Berndt, 1990). If intimacy is of great importance, how is this connected with communication about such a private matter as personal sexuality? We asked the boys and girls to identify those in whom they confided about their personal sexuality. Table 4 shows the answers.

More than one-third of the respondents (46, independent of social class and gender) did not wish to talk about this subject with their peers or with anyone else. Although, for adolescents, a friend must be somebody whom they trust and who is a partner in conversation, the results shown in Table 4 demonstrate that they do not communicate about such private matters as their own sexuality with those defined as friends. Courtship partners were exceptions; 33 respondents with partnerships answered that they confided in their partners about sexuality; however 10 respondents with partnerships belonged to the 46 "noncommunicators."

Only 10 adolescents, more girls than boys, mentioned their best friends as communication partners on this topic. As for parents, again, mothers were the ones with whom young people—especially lower-class girls—talked about sexuality, whereas fathers were not communication partners on this topic.

Table 4.   Who Is Your Confidential Communication Partner concerning Sexuality?[a]

My father	2
My mother	16
Both my parents	7
My best friends	10
My relationship/partner	33
Nobody	46
Others	6

[a] All data contained in this table are in absolute numbers. $N = 120$.

Regarding peer support, Table 2 indicates that most of the adolescents kept up
confidential relationships with peers; they could find help from their peers with
both daily problems and more severe difficulties. Respondents viewed their
peers' role as significant confidants with whom to discuss problems concerning
contacts with their contemporaries as the most important role. Sexuality did not
seem to play a major role in the mutual communication except within steady
relationships, and not all those respondents with lovers communicated about sex
with their partners. In other words, although peers are important to adolescents
for many reasons, the support they receive concerning their sexuality is more
often passive ("being young together and doing things together") than active
("Can you tell me how to use a condom?"). This pattern emerged independent of
social class and gender.

3. RESULTS ON PARENTAL SUPPORT PATTERNS

Youth researchers agree that relationships between parents and youngsters are
much more relaxed than they were in former times and are now characterized by
a liberal parental attitude toward the lifestyles and cultural needs of children and
by negotiation (Allerbeck & Hoag, 1985; du Bois-Reymond, Peters, & Ravesloot, 1990; Fisher et al., 1985). Several European studies have indicated that
parents are prepared to either permit or tolerate premarital sexual behavior in
their children, under one main condition: sexual relationships must be monoga-
mous and serious, based on feelings of true love (Neubauer & Melzer, 1989;
Ravesloot, 1992).

We were interested in parent-child relationships and the support functions of
parents today and especially focused on mutual perceptions of familial communication. To gain insight into the support functions of parents, we analyzed the
different styles of communication that could be discerned.[7] During the first
research year, we asked the youngsters and parents about parental expectations

and values concerning behavior. Topics included sanctions, freedom to choose peers, home rules, appearance, dress, and hairdos, education and work, personal relationships, and sexuality.[8] We categorized the patterns of parental communication that we found as a range from a traditionally grounded demanding (or command) attitude, whereby children had to obey unequivocally and parental support was given in the form of "one-way traffic," to a negotiation attitude, in which the balance of power was more equal and consensus between parents and children was of great importance.[9]

Negotiation implies that support is given independently of how parents judge a given situation or a particular behavior of their child. Both negotiation and command attitudes can include a warm and positive involvement and support. But in the case of a command attitude, the child's position is rather submissive, whereas in the case of a negotiation attitude, the child's position is much stronger. We also discerned two intermediate communication categories. Descriptions of the four patterns discerned with exemplary quotations from the interviews follow.

(1) A Demanding Attitude. Communication between parents and children is based on parental authority and children's obedience; the margins within which the adolescents can negotiate are very small or nonexistent: "My daughter is not allowed to sleep with her boyfriend and I will not discuss this." "My father forbids me to sleep with my boyfriend and I must obey."

(2) Feelings of Involvement without Interfering. The parents demonstrate interest in the (sexual) lives and choices of their sons and daughters without feeling obliged or justified to interfere: "Although I don't like my daughter's boyfriend . . . it's her life and I have to respect her choices, I will not say anything about it." "I know my mother does not like my boyfriend, but she says it's my own business . . . if there are problems I can count on her, I'm sure."

(3) A Negotiation Attitude. The parents negotiate about behavioral margins and both parents and children feel that it is important to reach consensus on controversial matters: "I don't like my daughter's boyfriend sleeping at my place . . . so I sit down with her and we'll discuss it." "We would like to sleep at my place but I know my parents don't agree . . . we must discuss this point this weekend . . . we'll find a solution."

(4) Feelings of Incompetence. Parents regard themselves as incompetent educators; they have no influence on the behavior of their children: "I have nothing to say to my son, he goes his way." "I don't care what my mother says, I am 16 years old and do what I want."

We first show the distribution of the different parental communication patterns (Table 5). Then, we address mutual perceptions by comparing the parents' and children's views on parental attitude and support, with special attention to gender

Table 5.   Descriptions of Parents' Educational Attitude concerning
             Sexuality from Parents' Perceptions[a]

Parents	Mothers	Fathers
Involved without interfering	28	32
Negotiation attitude	26	10
Command attitude	2	3
Feelings of incompetence	3	14

[a] All data contained in this table are in absolute numbers. $N = 59$ for both
mothers and fathers.

differences between sons and daughters (Tables 6–9). Such a comparison of
parents' and adolescents' viewpoints has not previously been carried out in the
Netherlands.

On the whole, we expected a high degree of negotiation between parents and
children, for, on the one hand, parents would have to face the reality that
sexuality belongs to the youth phase as a developmental task, and on the other
hand, they would want to transmit their own values and certain behavioral
standards. If a daughter asked permission to sleep with a boyfriend at her parental home, we assumed that her parents would rather try to convey their values and
negotiate the issue than simply forbid her to go her way, because they would be
sure that "it" would happen anyhow. We also expected that there would be
parents who did not negotiate, especially with girls. Those parents would try to
prevent problems such as early pregnancy or loss of good name by adopting a
restrictive attitude. Table 5 shows the different parental attitudes.

Generally speaking, most of the parents, independent of social class, did not
wish to interfere with their children's sexual behavior. "It's their life and their
body" seemed to be the liberal opinion of most of the parents; it was characteristic of fathers even more than mothers. One father remarked about his daughter
that "most of the time she finds her own solutions, she talks with all kinds of
persons, and I think, most of the problems are their business . . . if she gets into
trouble, she can come to me, I am her father, but actually . . . I mean, and
maybe that's stupid: why should I interfere, let her have a look first."

An *attitude of nonintervention* could mean two things: There were parents
within this group who honestly showed respect for the private lives of their
children. Another group told us about feelings of discomfort. These parents
sheltered behind liberal thoughts of nonintervention, but actually they were
afraid of discussing sexual matters openly with their children. Their reserved
attitudes show the still existing taboo on this topic. Neubauer and Melzer (1989)
also paid attention to this parental attitude.

Thirty-six parents, independent of social class, considered themselves *negotiators*. Their attitude was characterized by an active involvement in the sexual
development and behavior of their children. We found qualitative differences

between passive and active interfering, observing a passive subgroup of 5 fathers and 2 mothers "waiting" until their sons or daughters consulted them and an active subgroup of 4 fathers and 21 mothers who took the initiative if they felt the need to make clear their own values and to influence their children's behavior. Yet they had open minds and did not wish to enforce a certain behavior or obedience.

Finally, there was a small group of negotiators, consisting of 3 mothers and 1 father, who had a totally liberal attitude: "Whatever you do is o.k. under the condition that you tell me." As one mother said:

> I cannot say to my children, you must do this . . . but we discuss things openly— and they tell me, if something [sexual intercourse] has happened. I insist on that, or let me say, whatever they do, I want them to tell me. I never could do that with my mother when I was young. We never were able to say anything to our mother and that's what I want with my children . . . I insist.

Unlike the former category of nonintervention, the negotiation subgroup showed gender differences. Many more mothers than fathers considered themselves negotiators, a gender-specific outcome that corresponds with findings in other youth research (Meeus, 1989; Peters, 1992; van der Linden, 1991).

The parents in our study had largely been brought up in demanding households with strongly restrictive sexual codes. As can be seen, this kind of *restrictive attitude* belongs to the past. Only 2 mothers and 3 fathers, all from the lower and middle classes, did not wish to negotiate at all with their children about topics concerning sexuality. These parents did not allow any kind of countering or arguing about any decision they made in the interests of their children. As one Father said: "In my home I forbid my son to sleep with his girlfriend . . . and I tell him I do not want myself and him getting into trouble."

Let us now turn to the 17 parents from all social classes who told us about *feelings of incompetence* concerning sexuality. More fathers than mothers belonged to this group. Evidently, it is harder for men than it is for women to be "modern educators"; these parents know they cannot "demand" anymore (as their fathers could), but an alternative attitude is difficult to develop. They complained about their sons and daughters going their own way and sidestepping parental rules and control. "Talking" and "threatening with sanctions" had no influence, according to these parents. Most of the parents acquiesced in the situation; they wanted to avoid conflicts and keep their children from leaving home too early. Qualitative analysis showed that, within this group of "incompetent parents," a subgroup of 8 fathers (mostly from higher social classes) could be distinguished who did not wish to have any kind of responsibility. They wanted their wives to solve problems and answer questions on this "difficult topic," viewing sexuality as "women's business": "It's my wife who talks about that kind of thing with my son . . . about sexuality. . . . I don't want to talk about that . . . She is better about that than me. . . . I support my son with his homework and that kind of thing."

So far, we can conclude that the expected modern parental attitude of negotiation indeed prevails—although only to a certain degree and mostly among mothers—whereas the old-fashioned demand attitude has almost disappeared. If parents give support in an active way, they do it by means of negotiation rather than by defining unequivocally "what's best for you." This modern parental attitude is not exclusively found in the upper classes but is spread over all social levels, although it must be mentioned that the few demanding parents observed all belonged to the lower classes. A large group of parents was involved in the "do's and don't's" of their children's lives, without interfering. These fathers and mothers gave no active support but rather, created a safety net. They functioned in the background and hoped their children would approach them if problems occurred. Their support lay in "being there in case of emergency." Sexuality was a private domain for both them and their children. As was suggested, behind this liberal attitude there were still feelings of shame and embarrassment derived from their own youthful educational experiences. We now turn to the question of whether the parents were able to give support if their children needed it and how their children experienced parental support.

4. RESULTS: COMPARISON OF PERSPECTIVES

Do parents and adolescents have the same opinions about the character of their communication about sexual matters? We expected, first, that there would be a great amount of agreement between noninterfering parents and their children. In other words, adolescents with parents who regarded themselves as noninterfering would regard their parents in the same way. Second, we expected discrepancies between negotiating parents and their children because, although these parents regarded themselves as being much more liberal than their own parents, their children could not make such an intergenerational comparison and thus would not experience a liberal attitude.[10]

4.1. Mothers and Daughters

If we are to believe public opinion and research, modern mothers and daughters have relationships characterized by trust and equality ("My mother is my best friend") more than by inequality and demands, especially in such an emotional area as sexuality. Hence, we expected a high level of agreement between mothers' and daughters' perceptions of negotiation. Table 6 compares the perspectives of 31 mothers and their daughters.

Comparing the totals on the group level, we notice some disagreement: Most

Table 6. Comparison of Mothers' and Daughters' Perceptions of Educational Attitude of Mother concerning Sexuality[a]

According to Daughters	According to Mothers					
	Noninterfering	Negotiating	Demanding	Incompetence	No Answer	Total
Demanding	6	5	1	0	1	13
Negotiating	0	3	0	0	0	3
Noninterfering	5	7	0	2	0	14
No answer	0	1	0	0	0	1
Total	11	16	1	2	1	31

[a] All data contained in this table are in absolute numbers.

mothers told us about their "modern" attitude of negotiation (16) or about noninterference (11), but most daughters told us about their mothers' "old-fashioned," demanding attitude (13) or about a noninterfering attitude (14). There were 13 daughters who perceived their mothers as restrictive educators, whereas their mothers perceived themselves as noninterfering or negotiating. Only one mother-daughter couple agreed on a demanding attitude. As for the 14 daughters who perceived their mothers as noninterfering, 5 mothers agreed, and 7 mothers regarded themselves as negotiators.

Eleven mothers considered themselves as liberal and as not interfering with the sexual lives of their daughters; 5 daughters agreed, but 6 girls considered their mothers very restrictive and demanding. Sixteen mothers regarded themselves as negotiators, whereas only 3 daughters told us the same, and most of the daughters did not experience any kind of negotiation. In other words, mothers had the impression that they negotiated with their children to a greater extent than their daughters did, whereas daughters had the idea that they had to deal with demanding mothers or with an attitude of nonintervention. The different perspectives of mothers and daughters do not have to be contradictory. It cannot be said that a mother has a "wrong" perception and her daughter a "right" one on the issue. For a mother can—referring to her sexuality—consider her attitude as communicative, based on equality and openness, whereas the daughter does not experience freedom to the same extent. The difference in judgment can be illustrated with the following statement: "How my daughter wants to deal with sex is her problem, they all have to find out! I am not able to interfere in any way and I don't wish to."

This liberal attitude did not mean she did not worry about her daughter. Recently, problems had occurred between her daughter and her boyfriend. Her daughter refused to talk out her problems. The mother found the situation unpleasant for her daughter, but she did not take any action:

I hope my daughter will behave more freely, how can I put it, less shy, I hope she learns to communicate easier . . . that's really her problem . . . but I will not arrange anything, that's not my business. I will not say anything to her . . . she is

17 years old. I already hear her friends sneering about me and saying she is an idiot, she lets her mother phone us, no.

Her 17-year-old daughter experienced the situation quite differently, holding the view that her mother always interfered in her life:

I am not allowed to go out whenever I want to . . . sometimes I am home too late . . . sometimes I am not . . . [at what time do you have to come home?] . . . at midnight and if I am too late . . . I have to stay inside next day or I get a serious warning.

Another mother always talked to her daughter. Finding a consensus was the most important ideal in her educational beliefs: "I always say to my children: talk with each other and do not keep things to yourself you can communicate about . . . if something is the matter, we'll find a solution for it together . . . that's important." Her 18-year-old daughter said: "My mother thinks she knows what's good for me and I have to do her will . . . for my own good she says."

Our expectation of a high degree of agreement between mothers who negotiated and their daughters was not supported. From the mothers' points of view, a modern mother-daughter relationship concerning sexuality could be characterized in terms of nonintervention (background support) or active support, but the daughters did not experience motherly support and freedom to the same extent. It is therefore questionable whether such a daughter would turn to her mother for support if she got into trouble—that is, whether such a mother would be able to support her daughter adequately.

4.2. Mothers and Sons

We expected mothers to be less involved with the sexual behavior of their sons because of the gender-specific values that still exist: Daughters must and will behave decently, whereas sons are allowed more freedom. This difference was expected to be reflected in a high number of mothers of sons who stayed in the background. Consequently, we expected a high level of agreement between mothers and sons about nonrestrictive attitudes. Table 7 compares the perceptions of mothers and sons.

Most of the mothers considered themselves noninterferers, and most of the sons told us the same. But 11 sons whose mothers regarded themselves as not at all demanding experienced a restrictive education. The highest number of boys (13) experienced a noninterfering motherly attitude; 8 mother-son couples agreed on this attitude, whereas 4 mothers perceived themselves as more permissive than their sons saw them as being.

One mother told us that, in her opinion, sex and love were connected to each other. She hoped that her son would experiment sexually within the boundaries

Table 7. Comparison of Mothers' and Sons' Perceptions of Educational Attitude of Mother concerning Sexuality[a]

According to Sons	According to Mothers					
	Noninterfering	Negotiating	Demanding	Incompetence	No Answer	Total
Demanding	6	4	0	1	0	11
Negotiating	2	1	0	0	0	3
Noninterfering	8	4	1	0	0	13
No answer	1	1	0	0	0	2
Total	17	10	1	1	0	29

[a] All data contained in this table are in absolute numbers.

of a steady relationship with the prospect of marriage. But she would never impose her will on her son or forbid anything to take place. She also hoped her son would be polite to girls and that he would never go "further with sex than the girl wants to." But again, she would not force anything:

> I think the most important issue for me is that everything is going well with my children, with their relationships and their sex; I don't care for the formality of marriage. It's their choice and that's o.k. Who am I to judge?

Kees, her 18-year-old son, had a girlfriend. According to Kees, his mother was not very happy with the situation; he thought his mother was afraid he would enter into a relationship too early. Actually, he found his mother far too interfering with his life and with his commitment to his girlfriend: "She wants me to slow down, and she says 'Don't go too steady, you are too young for that kind of thing.' She expects me to give it up."

Another mother described herself as "always explaining why and how" and found herself willing to negotiate at any time. She had the idea that she had a healthy and open relationship with her son, and she wanted to explain to him why it was so important not to go to bed with a girl you don't know very well: "I hope he will not go to bed with someone until he really loves a girl." If she had the impression that her son really loved somebody, she found it no problem at all to "let him go." Her son, who was 17 years old, did not experience his mother's attitude as advising. On the contrary, he found himself confronted with clear demands: "They don't want me to go and sleep around with any girl . . . they think that's dangerous . . . too many risks . . . having a baby is no fun."

Ten mothers regarded themselves as negotiators, whereas their sons perceived their attitudes as noninterfering.

From the mothers' points of view, a modern mother-son relationship concerning sexuality could be characterized—just as was the case between mothers and daughters—by modern values of not interfering or negotiating, whereas most sons considered their mothers either as noninterfering or as demanding. Comparing the motherly attitudes toward sons and daughters, we found a gender-specific attitude: More mothers let their sons be free and negotiated with daughters, whereas more or less equal numbers of sons and daughters experienced their mothers as demanding or not interfering. Most adolescents hardly negotiated with their mothers. In terms of amount of support, it can be said that mothers regarded themselves as more supportive (on an equal footing as negotiators or on an unequal footing as demanders) than their children viewed them as being.

4.3. Fathers and Daughters

On the whole, we expected that fathers would not show an active intention to negotiate with their children about sexual behaviors. Fathers did not wish to interfere with sexual education, having an attitude that could be characterized as remaining in the background. We expected that their strategy of nonintervention would be reflected in the answers of their daughters. A look at Table 8 nevertheless reveals a number of fathers and daughters with opposite perceptions.

A global look confirms our expectations: Most fathers and daughters told us about a noninterfering educational attitude and, indeed, most fathers had a corresponding position. But a substantial group of girls experienced their fathers as authoritarian, even if the fathers regarded themselves as negotiators, which was the case with 5 fathers. The following father and his daughter agreed that they had a relationship based on negotiation:

> I want to talk to my daughter to reach a consensus . . . last year she wanted to go on a holiday with her boyfriend . . . we don't like that kind of thing, she is only 18 years old, but, you know, times are changing, we have to face the facts, when we were young, that kind of thing was impossible, you did not even ask your father. . . . Now we'll talk and talk . . . until a solution is found.

His 18-year-old daughter had the same opinion: "We talk it over . . . until we find a solution . . . when I don't live at home any more I can go my own way." She will negotiate with her father until she lives on her own.

Table 8. Comparison of Fathers' and Daughters' Perceptions of Educational Attitude of Father concerning Sexuality[a]

According to Daughters	According to Fathers					
	Noninterfering	Negotiating	Demanding	Incompetence	No Answer	Total
Demanding	3	0	2	6	0	11
Negotiating	3	1	0	0	0	4
Noninterfering	6	4	0	2	1	13
No answer	1	0	0	0	0	1
Total	13	5	2	8	1	29

[a] All data contained in this table are in absolute numbers.

In contrast to the mothers, there was a group of fathers with feelings of incompetence. These fathers were frustrated because they had no influence on their daughters' behavior. Their daughters did not agree; most of them told us about a demanding fatherly attitude. Note that these two attitudes did not exclude each other from the viewpoint of the fathers. They could try to give strict orders to their daughters, just because they felt powerless, but the daughters did not wish to obey. One father said:

> If there are problems, my wife warns me. . . . I do not interfere with any-thing. . . . I work very hard and I'm not at my home very often . . . it's my wife's task to handle it. . . . I am not able to do that . . . it's not my business.

His 19-year-old daughter gave a completely different account:

> No, I am not allowed to go upstairs to my bedroom for a few hours, we were never allowed to do that . . . at half past eight he wants us to come downstairs to watch t.v. . . . I'm using the pill in secret and that's annoying . . . he badgers the life out of me to come home early . . . always restrictions.

In terms of amount of support, it can be said that fathers did not regard themselves as active supporters concerning sexuality. Most of them either did not interfere or had feelings of incompetence. Most daughters told us the same, or they found themselves confronted with strict demands. On the whole, we found few differences between fathers and mothers, although more fathers had negative feelings and more mothers perceived themselves as negotiators.

4.4. Fathers and Sons

Concerning fathers and sons, we expected even less interference and, accordingly, a high degree of agreement.

A global look at Table 9 indeed shows a high level of agreement. Most sons and fathers perceived the fatherly attitude toward sexuality as liberal. But there was disagreement as well. Eleven sons experienced a high degree of demand from their fathers, but almost all of the fathers perceived themselves as noninter-fering: "I let my son free, the only thing I hope is that he gets a family and children, but it's his life and his choices." His 17-year-old son told us: "I cannot speak about the things I do. . . . He would not like that at all . . . if he should know I sleep with girls . . . I don't know . . . he surely would disapprove."

We found few contradictions between those 14 sons who felt no parental influence at all and their fathers, although 4 of these fathers regarded themselves as negotiators. The highest number of fathers (21) regarded themselves as non-interfering, whereas only 9 of their sons experienced no restrictions or demands at all:

Table 9. Comparison of Fathers' and Sons' Perceptions of Educational Attitude of
Father concerning Sexuality[a]

According to Sons	According to Fathers					
	Noninterfering	Negotiating	Demanding	Incompetence	No Answer	Total
Demanding	10	0	0	1	0	11
Negotiating	1	0	0	1	0	2
Noninterfering	9	4	1	0	0	14
No answer	1	1	0	0	0	2
Total	21	5	1	2	0	29

[a] All data in this table are in absolute numbers.

> About my son . . . that's his life, I have nothing to say about it, I hope he will be
> happy, that's my only fear . . . but how he wants to arrange everything . . . that's
> his business . . . that remains his choice . . . whatever he prefers to do.

His 19-year-old son did not experience this kind of liberal attitude at all: "I
cannot come home with a girlfriend I like . . . and I am not allowed to marry or
to cohabit too early . . . that's what my father tells me. . . ."

As can be seen, these fathers were not active negotiators. They did not interfere, especially with regard to sons, or they felt incompetent on the matter and
left it to their wives. It must be mentioned that the largest differences between the
attitudes of mothers and fathers toward their children were mostly mentioned by
the parents. Sons and daughters did not experience their fathers' or mothers'
attitudes so differently. Both boys and girls experience parental attitudes in terms
of demands or nonintervention. In any case, we cannot confirm the global notion
that sexual education in modern families is undoubtedly supportive and liberal.
The consequences of these findings are discussed in the last section.

5. DISCUSSION

In our introduction, we remarked that in the course of modernization, youth as
a phase in the life course of people has undergone a prolongation, whereas youth
as a concept has become connected to a growing number of individual choices.
For both reasons, youth is changing from a short transition to adulthood into a
life period that is experienced by young people as endowed with cultural values.
Starting from the well-established assumption that peers and parents are the most
significant others during the youth phase, we asked about the supportive roles
and functions of these two reference groups.

Our first findings show peers to be the main reference group adolescents turn
to concerning all affairs connected to youth-culture lifestyles. Young people

discuss these matters with their peers at large, but most exclude their personal sexual lives and problems from this communication. They will discuss these matters with their love partners; most discuss them with nobody at all. In other words, personal sexuality is discussed primarily within highly individualized peer relationships, and this finding holds true for all social levels.

Second, we looked for peer pressure to behave sexually in a certain way. We found gender differences, with girls being more controlled by peers of the same gender than boys. Girls watch other girls' sexual behavior and thus enforce standards of double morality. Yet times have changed in as much as girls are allowed (and allow themselves) to be sexually active once they have entered steady relationships. The supporting function of peers in the field of sexuality does not seem to be as all-encompassing as has been suggested by youth research stressing the peer group as the main reference point for all youth-culture-bound activities.

Third, we approached the topic of parental support by looking at patterns of familial communication. Starting from the theoretical notion that a liberalization of parental values and attitudes is part of the above-mentioned processes of modernization, we established different communication patterns in the families on empirical grounds. The patterns ranged from a "demand" to a "negotiation" attitude. Within this range, we discerned a communication pattern of parental involvement without interfering, one of active negotiation, one of feelings of incompetence, and a traditional pattern of demand.

Our expectation that we would observe familial communication based largely on negotiation and liberal parental attitudes toward the sexual lives of their children was confirmed, albeit with mothers being more willing and apt to communicate than fathers were.

As Table 4 shows, only a minority of adolescents talk to their parents confidentially about sex, and if they do, they turn to their mothers and hardly ever to their fathers. This finding does not fit the picture the parents drew. We explained this discrepancy by pointing to a generation gap: when they compared their own adolescent period with that of their children, parents (across social classes) were convinced that there was much more openness in communication about sexuality than was the case when they were young. In other words, the two generations started from very different experiences—and that brought them to different judgments about sexual education.

It follows that the pattern of "not interfering" is a convincing parental attitude in all social classes that bridges the generation gap. Behind this attitude, we discerned a certain embarrassment about communicating about sexuality among the parents. Their children feel this embarrassment and therefore refrain from confidential communication about their sexual lives. They get the message from their parents that sex is only permitted in a steady relationship. They themselves have internalized this value pattern, but a steady relationship nowadays means something different than it did when their parents were young. Insofar as they experience more sexual freedom, the adolescents are not sure about the extent to which their parents will agree to sexual behavior.

Embarrassment and taboo are not restraints for negotiating parents (mainly mothers); they represent the most modern fraction of present-day parent educators. Negotiation implies no restrictions whatsoever and confidential and open communication between parents (mothers) and their children.

A closer look at the mutual perceptions of children and parents concerning sexual education and communication (Tables 6–9) confirms the existence of a generation gap, in that the children systematically perceived their parents as being more restrictive in their attitudes on sexual matters than the parents saw themselves as being, and mothers were perceived as more liberal than fathers. At the same time, we found some consensus, mainly within the category "not interfering."

We would like to discuss why young people refrain from talking about their sexual lives with their parents and also refrain from talking openly with their peers on a more theoretical level. In the course of modernization, a dialectical relationship develops between informalization and individualization. Informalization is expressed by a loosening of restrictions on sexuality; individualization is characterized by increasing options and individual freedom to make personal choices, choices that have to be legitimated by the individual. Thus, communicating about intimate feelings such as choosing a sex partner and experiencing problems with sexuality will be restricted to self-created situations and contexts. *Within* a generation of contemporaries, the courtship relationship is the most highly individualized peer relationship. *Between* generations, parents, especially mothers, are the most intimate interlocutors for young people. If parents act and react as truly liberal and open educators, young people will turn to them for support. But, as was shown, by no means all parents are free of embarrassment concerning sexual matters.

There is thus no reason to assume that young people will simply seek and find parental support. Such support will largely depend on the communication patterns in a family. A noninterfering parental attitude might be sufficient if young people are not in trouble or are able to develop effective skills, such as the ability to negotiate with their partners about use of contraceptives. They are then capable of and willing to solve all sexual matters themselves or with their partners. But if the opposite occurs, it is doubtful whether young people will get enough support from either their peers or their parents.

NOTES

1. We did not define sexuality during the interviews, but asked the respondents to answer from their own perspectives; however, we emphatically referred to their own

sexuality. It is interesting to note that most of the boys and girls directly associated "personal sexuality" with having or not having had the experience of coitus.

2. The project, conducted at Leiden University, at the Center of Youth Studies and Youth Policy, was co-financed by the Dutch Ministry of Social Affairs and Employment and the Ministry of Welfare, Public Health and Culture. The research group consisted of the authors and Els Peters, Harry Guit, and Erwin van Rooijen.

3. To determine social class, the respondents were asked to disclose their parents' (father's and mother's) educational and professional status. We compressed these data to determine an average social level for each family, taking the higher status in cases of a discrepancy between mother and father. We identified social class as high, middle, or low (cf. van Rooijen & Guit, 1990).

4. We asked each respondent to identify his or her most important confidential communication partner in the last year at school and the period after final exams (one response). The answers can be interpreted as representing a longer period (1988 and 1989).

5. Altogether, 51 respondents told us about having heterosexual courtships. Thus, 30 (51−21) respondents did not mention their lovers as confidential communication partners. These respondents, mostly lower-class girls, mostly communicated with their mothers or best friends in a confidential way.

6. See, for further analyses, Ravesloot and du Bois-Reymond (1992).

7. In the first place, we developed the communication codes between parents and children from the adolescents' point of view. Secondly, in analyzing the parent interviews, we found that it was necessary to add one new code, feelings of incompetence.

8. We must take into account the question of social desirability, especially as an influence on the parents. Parents have their own past experiences and may be inclined to give answers that fit how "modern parents" should behave. We tried to solve this problem by creating a confidential atmosphere during the interview and by asking about the same topics several times.

9. This typology is derived from the civilization theory of N. Elias, who perceived social change in terms of shifts in the balance of power between genders and the generations (de Swaan, 1982).

10. In this section, we analyze two subgroups: (1) 60 mothers with 31 daughters and 29 sons and (2) fathers with 29 daughters and 29 sons. The families were from different social levels, and most of the fathers and mothers were born between 1938 and 1945.

REFERENCES

Allerbeck, K., & Hoag, W. (1985). *Jugend ohne Zukunft?* [Youth without a future?] Munich: Piper.

Coleman, J. (1989). The focal theory of adolescence: A psychological perspective. In K. Hurrelmann & U. Engel (Eds.), *The social world of adolescents: International perspectives* (pp. 43–56). Berlin: de Gruyter.

de Swaan, A. (1982). Uitgaansbeperking en Uitgaansangst. Over de Verschuiving van bevels huishouding naar Onderhandelingshuishouding [Restrictions on "going out" and fear of "going out". On the shift from authoritarian to negotiative home ecology]. In A. de Swaan (Ed.), *De mens is de mens een zorg* (pp. 81–115). Amsterdam: Meulenhoff.

du Bois-Reymond, M. (1992). Eltern und Kind Beziehungen zwischen 1900 und 1920 am Beispiel Sexualerziehung [Parent-child relations between 1900 and 1920 as reflected in sex education]. *Zeitschrift für Biographieforschung und Oral History, 1,* 49–62.

du Bois-Reymond, M., Guit, H., & Rooijen, E. van (1992). Lebensentwürfe von Jugendlichen und die Rolle der Eltern beim Übergang ins Ausbildungs—und Beschäftigungssystem. Eine Studie aus den Niederlanden [Life plans of youth and the role of parents in the transition into the training and employment system]. *Zeitschrift für Sozialisationsforschung und Erziehungssoziologie, 12*(2), 114–132.

du Bois-Reymond, M., & Peters, E. (Eds.). (1992). *Keuzeprocessen van Jongeren. Dersd Onderzoeks rapportage* [Decision process of youngsters. Research report.] Leiden, the Netherlands: University Press.

du Bois-Reymond, M., Peters, E., & Ravesloot, J. (1990). Jongeren en Ouders: Van bevels—naar onderhandelingshuishouding. Een intergenerationele vergelijking. [Youth and parents: From authoritarian to negotiative home ecology. An intergenerational comparison.] *Amsterdams Sociologisch Tijschrift, 17*(3), 69–100.

Fisher, A., Fuchs, W., & Zinnecker, J. (1985). *Jugendliche + Erwachsene '85, Band 3: Jugend der Fünfziger Jahre, Heute* [Youth and adults '85. Volume 3: Youth of the fifties, today]. Opladen, Germany: Leske + Budrich.

Ford, C., & Beach, F. (1952). *Patterns of sexual behavior.* London: Eyre & Spottiwoode.

Fuchs-Heinrintz, W., Kruger, H., & Ecarius, J. (1990). Feste Fahrpläne durch die Jugendphase? [Firm itineraries through the youth phase?]. In M. du Bois-Reymond & M. Oechle (Eds.), *Neue Jugendbiographie? Zum Strukturwandel der Jugendphase* (pp. 25–41). Opladen, Germany: Leske + Budrich.

Hurrelmann, K. (1989). The social world of adolescents: A sociological perspective. In K. Hurrelmann & U. Engel (Eds.), *The social world of adolescents: International perspectives* (pp. 3–26). Berlin: de Gruyter.

Hurrelman, K., & Lösel, F. (1990). *Health hazards in adolescence.* Berlin: de Gruyter.

Kinsey, A., Pomeroy, W., & Martin, C. (1948). *Sexual behavior in the human male.* Philadelphia: Saunders.

Kinsey, A., Pomeroy, W., Martin, C., & Gebhard, P. (1953). *Sexual behavior in the human female.* Philadelphia: Saunders.

Kooij, G. A. (1972). *Jeugd en Seksualiteit Tegen de Jaren Zeventig* [Youth and sexuality around the seventies]. Wageningen, the Netherlands: Veenman.

Meeus, W. (1989). Parental and peer support in adolescence. In K. Hurrelmann & U. Engel (Eds.), *The social world of adolescents: International perspectives* (pp. 167–184). Berlin: de Gruyter.

Meeus, W. (1990). Ouders en leeftijgenoten in het Persoonlijke Netwerk van Jongeren [Parents and peers in the personal network of youngsters]. *Pedagogisch Tijschrift, 15*(1), 25–37.

Neubauer, G. (1990). *Jugendphase und sexualität* [The youth stage and sexuality]. Stuttgart: Enke.

Neubauer, G., & Melzer, W. (1989). Sexual development of the adolescent. In K. Hurrelmann & U. Engel (Eds.), *The social world of adolescents: International perspectives* (pp. 321–336). Berlin: de Gruyter.

Oswald, H., Pforr, P., & Pippig, K. (1991, July). *Sexuality and AIDS: Attitudes and behaviors of adolescents in East and West Berlin.* Paper presented at the XIth Biennial Meeting of the ISSBD, Minneapolis.

Peters, E. (1992). *Veranderingen in de jeugdfase van meisjes. Generaties vergeleken* [Changes in girls' adolescence: Comparing generations]. Leiden, the Netherlands: DSWO Press.

Rademakers, J. (1990). *De Eerste Kennismaking met Anticonceptie* [First encounters with contraceptives]. NISSO studies nr. 5. Delft, the Netherlands: Eburon.

Ravesloot, J., & du Bois-Reymond, M. (1992). *Communicatie Tussen Ouders en hun Jong Volswassen Kinderen over Seksualiteit* [Dialogue between young adults and their parents about sexuality]. In J. M. R. Gerris (Ed.), *Opvoedingsen gezinsonderzoek Serie nr. 6* (pp. 165–189). Amsterdam/Lisse: Swets & Zeitlinger.

Ravesloot, J. (1992a). Jongeren an Seksualiteit [Youth and sexuality]. In M. du Bois-Reymond (Ed.), *Jongeren op Weg Naar Volwassenheid* (pp. 65–91). Groningen, the Netherlands: Wolters Noordhoff.

Ravesloot, J. (1992b). Jongeren, Relatievorming en Seksualiteit [Youngsters, relationship formation and sexuality]. In M. du Bois-Reymond & E. Peters (Eds.), *Keuzeprocessen van Jongeren. Derde onderzoeksrapportage* (pp. 91–119). Leiden, the Netherlands: University Press.

Savin-Williams, R. C., & Berndt, T. J. (1990). Friendship and peer relations. In S. Feldman & G. R. Elliott (Eds.), *At the threshold: The developing adolescent* (pp. 277–307). Cambridge, MA: Harvard University Press.

Schmidtchen, G. (1992). *Ethik und Protest: Moralbilder und Wertkonflikte junger Menschen* [Ethics and protest: Moral representations and value conflicts of young people]. Opladen, Germany: Leske + Budrich.

Schmid-Tannwald, I., & Urze, A. (1983). Sexualität und Kontrazeption aus der Sicht von Jugendlichen und ihren Eltern [Sexuality and contraception from the perspective of youth and their parents]. *Schriftenreihe des Bundesministeriums für Jugend, Familie und Gesundheit* (Vol. 132). Stuttgart: Kohlhammer.

Sinnige, P. S. M. (1992). Communication of adolescents with parents and peers: A review of recent literature. *Zeitschrift für Sozialisationsforschung und Erziehungssoziologie, 2*, 133–147.

van der Linden, F. (1991). *Adolescent lifeworld: Theoretical and empirical orientations in socialization processes of Dutch youth.* Lisse, the Netherlands: Swets & Zeitlinger.

van Roajen, E., & Guit, H. (1990). De jeugdfase binnen het levensperspectief van jongeren [The youth phase in youngsters' life perspectives]. *Comenius, 40*, 450–464.

Younniss, J., & Smollar, J. (1985). *Adolescent relations with mothers, fathers, and friends.* Chicago: University of Chicago Press.

9

Mentors in Adolescents' Lives

Stephen F. Hamilton and Nancy Darling

The word "mentor" evokes the image of a wise counselor—someone who is at the same time nurturant, challenging, and experienced. At a more concrete level, the mentor relationship connotes a special bond between an inexperienced or naive student and someone more skilled than him or her who is willing to act as a guide in a new or unfamiliar situation. The prototypic mentor is an unrelated adult who takes on responsibility for socializing a youth above and beyond that required by his or her social role. A professional teacher or counselor may become a mentor, but the two roles are not identical; being a mentor entails a depth of commitment and breadth of involvement that exceed professional norms. Parents ordinarily do many of the same things unrelated adult mentors do, but because they are obligated by kinship to teach and counsel their progeny, the term mentor is usually reserved for unrelated adults. Mentoring relationships are considered to be beneficial in promoting competence and providing self-assurance and support in the face of new situations. This chapter will primarily discuss adolescents' mentoring relationships with unrelated adults but will also examine the extent to which adolescents' relationships with parents, other relatives, and peers have similar characteristics.

1. MENTORS AND ADOLESCENT DEVELOPMENT

Writing in the 1930s, the Soviet psychologist Vygotsky (1978) argued that social relations and activities together advance human development. If mentors engage in activities with adolescents that expand their competence, encourage them to engage in other such activities, and extend the range of people with whom they interact, then mentors should have a positive impact on adolescents' development. Bronfenbrenner drew upon ideas of Vygotsky, Lewin, and others in his book *The Ecology of Human Development* (1979) to construct a framework for understanding human development that emphasizes contexts and interactions. Our research was guided by Bronfenbrenner's proposal that "activity, role, and interpersonal relation" (1979, p. 22) are key elements of the ecology of human development and by his hypotheses that development is facilitated by participating in "progressively more complex patterns of reciprocal activity" (p. 60) in an environment characterized by a "balance of challenge and support" (p. 288).

Bronfenbrenner (Bronfenbrenner & Crouter, 1981) has also stressed the importance of research guided by what he termed "person-process-context" models; that is, studies that not only examine differences in developmental indicators among subgroups of people but also document the processes responsible for creating these differences and how those processes may vary depending upon characteristics of the developing person and the person's environment. When applying these criteria, it is not enough to identify differences in the school performance of adolescents of different social classes, for example; the researcher must also determine what features of the environments inhabited by adolescents of different social classes account for the differences in school performance and how those differences operate to produce different outcomes for different people. Heyns's (1978) study demonstrating higher rates of learning loss over the summer among disadvantaged children is an example of this kind of research, though it lacks the attention to characteristics of persons that Bronfenbrenner urged. The person-process-context model guided our analyses of the retrospective data from the present study.

1.1. Previous Research

When we began our study, the empirical literature on adolescents' interpersonal relations was limited to descriptive studies and to investigations of relations with peers and parents. Two of the most substantial contributions were those by Garbarino, Burston, Raber, Russell, and Crouter (1978) and Blyth, Hill, and Thiel (1982). Both reported adolescents' responses to questions about the most important people in their lives. Both found that parents, other family members, and peers were the most consistently listed, in that order. A review of these and related studies (Galbo, 1986) pointed out that parents remain the most important people in most adolescents' lives but that unrelated adults become increasingly important in later adolescence.

By its scant reference to the developmental effects of significant others, Galbo's (1986) review demonstrated the need to move beyond descriptive studies to assessments of impact, as Foster-Clark and Blyth (1987) did by showing drug abuse to be related to the characteristics of adolescents' social networks. Using data from our pilot study, Darling (1987) confirmed the value of examining the developmental impact of adolescents' significant others. She found that eighth and eleventh graders who reported the presence of challenging adults in their lives performed better on tests of verbal, quantitative, and reasoning abilities, after other factors had been controlled. Challenging parents of the same gender had the strongest impact, but parental influence declined while nonparental influence rose as a function of subjects' age.

Although much has been written about the benefits of mentors, there is little empirical evidence on how often they appear in the lives of adolescents or on their influence, or even agreement as to how they should be defined. The term mentor has been used in many different ways. There is confusion about what mentors are and what they do. They have been operationally defined as everything from the most influential professor a student had in college (Erkut & Mokros, 1984), to a professional a young student is assigned to during an internship (Borman & Colson, 1984), to someone who fosters a young adult's development by "believing in him, sharing the youthful Dream and giving it his blessing, helping to define the newly emerging self in its newly discovered world, and creating a space in which the newly emerging self can work on a reasonably satisfactory life structure that contains the Dream" (Levinson, 1978).

It is important to distinguish the use of the word mentor as it describes a social role from its use describing a functional role. Several authors have used "mentor" to describe adults who participate in programs designed to initiate adolescents ("protégés") into the world of adulthood by providing youths with career internships (Booth, 1980; Borman & Colson, 1984; Colson, 1980), serve as advisors to college students (Brown & DeCoster, 1982; Daloz, 1986), or help students work on areas of personal growth (Blyth, Bronfenbrenner, Ceci, Cornelius, Hamilton, & Voegtle, 1987). When used in this way, "mentor" describes a social role (who the people involved are) rather than a functional role (what the people involved do). When the word is used to describe a social role, any two people involved in such a program will be defined as mentor and protégé, regardless of the extent to which their relationship is characterized by the qualities such a relationship connotes.

On the other hand, a "functional role" is defined by its content rather than by its structure. Defined in this way, a mentor is one who performs the act of mentoring. The social roles of the participants—whether the experienced person involved is a college professor or a janitor—are irrelevant. Thus, in the social role "mentor" the incumbent's functional role is ignored, but in the functional role "mentor," the incumbent's social roles are ignored, and only his or her behaviors and the emotional relationship within the dyad are considered. Edlind and Haensly (1985) highlighted the tension between the two types of roles in the following statement about a mentoring program: "Mentorships, however, are difficult to establish; it might be more appropriate to say that educators arrange for two individuals with similar interests, a student and a professional, to come together in order to provide an opportunity for a mentorship to develop." The social role is easily established, but the functional role may not follow. It is the latter concept with which we will be concerned.

1.2. The Functional Role of Mentor

Following Bell (1970), we can distinguish two major components of the functional role of mentor: the interaction the mentor engages in with the protégé, and the mentor's provision of a role model. Interviews with mentors and their protégés have furnished some information concerning the objective behavior evidenced by mentors. First, a mentor is involved in a one-on-one relationship with a younger person. Moore (cited in Edlind and Haensly [1985]), described this relationship as informed by an attitude of "You ought to do this, I'll show you how." Teaching may be formal, as in the case of a piano teacher or athletic coach who is a mentor, but it may also be informal, occurring incidentally as an adult and a young person pursue common interests together. Teaching occurs naturally when an adult and a younger person tinker with an automobile engine, go camping, or talk about personal relationships, fishing, or future plans. In addition to conveying specific knowledge or skills, a teacher opens new vistas and provides new perspectives on familiar scenes. When a mentor shares her stamp collection with a young person, the content of the protégé's learning may be facts about philately, but it may also be the geography of exotic nations or the fine points of engraving and color printing.

Mentors also challenge protégés (Daloz, 1986). This act entails both pushing protégés to perform at their best level and pointing out options that they may not have recognized as possible for themselves. A mentor's challenging behavior is related to a protégé's goals and their attainment, though often those goals may be unstated, perhaps unrecognized. More specifically, mentors encourage young people to set goals and to set them high. They help protégés make plans for achieving their goals and help them evaluate their actions in terms of their contributions to meeting those goals. The challenge mentors provide is complemented by their teaching, in that one provides the impetus and the other the means of achievement. Evaluation of actions might occur at the conclusion of an explicitly goal-directed activity, but it might also occur when a mentor urges a protégé to try harder at something she or he has been doing, such as school work or playing a musical instrument.

Immediate goals are inherent in certain kinds of activities. When a mentor plays anagrams with a protégé, for example, the immediate goal is for the protégé to come up with as many different words as possible. In the long term, this activity may be associated with the goal of increasing cognitive competence, but neither the mentor nor the protégé needs to have such a goal foremost in his or her mind; it may be more salient that they are jointly engaged in an enjoyable activity. In other words, the long-term goals related to some challenging activities may be subordinated to the more immediate goals inherent in the activity and to the immediate goal of enjoying each other's company.

1.3. Characteristics of the Mentoring Relationship

The characteristics of a mentoring relationship described thus far can be objectively observed and are demonstrated by the person playing the mentor role. However, another component of that role is not dependent on the mentor, but on the protégé. In order for an adult to act as a mentor, he or she must be acknowledged by the protégé as a role model (Daloz, 1986; Erkut & Mokros, 1984; Torrance, 1983).

As defined by Kemper (1968), a role model is one "who demonstrates for the individual how something is done in the technical sense. . . .[The role model] is concerned with the 'how' question. The essential quality of the role model is that he possesses skills and displays techniques which the actor lacks (or thinks he lacks) and [is someone] from whom, by observation and comparison with his own performance, the actor can learn." A role model provides a protégé with observational learning opportunities that include imitation of new behaviors, inhibition of unsuccessful behaviors through observation of negative consequences, disinhibition of formerly constrained behaviors, and increasing use of successful behaviors through observation of positive consequences (Bandura, 1969).

Although a mentor cannot force a protégé to accept him- or herself as a role model, because of the importance of role modeling to effective mentoring, good mentors conduct themselves as if their protégés regard them as role models. This requirement carries three implications: (1) Mentors behave in a manner that they would wish their protégés to emulate. Mentors cannot be expected to be saints, but they should demonstrate exemplary character and integrity. When they fall short of their own ideals, it is not for lack of trying. (2) Mentors tell their protégés about challenges, moral dilemmas, and difficult situations they have faced. They describe these and their responses in order to help young people appreciate the need to struggle, not to glorify themselves or promote their own particular views. Describing a situation that, in hindsight, might have been better handled can be as instructive as describing one in which a mentor made the best decision. (3) As they interact with their protégés, mentors exemplify how mature, thoughtful adults think about issues, solve problems, and confront challenges. Exemplification is not limited to moral issues but also includes the whole range of challenge and support discussed above. With respect to all issues regardless of their moral weight, the purpose of exemplification is not to teach specific values to young people but to demonstrate to them one way to be responsible and competent adults.

The mentoring role, then, is defined both by behaviors enacted by the mentor—challenging, teaching, and supporting—and by the adoption of the mentor as a role model by the protégé. It is thus the relationship between the two participants that defines mentoring, not simply the behaviors or the psychological events experienced by either participant.

The type of relationship described by mentoring is of particular relevance to adolescents and young adults. One factor contributing to the emotional force of mentoring relationships may be the young person's discovery of an adult who "sees me as I really am" (Daloz, 1986) at a point of identity formation. Erikson (1968) suggested that "adolescents look most fervently for men and ideas to have faith in, which means men and ideas in whose service it would seem worth while to prove oneself trustworthy" (p. 130). Mentors provide both the ideals that are necessary for identity formation and the skills that allow those ideals to be realized. Through their very existence, they also provide proof that a transition to adulthood can be made. Identification with mentors may help protégés believe that they can successfully negotiate the transition as well.

During adolescence, the importance of nonparental adults in general, and nonparental adults playing mentoring roles in particular, may increase. Several factors contribute to this likelihood. First, an adolescent's drive to differentiate him- or herself from parents may make the adolescent more open to the influence of an adult other than a parent. Second, as a young person's contact with the world outside of the immediate environment increases, the expanded social network that unrelated adults have the potential to bring to a relationship becomes more valuable. Third, for the same reason, skills and knowledge that a mentor might have that differ from those possessed by family members become more valuable as they offer insight into the larger world. Fourth, a close, meaningful relationship with an adult other than a parent allows the adolescent to be involved in a more informal adult relationship that paves the way for the time when he or she too will be an adult. Lastly, as children become adolescents and young adults, they gain opportunities to initiate relationships with associates who share their interests. We begin by describing the frequency and content of these relationships.

2. DESIGN AND METHODS OF THE EMPIRICAL STUDY

Retrospective accounts of important people were collected from 126 (57 male and 69 female) third-year students at Cornell University who were recruited from three academic areas: business, natural sciences, and the humanities. Approximately equal numbers of males and females were recruited in each area. Comparable data were collected from a second sample of 40 eighth and 34 eleventh graders (respectively, 13 to 14 and 16 to 17 years old) in a small town in rural New York State. The secondary school sample will be used here only to make an age comparison regarding the prevalence of unrelated adult mentors.

2.1. Procedures

Students filled out several questionnaires in group settings. Four types of information were collected: (1) a list of the people who were important in their lives before the students entered college, (2) a description of their relationship with each person listed, (3) activities they had engaged in and with whom they had engaged in those activities, and (4) background information. In addition, the college students completed a battery of cognitive tests.

These data gave us two ways in which to describe our subjects' significant others, or associates. Their responses indicating whether the people they named were related and in what connection they knew them defined the associates' social roles: mother, brother-in-law, teacher, coach, and so forth. Statements describing the relationships defined what we called associates' functional roles.

2.2. Defining Functional Roles

Associates' functional roles were derived from subjects' dichotomous responses to 26 questionnaire items describing relationships. Iterated principal component factor analysis was employed to identify six functional roles defined by these items, which we labeled Mentor, Supporter, Companion, Dependent, Antagonist, and Challenger (Darling, 1986). The PROMAX method was used to rotate the factors. Table 1 presents loadings of the functional role items on each factor. An arbitrary decision was made that loadings higher than or equal to .30 would be considered nonzero.

The six factors are correlated (see Table 2). Students who described associates as mentors were unlikely to feel that they had taught the associates a great deal (i.e., that the associates were dependents). Mentoring and support are related, however, as are companionship and support. The associates whom students described as dependents were considered to be companions as well. All of these associations seem sensible, lending face validity to the derived factors.

2.3. Conceptual Reworking of Derived Factors

Because mentors are the focus of this chapter, only the Mentor factor will be discussed. On the conceptual grounds discussed above, this factor was divided into three dimensions, captured by the following questionnaire items: (1) Teacher —"I learned how to do things by watching this person do them" and "I acquired knowledge, information, or skills from this person." (2) Challenger—"This person challenged my ideas," "This person pushed me to do a good job," "This person pushed me to do things on my own," and "This person gave me constructive criticism." (3) Role Model—"I got a lot of my values from this person," "This person served as a role model of achievement for me," and "I admired this person as a human being."

2.4. Assigning Functional Roles to Associates

Associates were classified as performing a particular functional role when the number of items a subject identified with them exceeded the sample median for

Table 1. Loadings of Functional Role Items on Six Factors

	F1	F2	F3	F4	F5	F6
Factor 1: Mentor						
44. I learned how to do things by watching this person do them.	.74*	.07	.03	−.13	.10	−.09
53. I acquired knowledge, information, or skills from this person.	.71*	.03	−.01	−.10	.01	.09
46. This person pushed me to do a good job.	.62*	−.21	.04	−.06	.03	.37*
51. This person pushed me to do things on my own.	.58*	−.16	.02	.04	.01	.20
65. I got a lot of my values from this person.	.57*	−.12	.09	.28	−.02	−.11
57. This person served as a role model of achievement for me.	.49*	.04	−.12	.00	−.07	.05
59. I admired this person's qualities as a human being.	.47*	.19	.09	.14	−.27	−.07
63. This person gave me constructive criticism.	.42*	.13	−.00	.06	−.03	.39*
Factor 2: Companion						
49. This person was fun to be with.	.07	.72*	.04	−.05	−.16	−.02
56. We shared a lot of interests in common.	−.00	.69*	.08	−.02	−.01	−.06
48. We did things that were new and exciting.	−.03	.61*	.02	.01	.06	.04
50. We talked together and shared ideas.	.00	.61*	.07	.11	−.09	.23
43. This person introduced me to new ideas, interests, and experiences.	.29	.34*	−.18	.09	.02	.11
Factor 3: Dependent						
52. I helped this person learn how to do things.	.05	.12	.67*	−.03	.09	.05
47. When we did things together, I usually took the lead.	−.13	.09	.64*	−.10	−.06	.02
68. I taught this person quite a bit.	.06	−.00	.63*	.12	.12	−.04
Factor 4: Supporter						
62. This person protected me from getting hurt emotionally.	.10	−.05	−.02	.61*	.01	−.06
64. I served as a source of emotional support for this person.	−.13	.15	.31	.43*	.13	−.02

(*continued*)

Table 1. (Continued)

	F1	F2	F3	F4	F5	F6
45. This person gave me emotional support, security, and encouragement.	.24	.15	.01	.40*	−.09	.08
54. This person gave me advice about my personal life.	.06	.33*	−.06	.34*	.10	.16
66. I was physically attracted to this person.	−.15	.08	.08	.16	.07	.09
Factor 5: Antagonist						
58. This person had some negative influence on me.	−.10	−.15	.02	.04	.53*	.10
67. This person and I would get angry at each other.	.18	−.02	.25	.04	.50*	.04
55. When we did things, this person usually took the lead.	.29	.13	−.33*	.08	.36*	−.04
60. I competed with this person.	−.19	.35*	.14	−.14	.34*	.04
Factor 6: Challenger						
61. This person challenged my ideas.	.24	.14	.01	−.05	.19	.39*

*Nonzero loadings.

the factor that represented that role. Operationally, then, a Mentor is an associate identified with four or more of the seven items composing the Mentor factor. (Such associates will be denoted as "Mentors" throughout the text to distinguish the use of the operational definition from other definitions of the word "mentor.") To be classified as a Teacher, an associate must have been identified with both of the items defining a Teacher: a Challenger classification required three or four

Table 2. Interfactor Correlations

	Mentor	Companion	Dependent	Supporter	Antagonist	Challenger
Mentor	—	.16	−.34*	.42*	−.03	.17
Companion		—	.38*	.42*	.21	.09
Dependent			—	.08	.16	−.06
Supporter				—	−.04	.26
Antagonist					—	−.02
Challenger						—

*Nonzero correlations.

items, and a Role Model classification, two or three. This procedure reflected our interest in the people in adolescents' lives rather than in the total or average quality of the adolescents' relationships with a range of people. We wished to know about the individuals who could be classified as Mentors, not the sum total of mentoring performed by various people. We recognized the argument against classifying associates dichotomously as either Mentors or not Mentors; in reality the characteristics of a Mentor are found to a greater or a lesser degree in different associates. Alternative methods, which treated functional roles as linear variables characterizing either associates or social environments, yielded similar results but greatly complicated interpretation and presentation. Using a median split to define functional roles operationally simplified interpretation of the data and assured that only associates who were strongly identified with the relevant items were classified in the role.

2.5. Questions

The empirical results that follow address five questions: (1) Who has Mentors? What proportion of the sample identifies unrelated adult associates as performing the Mentor role? Are there gender and age differences? (2) What components of the Mentor role are reported most frequently? Do these vary by gender? (3) What activities do Mentors engage in with adolescents? (4) To what extent do parents, other relatives, and peers interact with adolescents as Mentors do? and (5) Are adolescents whose parents act as Mentors more or less likely to have unrelated adult Mentors?

3. RESULTS: MENTORS IN THE LIVES
OF AMERICAN ADOLESCENTS

Eighty-two percent of the 127 college students in our sample named at least one unrelated adult as an important person in their lives (i.e., as an associate). Of those subjects, 45 percent had at least one associate who qualified as a Mentor by our criteria. Twenty-four percent of the students described more than one unrelated adult associate as a Mentor.

3.1. Who Has Mentors?

Females were less likely than males to have unrelated adult Mentors (37% vs. 54%, $p < .05$). Because females are more likely than males to name unrelated adults as significant others, this difference is further exaggerated when we look only at those students who named unrelated adults. Seventy-two percent of the males who named unrelated adults described at least one such individual as a Mentor, but only 43 percent of the females who named unrelated adults did. Thus, although males were less likely to have unrelated adults in their lives, an unrelated adult who became significant to a male was more likely to become a Mentor.

The sample of secondary school students allowed us to explore age trends in adolescents' descriptions of their relationships with unrelated adults. Approximately the same proportion (about 60%) of the eleventh graders and college students who named adult associates described at least one of them as a Mentor, but the eighth graders were less likely to do so (25%). The proportion of students who named unrelated adults as significant others grew larger with age as well. Few of the eighth graders (53 percent of the girls but only 6 percent of the boys), a larger number of eleventh graders (61%), and a still larger number of college students (82%) named unrelated adults as significant others. The rarity of students', especially male students', involvement with unrelated adults during early adolescence suggests that mentoring may be associated more strongly with middle and late adolescence.

3.2. What Components of the Mentor Role Are Most Commonly Reported?

The three components of the Mentor role are distributed almost equally, with Teacher being somewhat more frequent (68 percent with at least one in this role), followed by Role Model (67%), and Challenger (56%). However, the picture changes when the components are arrayed by gender, as in Figure 1. Males were more likely than females to have unrelated adult associates who fulfilled the instrumental dimensions of the mentoring role—Teacher and Challenger—but no more likely to see their unrelated adult associates as Role Models.

3.3. What Activities Do Mentors Engage in with Adolescents?

In view of Vgotsky's observation that people and activities together advance human development, activities should be examined along with relations. Do unrelated adult Mentors participate in a greater variety of activities with adolescents than other unrelated adult associates do? Our data indicate that Mentors engage in a greater range of activities with students than unrelated adults not classified as Mentors, but the difference is not statistically significant.

Unrelated adults, then, were not described as Mentors simply because of the number of activities that they engaged in with students. We have no data comparing the intensity with which Mentors and other associates engaged in activities with adolescents or indicating the importance adolescents placed on this participation. However, there were some activities that unrelated adults who were

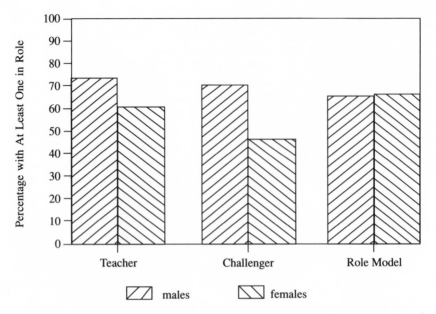

Figure 1. Percentages of males and females describing at least one unrelated adult associate as a Teacher, Challenger, or Role Model.

Mentors participated in more frequently than did unrelated adults who were not: (1) talking about personal matters you cared deeply about, (2) talking about family and friends, (3) talking about ideas, politics, the news, the future, and so forth, (4) playing word games, (5) listening to music, (6) cultural experiences (going to classical music concerts, plays, lectures, museums), (7) outdoor activities other than games, and (8) organized activities in or out of school.

The verbal and cultural content of these activities is notable. It is unclear whether this pattern of activities characterizes all Mentor-adolescent relations or simply characterizes those of our student sample. It may be that the kind of adolescent who enrolls in Cornell University is more likely to participate in such activities with adults who challenge, teach, and act as role models for them than are adolescents who become skilled machinists. The nature of the activities engaged in with Mentors may hold the key to explaining why having a Mentor appears to foster cognitive development.

3.4. Do Other Associates Relate
to Adolescents as Mentors Do?

Although we began by defining mentors as unrelated adults who act as informal teachers and counselors, our operational definition of a Mentor in terms of a functional role leaves open the question of whether persons in other social roles

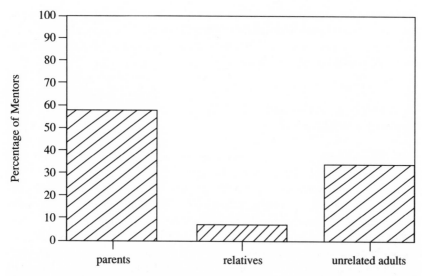

Figure 2. Percentages of adult mentors who are parents, and nonparental relatives.

are also described by adolescents as Teachers, Challengers, and Role Models. The answer to that question is yes. Of the 563 adults that students named as significant others, 52 percent were classified as Mentors. The majority of adult associates who met the operational definition were parents, who accounted for 58 percent of adult Mentors (see Figure 2). Unrelated adults were the next largest category, 34 percent, and relatives other than parents made up only 7 percent of the Mentors.

That most people who relate to adolescents as Mentors do are parents is unsurprising in view of our operational definition; one way of defining a mentor is as someone who stands in loco parentis (as the original Mentor did with Telemachus on behalf of Odysseus). One might suspect that the prominence of parents among mentoring associates results from the fact that most subjects named their parents as important people in their lives. Parents who were listed were also more likely than any other associates to be classified as Mentors. Unrelated adults were the next most frequently listed as adult associates, followed by relatives. Hence, there are more parents and fewer relatives in the pool of adult associates who might be described as Mentors. However, most parents named as associates (67%) were also classified as Mentors. Of the unrelated adults named as associates, 44 percent were Mentors, and only 27 percent of relatives other than parents fit our definition of a Mentor.

Subjects named 843 peers and siblings as associates. Peers who were no more than one year older or younger than subjects were classified as same-age peers. All siblings ($n = 247$) were coded as peers regardless of age, on the grounds that they belonged to the same generation as the subjects. Nearly all the siblings who were named were either close in age to or older than the subjects. No younger peers were described as Mentors. Siblings and same-age peers were described as performing the mentoring role in nearly equal proportions (about 48 percent), with the balance accounted for by older peers.

3.5. Mentoring Parents and Unrelated Adult Mentors

The predominance of parents among the associates of adolescents who filled the functional role of Mentor raises the question of whether adolescents whose parents function as Mentors are more or less likely to have unrelated adult Mentors than adolescents whose parents do not function as Mentors. According to one line of reasoning, unrelated adult Mentors complement parents; they reinforce the kinds of things most parents already do. A competing hypothesis is that adolescents whose parents do not do what Mentors do seek out other adults to perform those functions. In this case, unrelated adult mentors substitute for parents. Males who described at least one of their parents as a Mentor were more than twice as likely to describe an unrelated adult as a Mentor than were males whose parents were not Mentors. This finding was not true for females, however.

If unrelated adult Mentors substitute for parents, then adolescents whose parents are divorced would be more likely to have them than those in two-parent families. However, this was not the case; students who came from divorced families were no more likely to have unrelated adult Mentors than students from intact families. These findings suggest that nonparental Mentors complement parents rather than substitute for them. We suspect that males' parents who are Mentors are more likely to encourage their sons in the formation of positive relationships with other adults than are females' parents; the fact that more of the boys we invited to join the experimental mentor program accepted and received permission from their parents supports this assumption.

4. DISCUSSION

These results are useful for their descriptive content. With relatively little known about adolescents' relations with adults, researchers need to begin simply by learning how many and what kinds of adults adolescents consider to be important. The comparisons by gender, parental role, and age yielded important findings. Chief among these findings are that younger adolescents and females are less likely to have unrelated adult mentors than older adolescents and males and that unrelated adult mentors appear to complement rather than substitute for parents.

The age relationship seems easily explained. It is consistent with the vision of the developmental process in which adolescents gradually enlarge their social networks to include more people outside their families. The difference between males and females is less easily explained, though it is also consistent with what is known about gender differences in adolescent social relations. It is interesting to note that females were just as likely as males to describe their parents as Mentors. In fact, the principal difference between the boys' and girls' descriptions of their nonparental adult associates was that the girls identified fewer relatives and unrelated adults as being Teachers and Challengers, though they were equally likely to describe them as Role Models. These data suggest that some differences in male and female socialization might be attributable less to adolescents' relations with their parents (or to what adolescents contribute to their interpersonal relations) than to how other relatives and unrelated adult associates act toward adolescents. Our design was not powerful enough to support firm conclusions on these matters, but the suggestion is tantalizing.

Finding that unrelated adult mentors appear to complement rather than substitute for parents confirms results from the studies cited above (Blyth et al., 1982; Galbo, 1987; Garbarino et al., 1978) finding that adolescents continue to regard their parents as the most important people in their lives even as their social networks expand. It also constitutes a warning that unrelated adult mentors are unlikely by themselves to fill the gap left by absent or unavailable parents, at least in naturally occurring relationships. It is possible that mentors introduced to adolescents as part of a program could compensate for absent parents or parents who for other reasons do not function as Mentors. The scarcity of compensatory mentors in our sample, however, suggests that this substitution may not be easily accomplished.

This difficulty has been a major limitation to mentoring programs, including one developed in connection with the present study (Hamilton & Hamilton, 1992). Attempts to synthesize mentoring relationships between adolescents and adults have fallen short of their advocates' hopes (Freedman, 1993).The limitation results from the need for both parties to contribute to the relationship and, ironically, from the same barriers of distance, social class, and conflicting commitments that separate adolescents from adults in the first place.

Mentoring relationships with nonkin adults are likely to be beneficial to adolescents, especially when their parents are unable or unavailable to perform mentoring functions. However, as Freedman suggests, the most effective intervention is probably providing "mentor-rich environments" for youth rather than attempting to create mentoring relationships without appropriate contexts and without opportunities for mutual self-selection.

ACKNOWLEDGEMENT

An earlier version of this chapter was presented at the International Symposium on Unrelated Adults in Adolescents' Lives at Cornell University in March

1988. It is one product of a larger project supported by grants from the New York State College of Human Ecology, the Spencer Foundation, and an anonymous donor. Dale Blyth, Urie Bronfenbrenner, Stephen Ceci, and Steven Cornelius have been involved in that project, which was directed at its conclusion by the first author. Secondary school data were collected by Dr. David Smith and his students at Potsdam State College. A number of Cornell students have assisted in data collection, reduction, and analysis. All these people and others deserve our thanks. We would especially like to acknowledge the help and guidance of Urie Bronfenbrenner in this effort.

REFERENCES

Bandura, A. (1969). Social learning theory of identification process. In D. A. Goslin (Ed.), Handbook of socialization theory and research (pp. 213–262). Chicago: Rand McNally.

Bell, A. P. (1970). Role modelship and interaction in adolescence and young adulthood. *Developmental Psychology, 2*, 123–128.

Blyth, D. A., Bronfenbrenner, U., Ceci, S., Cornelius, S., Hamilton, S. F., & Voegtle, K. H. (1987). *Linking up: An experiment in building teenage competence.* Unpublished manuscript, Cornell University.

Blyth, D., Hill, J. P., & Thiel, K. P. (1982). Early adolescents' significant others. *Journal of Youth and Adolescence, 11*, 425–450.

Booth, L. (1980). An apprentice-mentor program for gifted students. *Education Digest*, December, 38–43.

Borman, C., & Colson, S. (1984). Mentoring—An effective career guidance technique. *Vocational Guidance Quarterly, 32*, 192–197.

Bronfenbrenner, U. (1979). *The ecology of human development: Experiments by nature and design.* Cambridge, MA: Harvard Unversity Press.

Bronfenbrenner, U., & Crouter, A. C. (1981). The evolution of environmental models on developmental research. In H. P. Mussen (Ed.), Handbook of child psychology, Vol. 1: History, theory, and methods (W. Kessen, volume editor) (pp. 357–414). New York: Wiley.

Brown, R. D., & DeCoster, D. A. (Eds.). 1982. *Mentoring-transcript systems for promoting student growth.* San Francisco: Jossey-Bass.

Colson, S. (1980). The evaluation of a community-based career education program for gifted and talented students as an administrative model for an alternative program. *Gifted Child Quarterly, 24*, 101–106.

Daloz, L. A. (1986). *Effective teaching and mentoring: Realizing the transformational power of adult learning experiences.* San Francisco: Jossey-Bass.

Darling, N. (1986). *The functional roles played by important people in developing lives: An exploratory factor analysis.* Unpublished manuscript, Cornell University.

Darling, N. (1987). *The influence of challenging and supportive relationships on the academic achievement of adolescents.* Unpublished master's thesis, Cornell University.

Edlind, E. P., & Haensly, P. A. (1985). Gifts of mentorships. *Gifted Child Quarterly, 29*, 55–60.

Erikson, E. H. (1968). *Identity: Youth and crisis*. New York: Norton.

Erkut, S., & Mokros, J. R. (1984). Professors as models and mentors for college students. *American Educational Research Journal, 21*, 399–417.

Foster-Clark, F. S., & Blyth, D. A. (1987). *Predicting adolescents' drug use: The role of personal and social network characteristics.* Paper presented at the Biennial Meeting of the Society for Research in Child Development, Baltimore.

Freedman, M. (1993). *The kindness of strangers: Adult mentors, urban youth, and the new voluntarism.* San Francisco: Jossey-Bass.

Galbo, J. J. (1986). Adolescents' perceptions of significant adults: Implications for the family, the school, and youth serving agencies. *Children and Youth Services Review, 8*, 37–51.

Garbarino, J., Burston, N., Raber, S., Russell, R., & Crouter, A. (1978). The social maps of children approaching adolescence: Studying the ecology of youth development. *Journal of Youth and Adolescence, 7*, 417–428.

Hamilton, S. F., & Hamilton, M. A. (1992). Mentoring programs: Promise and paradox. *Phi Delta Kappan, 73*, 546–550. (Reprinted in *New Designs for Youth Development*, 1992, *10*(2), 13–17.

Heyns, B. (1978). *Summer learning and the effects of schooling.* New York: Academic Press.

Kemper, T. (1968). Reference groups, socialization and achievement. *American Sociological Review, 33*, 31–45.

Levinson, D. (1978). *The seasons of a man's life.* New York: Knopf.

Torrance, E. P. (1983). Role of mentors in creative achievement. *Creative Child and Adult Quarterly, 3*, 8–15, 18.

Vygotsky, L. S. (1978). Mind in society: The development of higher educational processes. Cambridge, MA: Harvard University Press.

III

PROBLEM BEHAVIOR AND PROBLEMATIC ENVIRONMENTS

The selections in Part III explore adolescent problems with an emphasis on the kinds of social environments that elicit problem behavior. A brief description of the chapters follows.

Personality, Perceived Life Chances, and Adolescent Health Behavior

Jessor, Donovan, and Costa developed problem-behavior theory to understand delinquency and related adolescent behavior. In this chapter, they apply the theory to health behavior. They find correlations in their data between various health behaviors and other personality and behavioral patterns as well as adolescents' ecological locations.

The Development of Authoritarianism in Adolescence

Despite their tiny numbers, young neo-Nazis in Europe are frightening. Vollebergh provides some clues about the sources of their attitudes. Her longitudinal study found authoritarianism declined over time among students in more academic schools, with better-educated boys' authoritarianism declining toward girls' initially lower levels. Less-educated boys were the most authoritarian.

Youth in the Shadow of War, War in the Light of Youth

Much of the literature on youth and war has held that war is likely to be traumatic because it is a societal crisis that coincides with the individual crisis of becoming adult. However, interview responses of Israeli veterans of the Yom Kippur War who were exposed to battle as adolescents and young adults were very different from what might be expected. Lomsky-Feder found that war

217

seemed normal to them, and their youthfulness seemed a resource that helped them to cope with the experience, which most described as an opportunity to mature. These findings may reflect a situation unique to Israel, but they suggest that the way young people experience war and make sense of it as adults depends heavily on the meaning of war in their society. It may also depend upon the meaning of a particular war.

Youth in Dangerous Environments:
Coping with the Consequences

Physical danger is harmful by definition. James Garbarino points to the different contexts in which children and adolescents experience violence either directly or as witnesses, including war, civil unrest, crime, and domestic abuse. He gives examples of different ways of coping with violence, contrasting the political and ideological contexts and orientations accompanying war and insurrection with the nonpolitical context of crime. Political contexts have an advantage in that, unlike high-crime neighborhoods, they can provide emotional support and social sanction for adolescents who have been exposed to violence.

10

Personality, Perceived Life Chances, and Adolescent Behavior

Richard Jessor, John E. Donovan, and Frances Costa

Both societal and scientific concern with health among young people has grown substantially in recent years. Indeed, the World Health Organization selected "the health of youth" as the topic for global attention during its 1989 Technical Discussions in Geneva (Jessor, 1989). Among biomedical and social scientists, there is considerable consensus that adolescence is something of a crucible for the shaping of health in later life. Not only are many health-related behaviors— eating and exercise patterns, sanitary practices, safety habits, and substance use—initially learned and tried out in adolescence, but also, many of the values, beliefs, and self-concepts that influence and regulate the occurrence of health-related behaviors are acquired or consolidated in that period as well. Perhaps the most important advance has been the recognition that behavior plays a central role in health and that much of the variation in health derives from the actions and decisions and choices that individuals make. In short, there is now considerable agreement that behaviors are critically important risk factors for disease, disability, and death.

The behavioral perspective on health has been generative in several respects, especially in relation to youth. It has stimulated a large body of research on the psychosocial determinants of health behavior, determinants that refer to the immediate context or setting in which health behavior occurs. It has also stimulated inquiry about the organization of health-related behaviors, their interrelatedness, and the degree to which they covary in the maintenance of health or the etiology of disease. The behavioral perspective has also put on the scientific agenda the question of links between health behavior and other domains of adolescent life, such as school achievement, interpersonal relations, and problem behavior.

Salutary as these developments have been, they have not as yet enabled scientific understanding to "exceed its grasp" by as much as may have been hoped. The key limitations of the research conducted thus far would seem to stem from the unsatisfactory state of theory in the field of adolescent health. Much of the research appears to be entirely atheoretical. Where theory has been engaged, it has tended to be highly proximal, invoking concepts that are directly and immediately implicative of health, such as health beliefs and intentions, social support for health behavior, and internal versus external control of health. Although such work clearly advances understanding of factors that influence health behavior, the proximal nature of the concepts—their immediacy, and the commonsense obviousness of their linkage to behavior—does not yield a social psychology that can capture more remote regions of the causal network. Neither do such proximal concepts make apparent the relation of health behavior to other domains of adolescent behavior. Finally, such proximal conceptual efforts are unlikely to engage systematically the role of the larger social environment, an even more distal and yet enduringly important source of influence on behavior.

1. PROBLEM-BEHAVIOR THEORY AND ADOLESCENT HEALTH BEHAVIOR

Our own efforts have sought to explore the reach and the relevance of a particular social-psychological framework—problem-behavior theory—as an account of variation in adolescent health behavior (Costa, Jessor, & Donovan, 1989; Donovan, Jessor, & Costa, 1991; Jessor, 1978, 1982, 1984; Perry & Jessor, 1985). Originally formulated for a study of alcohol abuse and other social problem behaviors in a small, rural, triethnic community (Jessor, Graves, Hanson, & Jessor, 1968, pp. xi & 500), the theory was later revised and elaborated to guide a longitudinal study of problem behavior among cohorts of adolescents who were followed well into young adulthood (Jessor, Donovan, & Costa, 1991; Jessor & Jessor, 1977).

Since the general framework of problem-behavior theory has been explicated in other publications (e.g., Jessor, 1987; Jessor & Jessor, 1977, chapter two), only a brief description is warranted here. The theory is focused upon three major systems: *behavior*, both conventional behavior (e.g., church attendance, school achievement) and unconventional or problem behavior (e.g., problem drinking, illicit drug use, delinquency, aggression, precocious sexual intercourse, risky driving); *personality* (including values and expectations about achievement and autonomy, beliefs about the self and the social world, and attitudes about morality and normative transgression); and the *perceived environment* (perceived controls, and supports, models, and approval for problem behavior). Some of the concepts in the theory are theoretically proximal to problem behavior; examples are attitudinal intolerance of deviance and perceived models for drug use. Others are distal—for example, the value placed on academic achievement and perceived parental support. All of the concepts in each of the systems have an explicit directional implication for the likelihood of occurrence of problem behavior and reflect the underlying idea of *proneness to problem behavior*. In the logic of problem-behavior theory, it is possible to speak of personality proneness, or perceived environmental proneness, or, taking the two together, of overall psychosocial proneness to problem behavior. At whatever level, proneness is the fundamental explanatory notion in the theory.

The theory has by now been employed in a wide variety of studies, both cross-sectional and longitudinal, dealing with a wide variety of problem behaviors in a number of different societies, and it has consistently shown itself to be at least modestly useful. The key personality and perceived environmental variables have proved predictive of both cross-sectional and developmental variation and, taken together, they usually account for between 30 and 50 percent of the variance in behaviors such as illicit drug use or delinquency among adolescents. In addition, the relevant research has shown that there is significant covariation among problem behaviors and that they tend to be positively related among themselves but negatively related to conventional behaviors.

As mentioned earlier, the theory has been extended in recent years to explore its relevance for adolescent health behavior. Some comment needs to be made about the warrant for extending the theory beyond the problem behavior domain for which it was originally formulated; the rationale has been elaborated in more detail elsewhere (Donovan et al., 1991; Jessor, 1984). First, we have argued at the very outset of our work (Jessor et al., 1968) that a theory of deviance or problem behavior was, necessarily and simultaneously, an account of conforming behavior. To the extent that health behavior can be seen as conforming or conventional behavior, the theory ought, logically, to be relevant. Second, it is clear that there are widely shared social norms for engaging in health-enhancing behavior and for avoiding health-compromising behavior. Those norms are promulgated by the institutions of conventional society, and youths are regularly exhorted by parents, schools, and the media to comport themselves in accord with them. To the extent that failing to engage in health-enhancing behavior or actively engaging in health-compromising behavior represents the transgression of or departure from norms, the theory should be apposite, since accounting for normative transgression is its primary aim.

Third, several of the problem behaviors that the theory is concerned with—for example, cigarette smoking or alcohol abuse—are simultaneously defined as health-compromising behaviors by researchers in the health field. The theory's demonstrated utility in accounting for such health-compromising behaviors suggests the possibility of its relevance to other, nonproblem health behaviors. Finally, problem-behavior theory research showing the interrelatedness of various problems suggests the possibility of even larger organizations of behavior within an individual's repertoire, organizations at the level of lifestyle that may entail links between problem behaviors and health behaviors.

Given these various considerations as warrant, the exploration of adolescent health behavior within the framework of problem-behavior theory has the potential of providing a more distal account, one that embeds health behavior in a broader network of person-environment variables, one that illuminates the relation of health behavior to other domains of adolescent behavior, and one that can articulate its linkage with the larger social environment. These are the key issues in the present report.

2. DESCRIPTION OF THE STUDY

At the time of this writing, the research presented here had only recently been completed, and its data were not yet fully analyzed. Nevertheless, the study enabled us to address, at least in a preliminary fashion, the three key issues noted above. Data were collected during the spring of 1989 in six middle schools (grades 7 and 8) and four high schools (grades 9–12) in a large metropolitan school district in a Rocky Mountain state. The city's population numbered over half a million residents and was ethnically heterogeneous, with Hispanic citizens constituting its largest minority. Schools were assigned to the study from inner-city areas. Letters explaining the nature of the study were written to each student in each school and to the student's parents, and active signed consent was requested from both student and parent. Participation rates varied from school to school and between middle and high school students. The overall participation rate for the middle schools was 67 percent; for the high schools, it was 57 percent.

Data were collected in large group sessions, usually held in a school's library or cafeteria; students were released from their regular classes if they had obtained signed parental permission to participate. A 37-page questionnaire (the Health Behavior Questionnaire) was given to each student to fill out; average time for completion was 48 minutes at the middle school level and 42 minutes at the high school level. Upon completing the questionnaire, each student received a token payment of $5.00.

The Health Behavior Questionnaire was a revised and elaborated version of questionnaires used in our previous studies. It included well-established scales assessing the major variables in the personality, perceived environment, and behavior systems of problem-behavior theory. In addition, it included a variety of measures of health behavior in such areas as eating, exercise, safety, and sleep as well as measures of health-related psychosocial orientation such as value on health, health internal control, and models for health behaviors. At the end of the questionnaire, students were asked to evaluate it, and the great majority thought it was interesting and worthwhile.

In the present report, the data are based upon all those participants for whom ethnic status could be determined and who were classified as either White, Black, or Hispanic. At the middle school level, there were 258 White males,

126 Black males, and 265 Hispanic males; of the female middle school participants, 262 were White, 173 Black, and 305 Hispanic. At the high school level, there were 349 White males, 193 Black males, and 425 Hispanic males; of the female high school participants, 457 were White, 308 Black, and 583 Hispanic. Overall, there were 1,389 middle school youths and 2,315 high school youths; 1,326 were White, 800 were Black, and 1,578 were Hispanic.

The three key issues to be addressed in the remainder of this report rely on data drawn from the responses to the Health Behavior Questionnaire made by the subsamples just described. The first issue to be examined is the relationship of the distal measures in the personality system of problem-behavior theory to variation in adolescent health behavior. The second issue is the relationship of health behavior to other domains of behavior, especially problem behavior, in this adolescent population. And the third issue is the link of variation in adolescent health behavior to the larger social environment.

3. LINKING PERSONALITY VARIATION TO VARIATION IN ADOLESCENT HEALTH BEHAVIOR

The first step in examining all three issues was to establish an overall health behavior criterion measure. Measures were selected from four separate domains of health-related behavior: exercise, healthful eating practices, adequacy of sleep, and safety. Exercise was assessed by a four-item scale asking about the number of hours a week spent in organized sports participation, in working out as part of a personal exercise program, in pickup games, or in practicing physical activities (Cronbach's $\alpha = .70$). Healthful eating practices were measured by a nine-item scale asking how much attention adolescents paid to seeing that their diets were healthy, to limiting the amounts of salt and fat eaten, to eating healthful snacks like fruit, and so forth ($\alpha = .87$). Sleep adequacy was assessed by a two-item scale focused on the usual number of hours of sleep on school nights ($\alpha = .78$). Safety was measured by a single question regarding how much of the time a seat belt was used when riding in a car. Correlations among the four measures are positive and significant but small, generally less than .20. The measure of healthful eating practices has the strongest and most consistent associations with the other measures. A summary index of involvement in health behavior was constructed by summing *t*-scores on the four component behaviors; higher scores on the health behavior index reflected greater involvement in positive health behavior. Some indication of the construct validity of the health behavior index can be found in relation to five different measures of proximal psychosocial orientations to health: value on health, health internal control, health external control, parental models for health, and friends' models for health. As expected, all of the relationships were positive. Multiple correlations

Table 1.   Pearson Correlations between the Distal Personality System Measures and the
Health Behavior Index

	Middle School		High School	
Personality Measures	*Males*	*Females*	*Males*	*Females*
Value on independence/value on achievement disjunction	−.29*	−.26*	−.31*	−.27*
Expectations for academic achievement	.36*	.35*	.30*	.30*
Intolerant attitude toward deviance	.28*	.37*	.25*	.25*

*$p < .05$ (two-tailed test)

(r's) of these five measures of psychosocial orientations toward health with the
health behavior index were all above .50 for middle school and high school males
and females.

Table 1 shows the relationship of the distal personality system variables in
problem-behavior theory to adolescent health behavior. Bivariate correlations
between three personality measures and the health behavior index are presented
for males and females at the middle school and high school levels. The three
personality measures—all of them distal from health behavior—are (1) value on
independence/value on academic achievement disjunction (a discrepancy score
indicating the degree to which independence is valued more highly than academic achievement); (2) expectations for academic achievement (a 4-item scale
indicating the subjective probability of doing well in schoolwork; $\alpha = .85$); and
(3) intolerant attitude toward deviance (a 10-item scale indicating the unaccept-
ability of engaging in nonnormative behavior; $\alpha = .90$).

It is clear from Table 1 that, for all four subsamples, all three personality
measures relate to the health behavior index significantly and in the theoretically
expected direction. The more independence is valued over academic achievement, the less the involvement in positive health behavior; and the higher the
expectations for academic achievement and more intolerant the attitude toward
transgression, the greater the involvement in positive health behavior.

Although the magnitude of the correlations is modest, the consistency across
the three measures and across the different age and gender groups is noteworthy.
The predictiveness of the personality system as a whole can be determined from
the multiple correlations of the three personality measures, taken together, with
the health behavior index. For the middle school males and females and the high
school males and females, the respective correlations are .42, .46, .41, and .38.
Multiple correlations carried out within the three ethnic groups yielded similar
results with the single exception of the Black high school males.

With respect, then, to the first issue addressed in the present study, it is
apparent that there are systematic relations between personality measures that are

distal from health behavior and a composite measure of health behavior itself. The relationship shown when the three personality measures are combined is not trivial; the amount of variance accounted for in the health behavior index is around 15 to 20 percent for the various gender-by-grade groups and the three different ethnic groups.[1]

These data provide the first replication of our previous findings (Donovan et al., 1991). The present data extend those earlier findings to a large urban sample and to minority ethnic groups not represented in the previous study. What the results permit is the linking of adolescent health behavior to a larger network of individual difference variation—individual difference attributes with no immediately obvious implication for health behavior. In addition, the findings show that measures originally designed to explain variation in problem behavior are also predictive of health behavior. Such findings strengthen the inference that involvement in health behavior is normatively regulated, just as involvement in problem behavior is, and that variables that account for normative adherence or transgression can significantly enhance understanding of variation in health behavior.

4. LINKING ADOLESCENT HEALTH BEHAVIOR AND ADOLESCENT PROBLEM BEHAVIOR

In prior work on problem-behavior theory, research that was focused on the behavior system helped to illuminate its structure and organization. Several studies have demonstrated a significant degree of relatedness among different problem behaviors and their negative relation with conventional behaviors (e.g., Jessor & Jessor, 1977). It has also been shown that covariation among problem behaviors holds in young adulthood as well as in adolescence and that a single underlying factor can explain the obtained pattern of correlations among them (Donovan & Jessor, 1985; Donovan, Jessor, & Costa, 1988).

The second key issue to be addressed in the present study is whether involvement in health behavior has any systematic relation to involvement in problem behavior. Evaluating the evidence for covariation between health behavior and problem behavior would contribute to an understanding of the larger organization of behavior in adolescence. To examine this issue in a rather preliminary fashion, we correlated four measures of problem behavior (delinquent-type behavior, involvement with marijuana, frequency of drunkenness, and sexual intercourse experience) with the four measures of health behavior discussed earlier (exercise, healthful eating practices, adequacy of sleep, and seat belt use). As expected, the correlation matrix shows negative associations between each of the problem behaviors and each of the health behaviors; the correlations are again small, generally about .20, but almost all are statistically significant. The exercise

Table 2. Pearson Correlations between the Health Behavior Index and the Multiple Problem Behavior Index

	Total Sample	Whites	Blacks	Hispanics
Middle school				
Males	−.28*	−.22*	−.23*	−.31*
Females	−.35*	−.29*	−.34*	−.33*
High school				
Males	−.31*	−.32*	−.13	−.35*
Females	−.29*	−.39*	−.14*	−.27*

*$p < .05$ (two-tailed test)

measure is the one with the smallest correlations, almost none significant, when the analysis is carried out by gender and school level.

A more general and more stable appraisal of the issue is obtained by examining the relation between the summary health behavior index and a comparable composite index of the four problem behaviors constructed in the same way as the health index. Table 2 presents the relevant data by gender and school level for the total sample as well as for the three ethnic subsamples.

As can be seen, there are consistent and significant correlations between involvement in health behavior and involvement in problem behavior. The correlations between the health behavior index and the multiple problem behavior index are negative, as expected, and they hold for all the gender-by-school-level groups and for all the ethnic subgroups except for the Black high school males. The data, again, serve as an independent replication of earlier findings (Donovan et al., 1991) and extend them to an urban and ethnically heterogeneous population.

It is of further interest to examine, for the same groups, the relations of the health behavior index and of the multiple problem behavior index to a measure of another behavioral domain, namely, involvement in school achievement. This measure of a conventional behavior is indexed by self-reported grade point average. The correlations with the health behavior index are, as expected, all positive and significant; they range between .16 and .32. The correlations of grade point average with the multiple problem behavior index are, again as expected, all negative and significant; they are higher and range between .17 and .46. These findings not only add to the construct validity of both indexes, but also reveal the link, albeit modest, of health behavior to yet another domain of behavior, school achievement.

The correlations in Table 2 are small in magnitude, the common variance being, at best, no more than about 15 percent, but the consistency of their direction and of their statistical significance across the multiple subsamples is of major theoretical importance. They strongly suggest that health behavior is not isolated from the rest of an adolescent's behavioral repertoire. Indeed, they suggest that a full understanding of health behavior will require consideration of an adolescent's involvement in other conventional behaviors, such as school achievement, as well as in a variety of youthful problem behaviors. We have also conducted further analyses of the structure of health and problem behavior in this data set, using latent variable procedures (Donovan, Jessor, & Costa, 1993).

5. LINKING ADOLESCENT HEALTH BEHAVIOR WITH THE LARGER SOCIAL ENVIRONMENT

The third and final issue to be addressed in this report focuses on the role that problem-behavior theory can play in articulating the relationship between adolescent health behavior and the larger social environment. In its earliest formulation (Jessor et al., 1968), the theory sought to construct a bridge between society and the person by elaborating isomorphic conceptual structures for both. The opportunity structure, the normative structure, and the social control structure were elaborated for the social environment, and, as parallels, the perceived opportunity structure, the personal belief structure, and the personal control structure were elaborated for the person. In that early research, an important personality variable referred to the "perception of life chances in the opportunity structure." It was a variable designed to reflect, at the subjective level, Max Weber's concept of the objective position that a person occupies with respect to access to societal rewards such as status, respect, income, power, and the like (cf. Dahrendorf, 1979). Objective position in the opportunity structure is often indexed by proxy measures of socioeconomic status. Because of our interest, in the present study, in the relation of health behavior to poverty and disadvantage, we again turned to the perception-of-life-chances variable and developed a new measure to assess it. Our initial findings with this measure of perceived life chances enable us to explore, in a preliminary fashion, the linkage of adolescent health behavior to the larger social environment.

The 10-item perceived life chances scale represents a variety of future states that are widely endorsed as desirable and assesses the subjective likelihood of their future attainment. Taken together, the items yield a measure of an adolescent's belief about the future and about the overall likelihood that it will be benign or malignant. In problem-behavior theory, the perceived life chances variable is considered to be a generalized expectancy and to occupy a place in the personal belief structure of the personality system.

The 10 items in the perceived life chances scale follow. Items were preceded by the stem "Think about how you see your future; what are the chances that. . . ." Five response options were offered, ranging from ["I think the chances are"] "very high" to "very low": [What are the chances that] you will graduate from high school?, you will go to college?, you will have a job that pays well?,

Table 3.   Pearson Correlations Between the Measure of Perceived Life Chances and the
Health Behavior Index

	Total Sample	*Whites*	*Blacks*	*Hispanics*
Middle school				
Males	.35*	.34*	.20*	.43*
Females	.40*	.35*	.41*	.36*
High school				
Males	.27*	.31*	.32*	.23*
Females	.30*	.32*	.26*	.30*

*$p < .05$ (two-tailed test)

you will be able to own your own home?, you will have a job that you enjoy doing?, you will have a happy family life?, you will stay in good health most of the time?, you will be able to live wherever you want to in the country?, you will be respected in your community?, you will have good friends you can count on?

The perceived life chances scale has excellent psychometric properties. Cronbach's alpha reliability ranges between .88 and .92 for the four gender-by-school-level subsamples. Table 3 shows the relation of the perceived life chances measure to variation in the health behavior index. As can be seen, there is a consistent, positive relation between perceived life chances and the health behavior index: the greater the perception of access to future opportunity, the greater the involvement in positive health behavior.[2] Though modest, the correlations are statistically significant for all of the gender-by-school-level subsamples as well as for the three ethnic groups. The magnitude of the correlations is similar to that of the other three personality measures presented earlier in Table 1, and in the total sample, the perceived life chances measure accounts for between 7 and 16 percent of the variance in health behavior. Perceived life chances constitutes, then, another distal personality measure that is systematically linked to health behavior in youth.

To establish whether this new measure contributes any unique personality variance beyond that accounted for by the other three distal personality measures discussed earlier, we carried out hierarchical regression analyses in which the perceived life chances measure was added to the regression after the other three personality measures had been entered. The multiple correlations for the total sample and the three ethnic subsamples are shown in Table 4. The measure of perceived life chances does, indeed, add a significant increment to the multiple correlations for all but two of the subsamples, the Black middle school males and the Hispanic high school males. Although the increases in the correlations are generally small, they represent a *relative* increase in the amount of variance accounted for of as much as 39 percent (e.g., for the Black high school males).

Having established, thus far, that the distal personality measure of perceived life chances is relevant to variation in adolescent behavior, we turn to the issue of

Table 4. Multiple Correlations of the Distal Personality System Measures and the Perceived Life Chances Measure with the Health Behavior Index

	Total Sample	Whites	Blacks	Hispanics
	Middle School			
Males				
Personality measures	.42	.37	.46	.46
With perceived life chances added	.47[b]	.42[b]	.46	.54[b]
Females				
Personality measures	.46	.46	.42	.43
With perceived life chances added	.50[b]	.49[b]	.48[b]	.47[b]
	High School			
Males				
Personality measures	.41	.43	.19[a]	.48
With perceived life chances added	.43[b]	.46[b]	.32[b]	.48
Females				
Personality measures	.38	.42	.28	.37
With perceived life chances added	.41[b]	.46[b]	.33[b]	.40[b]

[a] This multiple correlation is the only 1 of the 16 based on the three distal personality measures that did not reach significance at the $p = .05$ level.
[b] The increment in R yielded by the addition of the perceived life chances measure is statistically significant at $p < .05$.

linking adolescent health behavior to the larger social environment. Our efforts in this direction were still quite preliminary, but as initial steps they were promising and of interest. They entailed examining whether the health behavior index and the measure of perceived life chances *both* varied according to position in the social system. To the extent that that was indeed the case, it would be reasonable to consider perceived life chances as mediating between the larger social environment and health behavior.

The approach to indexing location in the social system was to employ three standard measures of socioeconomic status: father's occupation, father's education, and mother's education. The large amount of missing data on father's occupation led us to develop an index of socioeconomic status that was based, for each participant, on the average of whichever of the three measures was available. We carried out all of the analyses to be reported both using the index and using the three component measures separately. The findings are almost identical, their robustness providing greater confidence in the socioeconomic status index.

The data in Table 5 present mean scores on the health behavior index by three

Table 5. Mean Scores on the Health Behavior Index and the Measure of Perceived Life Chances by Low, Medium, and High Socioeconomic Status

| | Index of Socioeconomic Status | | | | |
	Low	Medium	High	F	Eta-Square
	A. Health Behavior Index				
Middle school					
Males	194.7	199.5	205.0	9.3***	.031
Females	193.0	198.5	206.5	18.3***	.052
High school					
Males	196.5	199.1	204.9	10.0***	.021
Females	195.1	199.9	204.4	15.6***	.024
	B. Perceived Life Chances				
Middle school					
Males	41.0	42.0	44.5	13.6***	.046
Females	39.8	42.8	44.1	27.7***	.077
High school					
Males	40.4	42.5	43.2	15.3***	.033
Females	40.7	42.0	43.9	27.9***	.042

$*p < .05, **p < .0, ***p < .001.$

categories of socioeconomic status (low, medium, and high) for the four gender-by-school-level subsamples. They also present a comparable appraisal of the perceived life chances scale. As can be seen, both the health behavior index and the perceived life chances scale vary significantly with the measure of socioeconomic position. The higher the socioeconomic status, the greater the involvement in health behavior *and* the greater the perception of access to future opportunity. The findings are consistent for all four gender-by-school-level subsamples.

Since we have already shown (Table 3) that perceived life chances is linked to health behavior, the present findings suggest that the link between adolescent health behavior and the larger social environment may be mediated, at least in part, by the perception of life chances in the opportunity structure. In pursuit of greater conviction about the role of perceived life chances as a mediator between the larger social environment and health behavior, we carried out analyses of covariance by gender and school level. In these analyses, perceived life chances was controlled as a covariate while we examined the relationship between the index of socioeconomic status and the index of health behavior. That relationship should be reduced by controlling for perceived life chances if the latter is, in fact, mediating the relationship. The results of the analysis of covariance support the mediating role of perceived life chances for all four gender-by-school-level groups. In all cases, the value of *F* is sharply reduced, and the percentage of variance in health behavior accounted for by the measure of socioeconomic status is lowered by about half when compared to the etas already shown in Table 5.

6. SUMMARY AND CONCLUSIONS

The major aim of this report has been to enlarge understanding of adolescent health behavior by embedding it in a broader social-psychological framework. That framework, problem-behavior theory, is concerned with distal as well as proximal determinants of behavior; it is concerned with the structure and organization of behavior; and it is concerned with the impact of the larger social environment on behavior. All three of those concerns were addressed in the present study. The findings show that personality measures that are distal from adolescent health behavior—values about academic achievement and autonomy, expectations for academic achievement, and attitudes about normative trangression—are all relevant to an account of its variation. The findings also show that involvement in health behavior is positively related to other conventional behavior such as school achievement and negatively related to involvement in problem behavior. Finally, the findings suggest that the perception of access to future opportunity, another personality variable that is distal from health behavior, may mediate between a disadvantaged position in the larger social involvement and the lesser involvement in health behavior. Position in the opportunity structure was related to both involvement in health behavior and the perception of future life chances, and, as would be expected if it actually served as a mediating variable, controlling for perceived life chances weakened the link between the larger social environment and health behavior.

Overall, the findings indicate that it is useful to consider adolescent behavior as normatively regulated, as linked to other domains of behavior, and as reflecting the impact of location in society. To the extent that such knowledge enlarges understanding of adolescent health bevavior, it calls attention to the positive role that theory can play in research on social behavior among youth.

ACKNOWLEDGEMENT

The research reported in this chapter was supported by Grant No. 88-1194-88 from the William T. Grant Foundation. The data could not have been collected without the exceptional cooperation of the school district central administration and the building principals of the schools involved. The generous assistance of our colleague, Jill Van Den Bos, in the data collection and, especially, in the analyses presented here is gratefully acknowledged.

NOTES

1. In this chapter, we restrict our focus to the personality system and to its distal variables. A substantial increment in the amount of variance in the health behavior index

could be achieved by engaging the distal variables in the perceived environment systems as well. However, our aim in this presentation is not to try to exhaust the variance in adolescent health behavior but rather, to illustrate the general point about the explanatory relevance of more remote regions of the causal network. For that purpose, reliance on the distal measures in the personality system alone is sufficient.

2. Since one of the items in the perceived life chances scale, item 7, refers directly to "good health," it could have inflated the correlations shown in Table 3. The correlations were generated again with item 7 deleted, and the magnitude of the difference in r is trivial, ranging from .00 to .03.

REFERENCES

Costa, F., Jessor, R., & Donovan, J. E. (1989). Value on health and adolescent conventionality: A construct validation of a new measure in problem-behavior theory. *Journal of Applied Social Psychology, 19*, 841–861.

Dahrendorf, R. (1979). *Life chances: Approaches to social and political theory*. Chicago: University of Chicago Press.

Donovan, J. E., & Jessor, R. (1985). Structure of problem behavior in adolescence and young adulthood. *Journal of Consulting and Clinical Psychology, 53*, 890–904.

Donovan, J. E., Jessor, R., & Costa, F. (1988). The syndrome of problem behavior in adolescence: A replication. *Journal of Consulting and Clinical Psychology, 56*, 762–765.

Donovan, J. E., Jessor, R., & Costa, F. (1991). Adolescent health behavior and conventionality-unconventionality: An extension of problem-behavior theory. *Health Psychology, 10*(1), 52–61.

Donovan, J. E., & Jessor, R., & Costa, F. (1993). Structure of health-enhancing behavior in adolescence: A latent-variable approach. *Journal of Health and Social Behavior, 34*(4), 346–362.

Jessor, R. (1978). Health-related behavior and adolescent development: A psychosocial perspective. In National Academy of Sciences, *Adolescent behavior and health: A conference summary* (pp. 39–43). Institute of Medicine Publication No. 78-004. Washington, DC: National Academy of Sciences.

Jessor, R. (1982). Critical issues in research on adolescent health promotion. In T. J. Coated, A. C. Petersen, & C. L. Perry (Eds.), Promoting adolescent health: A dialog on research and practice (pp. 447–465). New York: Academic.

Jessor, R. (1984). Adolescent development and behavioral health. In J. D. Matarazzo, S. M. Weiss, J. A. Herd, N. E. Miller, & S. M. Weiss (Eds.), Behavioral health: A handbook of health enhancement and disease prevention (pp. 69–90). New York: Wiley.

Jessor, R. (1987). Problem-behavior theory, psychosocial development, and adolescent problem drinking. *British Journal of Addiction, 82*, 435–446.

Jessor, R. (1989). The health of youth: A behavioral science perspective. *Proceedings, technical discussions on the health of youth*. Geneva: World Health Organization.

Jessor, R., Donovan, J. E., Costa, F. (1991). Beyond adolescence: Problem behavior and young adult development. New York: Cambridge University Press.

Jessor, R., Graves, T. D., Hanson, R. C., & Jessor, S. L. (1968). *Society, personality, and deviant behavior: A study of a tri-ethnic community*. New York: Holt, Rinehart & Winston (Reprinted by Kreiger, Melbourne, FLA.).

Jessor, R., & Jessor, S. L. (1977). *Problem behavior and psychological development: A longitudinal study of youth*. New York: Academic Press.

Perry, C. L., & Jessor, R. (1985). The concept of health promotion and the prevention of adolescent drug abuse. *Health Education Quarterly, 12*, 169–184.

11

The Development of Authoritarianism in Adolescence: Longitudinal Change and the Impact of Age, Gender, and Educational Level

Wilma Vollebergh

1. INTRODUCTION

Studies of the social and historical background of authoritarianism have shown a decrease in this characteristic over recent decades in some Western countries (for the Netherlands, see Middendorp [1978] and Meloen and Middendorp [1985]; for the United States and Germany, see Ledere [1982]), particularly in the authoritarianism scores of youngsters (Meloen & Middendorp, 1985; Middendorp, 1978; Reddy, 1983). Young people in general tend to be far less authoritarian than the older generation. However, the question is whether this difference holds for the whole generation of youngsters. Especially in Germany, the decrease in authoritarianism in youngsters as a generation has been questioned and contradicted by the empirical fact that right-wing extremism and neofascism seem to attract sections of the younger generation as well (Heitmeyer, 1987, p. 39), although always to a lesser extent than they attract older people (Stöss, 1989).

Longitudinal data on different age groups in the Netherlands and in the United States suggest that authoritarianism is already quite firmly established by early adulthood (18 years plus); in other words, an authoritarian or nonauthoritarian preference at that age is likely to persist into later adulthood (Meloen & Middendorp, 1985). Altemeyer (1981, 1988), however, demonstrated some changes in authoritarianism levels in students as effects of, for example, educational level and occupational choice. In this respect, researchers need to look at the influence of educational level, as correlations of authoritarianism with educational level

235

seem to be even more important than correlations with occupational status (Eisenga & Scheepers, 1989; Grabb, 1980; Meloen & Middendorp, 1985). Higher educational levels lead to a lower level of authoritarianism, but this relationship is not observed cross-culturally: education tends to reduce authoritarianism only in countries with a Western culture (Western European countries, the United States), where the educational systems place major emphasis on cognitive learning (Simpson, 1972).

If authoritarianism is assumed to characterize the worldview of particular groups in society, it seems probable that authoritarianism is stabilized as a corollary effect of the stabilization of social and occupational positions. That leads to the assumption that changes in adolescence, when the stabilization of social positions is likely to take place, are constitutive for the stabilization of authoritarianism. If psychological and social changes in adolescence do have a significant influence on the development of authoritarianism, two different aspects would seem to be important: (1) the development of cognitive capabilities that enable adolescents to develop a more sophisticated view of society, and (2) changes in social position.

1.1. Age as an Indication of Level of Cognitive Development

Following Piaget, cognitive developmentalists assume that in early adolescence a fundamental change in cognitive capabilities can occur: a transition from the use of concrete operations to the use of formal operations, prerequisite for the use of formal logic, which is necessary for abstracting from concrete data, arguing with the help of propositions and hypotheses, and envisaging "the possible" as opposed to "reality" (Inhelder & Piaget, 1958). Although these cognitive changes were initially investigated in formal logic only, Kohlberg (1969) showed that the development of modes of moral reasoning in the social domain also seemed to have its origin in cognitive development. Later research has supported this thesis; logical operations appear to serve as a "pacing" mechanism in moral development, so that moral development never exceeds certain limits imposed by the individual's level of logical operations (Kuhn, Langer, Kohlberg, & Hahn, 1977, p. 178; Tomlinson-Keasy & Keasy, 1974). Other studies have found comparable relations between cognitive development and the development of an identity during adolescence, as operationally defined by Marcia (Adams, 1985; Bosma & Graatsma, 1982; Marcia, 1980), the development of social cognition (Gallatin, 1980), and the development of conceptions of social order (Adelson & O'Neill, 1966; Torney, 1971). Without going into too much detail now, and so for the time being putting aside the controversies about these relationships, I can note that the overall results of these studies confirm that the development of more sophisticated cognitive operations in adolescence is a prerequisite—though not a sufficient—condition for advanced modes of moral judgment, the use of abstract conceptions and principles, and the development of a more or less coherent ideology.

These changes in cognitive capacities can be important in the development of authoritarianism, too, since the development of advanced modes of moral reasoning and less authoritarian thought tend to be related. Altemeyer discovered a very solid relationship between authoritarianism and modes of moral reasoning, as measured by the classic Kohlberg procedure (1981, pp. 192–193).

So, on average, changes in adolescence seem to run alongside the growth of political interest, cognitive sophistication, and a *decrease in authoritarianism* (Adelson & O'Neill, 1966, p. 304; Fischer, 1982; Jaide, 1982, p. 50; van der Linden & Hagen, 1977). This suggests that authoritarianism can be characterized as a less sophisticated, less abstract, and more concrete way of thinking that may be related to limited cognitive development.

However, this relationship need not depend on age alone. On average, political interest grows and authoritarianism decreases as a function of educational level and therefore of social class: More education leads to a higher level of political interest and to a lower level of authoritarianism (Altemeyer, 1988, p. 97; Wassmund, 1982, pp. 66–67).

1.2. Social Change

The development of cognitive capabilities is stimulated by social changes as well as age. Participation in education or in vocational training for professional occupations in the sociocultural domain tends to *lower* the level of authoritarianism to a considerable degree (Altemeyer, 1981, 1988; Meloen, 1983). Thus, these background factors seem to be important for levels of (non)authoritarianism, shaping an adolescent's present and future opportunities to prepare for and occupy an autonomous, active social position.

Furthermore, research in Germany and the Netherlands has systematically shown significant differences between girls and boys in their susceptibility to authoritarianism: boys are more susceptible than girls (Fischer, 1982; Hagendoorn & Janssen, 1983; Raaijmakers, Meeus, & Vollebergh, 1986). No comparable differences in authoritarianism were found in adults, although analysis of longitudinal data from the Netherlands revealed a *decline* in more conservative political opinions in women but not men (Meloen & Middendorp, 1985).

On the whole, the same social differences that characterize the political thought of parents seem to be encountered in their children, although to a lesser extent (Sigel & Hoskin, 1981, p. 194). In general, children who have benefitted from a well-to-do social background develop fewer authoritarian leanings. However, youngsters may break away from their parents' homes in adolescence by leaving the house, postponing their active entry into society, and prolonging their educations. English research, for example, has shown that the political opinions of students from blue-collar backgrounds resembled the opinions of their white-collar student colleagues more than the opinions of blue-collar nonstudents, and white-collar nonstudents were more like blue-collar nonstudents in this respect (Kasschau, Ransford, & Bengston, 1974). The educational level of youngsters seems to have its own effect in this period of life and so may partly outweigh the influence of their original socioeconomic backgrounds. As receiving higher levels of education is one of the ways in which youngsters can improve their future positions in society, it may exert a considerable influence on their views on society (Fischer, 1982; Heitmeyer, 1987, p. 37; Raaijmakers et al., 1986; SINUS, 1983; Vollebergh, 1986).

Two possible explanations of this phenomenon are readily available. First of all, prolonged education may lead to the development of more sophisticated cognitive capacities and more complex ways of reasoning that, by implication, include the use of more abstract concepts, a more coherent ideology, and a decrease in the "taken-for-granted" law-and-order orientation that characterizes less abstract reasoning on social issues, especially when education in the social professions is at stake. Secondly, a higher level of education may have the effect of "anticipatory socialization" (Kohlberg, 1969, p. 401): as the educational level rises, it increasingly prepares youngsters to take up future positions in society in which they will and should be able to make decisions on their own, without relying on external authorities to tell them what to do. Receiving higher forms of education leads youngsters to adopt the kind of reasoning that is characteristic of the more highly educated members of society (Sigel & Hoskin, 1981). As the demand for internal social control is a major characteristic of many professions in Western countries, the adoption of nonauthoritarian ways of thinking can be seen as the appropriation of the "cultural capital" (Bourdieu, 1989) essential to qualify for modern professions.

1.3. The Research Problem

Most research on the origins of authoritarianism has tended to support the notion that the social background of both parents and their children plays an important part in levels of authoritarianism. Parents and their children share the same social conditions and will therefore tend to share the same worldview. It is furthermore in accordance with most research results to suggest that adolescence is a relevant stage of life for the establishment of authoritarianism. Not until adolescence will children have acquired the information and the cognitive capacities necessary to articulate more or less coherent opinions about social and cultural issues. As adolescence is also a most important time of life for the establishment of an autonomous social position—autonomous in the sense that it may differentiate youngsters from the social positions of their parents—adolescence will be relevant for the establishment of an accompanying coherent worldview.

Empirical research on political opinions in adolescents supports these notions, but it also leaves some questions unanswered: (1) The development of a political ideology and more sophisticated lines of reasoning on social and cultural issues seems to be related to the growth of cognitive capacities, and therefore to *age*. This relationship may be the main reason that authoritarianism tends to decrease as adolescents grow older. (2) However, differences between social positions, like *educational level and gender*, have their impact on levels of authoritarianism in adolescence as well, and they might also explain the supposedly age-related phenomenon. It may be that the decrease in authoritarianism with age should be seen as an effect of prolonged education.

The issue to be addressed in the present research therefore concerns on the one hand the effect of age as an indicator of individual development, and on the other hand the effect of social background characteristics as indicators of societal influences on levels of authoritarianism. Two key social background characteristics are examined in this chapter: gender and adolescents' educational level. The question is, how are these effects related? I explore some changes in authoritarianism in adolescence and early childhood and present the results of a longitudinal survey of political attitudes in which more than 2,500 pupils at different educational levels were studied with respect to their social and political worldviews. These data will enable me to highlight the relevance of social factors for changing levels of authoritarianism in adolescence.

2. METHODS

2.1. Sample Survey

The research was carried out between 1986 and 1990. In 1986, several schools were selected in the Netherlands, in both towns and rural areas. The survey team questioned approximately 2,700 girls and boys by distributing questionnaires in classrooms. We wanted to follow youngsters in their passage from school to further education or the labor market, so we selected approximately the same number of pupils from the four major educational levels in Holland: (1) LBO, lower technical and vocational training (12–16-year-olds); (2) MAVO, lower general secondary education (12–16-year-olds); (3) HAVO, higher general secondary education (12–17-year-olds); and (4) VWO, preuniversity education (12–18-year-olds). Since we approached the pupils in their last year of school, age differences in our sample correlate with educational level (the oldest ones were the VWO pupils).

Two years after this first measurement, a second survey was conducted. We had asked the pupils to write their names on the original questionnaires if they

Table 1. Characteristics of the Survey Sample

| | Educational Level[a] | | | | | | | |
| | LBO | | MAVO | | HAVO | | VWO | |
Age	Male	Female	Male	Female	Male	Female	Male	Female
≤ 15	152	142	147	247	0	1	1	—
16	197	135	99	141	48	79	1	5
17	86	59	42	36	99	171	136	123
18	22	8	4	3	75	105	90	88
≥ 19	3	0	1	2	33	22	64	34
n	460	344	293	429	255	378	292	250

[a]LBO = lower technical and vocational training. MAVO = lower general secondary education. HAVO = higher general secondary education. VWO = preuniversity education.

were prepared to take part in further investigations. Approximately 50 percent of them did so. Table 1 gives characteristics of the original survey sample.

These youngsters were contacted by mail and given a second questionnaire. Those who did not respond were contacted by telephone at a later date. In this way, we managed to track down over 30 percent of the original population. Table 2 compares the characteristics of the population and the two subsamples, one measured only once, the other measured twice. The less-educated individuals (LBO pupils) are somewhat less well represented in the second measurement. I do not know whether this difference has much impact on the analysis of the change in authoritarianism over time, as it is impossible to compare the two subsamples with respect to this change. It is clear, however, that—for example—a lowering of authoritarianism scores after two years is *not* due to a lower level of authoritarianism in this subsample, as the comparison between the first and second score was made with respect only to the twice-questioned youngsters.

Table 2. Characteristics of the Survey Sample in the Second Measurement

Sample	All	Only 1st Measurement	Two Measurements
Gender			
Female	1,308	885 (68%)	423 (32%)
Male	1,408	912 (65%)	496 (35%)
		$\chi^2 (1) = 2.40$, n.s.	
Educational level			
LBO	813	589 (72%)	224 (28%)
MAVO	729	456 (63%)	273 (37%)
HAVO	638	413 (65%)	225 (35%)
VWO	545	347 (64%)	198 (36%)
		$\chi^2 (3) = 20.70, p < .001$	

2.2. Measurement Instrument

The questionnaires contained questions concerning background characteristics and several attitude scales, among these a scale measuring authoritarianism. This scale initially consisted of the Dutch version of the original F-scale (Hagendoorn & Janssen, 1983). In previous research, these items were factor-analyzed and a shortened version of the scale, consisting of the highest-loading items, was constructed (Raaijmakers et al., 1986). Respondents indicated agreement with the items by circling a precoded answer; responses ranged from 1 (fully disagree) to 5 (fully agree). The items of the authoritarianism measure ($\alpha = .77$) were as follows: (1) Obedience and respect for authority are the most important virtues children should learn, (2) Young people sometimes get rebellious ideas, but as they grow up they ought to get over them and settle down, (3) Most of our social problems would be solved if we could somehow get rid of squatters and caravan-dwellers, (4) There has to be order in a group in the first place, (5) Rioters and trouble-makers should be treated much more forcefully than is usually the case, (6) What a youth needs most is strict discipline and strong determination, and (7) A strong person does not show his feelings.

2.3. The Measurement of Change

The analysis of a change in scores on the authoritarianism scale over two years is not without technical and statistical problems. It seems easy to simply calcu-late a differece score by subtracting the first score from the second, but this procedure has a lot of disadvantages. Most noteworthy is subjects' tendency to regress toward the mean (that is, to give a second score that is less extreme and closer to the mean) as an effect of *measurement errors*. Correction of measure-ment errors has to take into account that different groups will tend to regress toward different means, if considerable differences in mean scores are found. As the mean scores within the different educational levels proved to be most note-worthy in prior research, a correction for regression toward the mean in this sample was carried out for the four educational levels separately (see Appendix A in Vollebergh [1991]). In this report, only these regressed scores are used.

3. RESULTS

3.1. Authoritarianism, Age, Gender, and Educational Level

As adolescents grow older, their authoritarianism is thought to decrease sub-stantially. However, most of the research in which this relationship has been

Table 3. Results of MANOVA for Authoritarianism and the Effect of Educational Level, Age, and Gender.

Variables	df	F	p
TIME 1[a]			
Educational level	3	219.27	.000
Gender	1	15.54	.000
Age	2	0.95	n.s.
Educational level × gender	3	1.86	n.s.
Educational level × age	6	1.57	n.s.
Gender × age	2	2.45	n.s.
Educational level × gender × age	6	2.76	.01
TIME 2[a]			
Time	1	46.19	.000
Educational level × time	3	6.83	.000
Gender × time	1	11.92	.000
Age × time	2	0.37	n.s.
Educational level × gender × time	3	2.68	.05
Educational level × age × time	6	1.36	n.s.
Gender × age × time	2	3.39	.05
Educational level × gender × age × time	6	0.85	n.s.

[a] Tests of significance using sequential sums of squares are shown.

found was cross-sectionally designed. As was already mentioned, educational level and age are correlated in this sample, since we selected youngsters in their last year of school. This same correlation might be found in other research too, if the selection of subjects has not been controlled for educational level. As adolescents are usually selected from schools, less-educated youngsters, once they leave school and go to work, will increasingly be excluded from samples automatically, thus transforming the subsamples of older adolescents to subsamples of the highly educated.

When we analyzed the effect of age together with the effect of gender and educational level, using a MANOVA repeated measures procedure with authoritarianism scores corrected for the regression phenomenon, we saw only a direct effect of educational level and gender. There was a small but significant *decrease* in authoritarianism over the two years (mean 1 = 3.07, mean 2 = 2.96, $F_{1,885} = 44.71$, $p < .001$). This finding might suggest the decrease is an age-related phenomenon: adolescents tend to become less authoritarian as they grow older. However, inspection of the effect of age on the change over time does not support this interpretation.

However, the possible importance of age is indicated by both the significant three-way interaction between educational level, age, and gender and by the interaction among gender, age, and time. As a significant interaction effect between gender and educational level also emerged, separate analyses of patterns within different educational levels were called for. There was also a second reason to do such analyses. Because of the correlation between age and educational level (see Tables 1 and 2 on the survey sample), we had to take 15- and 16-year-olds together, and also subjects of 18 years and more. This is a major disadvantage, since in the lowest and in the highest educational levels pupils of the younger and the older ages are respectively overrepresented. Proper analysis of the effect of age therefore had to be done within the different educational levels. Such an analysis would also reveal details on the effect of gender, which did not seem to be the same within educational levels either. I present our analysis in two steps. First, the effect of educational level on levels of authoritarianism is reviewed to give an indication of the former's importance. After that, the effect of age and gender within educational levels is examined to show the possible additional importance of these two variables.

3.2. The Effect of Educational Level

Figure 1 shows the effect of educational level on levels of authoritarianism. These data confirm what is well known already: pupils engaged in lower forms of education show higher levels of authoritarianism. What is new is that we can show that they continue to do so after two years, and the difference between lower and higher levels of education tends to become even larger over this

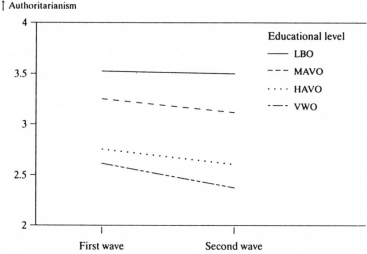

Figure 1. Educational level and change in authoritarianism.

Table 4.   Correlations over Time

Educational Levels	r	First Mean	SD	Second Mean	SD
LBO	.33	2.48	.36	2.49	.35
MAVO	.47	2.75	.48	2.85	.49
HAVO	.63	3.20	.63	3.34	.62
VWO	.54	3.36	.57	3.59	.50

period. Figure 1 shows that as level of education increases, the lowering of authoritarianism scores tends to become stronger. VWO pupils on the whole were less authoritarian after two years, but LBO pupils remained as authoritarian as they had been. This is *not* to say that the scores of the LBO pupils are more stable.

Table 4 shows that the correlation between the first and the second score tends to be far lower in the LBO pupils, which is in accord with many previous analyses of the effect of educational level (Raaijmakers et al., 1986; Vollebergh, 1991). But it does show that the differences between educational levels are firmly established by this age and even tend to become more prominent.

3.3. The Effect of Gender and Age within Educational Levels

We analyzed the effect of gender and age for each educational level, again using a repeated measures MANOVA, on the regression-corrected scores of pupils within educational levels. Figures 2, 3, 4, and 5 and Table 5 show results.

In the group of LBO pupils, no significant effects at all were found. They

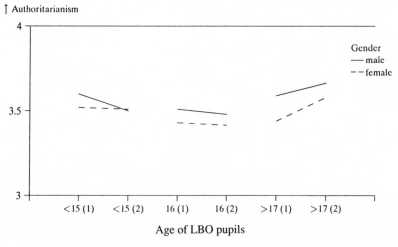

Figure 2.   Age, gender, and change in authoritarianism in LBO pupils.

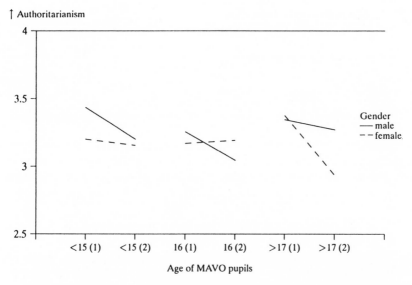

Figure 3. Gender, age, and the change in authoritarianism in MAVO pupils.

constituted the most authoritarian group and remained the most authoritarian group. No significant differences were found between girls and boys or with respect to age. Furthermore, this is the only group that showed no decrease in authoritarianism scores in the course of two years. We seem to encounter a broad consensus within this group of pupils with respect to opinions on law and order.

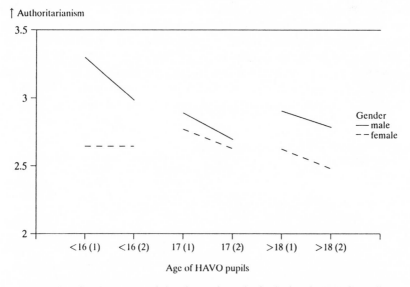

Figure 4. Gender, age, and the change in authoritarianism in HAVO pupils.

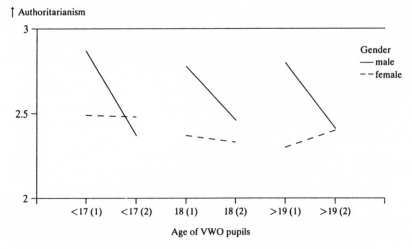

Figure 5. Gender, age, and the change in authoritarianism in VWO pupils.

In the MAVO pupils, we see a slightly different pattern. This group lowered its authoritarianism score over two years. However, it is not clear whether we can attribute this change to a particular segment within the group. Boys of all ages tended to lower their scores somewhat, but among girls only the 17-year-olds did so. It is difficult to interpret this finding. This age difference within the group of girls is the only deviant pattern we found.

The HAVO pupils lowered their authoritarianism scores over the two years as well. This is the first group that showed a manifest difference between girls and boys in levels of authoritarianism. The boys were far more authoritarian than the girls and, although it seemed that the boys' scores declined to a somewhat larger degree than the girls', this difference did not reach a level of significance. The girls remained less authoritarian after two years, and neither age nor gender had a significant effect on the change over time.

In the VWO pupils, we see an effect of gender not only on level of authoritari-

Table 5. Effects on Change in Authoritarianism

Educational Level	Effect of Gender	Effect of Age	**Change over Time**	Gender Affects Change	Age Affects Change
LBO	No	No	No	—	—
MAVO	No	No	**Yes**	No	No*
HAVO	**Yes**	No	**Yes**	No	No
VWO	**Yes**	No	**Yes**	**Yes**	No

*Significant interaction between gender and age.

anism, but also on change over time. The VWO pupils on the whole were also less authoritarian after two years, but in this group this lowering is clearly an effect of the lower scores of the boys. The girls were by far the most non-authoritarian group of all the respondents reviewed to this point, and they remained about as nonauthoritarian as they already were.

Table 5 summarizes the results.

Thus, for the LBO group (lower technical and vocational trainees), there were no significant effects; authoritarianism scores remained the same for both boys and girls of all ages. For the MAVO pupils (lower general secondary education), scores were lower after two years, but no clear effect of gender or age emerged. Among the HAVO pupils (higher secondary education), the girls were less authoritarian than the boys, and authoritarianism scores were lower after two years for boys and girls of all ages. Finally, for the VWO (preuniversity education) pupils, the girls were less authoritarian than the boys, and scores were lower after two years for the boys only.

4. CONCLUSION AND DISCUSSION

In this chapter, the social background of authoritarianism was investigated in adolescents. I assumed that adolescence is an important time in life for the establishment of an autonomous social position that may differentiate youngsters from the position of their parents and lead them to participate in other social groups that will gain relevance in shaping their worldviews. I was able to show that the educational level of adolescents is the most relevant predictor of their level of authoritarianism. Within educational levels, the effect of age differences almost completely disappears. If age itself, as an indicator of individual development, is of any relevance for authoritarianism, it is earlier, before youngsters reach the age of 14 or 15. Gender differences in authoritarianism within educational levels do exist, but these are not as relevant as the effect of the level of education itself and only manifest themselves at the higher levels of education (here, among the HAVO and VWO groups).

An analysis of longitudinal change in authoritarianism scores in the first two years after our subjects left school revealed that the influence of educational level tends to be reinforced by this passage. On average, the pupils engaged in higher forms of education prolonged their academic careers by going on to further education after leaving school, thus making the already existing differences between the pupils in the different educational programs even larger. There was a substantial decrease in authoritarianism, but only in the pupils pursuing higher education. In particular, boys tended to lower their scores, making the difference between the sexes smaller, and better-educated youngsters in particular tended to lower their scores, thus increasing the effect of educational level on authoritarianism. Boys became less authoritarian, and since the more highly educated also became less authoritarian, this effect was most conspicuous in the more highly educated pupils.

How are these results to be understood? The pupils in educational programs that place a major emphasis on cognitive learning (general education, MAVO) had lower authoritarianism scores over time, but the pupils engaged in lower vocational and technical training (LBO) did not. This pattern is in accord with the thesis of Simpson (1972). Furthermore, we see significant gender differences, but only at the highest levels of education (HAVO-VWO). This result is in accord with prior research demonstrating that girls tend to become less authoritarian than boys when a particular level of consciousness regarding the sociocultural implications of authoritarian views (i.e., ethnocentrism, sexism and masculinity, racism) has been reached. Whether or not authoritarianism is equivalent to ethnocentrism or sexism as such is not at stake here. What is important is that authoritarianism is *seen and interpreted* as such by the pupils when filling in our questionnaires. Better-educated pupils tend to associate authoritarianism to a greater extent with more violent forms of intolerance than less-educated pupils do: correlations between authoritarianism and intolerant attitudes toward minorities or women have repeatedly been shown to be higher among the more educated (Vollebergh, 1991), indicating that authoritarianism is seen as "bad" mainly by that group. Their scores are therefore better understood in terms of a growing rejection of the scale items. I might even suggest that the authoritarianism scale does not measure the same concept in those with lower and higher educations (cf. Raaijmakers et al., 1986; Vollebergh, 1991): the more highly educated especially tend to respond to its specific intolerant nature. Prior research has suggested that girls will be especially sensitive to this violent, and in a way masculine, aspect of authoritarianism and therefore will reject the items of the scale to a larger extent. Boys tend to follow the girls in these opinions but, it seems, only after a period of time. Both girls and boys at the higher educational levels are acquiring the nonauthoritarian worldview that is characteristic of the better-educated in society, but in doing so the boys have to "outgrow" the "masculinity" inherent in authoritarian thought.

One worrying result is left to be considered: the LBO pupils constituted the most authoritarian group. Their authoritarian worldview may not be very stable, considering the fairly low correlations between the first and second times of measurement, yet no decrease in authoritarianism was found at all over the two years. The most authoritarian group is therefore also the group that shows no tendency to comply with the nonauthoritarian norms existing in the Netherlands. Thus, the fairly optimistic conclusion that lengthened education will lower authoritarian forms of intolerance does not include the most authoritarian youngsters, but this seems to be the group raising most concern.

Still, in the context of social intolerance, it is probably ill advised to worry about authoritarian youngsters only. Nonauthoritarian youngsters might manifest other forms of social intolerance that are not yet touched upon in research on political attitudes (cf. Vollebergh, 1991).

REFERENCES

Adams, G. R. (1985). Identity and political socialization. In A. S. Waterman (Ed.), *Identity in adolescence: Processes and contents. New directions for child development*, No. 30 (pp. 61–77). San Francisco: Jossey-Bass.

Adelson, J., & O'Neill, R. P. (1966). Growth of political ideas in adolescence: The sense of community. *Journal of Personality and Social Psychology, 4*, 295–306.

Altemeyer, B. (1981). Right-wing authoritarianism. Manitoba: University of Manitoba Press.

Altemeyer, B. (1988). *Enemies of freedom*. San Francisco: Jossey-Bass Publishers.

Bosma, H. A., & Graafsma, T. L. G. (1982). *De ontwikkeling van identiteit in de adolescentie* [The development of identity in adolescence]. Nijmegen, the Netherlands: Dekker & Van de Vegt.

Bourdieu, P. (1989). *Opstellen over smaak, habitus en het veldbegrip* [Essays on taste, habit and the field concept]. Amsterdam: Van Gennep.

Eisinga, R. N., & Scheepers, P. L. H. (1989). *Etnocentrisme in Nederland* [Ethnocentrism in the Netherlands]. Nijmegen, the Netherlands: ITS.

Fischer, A. (Ed.). (1982). *Jugend '81 (Youth '81)*. Opladen, Germany: Leske + Budrich.

Gallatin, J. (1980). Political thinking in adolescence. In J. Adelson (Ed.), *Handbook of adolescent psychology* (pp. 344–382). New York: Wiley.

Grabb, E. G. (1980). Marxist categories and theories of class. The case of working-class authoritarianism. *Pacific Sociological Review, 24*, 359–376.

Hagendoorn, L., & Janssen, J. (1983). *Rechtsomkeer* [Turn about right]. Baarn, the Netherlands: Ambo.

Heitmeyer, W. (1987). *Rechtextremistische Orientierugen bei Jugendlichen. Empirische Ergebnisse und Erklärungsmuster einer Untersuchung zur politischen sozialisation* [Extreme rightist orientations of youth: Empirical results and explanatory frameworks from an investigation of political socialization]. Munich: Juventa Verlag.

Inhelder, B., & Piaget, J. (1958). *The growth of logical thinking from childhood to adolescence*. New York: Basic Books.

Jaide, W. (1982). *Achtzehnjährige zwischen Reaktion und Rebellion* [Eighteen-year-olds between reaction and rebellion]. Opladen, Germany: Leske Verlag.

Kasschau, P. L., Ransford, H. E., & Bengston, V. L. (1974). Generational consciousness and youth movement participation: Contrasts in blue-collar and white-collar youth. *Journal of Social Issues, 30*, 69–94.

Kohlberg, L. (1969). Stage and sequence: The cognitive-developmental approach to socialization. In D. A. Goslin (Ed.), *Handbook of socialization: Theory and research* (pp. 347–480). Chicago: Rand McNally.

Kuhn, D., Langer, J., Kohlberg, L., & Haan, N. S. (1977). The development of formal operations in logical and moral judgement. *Genetic Psychology Monographs, 95*, 97–188.

Lederer, G. (1982). Trends in authoritarianism: A study of adolescents in West Germany and the United States since 1945. *Journal of Cross-Cultural Psychology*, *13*(3), 292–314.

Marcia, J. E. (1980). Identity in adolescence. In J. Adelson (Ed.), *Handbook of adolescent psychology* (pp. 159–187). New York: Wiley.

Meloen, J. D. (1983). *De autoritaire realtie in tijden van welvaart en krisis* [Authoritarian reactions in times of economic peaks and slumps]. Amsterdam: Univesiteit van Amsterdam.

Meloen, J. D., & Middendorp, C. P. (1985). Potentieel fascisme in Nederland [Potential fascism in the Netherlands]. In *Jaarboek van de Nederlanse verenigung van marktonderzoekers* (pp. 93–108). Haarlem: De Vriesborch.

Middendorp, C. P. (1978). *Progressiveness and conservatism*. The Hague: Mouton.

Raaijmakers, Q., Meeus, W., & Vollebergh, W. (1986). Extreme politieke opvattingen bij LBO-MAVO-scholieren [Political extremism among MAVO and LBO students]. In H. Dekker & S. Rozemond (Eds.), *Politieke socialisatie* (pp. 83–102). Culemborg, the Netherlands: Educaboek.

Reddy, K. S. (1983). Generation gap: Attitudes of the youth and adults toward authoritarianism. *Journal of Psychological Research*, *27* (1), 45–47.

Sigel, R., & Hoskin, M. B. (1981). *The political involvement of adolescents*. New Brunswick, NJ: Rutgers University Press.

Simpson, M. (1972). Authoritarianism and education: A comparative approach. *Sociometry*, *35*, 223–234.

SINUS. (1983). *Die verunsicherte Generation. Jugend und Wertewandel* [The insecure generation: Youth and changing values]. Opladen, Germany: Leske Verlag.

Stöss, R. (1989). *Die extreme Rechte in der Bundesrepublik* [The extreme right in the Federal Republic]. Opladen, Germany: Westdeutscher Verlag.

Tomlinson-Keasy, C., & Keasy, C. B. (1974). The mediating role of cognitive development in moral judgement. *Child Development*, *45*, 192–298.

Torney, J. V. (1971). Socialization of attitudes toward the legal system. *Journal of Social Issues*, *27*, 137–154.

Van der Linden, F., & Hagen, J. (1977). Politieke betrokkenheid van jongeren [Political engagement of youth]. *Juegd en Samenleving*, *7*, 254–271.

Vollebergh, W. (1986). De politisering van sexisme [Sexism politicized]. In M. Matthijssen, W. Meeus, & F. van Wel (Eds.), *Beelden van juegd* (pp. 68–89). Groningen, the Netherlands: Wolters-Noordhof.

Vollebergh, W. (1989). Politische Interesse und politische Intoleranz bei Heranwachsenden [Political interests and political intolerance among older youth]. In B. Claussen (Ed.), *Politische Sozialisation Jugendlicher in Ost und West* (pp. 238–252). Darmstadt, Germany: May & Co.

Vollebergh, W. (1991). *The limits of tolerance*. Unpublished doctoral dissertation, Utrecht University.

Vollebergh, W., & Raaijmakers, Q. (1989). De masculiene parade in de adolescentie [The masculine parade in adolescence]. *Juegd en Samenleving*, No. 6/7, 373–388.

Vollebergh, W., & Raaijmakers, Q. (1991). De intergenerationele overdracht van autoritarisme [Intergenerational transmission of authoritarianism]. In P. Scheepers & R. Eisniga (Eds.), *Onderdanig en intolerant: Lacunes en controverses in auto-*

ritarisme-studies (pp. 61–78). Nijmegen, the Netherlands: Instituut voor Toegepaste Sociale Wetenschappen.

Wassmund, K. (1982). Was wird wie und wann im Prozess der politischen Sozialisation gelernt? [What is learned, when and how, in the process of political socialization?] In B. Claussen & K. Wassmund, *Handbuch der politischen Sozialisation*. Braunschweig, Germany: Pedersen.

12

Youth in the Shadow of War, War in the Light of Youth: Life Stories of Israeli Veterans

Edna Lomsky-Feder

A basic fact of all modern wars is that a large proportion of the soldiers are youths recruited into an army before integrating into adult society. This chapter investigates the cultural interpretation of the relationship between war and youth as expressed in the life stories of veterans.

The relationship between war and youth is interesting since each phenomenon involves a potential crisis on both a psychological and a social level. This potential crisis has been stressed in the literature, particularly in studies of Vietnam veterans. War is portrayed as an experience that disrupts the transition to adulthood; thus, the relationship between youth and war is perceived as painful and traumatic (Borus, 1976; Card, 1983; Figley, 1978; Laufer, 1988a, 1988b; Lifton, 1973; Modell & Haggerty, 1991). Yet this explanation of the encounter between war and youth is limited and unsatisfactory since it is founded on problematic theoretical assumptions about the natures of the war experience and youth.

One such assumption is that war is an exceptional event in the life of society and an isolated experience in the life course of an individual. War is thus defined as an extreme, stressful experience that exposes individuals to aggression and violence. As such, it is believed to have severe destructive effects on those who participate in it. On a macro level, war is viewed as reinforcing elements that threaten the social order and is also considered an expression and metaphorical portrayal of the sinister, violent side of society (Fussell, 1975). This assumption about war, which has undoubtedly been influenced by the antiwar ideology that developed as a result of the Vietnam War (Modell & Haggerty, 1991), does not frame the elements that connect society and soldiers with war positively. But alongside the aggressive elements that undermine society are aspects of war that actually reinforce or transform it. Similarly, one cannot disregard the aspects of war that strengthen individuals and enhance their ability to incorporate such an experience into their lives. The literature disregards the complex dual relationship between human society and war, a relationship that has taken various forms since the earliest days of Western culture. In the modern state, this duality is embedded in the definition of nationalism, which binds the soldier's role and the civilian's role together (Janowitz, 1976, 1983). Participation in war is not only an obligation but also a right, and it constitutes a maximal expression of a citizen's affiliation with society (Mosse, 1990). Against this background, there is a need to consider the heroic aspects of the war experience—aspects that strengthen the ties between individual and social environment—and intensify commitment to cultural values. The centrality of this relationship between the soldier's role and the civilian's role has varied from culture to culture and from period to period. It is undoubtedly stronger in societies in which war is relatively frequent.

The second problematic assumption underlying studies of the encounter between youth and war lies in their definition of adolescence. According to this assumption, young soldiers are exposed to the experience of war at a problematic stage in their development. Hence, their encounter with war is painful and even traumatic. These studies emphasize the vulnerability, sensitivity, and instability of youth—elements that are highlighted in research on developmental psychology (Peterson, Silbereisen, & Sörensen, 1992). They do not give enough attention to the flexibility, vitality, and openness of youth, which may help soldiers cope with difficult experiences such as war.

The researchers' etic interpretations of war as a traumatic experience and of youth as a vulnerable stage of life predominate to such an extent that emic interpretations (those formulated by soldiers themselves) are hardly heard. The literature has dealt primarily with the "objective" implications of war for veterans. It has emphasized how war affects adjustment in society, in terms of the incidence of behavior defined (by researchers) as socially or psychologically maladaptive, such as unemployment, use of drugs or alcohol, delinquency, emotional disorders, and divorce. Studies have focused on the statistical relationship between background variables and behavioral variables, but the meaning of the war experience for veterans has remained vague. For example, perhaps divorce after war is not perceived by veterans as the result of problematic relationships (as existing research has defined it); rather, they may view it as a release from family and social pressures. Without entering into the complex question of which is the true explanation for such behavior, it is undoubtedly worthwhile to reveal the soldiers' interpretations of their own behavior. If researchers place more emphasis on listening to the soldiers, they may be able to enhance their understanding of the encounter between war and youth, particularly its cultural interpretation, because the soldiers' emic interpretations of their experience are not isolated from the cultural-historic context. Rather, they are closely linked with the collective meaning attached to this issue. Hence, veterans' interpretations can serve as a means to explore the following: (1) how youth is defined in various social contexts and whether youth is necessarily perceived as a problem in coping with war, and (2) how war is culturally defined and whether soldiers perceive it as a painful, traumatic experience.

It is particularly interesting to explore this issue among Israeli soldiers because of the special meaning of the encounter between youth and war in Israeli society, which has experienced frequent wars. Hence, in Israel war is neither an exceptional event in the life of society nor an isolated experience in the life course of the individual. War plays a central social and ideological role in Israeli society and maintains social solidarity (Eisenstadt, 1985; Horowitz & Lissak, 1989; Kimmerling, 1985). Moreover, military service is a dominant part of adolescence in Israeli society (Azarya, 1983; Lieblich, 1989). Jewish youths are inducted into the army at the age of 18, and regular military service is obligatory, universal, and prolonged; it lasts three years for males, who then continue reserve duty until the age of about 50. Thus, military service plays a central role in Israeli youth culture. It constitutes a common experience for all, transcending socioeconomic and ethnic differences. Since Israeli society is in a continuous state of war, young soldiers are actually exposed to armed conflict, and military service is not merely a civil ceremony.

This study focused on soldiers who fought in the 1973 Yom Kippur War in the framework of their regular service. The Yom Kippur War is a particularly interesting topic in that it is socially defined as the most traumatic of all of Israel's wars. It destroyed the absolute confidence in the power of the Israel Defense Forces that had prevailed following the Six Day War, which occurred in 1967. Thus, the Yom Kippur War brought back a previous sense of existential insecurity and instability, on both individual and collective levels.

1. METHODS

The perceptions of Israeli soldiers regarding the encounter between youth and war were examined through life stories. This approach focuses on an interviewee's narration of his life course.[1] Through this method, I seek to understand how the narrator interprets and perceives what he experienced. In so doing, I neither intend nor claim to reconstruct a true picture of reality.

This approach is based on two assumptions that render the life story a sociocultural document: First, it is assumed that a person's life story reveals the meaning and interpretation he attributes to major events in his life. Second, it is assumed that the life story is not merely personal and idiosyncratic but that it reflects a social, cultural, historical context and is influenced by that context. Hence, the life story is largely a cultural mechanism mediating between individual and collective meaning (Bertaux & Kohli, 1984; Frank & Vanderburgh, 1986; Runyan, 1984).

The life story approach was appropriate for this research since it reveals the emic meaning of the war experience. The way life stories were narrated and worded—what was emphasized and what was played down, what images were used to describe the war, how war was presented in comparison with other life events—exposed how the encounter between youth and war was interpreted in the context of individuals' life courses.

Sixty-three males born between 1952 and 1954 who fought in the Yom Kippur War in 1973 during their regular army service were interviewed in the study. Interviewees were selected through the snowball method. All of them were from secular, middle-class homes and had gone to high school in urban centers. They had held various positions in the army and served in different units (combat and rear-line).

The life stories were elicited in open-ended interviews conducted 15 years after the war, so the descriptions are retrospective. The fact that the interviews are removed from the event may seem problematic, but it is actually very important. Since the aim was to reveal how the individuals interpreted their past, the reliability of the narrative is relatively unimportant, but the time perspective adds a special quality to the interviews. The passage of time allows for more reflexive contemplation and gives a broader perspective that enriches the interpretations of the event. This factor is particularly meaningful for our interviewees, who went through additional wars, including the Lebanon War (1982) and the Palestinian uprising (1987) on an active or passive level later in their lives. The comparative perspective lends a special dimension to the meaning the soldiers attribute to the encounter between war and youth since they experienced war both as youths and as adults.

The findings are based on a content analysis of the interviewees' life stories. Two aspects of the encounter between youth and war were explored: First, the meaning the soldiers attributed to the experience of war in light of being young and second, their interpretation of their own youths in the shadow of being soldiers.

2. RESULTS

Two major points emerge with regard to the meaning of war for the interviewees in light of their experiences as adolescents: (1) war as a maturing experience, and (2) war as a chapter of life that epitomizes the stage of adolescence.

2.1. War as a Maturing Experience

The maturing quality of war is centered on the formulation of self-identity. One of the dominant interpretations deriving from the life stories is that war was an experience that brought the soldiers face-to-face with the biological, psychological, and social limits of the self. The veterans talked about the encounter with death, suffering, and bereavement and about coping with situations of physical and psychological stress. However, the most powerful stories were those in which veterans talked about how their social awareness was enhanced by the war experience and how the war led to reflexive examination of the link between self and society. The soldiers talked about understanding the price of war, recognizing the discrepancy between myth and reality, and realizing what it meant to serve in a shaken army that was paying a price for its arrogance. They described how they handled their disillusion with political leaders—leaders who failed—both on an operational and a moral level. They also talked about how they began to question the relationship, once taken for granted, between citizens, soldiers, state, and war. War brought the soldiers face-to-face with the limits of the social self, in the sense that it aroused political awareness, shook "sacred cows," and shattered social truths.

The salience of this issue is reflected not only in the extent to which it is emphasized but also in the form and tone of the soldiers' narratives. Its importance comes through clearly when the narratives are compared with the fighters' descriptions of how they coped during the battles. The latter stories focus on the encounter with the biological and psychological limits of the self. Usually, they were either told in a laconic tone, as if they were dry, factual reports, or they reflected self-acceptance and a tendency to overlook the weaknesses exposed. There are almost no motifs of guilt feelings and disappointment with one's self, but there are also no descriptions of heroism and sacrifice. The tone of the stories is restrained and controlled. However, the stories of the encounter with the limits of the social self are, for the most part, emotionally loaded, dramatic, and intense. The conclusions discussed are extremely harsh and painful, as exemplified in the story of Y. S.:[2]

> (. . .) But in the Yom Kippur War I definitely learned that you can't depend on anyone—neither commanders nor commands. It's bullshit and the army is an anarchistic institution, it's . . . run by all kinds of people with power mania on the one hand and others who are dedicated and others who are no-goods and lots of that kind of thing. (. . .) Myths like: "Don't leave the wounded behind, don't leave anyone on the battlefield, the commanders are all like that . . . " all of that disappears (. . .), when you see how wounded soldiers are left, how dead bodies are left behind, how commanders are hysterical, how commanders are unable to control the situation, how soldiers don't believe their commanders, how soldiers run away in order to avoid getting wounded, so . . . myths aren't shattered, they just fade out, fade out.

Another example was given by R.Y., an artillery commander:

> (. . .) a society that talks about the sanctity of life, but which is really totally indifferent to blood. Neither our blood nor the blood of the other side. What it comes downs to is, human life has no value. (. . . .) I had a clear sense that Israeli society didn't care about me at all on Yom Kippur. They care that I win so that the country will be saved. But they don't care about me.
> Q: You felt betrayed?

A: By all means, yes. The worst thing is I believed everything I had been fed—and I was fed lies. In retrospect it turns out that I was fed lies.

The voice of sons who were betrayed and abandoned underlies the interviewees' descriptions. This realization was painful and difficult, as it caused the soldiers to part with former beliefs and undermined their previous sense of security. At the same time, however, it strengthened each individual's autonomy vis-à-vis coercive frameworks of society. It detached them from their strong, uncritical, dependent relationship with myths of their culture and its carriers. In view of the soldiers' stories, war can be said to lead to a process of individuation (Blos, 1979) vis-à-vis an individual's collective parents. The extensive use of metaphoric images of fathers and sons in the context of reflexive examination of the war experience supports this contention. For example, A. S., a paratrooper, described soldiers as abandoned children:

(. . .) I knew my private war was one big mess, as I said, I wandered around without a father or mother, and . . . some of us kids went off to look for the enemy. That's pretty much it, from beginning to end. That's how it looks, that's how it looks.

Another image invoked in the stories is that of sons brought to war as sacrifices. This image is invoked from the biblical story of the sacrifice of Isaac. This sense of being betrayed sons is also expressed in recurring descriptions of difficult, disappointing encounters with commanders who, during the course of the war, were supposed to have played a fatherly role. The soldiers talk about how the true colors of their commanders came out in combat. When the soldiers should have been protected, the commanders sent them to fight, prompted by childish irresponsibility and fervor for battle or by a desire to prove their professionalism and advance their own careers.

Although war is interpreted by the soldiers as a maturing experience from a personal perspective, it is portrayed at the same time as an experience that delayed entry into adult roles. After the war, most of the veterans chose to go on extended trips abroad, take short-term jobs, or enroll in institutions of higher education. In most cases, even higher education was described as a way to pass time and not as a step toward the pursuit of a career. Prolongation of the social moratorium is expressed in the stories primarily through postponement of decisions about entering a professional career, and less through postponement of decisions about establishing a family. The interviewees explained their delayed entry into adult roles as part of a need to withdraw and retreat after the experience of war, or as a desire to enjoy life to the fullest before they tied themselves down. Although their explanations of the gap between psychological and social maturity focus on the individual level, that gap can also be viewed as an expression of passive social protest. Delayed entry into adult roles can also be explained as rejection of that world or as a manifestation of difficulty integrating into adult life. This point was reinforced when the interviewees compared themselves with the heroic generation of the Six Day War, whom they perceived as much more integrated and committed than themselves. The Yom Kippur War veterans described themselves with images such as "lost generation," "wanderers," and "crisis generation." These images reflect a problematic attitude toward the social order, an attitude explained by the interviewees as resulting from their entering the adult world at a difficult and traumatic time in the collective life course of Israeli society.

In light of the dramatic images invoked by the interviewees and the painful connotations of war in their descriptions of social maturation, one would have expected them to interpret the experience as a crisis that disrupted the normal life course. However, in the life stories the veterans primarily interpreted war as an experience that did not disrupt or curtail the natural, expected process of maturation; rather, it was perceived as an integral part of the process. According to them, war intensified or expedited processes that naturally occur in the lives of Israeli males, for whom military service is an inherent part of maturation. War epitomizes the process to the point that it is often defined as a rite of passage. Like every other story of maturation, the veterans' stories describe how they experienced growth, pain, and anger. Even though everything is more dramatic and painful, the dominant voice does not wish to express the experience as a crisis. Yet in some of the life stories war is nevertheless portrayed as a crisis. This interpretation is not voiced often in the narratives, but it cannot be ignored since it is expressed with considerable emotional intensity and invokes dramatic images. According to the crisis interpretation, war interfered with the gradual, predictable process of normal development and hence disrupted the normal maturation process. This disruption was defined in different ways. For example, war was defined as an aging experience—one that caused the soldier to skip intermediate stages of maturation and prematurely enter adulthood. In another definition, war was an event that caused one to become "stuck," that delayed growth and development. In yet another view, war was a turning point—after the war, things were not the same as before, nor did life continue as would normally have been expected. In this context, the disruption was also interpreted in a positive light, as an experience that released the interviewee from personal and social constraints. These voices constitute the antithesis of the noncrisis interpretation that predominates in the stories. Paradoxically, since the crisis interpretation is rare and contradictory, it emphasizes the other, more dominant voice.

An attempt to understand why some interviewees perceived war as a trauma may elicit a further dimension of the cultural meaning of the encounter between war and adolescence. These soldiers attributed the crisis interpretation to the intensity of the experience they went through in combat. In fact, this interpretation was only offered by soldiers who served in combat units and experienced the war on an intense level, and it was primarily offered by those who completed their service toward the end of the war. This latter characteristic suggests that their interpretation of the war as a crisis can also be attributed to their social position after the war—the fact that they were removed from the military framework. It seems that the encounter with civilian life upon completion of army service intensified the soldiers' realization of the meaning of the war. As a result, the experience was viewed as more of a crisis. This interpretation is also undoubtedly related to the fact that these interviewees were removed from the protected military framework as they separated from their comrades and their organic units. In addition, outside of the army they were more exposed to the public discourse regarding the 1973 war and its definition as a traumatic event on the collective level. The claim that the military framework was protective is corroborated by the fact that combat soldiers who continued serving in the army for over a year after the war had ended tended to interpret the experience as integrated into the process of maturation. These soldiers claimed that the military framework mitigated the trauma of the experience.

Up to this point, I have shown that the noncrisis interpretation of war prevails in the life stories of Israeli veterans. This interpretation is also manifest in the perception of the experience as epitomizing youth.

2.2. War as Epitomizing Youth

The meaning of war as an experience that epitomizes youth is exemplified in the story of Y. Sh., a pilot:

(. . .) I had the same spirit of Zionism and heroism, which I see today as a bit idiotic. But I remember that because I was young they didn't let me fly during the first two days [of the war] and I went on a hunger strike. I wouldn't shave and I went barefoot [customs of mourning in the Jewish religion that are practiced on the Yom Kippur holiday], until they let me fly. I was slightly injured once, friends died, friends were taken prisoner . . . but the whole thing wasn't even traumatic because it was all under the flag of Israeli heroism . . . that's it. (. . .)

Q: About the Yom Kippur War, you mentioned before that even though a lot of people died the event was not traumatic.

A: It was like—it may be cruel to say this—but it was like field exercises [practiced in youth movements]. We were kids. I was a boy, a little over 20, a boy of a little over 20 who . . . who did all kinds of things, all kinds of things that were fun; things like I dared—I was really daring. I think I'm a gambler by nature. I felt it was like, you know, like jumping off a motorcycle along the Yarkon [a river in Tel Aviv]. We would jump off, flip our motorcycles into the air and crash into a tree. I think I was just a boy. I didn't understand when I was in the war, I didn't feel anything, it didn't traumatize me.

Y. Sh., like other interviewees, defined war as an arena that gave him an opportunity to fulfill typically adolescent desires, for intense thrills, adventure, and peril. The behavioral manifestations of these desires are defined in other social contexts as irresponsible and rebellious. In Israeli society, these characteristics are channeled into military service, which legitimizes and even encourages them. Danger, adventure, and guts are meaningful in Israeli society not only in the context of being young; they are also central elements of the social definition of being a man. Hence, army service was perceived by the veterans as an essential phase in the formulation of masculine identity. They defined participation in war as an opportunity for maximal fulfillment of masculinity, as it translated into the ethos of heroism and the Israeli warrior.

The ethos of heroism emphasizes courage, but also sacrifice and total social involvement. Thus, internalization of the ethos also means identifying with central values of society. Against this background, the soldiers' accounts indicate that they perceived participation in war as an opportunity to express their patriotic commitment to the values of society in the most naive sense, without any reservations or criticism. War gave them an opportunity to contribute their share to society and realize all of the heroic tales they were brought up with. This point also sheds light on intergenerational relations in Israeli society, as exemplified in the story of H. Sh., an officer in the armored corps:

> (. . .) The very fact that we went through this [the war], that we contributed our share, is also . . . for us it's a kind of hurdle . . . by integrating here, now we've also done our share. (. . .) The first time, like I agreed to accept concern and warmth [from parents]—things which would have . . . irritated me before . . . and I think . . . I think it's not only true for me, the very fact that you are at the front and they [the parents] are at the rear, for the first time completely changed the balance of power within my family, you're the one who . . . is standing alone and doing the same things they always made you feel you would never be able to do, because of what they went through in 1948 [the War of Independence]. I think that was the point . . . in my relationship with my parents it was definitely the turning point . . . and it brought us closer than we had been before (. . .) anyhow, I think for all of us it was a ceremony in which we broke away from our parents, because . . . because we were the ones doing the . . .
> Q: Breaking away? It's actually coming back, becoming closer.
> A: Yes. That's why I call it growing up.

This description reflects the mood of quite a few interviewees who were influenced by the tales of heroism, primarily tales from the 1948 War of Independence, told by members of their parents' generation. In this case, the dialogue between parents and offspring also largely reflects the dialogue between the different generations on the history of wars in Israeli society.

An additional manifestation of the importance of war in the formation of Israeli youth is found in the descriptions of several interviewees who, contrary to their wishes and expectations, were not combat fighters. These individuals defined war as an experience that passed them by, as a missing chapter in their personal biographies and maturation processes. Moreover, they did not talk about this ethos from a cynical perspective like most of the others, but rather out of a sense of identification. Most of them sought compensation later in life for this loss; some fought in the Lebanon War, others went on dangerous trips abroad. Such trips were usually described in terms similar to those used to describe combat situations.

To sum up, most of the interviewees, particularly those who served in combat units, mentioned that when the war broke out, they were eager to fight. They felt they had been given an opportunity to fulfill their youth. Thus, youth was not interpreted as a vulnerable stage of life that made the encounter with war difficult, but as an attribute that gave them strength to cope and lent meaning to the experience. In this connection, the veterans largely defined youth as a resource enabling them to perform the role of fighter.

2.3. Youth as a Resource in War

The dominant perception in the life stories is that in the shadow of war youthfulness gave the younger soldiers an advantage over the older ones. The veterans claimed that psychological attributes affecting formulations of self-identity (as shown above) made it easier for them to assume the role of fighter; in the same connection, they mentioned social attributes inherent in the social status of youth. The interviewees emphasized, in various ways, the importance of being released from social commitments such as career and family, which strengthened their feeling that they had nothing to lose. A second social attribute associated with youth that the interviewees mentioned as facilitating participation in combat was the centrality of the peer group—comrades in arms and friends at home. The desire to be like everyone else, to be "in" and to benefit from social rewards, was a central motivation for participating in war. An additional point mentioned was the fact that during the Yom Kippur War they were doing regular army service. In their opinion, soldiers doing regular service ask fewer questions and respond more mechanically than reservists. Identification with the organization and with the organic units is particularly strong during the period of regular service. This sense of identification with the military framework and their removal from the outside world made it more difficult for them to criticize the army. In this sense, the veterans kept saying "we were kids"—as opposed to adults— since adults are supposed to be more aware, more conscious, and hence less adaptable. Youth was thus defined by the interviewees as an important resource possessed by fighters. They contended that the psychological and social attributes of youth not only facilitated participation in war but to a large extent protected the soldiers against war's traumatic effects. This argument is reinforced by the fact that all of the interviewees actively or passively grappled with the Lebanon War at a later stage of life. Take, for example, the story of the paratrooper Sh.A., who had a psychological breakdown during the Lebanon War and underwent therapy. In the course of his therapy, he sorted out the meaning of the war experience. In his life story, he mentions the difference between the wars:

(. . .) All in all, when I did my regular army service I was not—we and I were not—at all aware of what was happening to us. We were fools. And you're talking about soldiers doing regular service—their life is not in their hands. I don't think . . . maybe it's because of their age but it's also the situation of being a soldier doing regular service, you don't figure the profits and losses. (. . .) In Lebanon I was suddenly an adult, I was familiar with the stages [of the war]. I was with younger comrades, and I said: In the next stage this is what will happen. I also didn't believe how much I could anticipate. (. . .) And when I started analyzing things after Lebanon with the help of a psychiatrist, I also . . . I really started to see . . . the true meaning of things. In Lebanon I had more healthy senses. I definitely have healthy senses all the time, because even when I had an opportunity to raise my profile [of military fitness] . . . and go through a corrective experience—I didn't want a corrective experience, I was in a position of self-defense, I didn't want the corrective experience, I simply swore to myself in Lebanon. There were situations where I said I'll do anything to avoid being in that situation again. I'll do anything I can.

Even if this is an extreme case in the sense that Sh.A. was incapable of handling a second war, he definitely reflects the prevailing view of the interviewees that the encounter with the Lebanon War was difficult and even traumatic for some. In this connection, stories about the attempts to evade serving in Lebanon are not uncommon. Take, for example, the story of Y. S., an artillery fighter:

(. . .) Look, the experience I went through [during the Yom Kippur War] caused me to become almost paralyzed and develop strong antagonism toward the war [in Lebanon]. As a result, two or three of my friends messed around so much in our unit that we were thrown out (. . .) I think you can fight well once. In the next war you'll be washed out.

Combat at a late stage of life is perceived as more difficult than combat in youth. Even as one gains experience from war to war, one does not become inured to war's effect. On the contrary, according to the interviewees, older soldiers are more fearful and vulnerable.

Adult soldiers were viewed as not only more fearful, but also as less naive and more cynical. Thus, youth appeared to be an important resource for fighters not only from a psychological but also from a social perspective. Although the adult soldiers claimed that it was easier for the young to participate in war, it was clear to them that youth constitutes a social group that is easy to mobilize and manipulate. As adults, how did the interviewees cope with the recognition of this meaning of youth? Some reconciled themselves to the rules of the game and largely accepted them as facts of life. These soldiers emphasized the personal, experiential facet of the encounter between youth and war. Others expressed more anger, bitterness, and irony. They made cynical statements, such as how society exploits its youth—statements that constituted another facet of the process of gaining social awareness and shaking the war myth. At the same time, most of those who were angry and cynical did not remove themselves from the "game," and only a few refused to participate in war as a matter of principle or for ideological reasons. The same approach is evident in the attitudes they expressed about their children's educations and about their children's serving in the army. Only a few of them openly argued that they would educate their children not to serve in fighting units or stated that they would take action to prevent their sons from being drafted. The majority accepted the fact that as long as they stayed in Israel, military service and wars would be an integral part of their children's upbringing.

The interpretation of war as an experience that epitomizes youth would, at first glance, contradict the interpretation of war as a maturing experience that largely takes away from the soldiers' youthfulness. How do these two interpretations coincide?

The most common resolution of this inconsistency is inherent in the construction of the narrative of war as a story of growing up. At first soldiers are excited about fighting and, as the war goes on, they sober up. The story of war as a passage to adulthood often emphasizes the "first chapter" over what follows. The more the narrator stresses his enthusiasm about fighting at the beginning of the war, the more dramatic the encounter with reality afterwards and the greater the impact of maturation.

In other narratives, awareness of the maturing effect of war was described as occurring at a later stage in life. These stories emphasized that the military framework prevented soldiers from contending with the war experience. Only later, when they had completed their service and entered civilian life, were they able to connect with the experience. At that point, the maturing effect of war became part of retrospective consciousness. Some of the veterans came to this realization when they participated in a second war as adults. In these life stories, the dramatic elements of the description of war and the description of maturation are weaker and vaguer.

Another solution that reconciles the conflicting interpretations is not inherent in the narratives but rather in the way the interviewees described war as an exciting experience that epitomized youth. The tone of a 35-year-old man reminiscing about his young, vital, enthusiastic self is almost always cynical. Such cynicism can be understanding and patronizing (as in the story of the pilot); or it can be ironic, mixed with bitterness and pain—as in the story of Y. C., the artillery fighter:

> . . . I was wounded, and they took me away for a day. (. . .) They took me to
> Bluza [an army base], to headquarters, and I felt like a real hero . . . of course I

said "No! I won't go!" but I was really glad when they took me. I felt really scared, really scared.

The tone of this presentation is an outcome of maturation. Only a person who has "sobered up" from youthful enthusiasm can view it from an ironic perspective.

3. DISCUSSION

The life stories of these Israeli soldiers show that, contrary to the theoretical assumptions prevailing in the relevant literature, the veterans did not perceive war as a traumatic experience; rather, it was construed as part of the normal, expected course of maturation. By the same token, youth was not defined as a factor that hindered their ability to cope with the experience, but as a factor that protected young soldiers against war's traumatic effects. This perception of the relationship between youth and war can be understood against the background of Israeli society.

In Israel, where wars are frequent, young people are often recruited to fight for their country. Hence, since the establishment of the Israeli national entity, it has been necessary to construct a myth that Mosse (1990) calls "the myth of participation in war." Israeli society has consistently glorified military service and war and developed a myth of heroism (Gal, 1986; Sivan, 1991). Heroism in war is culturally constructed in the ethos of the Israeli soldier, which is part of the ethos of the *sabra* (native-born Israeli), as well as in the image of the "new Jew." The myth of heroism has served as a model for generations of young Israelis and is highly significant for the cohort participating in this study, whose adolescence was influenced by the euphoria of the heroic Six Day War. It is easy for young people to identify with the myth of heroism, since it incorporates such attributes of adolescence as courage, unyielding adherence to goals, ability to withstand physical and emotional pressure, and loyalty to friends. In Israeli society, youthful desires are channeled into army service, and the traits of youth are structured as part of the myth of heroism and the role of the soldier. Notwithstanding public discourse about the nature of this myth and the extent to which it has eroded or changed (Friedlander, 1992), research has shown that Israeli youth have always been highly committed to military service (Gal, 1986; Lieblich, 1989). In this connection, the war experience is defined, both on the individual and collective levels, as part of maturation and, to a large extent, as a "rite of passage" (Azarya, 1983). By the same token, adolescence is not described as a vulnerable period. Rather, youth is culturally perceived as providing a sense of power and commitment that enables soldiers to fulfill their role and cope with the war experience. The empirical finding that reserve soldiers have a higher rate of combat stress reactions than regular soldiers (Gal, 1986) suggests that the cultural definition may also have behavioral implications.

Perceptions of the war experience among Yom Kippur War veterans cannot be understood merely in light of the cultural meaning of war as a general phenomenon; they should also be viewed in light of their specific war experience and its collective meaning. The collective meaning of the Yom Kippur War is expressed primarily through the content of the veterans' stories of maturation. Comparison of the narratives of the Yom Kippur War veterans with those of veterans of the Six Day War (*Siah Lohamim*, 1968), the Lebanon War (Lieblich & Perlow, 1988), or the Vietnam War (Lifton, 1973; Wikler, 1980), indicates that the Yom Kippur War was different. Its veterans do not express personal remorse or guilt. Rather, they point an accusing finger at others. In so doing, they speak as victims and not at all as aggressors. In their reflexive examination of the Yom Kippur War, the significant other is not the enemy but their own leaders. The intensity of the war experience, according to the veterans, does not lie in the fact that it revealed a sinister, immoral side of their personalities—a fact that is difficult to integrate into the domain of the ego. Rather, it lies in the fact that they faced harsh questions about where they stood in their social milieu and how they could formulate their identities as civilians.

Emphasis on these points in the veterans' descriptions of maturation reflects the public discourse that ensued in Israel after the Yom Kippur War, which essentially expressed a basic breach of trust with respect to the political and military leadership. This collective crisis was one of the main factors that led to the fall of the Labor Party, which was identified with the founding fathers of Zionism and the establishment of the state. This background illuminates the metaphoric references to father-son relationships that appear in the descriptions of social maturation during the war. The interviewees likened themselves to sons who were abandoned, deceived, and betrayed by their collective parents. At the same time, however, they perceived themselves as having gained autonomy and social awareness. According to their stories, the Yom Kippur War released them from dependent, uncritical links with the heroes of the culture and the carriers of its values. These stories of personal maturation are, undoubtedly, among the cultural mechanisms underlying the construction of the collective discourse about the Yom Kippur War. Yet these stories are influenced by that discourse and reflect it accordingly.

This dialogue between the individual and collective story of the Yom Kippur War is also expressed in narratives that depict the war as a trauma. The crisis interpretation, which rejects the dominant interpretation of war as part of maturation, is more connected with the cultural definition of the Yom Kippur War as a collective trauma. Although the War of Independence was much more traumatic from an objective point of view (e.g., number of casualties; Sivan, 1991), the Yom Kippur War is socially defined as *the* traumatic war because, after the euphoric period that followed victory in the Six Day War, the country was exposed once again to real existential threat (Eisenstadt, 1985; Horowitz & Lissak, 1989). These narratives, which represent the war as a personal crisis, were created by soldiers who served in combat units and experienced the war intensely. The definition of war as a trauma in their private lives is undoubtedly related to their painful experiences. However, compared with their comrades who went through the same painful experiences but did not define the war as a crisis, these soldiers were more exposed to the public discourse that structured the traumatic meaning of the Yom Kippur War. They completed their army service immediately after the war and worked through this experience outside of the protected army framework. Hence, just as their stories contributed to the construction of the traumatic meaning of the Yom Kippur War, these soldiers were also more affected by it.

In sum, the life stories of these Israeli veterans shed light on the complex relationship between the personal experience of war and the cultural interpretation of that experience. The collective meaning of the encounter between youth and war is closely related to the personal interpretations of veterans. Thus, the young soldier's confrontation with war is structured and sustained by cultural factors, and these factors contribute to personal interpretations of the war experience. If personal interpretations of war help soldiers cope with that experience, the inherent cultural meaning of war is also crucial. The way society defines the meaning of youth in the context of war and the meaning of war in the context of youth affects the young soldier's ability to cope with war and its consequences. Although this study focused on the phenomenological aspect of coping, I submit that the cultural meaning of the encounter between youth and war may also affect behavior. However, this issue requires further research.

NOTES

1. All participants in this research were male.
2. Ellipses in parentheses indicate an editorial cut. Ellipses without parentheses indicate a pause made by the interviewee.

REFERENCES

Azarya, V. (1983). The Israeli armed forces. In M. Janowitz & S. D. Westbrook (Eds.), *The political education of soldiers* (pp. 99–127). London: Sage.
Bertaux, D., & Kohli, M. (1984). The life history approach: A continental view. *Annual Review of Sociology, 10*, 215–237.
Blos, P. (1979). *The adolescent passage: Developmental issues.* New York: International University Press.
Borus, J. F. (1976). The reentry transition of the Vietnam veterans. In N. L. Goldman & D. R. Segal (Eds.), *The social psychology of military service* (pp.27–43). London: Sage.

Card, J. (1983). *Lives after Vietnam*. Toronto: Lexington Books.

Eisenstadt, S. N. (1985). *The transformation of Israeli society* (pp. 387–402). London: Weidenfeld and Nicolson.

Figley, C. R. (1978). Psychology of adjustment among Vietnam veterans: An overview of the research. In C. R. Figley (Ed.), *Stress disorders among Vietnam veterans* (pp. 57–70). New York: Brunner Mazelin.

Frank, G., & Vanderburgh, R. M. (1986). Cross cultural use of life history methods in gerontology. In C. L. Fry & J. Keith (Eds.), *New methods for old age research* (pp. 185–212). South Hadley, MA: Bergen and Garey.

Friendlander, N. (1992) The sabra died in Lebanon. *Ma'ariv Newspaper*, January.

Fussell, P. (1975). *The great war and modern memory*. New York and London: Oxford Unversity Press.

Gal, R. (1986). *The portrait of the Israeli soldier*. New York: Greenwood Press.

Janowitz, M. (1976). Military institutions and citizenship in Western societies. *Armed Forces and Society*, 2, 185–203.

Janowitz, M. (1983). Civic consciousness and military performance. In M. Janowitz & S. D. Wesbrook (Eds.), *The political education of soldiers* (pp. 57–80). London: Sage.

Kimmerling, B. (1985). *The interrupted system*. New Brunswick and Oxford: Transaction Books.

Laufer, R. S. (1988a). The aftermath of war: Adult socialization and political development. In R. S. Siegel (Ed.), *Political learning in adulthood* (pp. 415–457). Chicago and London: University of Chicago Press.

Laufer, R. S. (1988b). The serial self. In J. P. Wilson (Ed.), *Human adaptation to extreme stress* (pp. 33–53). New York: Plenum Press.

Lieblich, A. (1989). *Transition to adulthood during military service: The Israeli case*. Albany: State University of New York Press.

Lieblich, A., & Perlow, M. (1988). Transition to adulthood during military service. *The Jerusalem Quarterly*, 47, 40–76.

Lifton, R. J. (1973). *Home from the war*. New York: Simon and Schuster.

Modell, J., & Haggerty, T. (1991). The social impact of war. *Annual Review of Sociology*, 17, 205–224.

Mosse, G. L. (1990). *Fallen soldiers*. New York and Oxford: Oxford University Press.

Petersen, A. C., Silbereisen, R. K., & Sörensen, S. (1992). Adolescent development: A global perspective. This volume.

Runyan, W. M. (1984). *Life history and psychobiography*. New York and Oxford: Oxford University Press.

Siah lohamim [The seventh day]. (1968). Tel Aviv: The Kibbutz Movement.

Sivan, E. (1991). *The 1948 generation: Myth, profile and memory*. Tel Aviv: Marachot.

Wikler, N. (1980). Hidden injuries of war. In C. R. Figley & S. Leventman (Eds.), *Strangers at home: Vietnam veterans since the war* (pp. 87–106). New York: Praeger.

13

Youth in Dangerous Environments: Coping with the Consequences

James Garbarino

How do we understand danger in the lives of youth? How do we understand the origins, mechanisms, and coping processes employed by youth in dealing with danger? What happens when a youth is hurt?

The consequences can range from minor injury to death, with the outcome reflecting a host of organic and situational factors. Physical disability has certain objective realities, of course, but I will be concerned in this chapter with the psychological and moral consequences of danger, which depend in part on the meanings given to injury and death (Garbarino, 1988).

The same physical consequences can have very different life-course effects, depending on cultural, social, and psychological influences. Thus, for example, it matters developmentally whether a teenager is hurt by a parental assault or through play, in the course of running away from a fight, or in the course of standing up for a friend.

1. POSTTRAUMATIC STRESS DISORDER

Of particular developmental interest is whether danger results in psychological disruption. The emergent field of traumatic stress studies is increasingly recognizing the importance of understanding the phenomenon of posttraumatic stress disorder (PTSD) as a response to childhood trauma (van der Kolk, 1987). This recognition follows upon the inclusion of PTSD as a category for official diagnosis in the third edition of the American Psychiatric Association's *Diagnostic and Statistical Manual*, published in 1980. Diagnostic criteria for PTSD include existence of a recognizable stressor that would evoke significant symptoms of distress in almost everyone, re-experiencing the trauma, and numbing of responsiveness.

These developments have helped establish a foundation upon which to build understanding of the relationship between danger and trauma. One element of this foundation is the distinction between acute danger, such as a situation in which a deranged individual enters a normally safe school and opens fire with a rifle, and chronic danger—such as when soldiers regularly attack students and teachers in or around a school as a means of disrupting day-to-day academic life.

Acute danger requires a process of adjustment through some measure of objective change in the conditions of life or subjective alteration of one's stance toward life events. Acute incidents of danger often simply require *situational* adjustment by normal youths leading normal lives—the assimilation of the traumatic event into the youths' understanding of their situation. The therapy of choice is reassurance: "You are safe again; things are back to normal."

This is not to deny that traumatic stress syndrome in children and youths exposed to acute danger may require processing over a period of months (van der Kolk, 1987). And, if the traumatic stress is intense enough, it may leave permanent "psychic scars," particularly for children made vulnerable because of disruptions in their primary relationships, most notably, those with parents. These effects include excessive sensitivity to stimuli associated with the trauma and diminished expectations for the future (Terr, 1990).

But chronic danger imposes a requirement for *developmental* adjustment—accommodations that are likely to include persistent PTSD, alterations of personality, and major changes in patterns of behavior or articulation of ideological interpretations of the world that provide a framework for making sense of ongoing danger—particularly when that danger comes from a violent overthrow of day-to-day social reality, as occurs with exposure to war, communal violence, or chronic crime (Garbarino, 1995).

The therapy of choice in situations of chronic danger is one that builds upon a child's primary relationships to create a new positive reality for the youth that can stand up to the "natural" conclusions a severely traumatized youth is likely to draw otherwise about self-worth, the reliability of adults and their institutions, and safe approaches to adopt toward the world.

There is a growing body of research and clinical observation based upon a concern that youths caught up in war and other forms of social crisis will adapt in ways that produce developmental impairment, physical damage, and emotional trauma and will be "missocialized" into a model of fear, violence, and hatred as a result (Garbarino, Kostelny, & Dubrow, 1991; Goleman, 1986; Rosenblatt, 1983).

This growing concern is fueled by the recognition that the demographics of war dangers have shifted as the 20th century has progressed. According to a 1986 UNICEF report, the ratio of soldiers to civilians killed in armed conflict has shifted; it was approximately 8:1 in the early decades (for instance, in World War I) and has been 1:5 in recent conflicts (such as the war in Lebanon).

Some observers have noted a similar trend in the case of the high-crime neighborhoods of American cities—that is, increasing victimization of women and children. However, epidemiological data continue to portray young males (the "soldiers") as the predominant casualties in neighborhoods saturated by crime, particularly gang- and drug-related crime. Young children are still "innocent bystanders" or "in training" for the front lines of violent conflict. Nonetheless, their experiences can be traumatic if the danger is chronic.

Political conflict, racism, and poverty create potentially dangerous threats to children's development. These evils provide a context in which researchers can seek to understand the dynamics of youth in dangerous and stressful environments and the relationship between danger and trauma. But the presumption that danger leads to developmental impairment is clearly not the whole story.

2. THE ROLE OF SOCIAL CRISIS IN MORAL DEVELOPMENT

A second theme in studies of youth in danger is the role of social crisis in stimulating moral development. As Coles (1986) noted in his study of political crisis, *some* children and youths develop a precocious and precious moral sensibility. This is a theme to which I shall return in seeking to understand the mediators between danger and trauma, on the one hand, and between danger and moral development, on the other.

Anna Freud's report on children exposed to trauma during World War II concluded that, at least in the short run, children in the care of their own mothers or familiar mother substitutes were not psychologically devastated by wartime experiences, principally because parents could maintain day-to-day care routines and project high morale (Freud & Burlingham, 1943).

This is not to say that such children escaped unscathed, however. Indeed, follow-up studies of severely traumatized children cared for by Freud and her colleagues revealed a significant proportion who evidenced chronic and profound problems despite receiving compensatory care. When such a "sleeper effect" occurs, life adjustment problems may emerge 10 or more years after family dissolution.

Convergent findings from several studies of life-course responses to stressful early experience suggest a series of ameliorating factors that lead to prosocial and healthy adaptability (Lösel & Bliesener, 1990): (1) actively trying to cope with stress (rather than just reacting), (2) cognitive competence (at least an average level of intelligence), (3) experiences of self-efficacy and a corresponding self-confidence and positive self-esteem, (4) temperamental characteristics that favor active coping attempts and positive relationships with others (e.g., activity, goal orientation, sociability) rather than passive withdrawal, (5) a stable emotional relationship with at least one parent or other reference person, (6) an open, supportive educational climate and parental model of behavior that encourages constructive coping with problems, and (7) social support from persons outside the family.

These factors have been identified as important when the stresses involved are in the normal range found in the mainstream of modern industrial societies—for example, poverty, family conflict, childhood physical disability, and parental substance abuse. Nonetheless, they may provide a starting point for efforts to understand the special character of coping in the stressful circumstances of prolonged violence (war, communal conflict, and pervasive violent crime), where the risk of socially maladaptive coping is high.

Adolescents forced to cope with chronic danger may adapt in ways that are dysfunctional. The psychopathological dimensions are equally worthy of attention, however. Youths may cope with danger by adopting worldviews or personae that may be dysfunctional in any normal situations in which they are expected to participate, such as school. For example, adaptive behavior in the abnormal situation of chronic crisis may be maladaptive in school if youths defend themselves by becoming aggressive, which stimulates rejection at school.

What is more, some adaptations to chronic danger, such as emotional withdrawal, may be socially adaptive in the short run, but become a danger to the next generation when the individual becomes a parent. This phenomenon has been observed in studies on families of Holocaust survivors (Danieli, 1985).

Even in the absence of this intergenerational process, however, the same links between danger and trauma observed in children may operate directly among parents. Their adaptations to dangerous environments may produce childrearing strategies that impede normal development. The fear felt by parents of children in high-crime environments may manifest in a very restrictive and punitive style of discipline (including physical assault) used in an effort to protect the child from falling under the influence of negative forces in a neighborhood.

Unfortunately, this approach is likely to have the result of heightening aggression on a child's part, with one consequence being difficulty in succeeding in contexts that provide alternatives to the gang culture and endorsing an acceptance of violence as the modus operandi for social control (which in turn rationalizes the gang's use of violence as the dominant tactic for social influence). Holding a child back from negative forces through punitive restrictiveness is generally much less successful as a strategy than promoting positive alternatives to the negative subculture feared by the parent (Scheinfeld, 1983).

In addition, early adaptation may lead to a process of "identification with the aggressor" in which children model themselves and their behavior on those powerful aggressive individuals and groups in their environment that cause the danger in the first place, such as gangs in a public housing project or enemy soldiers in occupied territories. And children exposed to the stress of extreme violence may reveal mental health disturbances years after the immediate experience is over (Goleman, 1986). For example, a follow-up study of Cambodian children who experienced the moral and psychological devastation of the Pol Pot regime in the period 1974–79 revealed that four years after leaving Cambodia, 50 percent developed PTSD. Of particular interest for the present study is the fact that those children who did not reside with a family member were most likely to show this and other psychiatric symptoms (Kinzie, Sack, Angell, Mauson, & Rath, 1986).

When coupled with political ideology reflecting violent communal conflict, experience of chronic danger appears to be a primary force serving to generate probable recruits for participation in terrorist violence (Fields, 1987). More broadly, it appears to be associated with truncated moral development in which a vendetta mentality predominates. Fields's research in Northern Ireland and the Middle East revealed children stuck at primitive stages of moral development compared to children of the same age in less violently conflictual communities, who had progressed to advanced moral reasoning. For example, while 27 percent of 11- to 14-year-olds in normal social environments typically respond at the "rational/beneficial/utilitarian" level, almost none of the 11- to 14-year-olds studied in Northern Ireland or Lebanon did (Fields, 1987). Why?

From what is known of the development of moral reasoning and ego generally (Loevinger, 1976), the most likely answer is one that mixes cultural, temperamental, and social forces. For example, it may well be true that males and females are inclined to approach moral issues somewhat differently as a function of their characteristically different early experiences, cultural expectations, and perhaps even innately different sensibilities. This is the basis for Gilligan's (1982) feminist alternative to standard "masculine" approaches to moral development, which concentrate on morality as the assertion of "objective" principles and rights. In her view, such masculine models are too narrowly rational and disregard the importance of moral reasoning based upon empathy and attempts to sustain and repair relationships.

Given that "feminine" approaches to morality seek to minimize hurt as the primary goal, they may provide an important resource for children encountering extreme danger. In such a situation, masculine models of asserting rights may lead directly to the arrest of moral development at the stage of vendetta. Movement beyond vendetta may depend upon the social environment stimulating a process of dialogue that can move victimized children and youths to an appreciation of abstract principles that provide an intellectual basis for empathy.

Advanced moral reasoning of the type measured by the Tapp-Kohlberg assessment seems to reflect the degree to which children are supported in engaging in issue-focused discussions and social interactions. These interactions invoke the child's emergent cognitive capacities and stimulate perspective taking and intellectual encounters with values and principles.

More generally, Vygotsky (1962) referred to this as a process that is operating in the "zone of proximal development," the developmental space between what a child can do alone and what he or she can do with the help of a teacher. Developmentalists have come to recognize that it is the dynamic relationship between a child's competence alone and the child's competence in the company of a guiding teacher that leads to forward movement.

This reinforcement seems particularly important in the case of moral development. The key here is a process of "optimal discrepancy" in which a child's moral teachers, be they adults or peers, lead the child toward higher-order thinking by presenting positions that are one stage above the child's characteristic mode of responding to social events as moral issues.

When all this happens in the context of a nurturant affective system—a warm family, for example—the result is ever-advancing moral development, the development of a principled ethic of caring (Gilligan, 1982). What is more, even if parents create a rigid, noninteractive, authoritarian family context (and thus block moral development), the larger community may compensate: "The child of authoritarian parents may function in a larger more democratic society whose varied patterns provide the requisite experiences for conceptualizing an egalitarian model of distributive justice" (Fields, 1987, p. 5).

However, this formulation becomes problematic in view of findings that only a minority of adults ever achieve the highest levels of moral reasoning in the Kohlberg system. Thus, the issue of stimulating moral development beyond the lower levels becomes in large measure a social issue: Do adults in the community outside the family (most notably, school teachers) demonstrate the higher-order moral reasoning necessary to move children from the lower to the higher stages?

3. THE ROLE OF IDEOLOGY

The arguments made above imply that ideology is highly important to the process of moral development. If school teachers and other adult representatives of a community are disinclined to model higher-order moral reasoning or are intimidated if they try to do so, then the process of moral truncation that is "natural" to situations of violent conflict will proceed unimpeded. This appears to have happened in Northern Ireland, for example, as both Protestant and Catholic teachers learned that if they tried to engage their students in dialogue that could promote higher-order moral reasoning, they would be silenced by extremist elements (Conroy, 1987).

Thus, situations of chronic danger can stimulate the process of moral development if they are matched by an interactive climate created by adults—and endorsed, or at least not stifled by, the larger culture through its political, educational, and religious institutions—and if the children are free of debilitating psychopathology (e.g., PTSD).

Families can provide the emotional context for the processing needed for children to make positive, moral sense of danger (and even trauma itself). Communities must usually carry things to the next step, stimulating higher-order moral development. They do so by presenting a democratic milieu in, for example, schools. Such a model is all the more important for adolescents, who characteristically operate outside the home and in the community to a larger extent than children.

However, when danger derives from political conflict in an antidemocratic social context and occurs in an authoritarian social climate as manifest within the family, the result is likely to be the truncated moral reasoning observed by Fields, particularly among boys, who are more vulnerable than girls to this consequence of living at risk, as they are to most others (Werner & Smith, 1982).

Some observers point to the importance of ideological factors in sustaining the ability to function under extreme stress. In his observations of life in Nazi concentration camps, Bettelheim (1943) noted that those who bore up best were people with intense ideological commitments (most notably, the ultrareligious and Communists), as their commitments offered meaning impervious to day-to-day brutalization.

Among inner-city Black Americans living in a racist society and contending with crime-plagued environments, fundamentalist religious groups offering a political ideology (e.g., the Black Muslims) serve the same function. In the Israeli-Palestinian conflict in the Gaza Strip and West Bank, Moslem fundamentalist groups (e.g., Hamas) play this role for Palestinians, and extreme Zionist groups do so for Jewish Israelis.

Documentation for this phenomenon can be found in a study conducted in Israel reporting that highly orthodox Jews suffered less from stress as a result of the Palestinian uprising of the 1980s than did more secular Jews (Pines, 1989). The former tended to see the issue in simplistic ideological terms (for instance, as a necessary prelude to fulfilling their Zionist dream of "Greater Israel"). The latter were suffering from the stress of being battered by their consciences as they sought to balance competing loyalties and values (their commitment to a democratic ethic, the ethical imperatives of Judaism, and their concern for national security). One dramatic expression of this conflict was the fact that hundreds of Israeli soldiers refused on grounds of conscience to participate in the military and police activities involved in combating the Palestinian uprising in the West Bank and Gaza Strip.

On the other side of the conflict, Palestinian Islamic fundamentalists take comfort in their extremist ideology, promising an end to Israel and the return to them of lands taken by the Israelis in 1948, and democratic-humanistic Palestinians must contend with stressful moral ambiguities as they seek ethically acceptable ways to participate in the nationalist struggle. Thus, stress, even moral tension, is the necessary price one pays for moral sensibility in the midst of extreme conflict.

Ideology is a psychological resource, and the more powerful it is as a psychological resource the more it serves to truncate moral development and even impede political settlement (and thus, to prolong situations of conflict). This ideological dimension has emerged repeatedly in accounts of families under stress. Political and religious interpretation can play an important role in shaping the consequences of experience, particularly when they are held to with fanatic intensity, which is perhaps needed to defend against the crushing weight of reality in a concentration camp, a prison, or a refugee camp.

Punamaki (1987) saw exactly this process at work in the case of Palestinians under occupation and in refugee camps, where every feature of day-to-day stress and physical deprivation was met with a process of ideological response that mobilized social and psychological resources:

> The psychological process of healing the traumatic experiences drew strength from political and ideological commitment. Nationalistic motivation was present at all stages of the stress process: The meaning and harmfulness of an event as well as sufficiency of one's own resources to cope with stressors were approaches in the wider social and political context of a victimized and struggling nation. (pp. 82–83)

The concept of determined struggle to persist (*sumud*) figures prominently in analyses of Palestinian culture and community life (Grossman, 1988) and in the resilience of children in the face of awesome stress, such as was experienced by Palestinian families under siege in the refugee camps in Lebanon during the conflicts there (Cutting, 1988). The parallels with Zionism as a sustaining ideology for Jews seeking to create the State of Israel is clear. Parallels of a sort have also existed in the several nationalist ideological movements among Blacks in the United States, such as the Black Panther Party and the Black Muslims.

Ideology is a resource for adults, but it does not stop there. Adolescents are very open to ideology as an influence on identity. The role of ideology is clearly evident in the psychosocial development of adolescents, for as development proceeds, a child is less and less dependent upon the narrow confines of the parent-child relationship. The adolescent lives in response to the world beyond the family, as a kind of social weather vane.

The normal issues of adolescence, particularly as they play out in identity formation, get bound up in the *ideological* events in the society in which young people are growing to maturity. The role of ideology is taken for granted as a natural feature of political socialization in normal times and places, where the ideology of youth is normative in the sense of being consonant with the political institutions that ultimately determine their fate (Coles, 1986).

As such, it blends in with the cultural background and may even seem to disappear. However, when children and youths are involved in struggles in which they are pitted against those political institutions, such as the movement to end racial segregation in the American South in the 1960s, they participate in a much more articulated ideology and are much more likely to be articulate about that participation (Coles, 1986).

There is growing recognition among developmental psychologists that where an individual is developmentally has a lot to do with how and how much historical events in the society and the community influence his or her personal development. For example, Stewart and Healy (1989) found that the effects of changed roles for American women during World War II "took" for women who came of age during the war to a larger degree than they did for their younger or older counterparts. Late adolescence is a time when sociopolitical influences on identity seem particularly powerful.

The openness to social redefinition that accompanies role changes at the heart of normal adolescence makes adolescents acutely susceptible to ideology as an influence on development and identity—and especially able to make use of it as a personal resource and as a source of resilience (Elder, 1980). This phenomenon is evident over and over again, as young people are the vehicles for social movements. Social history is important for adolescents because developmental outcomes for them depend less upon the day-to-day character of the infrastructure of families and more upon the ideologically driven activities available in the community and the larger society. It appears that adolescents encounter social conditions and culture more directly than do young children and that adolescents incorporate social events into their repertory of "identity alternatives" and then use them as resources in forming a coherent identity in early adulthood (cf. Stewart & Healy, 1989).

Studies of the life courses of youths exposed to violent danger support this view in differentiating between the paths followed by criminals and those followed by terrorists. The two groups are similar in their experience with brutalization but are differentiated by the ideological meanings available to the latter (Fields, 1987).

For all that adolescence is considered a time for focusing on the here and now, on the present, it is the relation of the present to the future that really drives most adolescents (Garbarino & Associates, 1985). In social movements and ideology, they seek to find a path to meaningfulness that fits into individual identity. Thus, one measure—perhaps *the* measure—of a good society for adolescents is its capacity to provide constructive social movements, movements that assist young people in developing identity without exploiting that need for narrow political or economic interests.

It is for historians, political scientists, and moralists to evaluate the legitimacy of the social movements to which adolescents are attracted, of course. Nonetheless, the psychosocial dynamic seems clear. Ideology plays into identity, and adolescent energy is mobilized through dramatic action that engages the critical process of identity formation.

4. THE DYNAMICS OF DANGER AND TRAUMA

The conflict between Israelis and Palestinians in the Middle East provided a context for my efforts to understand the dynamic relationship between danger and trauma. For the record, Punamaki's 1979 study of Israeli and Palestinian children living near the "Green Line" that divided pre-1967 Israel from the West Bank found that 45 percent of the Israeli children had seen or heard a bomb explosion or terrorist raid, and 21 percent had lost a family member in war or in other violence.

By comparison, 87 percent of the West Bank Palestinian children had been personally involved in at least one violent confrontation with Israeli forces, 66 percent had had a member of their family imprisoned, and 39 percent had lost a family member in war or other violence. Since 1988, the dangers to Palestinian children have increased dramatically. Thus, the Middle East presented a social laboratory in which to explore the dynamics of danger and risk. My experiences and observations with children and youths in the Middle East complement my study of inner-city youth in Chicago, where, according to Bell's (1991) survey, 25 percent of children have witnessed a murder by age 18.

In a village near the city of Hebron in the West Bank, a 12-year-old Palestinian boy involved in the uprising was interviewed. As the research team approached the town, we found him ready to attack the Israeli forces with a handful of rocks. Around his head was the traditional Palestinian headdress (*kafiyah*), wrapped so that only his eyes were showing (to prevent identification). Once he discovered that we were not the military, he was willing to be interviewed. While we talked, villagers down the road prepared for a confrontation with the soldiers who were reported to be waiting nearby (and who had entered the village in force the day before).

During our meeting, an Israeli military helicopter circled overhead, observing. Given press reports of the army's tactics, it seemed likely that the helicopter was there to provide a mobile command post and perhaps to drop tear gas bombs in support of the troops when they entered the village. This young boy dramatized the role of youth in the Palestinian uprising. His 16-year-old brother had already been taken away to prison for opposing the Israeli army and police. His father stood nearby and expressed pride in what his sons were doing. When the boy was asked what he wanted to be when he grew up, his answer was "I want to be free in my homeland or I want to be dead."

Many thousands of young Palestinians express the same conviction, and events have tended to validate that stance. From their point of view, the disturbances represent a nationalist uprising. This provides the context in which young people develop their identity as adolescents; it is fused with the ideology of nationalist struggle, and social conditions validate this fusion.

By 1989, it was obvious that a young person's relation to the Intifada was the dominant feature of adolescence for Palestinians. It dominated issues of schooling (as schools were closed most of the time and students were thus prevented from graduating), vocational development (traditional work patterns were disrupted by continuing strikes), physical well-being (more than 7,000 youths were seriously injured), sex roles (girls and women took an increasingly active public role in demonstrations and the larger struggle), peer status (arrest became a high-prestige badge of courage among teenagers, reluctance to confront the Israelis causing one to be scorned as a "KitKat," a pampered, effete wimp), residential patterns (thousands of adolescents were in jail or on the run to escape arrest by the Israelis), and even romance (boys and girls associated on new terms, in some cases as a result of the changing sex roles and general liberation from traditional adult constraints). These features form the social context for Palestinian adolescents and for adolescence itself.

By January 1989, boys and girls under 15 years of age constituted 40 percent of the casualties, and the average age of the Palestinians killed was 16 (Garbarino, Kostelny, & Dubrow, 1991). Sometimes injuries are incidental or even accidental. Some injuries reflect the development of personal vendettas (involving, for instance, Palestinians settling old scores with individuals thought to be collaborators with the Israelis, Israelis singling out specific individuals for personal reprisal, and Palestinians singling out individual soldiers for revenge attacks). Indeed, with the leadership of the Palestinians being primarily adolescent and so many of the soldiers being young, the conflicts in the street often resemble gang warfare, highly personal and charged with adolescent ambience.

Many youths retain a sense of humor about their experiences, at least as long as they are not directly involved in a terrifying or painful encounter. In this, the children seem to be replicating the experience of other children in times of war. The film *Hope and Glory* tells the story of a young boy and his peers living in London during the World War II blitz. It chronicles the way children played at war, in the rubble of bombed-out buildings and with pieces of antiaircraft flak that fell in the streets. But it makes clear the emotional upheaval involved when the war disrupted their intimate relationships—most particularly when *their* houses were bombed or *their* parents were hurt. Many Palestinian children have had precisely these experiences.

Of course, Israeli society being what it is, there are touching stories of decency to complement accounts of brutality and misuse of power—for example, soldiers refusing to obey orders that would put children in jeopardy, including the nearly 500 who have faced prison rather than serve in the West Bank or Gaza. One Palestinian mother told of confronting a soldier who entered her house late at night and frightened her children by yelling at him: "How can you do this! How do you think your children would feel if this happened to them!" The soldier left in tears.

In another incident, a 12-year-old boy was stopped at a checkpoint on the way home from school. The boy panicked and started to run. The soldier yelled, "Stop or I'll shoot." The boy didn't stop, but when the soldier aimed his gun at the boy the soldier deliberately released his ammunition clip so that the weapon would not fire. Though spared from being shot, the boy now refuses to travel out of sight of his home. Some children included pictures of soldiers accosting children at checkpoints as part of their drawings of "where I live and what it is like to live here."

Palestinian adults represent two themes in their interpretation of these events.

On the one hand, they are outraged that children and youths should be harmed and that they may feel powerless to provide protection. On the other hand, they portray the harm coming to youths as being a "necessary" feature of the larger political context created by occupation and the struggle to resist it. Giving up the struggle to provide immediate safety to children and youths does not seem to be an option for most, even in the face of daily threats to safety and Israeli efforts to make parents pay stiff fines when children and youths participate in demonstrations and acts of opposition.

It must be noted that a significant emigration of Palestinians concerned about the immediate and long-term prospects for their children occurred in response to the conflict. (This increase was matched by a similar increase in Israelis emigrating in search of brighter and more peaceful circumstances.) But what of those who stay and steadfastly continue the struggle? The issues for youth cut to the heart of adolescent development, in which a search for identity is paramount.

The current danger does not represent a historical discontinuity for Palestinian children, or for Israeli children, for that matter. The data cited earlier make that clear—recall that in 1979, 21 percent of Israeli children and 39 percent of Palestinian children reported having lost a family member in war or other political violence. Just as Israelis have lived in a state of siege since 1948, protest in the West Bank and Gaza has occurred for 20 years or more, beginning under the repressive Jordanian administration of the territories.

Children do participate in direct confrontations, and by most accounts this direct participation was growing at the time of this writing, in part because of depletion of the ranks of adolescents and young adults—more than 10,000 had been injured and a similar number imprisoned. This shift was evident in early 1989, as the average age of the wounded and killed decreased. Preadolescent rock throwers were common, and many children were quick to flash the prohibited "V" sign and sing outlawed patriotic songs. And there were numerous reports of children being detained by the military in an attempt to gather information on teenagers and adults.

A human rights group has published a report on children in jails that draws some of the same conclusions drawn by the Children's Defense Fund (1976) in the United States in its report *Children in Adult Jails,* namely, that jail is no place for children in the best of circumstances, let alone when they are subject to physical and sexual intimidation. Observers have recounted tales of degradation and intimidation among thousands arrested for political activities ranging across the spectrum from paramilitary acts of rebellion ("terrorism") to simple acts of political protest (e.g., displaying the Palestinian flag). Some of those arrested have been quite young (Shipler, 1985; Sifry, 1988).

Punamaki's (1987) study reported that the more children were exposed to traumatic events linked to the military occupation, the more psychological disorders they manifested. These included aggressiveness, severe nervousness, severe withdrawal symptoms, enuresis, severe anxiety, and phobias. Pictures of children taken in Gaza and the West Bank, and the pictures drawn by children, evidenced this darkness.

However, the effects of parental buffering were evident. Prior to the focal uprising, exposure to traumatic events linked to military occupation varied significantly from family to family and from village to village. Specific acts of retaliation on the part of the Israeli police, military, and secret police tended to be linked to specific acts of opposition on the part of Palestinians. However, the correlation between acts of opposition and acts of reprisal was far from perfect (Shipler, 1985). This disjunction fed the flames: if people are holding back from open opposition to the authorities for fear of reprisal and then observe that they can be punished for doing nothing, they may as well do something consistent with their underlying feelings and beliefs.

Punamaki's study was conducted during the period of "chronic conflict" that had obtained for the previous 20–40 years. At the time of this research, however, virtually all families and villages were touched directly by the acute crisis associated with the uprising, although there was still some variation in intensity, with the city of Nablus being a persistent "hot spot," a fact that was reflected in the degree of children's and parents' negative feelings toward Israelis evident in the interviews and children's drawings obtained there. One would be hard-pressed to find a single family or village that has not directly experienced the revolt and military efforts to combat it—that has not participated in rock throwing and tire burning or met with shootings, arrests, beatings, house demolitions, and tear gas.

5. EVIDENCE FROM DREAMS

Evidence that there is widespread mobilization of social support among the Palestinian community, support that reaches to children and youths, comes from an analysis of the dreams of Palestinian children and youths. The dreams of children reflect several processes. Dreams can reflect simple cognitive processing of information, but they can also reflect a child's efforts to wrestle with life issues. Children's dreams thus can indicate what is left over from conscious, overt processing occurring during the children's awake time. What is more, the narrative rendering of dreams, as in a journal or diary, allows or gives permission to a child to communicate messages that might otherwise be taboo as well as to make the dream conform to socially approved standards.

It is easy to make too much of a child's dream—particularly where one is imposing patterns and meanings rather than detecting them. The following summary reports themes in the dreams of 24 twelve-year-old Palestinian children who recorded two to five dreams each in special "dream diaries" in the mornings over a two-week period (Nixon, personal communication). (1) *Attack*. Only 1 of the children had no attacks in any of the dreams reported. On the other hand, 14 of the children had at least one dream in which there were no attacks. Sixteen children had dreams in which only the Israelis engaged in attacks. Five had dreams in which only the Palestinians attacked. Nine had dreams in which both sides engaged in attacks. A few children had dreams in which there were fantasy threats (6) or attacks (4). (2) *Emotions*. Half the children had dreams in which the emotional tone was idyllic; only 8 had dreams in which the tone was fearful. Three had dreams in which they expressed steadfastness, and 3 had dreams in which both emotions were expressed. (3) *Support*. Most of the children (21) had dreams in which a supportive relationship was present. Only one child had a dream in which there was betrayal. (4) *Injury*. More than half of the children had at least one dream in which someone other than the child was injured. Only 6 had dreams in which they were injured. And only 5 of the children had no one injured in any of their dreams.

What do these dreams say about the children who dreamed them? It seems clear that the youths were using their dreams (or at least their accounts of the dreams) as an opportunity to reflect upon the Intifada. They focused heavily (but not exclusively) on the political conflict. They dreamt about the violence. But the fact that they did not always dream about attacks (more than half had at least one dream in which there was no attack) probably reflects the fact that they had lives apart from it.

That more than half had at least one dream in which the emotional tone was idyllic is probably a sign of their need for peace in the midst of their commitment to struggle. Imagining idyllic scenes seems one appropriate and healthy way of coping with stressful day-to-day life. Similarly, that most kids had dreams about supportive relationships in which they were protected or helped is also a good sign, and it probably reflects the reality of their lives (there has been a mobilization of social support among Palestinians during the Intifada).

The frequency of injuries in the dreams is probably a reflection of the disturbing frequency of attacks in the dreams and injuries in real life. Injuries were a fact of life for these children, like the political conflict itself. That only 25 percent of the kids had dreams in which they were injured could mean they were not appreciating the risk they faced. On the other hand, it was an accurate appreciation of the probabilities of injury—even in real life, the injury rate for children was not higher than 25 percent.

6. EMPIRICAL OBSERVATIONS

Dreams offer one important expression of children's experience of coping with danger. Clinical observations offer another. Some professionals believe the trouble focused on here has had a therapeutic aspect. As they see it, demonstrations of group pride and identity by Palestinian nationalists help counter the hopelessness and despair children have seen all around them in Gaza and the West Bank in the absence of a political solution to the region's problems. This is particularly true for adolescents.

It seems fair to say that the uprising provides adolescents with a strong and unambiguous arena in which to play out the "melodramas of adolescence" (Garbarino & Associates, 1985). These melodramas center around testing limits, being "bad," being noble, challenging childhood roles within the family and the community, and making a statement about one's relationship to the future. In this sense, the Intifada has been exhilarating for many Palestinian adolescents. It channels energy into action and simplifies some issues of day-to-day life.

Of course, the current situation may mobilize anger in a negative way as well and lead to increased violence by Palestinians against Israeli civilians and by Palestinians against each other. Evidence of this latter concern is found in the games children play. It has become common for children to play the game of "soldiers and demonstrators," complete with real rock throwing and beatings. Children have been injured in these games.

How will the aggression associated with the Intifada affect children and youth? Some social scientists believe there is evidence of a general contagion effect: Any act of violence—no matter how it is intended or justified—has the effect of increasing the overall level of violence (Straus, 1994). Others take a somewhat different view.

After reviewing a large body of research dealing with violence and aggression, Goldstein concluded that "aggressive behavior used to achieve a personal goal, such as wealth and power, and that may be perceived by the actor as justified (or even non-aggressive) is a primary cause of the aggressive and criminal behavior of others" (1986, p. ix).

This conclusion suggests the problem of spillover and contagion will be small so long as the aggression of the Intifada is under social control on both sides. It limits concern that there will be spillover into Palestinian society to the extent that Goldstein's conclusion about aggression "used to achieve a personal goal" applies to socially validated aggression, like most of the violence occurring within the context of the Intifada.

A preliminary analysis of Israeli society found no general increase in criminal violence inside Israel in the wake of 1988, a year of massive involvement of adult males in violent activity in the West Bank and Gaza (Fishman, personal communication). Whether this would remain true or not was, of course, undetermined. The psychological and social dynamics of violence are neither simple nor fully understood.

Palestinian youths have grown up in the midst of a conscious policy designed to produce compliance with occupation through a campaign of intimidation and inducements to cooperation (Sifrey, 1988). When a campaign of fear succeeds, it "keeps the lid on" and may produce a high level of self-hatred, self-inflicted victimization, and within-group assault, as some have observed at various times and places among Black Americans and Native Americans.

But if a campaign of fear does not succeed in suppressing attacks against the dominant group, it can serve to stimulate and intensify them. In the case of Palestinians, and prior to the current uprising, it has certainly provided the fuel for revenge attacks against Israelis, some of which have had a pathologically desperate character to them. The home of a youth who was serving a nine-year prison sentence for firebombing an army bus demonstrated this process. The family's house had been razed by the Israelis as collective punishment for the family. His picture hung prominently in a place of honor in their current dwelling, and his younger siblings spoke of him with pride. When asked to draw a picture of where she lived and what happens there, his younger sister drew a scene involving a confrontation between soldiers and rock-throwing youths. When asked how the children in the picture would feel if a rock hurt one of the soldiers, she smiled shyly and said, "They would feel good, because the soldiers tried to hurt them."

In her research on the recruitment of terrorists in Northern Ireland, Fields (1987) found that

> even though the experience of violent trauma was common to all the children in the sample in Northern Ireland, those who became activists in organizations that advocate terror tactics, had usually suffered personal physical and psychological pain and humiliation at the hands of the authorities. In some cases they had been helpless on-lookers when parents or siblings were beaten and dragged off to interrogation centers or imprisonment. Very few who had that experience did not volunteer. (p. 8)

However, she also reported that it was clear from her Middle East data that "a child can be traumatized vicariously through his or her identification with a victimized group." She continued, "This finding underscores the importance of identity and self-image in relation to the larger society as a determinant of motivation and consequently of behavior" (1987, p. 9). Some observers have suggested a similar process at work for Israelis as a "traumatized society." The history of anti-Semitism shapes the worldview of even those who have not experienced it directly but whose strong communal identification produces vicarious traumatization. The parallels between Israeli and Palestinian experience in this regard provide much of the imagery underlying the struggle there.

Conflicts between parents and adolescents about participating in demonstrations and confrontations with soldiers are another issue. In the first weeks and months of the Intifada, some parents tried to prevent their teenagers from participating, to spare them from physical injury and arrest. Starting in 1988, Israeli authorities tried to increase this pressure by imposing stiff fines on parents whose children participated in rock throwing and other acts of opposition.

On the other hand, many teenagers (and, increasingly, children) were drawn irresistibly to join their peers "on the front lines," and those who did so were viewed as heroes. Parents often similarly glorified such heroics (even as they felt deeply the pain their children felt when injured). In hospitals and in homes, interviews with parents whose children and adolescents had been beaten and shot revealed clearly this mixture of pride and pain.

A 14-year-old boy who had been shot in the hand with a plastic bullet spoke for many youths in his affirmation of struggle. Even more to the point was his best friend, who sat with him and spoke of the injury with a mixture of anger (that his friend had been shot), pride (that they together were standing up to the Israelis), and envy (that he had not attained the heroic status achieved by his pal). Palestinian children and youths living in the Intifada are imbued with ideology. For example, the drawings they made almost invariably featured Palestinian flags, often in ingenious ways—for example, the flag as the window of a house, the flag worked into clothing, the flag attached to a balloon, and so forth. A systematic content analysis of a collection of such drawings documents the pervasiveness of nationalism and struggle as defining characteristics of the way Palestinian children and youth identify themselves.

Indeed, when asked to draw a picture of "where you live and what it's like to live there," a few children and youths simply drew a picture of the flag that covered the entire paper. This is not unique to Palestinian children. Some of the Jewish Israeli children living in a West Bank settlement approached the task in a similar manner.

For example, one child simply drew a map of "Greater Israel" (i.e., including all the land from the Mediterranean to the Jordan River) and wrote on it, "Israel is for the Israelis." When posed with the same task, a group of gifted 10-year-old Israeli children in Haifa responded with a wide variety of images, many reflecting political concerns, but others reflecting concern with an outbreak of automobile accidents and suicide attempts among local children.

How has the uprising affected Israel's Jewish children in general? Thus far, effects appear to be indirect, mediated through press reports and the experience of adults (teachers, parents, etc.). With few exceptions, the buffering process appears to have worked extremely well. One could see that descriptions of Israel as a very child-oriented society are valid. Parents and other adults have worked hard, and generally succeeded, in protecting most Israeli children from extreme stress most of the time for more than 40 years, through numerous wars and terrorist incidents.

As Shipler (1985) and other observers (e.g., Grossman, 1988) have pointed out, dehumanization and depersonalization of "the other" are common in the Middle East conflict. The reality of Palestinian Arab dehumanization of Israeli Jews is well known and publicized; Jewish Israeli dehumanization of Palestinian Arabs is less well recognized (Shipler, 1985).

Some mothers of Jewish children interviewed in West Bank settlements were appalled to learn that we had spoken to Arabs, with one responding,

Those people don't even deserve to be considered. They are subhuman; they are worse than dogs. It's like the child who murders his parents and then pleads for mercy from the judge because he is an orphan. They deserve no sympathy.

She was not alone in that assessment.

What is more, the study by Pines (1989) noted earlier suggests that those who have such a view find the Intifada less stressful than those who do not. The former respond with "justifiable rage"; the latter are profoundly troubled by the conflict between their image of themselves and their society as humanistic and the reality of the oppression they represent in the West Bank and Gaza.

Children and youths show some of the same complexity in their sociopolitical thinking. The truth of this assertion has emerged in violent political conflicts in many settings. Coles (1986) reveals the surprisingly sophisticated political moral analysis evident when children and youths are interviewed in-depth and over an extended period of time concerning their views; simplistic questionnaires seldom reveal this sophistication.

As a persecuted minority, Jews have had to learn to protect their children from horror, whether it be day-to-day anti-Semitism, pogroms, or concentration camps. It is difficult to respond to persecution and oppression in a humanistic way, despite the fact that most religious traditions ask people to do so. Palestinians have faced some of the same issues in recent decades, in Israel, Lebanon, Jordan, and elsewhere.

It is unclear how the round of confrontations discussed here will affect Israeli children in the long run. Just as analysts of race relations in the United States have long worried about the effects of segregation, so some contemporary Israeli observers are concerned about diminishing normal contact between Jewish Israelis and Palestinians (some 10 percent of whom are Christian). As Grossman (1988) pointed out, the contacts most Israeli children now have with Palestinians are limited to two kinds. The first is violent confrontation, and the second is subordination. Most Israeli children only encounter Palestinians as servants and menial workers. Many have no appreciable contact whatsoever.

When asked to draw "where you live and what it is like to live there," Israeli children living in settlements drew lovely pictures that almost never included any evidence of a Palestinian presence, unlike the Palestinian children, who sometimes included settlements in their drawings and usually included soldiers or settlers. In one settlement, the one picture that seemed to recognize the presence of the Arabs did so by including a bus with broken windows and an Arab taxi on the road.

For Palestinian children, contact with Jewish Israelis is generally confined to soldiers, police, bosses, and settlers. When pressed about whether they would like to meet Israeli children, many Palestinian children who were interviewed responded in a way that was generally evasive and apprehensive. Their pictures of "where the Israelis live and what it is like to live there" revealed an idyllic landscape with birds flying and the sun shining (something that rarely appeared in their pictures of life for Palestinians).

The pre-Intifada analysis of the dreams of 643 eleven- to thirteen-year-old Israeli and Palestinian children reinforces this point (Grossman, 1988). This research revealed that Israeli and Palestinian children often dreamt about the conflict between their two peoples. In these dreams, the children confronted stereotypical images of "the other"—Arabs as "terrorists" versus Israelis as "Jewish oppressors." Most of these dreams involve violent and aggressive confrontations and often ended in death.

Racist themes are evident in these dreams, as they are in relations between Israelis and Palestinians. Of course, as noted earlier, the images and themes evidenced in these pre-Intifada dreams have been displaced by the themes of assault and support noted above.

From one perspective, it is fair to say that Israeli children typically are not involved directly in the disturbances unless they live in settlements in the West Bank or Gaza, which are usually under armed guard. There, they may observe or be involved in direct confrontations with Palestinians—for example, having rocks or even firebombs thrown at their cars or school buses. Such impersonal attacks have occurred sporadically for many years and continue as do knife assaults and similarly personal attacks as well. However, Israeli youths are much more directly engaged; in settlements, it is they who often travel through dangerous areas to attend school, and inside the pre-1967 boundaries they are very much engaged in the moral and political issues of occupation as they contemplate imminent involvement as part of mandatory military service that can include service with occupation forces in "the territories."

But the frequency and intensity of dangerous encounters is not comparable for Israeli and Palestinian children. The death and injury statistics make this difference clear, and it was evident in my interviews with parents, in which some settlers said their children were safer now than they had been living in the city under "normal" conditions, a finding consistent with those of other observers.

From a broader perspective, however, it seems that many, if not all, Israeli youths are involved psychologically with the Intifada. This involvement comes from the challenge it poses to the national identity of Israelis. It comes from the fear that male relatives and friends will be hurt serving in "the territories." It comes from being a part of a traumatized people.

As with adults, the youths most affected by all this are those for whom the Intifada evokes moral dilemmas—most notably, those who come from families in which there is open discussion of the conflict posed by the pitting of national security concerns against ethical imperatives. This dilemma was very evident in a classroom of 10-year-olds in Haifa.

The teacher reported that students engaged in a lot of political discussion at home: they came from politically "aware" families. When asked to draw pictures of "where you live and what it is like to live there," most children drew what might be called political cartoons. These drawings reflected their profound involvement with the Intifada as a moral and political issue. Their emerging identity was clearly bound up in resolving what the conflict meant for them personally and politically.

In this, they were very much like the articulate children whose political life Coles (1986) studied. These children had a strong need to process their experience in a way that parallels the processing of their Palestinian counterparts on the front lines of the conflict. By virtue of living in a democratic society, Israeli children experience this necessary processing.

In the case of Palestinian youths, the prospects are less sanguine in this regard. They generally attend much more authoritarian schools and face an authoritarian political climate, derived in part from living under conditions of occupation in which they have very little in the way of political rights. Indeed, it is the great hope of many that the prevalence of such processing can be increased via democratization of family, school, and community achieved through the Intifada. The characteristic commitment of Palestinians to education is a crucial resource in this regard.

7. CONCLUSIONS

Whenever youths are faced with and involved in chronic danger, there are two alternative models for responding. The first accentuates ideological interpretation and giving meaning to dangerous events and thus provides social structure and significance to danger. This response may well shield youths from some mental health problems. The second model is devoid of political significance and is likely to produce a situation in which hopelessness and despair translate into within-group violence, depression, and self-hatred. These two models force dominant groups and professionals concerned with the mental health of children and youths to choose between the challenges of contending with revolutionary politics and the convenience of coping with the fruits of acquiescence. Neither comes without costs. That there are reserves of humanism among youths living in political conflict and day-to-day danger and that they can speak with an advanced moral voice are good signs. Amidst all the darkness, there are glimmers of sunshine. Finding these glimmers and nurturing them depends upon being able to hear what youths are saying about their efforts to cope with the consequences of living in danger (Garbarino, Stott, & Faculty of Erikson Institute, 1989).

ACKNOWLEDGMENT

The author acknowledges the assistance of Kathleen Kostelny and Nancy Dubrow.

REFERENCES

Baider, L., & Rosenfeld, R. (1974). Effect of parental fears on children in wartime. *Social Casework*, *47*, 498–503.

Bell, C. (1991). Traumatic stress and children in danger. *Journal of Health Care for the Poor and Underserved*, *2*, 175–188.

Bettelheim, B. (1943). Individual and mass behavior in extreme situations. *Journal of Abnormal and Social Psychology*, *38*, 417–452.

Bishop, P. (1989). Palestinian children are main victims of Israelis. *Daily Telegraph*, January 23, 1ff.

Children's Defense Fund. (1976). *Children in adult jails*. Washington, DC: Children's Defense Fund.

Coles, R. (1986). *The political life of children*. Boston: Houghton Mifflin.

Conroy, J. (1987). *Belfast diary*. Boston: Beacon Press.

Cutting, P. (1988). *Children of the siege*. London: Heinemann.

Danieli, Y. (1985). The treatment and prevention of long-term effects and intergenerative transmission of victimization. A lesson from Holocaust survivors and their children. In C. R. Figley (Ed.,) *Trauma and its wake* (pp. 23–51). New York: Brunner/Mazel.

Elder, G. (1980). Adolescence in historical perspective. In J. Adelson (Ed.), *Handbook of adolescent psychology* (pp. 3–46). New York: Wiley.

Fields, R. (1987). *Terrorized into terrorist: Sequelae of PTSP in young victims*. Paper presented at the Society for Traumatic Stress Studies, New York, October.

Freud, A., & Burlingham, D. (1943). *War and children*. New York: Willard.

Garbarino, J. (1988). Childhood injury prevention. *American Journal of Orthopsychiatry*, *58*, 25–45.

Garbarino, J. (1995). *Raising children in a socially toxic environment*. San Francisco: Jossey-Bass.

Garbarino, J., & Associates. (1985). *Adolescent development: An ecological perspective*. Columbus, OH: Merrill.

Garbarino, J., & Associates. (1992). *Children and families in the social environment*. New York: Aldine.

Garbarino, J., Kostelny, K. & Dubrow, N. (1991). *No place to be a child*. New York: Lexington/MacMillan.

Garbarino, J.. Stott, F., & Faculty of the Erikson Institute. (1989). *What children can tell us*. San Francisco: Jossey-Bass.

Gilligan, C. (1982). *In a different voice*. Cambridge, MA: Harvard University Press.

Goleman, D. (1986). Terror's children: Mending mental wounds. *New York Times*, September 2.

Grossman, D. (1988). Report from Israel: The yellow rain. *New Yorker*, February 8, p. 41ff., & February 15, p. 58ff.

Kinzie, J. , Sack, W., Angell, R., Mauson, S., & Rath, B. (1986). The psychiatric effects of massive trauma on Cambodian children. *Journal of American Academy of Child Psychiatry*, *25*, 370–376.

Lösel, F., & Bliesener, T. (1990). Resilience in adolescence: A study on the generalizability of protective factors. In K. Hurrelman & F. Lösel (Eds.), *Health hazards in adolescence* (pp. 299–320). Berlin: Walter de Gruyten.

Pines, R. (1989). *Why do Israelis burn out—The role of the Intifada*. Paper presented at the International Conference on Psychological Stress and Adjustment, Tel Aviv.

Punamaki, R. (1987). Psychological stress responses of Palestinian mothers and their children in conditions of military occupation and political violence. *Quarterly Newsletter of the Laboratory of Comparative Human Cognition*, April 9, 76–84.

Rosenblatt, R. (1983). *Children of war*. New York: Doubleday.

Shipler, D. (Ed.). (1987). *Through different eyes*. Bethesda, MD: Adler & Adler.

Sifry, M. (1988). After the "iron-fist"—What? *Nation*, 246, 186 ff.

Stewart, A., & Healy, J. (1989). Linking individual development and social changes. *American Psychologist*, *44*, 30–43.

Straus, M. (1994). *Beating the devil out of them*. New York: Lexington/MacMillan

Terr, L. (1987). *Too scared to cry*. New York: Harper-Collins.

van der Kolk, B. (1987). *Psychological trauma*. Washington, DC: American Psychiatric Press.

Vygotsky, L. (1962). *Thought and language*. Cambridge, MA: MIT Press.

Werner, E., & Smith, R. (1982). Vulnerable but invincible. New York: McGraw-Hill.

Index